MONUMENTAL HARM

Monumental Harm

Reckoning with
Jim Crow Era
Confederate
Monuments

Roger C. Hartley

THE UNIVERSITY OF
SOUTH CAROLINA PRESS

© 2021 University of South Carolina

Published by the University of South Carolina Press
Columbia, South Carolina 29208

www.uscpress.com

Manufactured in the United States of America

30 29 28 27 26 25 24 23 22 21
10 9 8 7 6 5 4 3 2 1

Library of Congress Cataloging-in-Publication Data
can be found at http://catalog.loc.gov/.

ISBN: 978–1-64336-168-0 (hardcover)
ISBN: 978–1-64336-169-7 (paperback)
ISBN: 978–1-64336-170-3 (ebook)

To Cathy

Contents

List of Illustrations.. ix
Preface... xi
Acknowledgments xv

Introduction... 1

PHASE I. Act or Leave the Monuments Undisturbed?

1. History and Memory Distinguished 19
2. The Distortion-of-History Approach: The Cult of the Lost Cause 24
3. The Warping-of-History Approach: The Rise of Monument Mania 53
4. The Racial-Reckoning Approach: The Stereotyping and
   Erasure Functions of Confederate Monuments........................ 92
5. Confederate Monuments and Contemporary Institutional Racism........ 109

PHASE II. The Disposition: Destroy, Contextualize, or Relocate
the Confederate Monument?

6. The Case Against Monument Destruction 129
7. The Trouble with Contextualization 135
8. Relocation and Its Critics.. 145

PHASE III. Who Decides?

9. The Legal Framework Protecting Confederate Monuments 163

Conclusion... 181

Cases Cited 185
Notes 187
Bibliography 237
Index.. 247

Illustrations

Robert E. Lee Monument, Charlottesville, VA................................. x

Confederate Memorial, Stone Mountain, GA 13

Stonewall Jackson Monument, Richmond, VA.............................. 40

Robert E. Lee Monument, Richmond, VA..................................... 43

Confederate Soldiers and Sailors Monument, Richmond, VA 47

Confederate Soldiers Monument, Raleigh, NC............................... 51

Lynching of Henry Smith (1893)... 62

Dedication of Confederate Monument, Arlington National Cemetery (1914)..... 76

Ulric Stonewall Jackson Dunbar and model of "Mammy Monument" (1923).... 81

Unveiling of "Silent Sam" monument, University of North Carolina (1913) 94

Confederate Monument, Augusta, GA..................................... 107

Robert E. Lee Monument, Charlottesville, VA.
Photo credit: Cville dog (via Wikimedia Creative Commons).

Preface

In the summer of 2017, James Fields, an avowed White supremacist, set out from Ohio to Charlottesville, Virginia, to attend a rally that drew hundreds of White nationalists to protest that city government's plan to relocate an equestrian statue of Confederate General Robert E. Lee. That road trip resulted in a sentence of life in prison plus 419 years for Fields who deliberately accelerated his car into a group protesting against racism. This punishment was in addition to a life sentence previously imposed on Fields following a conviction on twenty-nine federal hate crime charges. Fields's vehicular rampage killed Heather Heyer and injured more than two dozen others at the August 2017 "Unite the Right" rally. Those whom Fields killed and injured were among the hundreds who counterprotested against the anti-Black/White supremacist racism that animated objections to the proposed removal of the Lee statue.[1]

Hundreds of Confederate monuments currently dot the South. Most were raised at the turn of the twentieth century, at the height of Jim Crow racial segregation, by White-supremacist-controlled local governments. These monuments are located in prime public spaces—courthouse squares, public parks, and major street intersections. Now, in many of the municipalities where these monuments are located, African American political influence is on the rise, and residents, Black and White, aspire for their Southern communities to be identified as inclusive and welcoming diversity.[2] Accordingly, there is a growing insistence among residents of Southern municipalities that something be done with their local Confederate monument. The objective is to sever the town's past association with the monument's pro-Confederate message.

A mostly White resistance has developed. The Unite the Right rally in Charlottesville evidences that racial bigotry can account for an insistence that Confederate monuments remain undisturbed—so that they can continue their historic role as symbols that perpetuate racist stereotypes and symbolically exhort and encourage an ideology of White supremacy. If racial animus were the *only* motivation for opposing removal of Confederate monuments, the question presented to Southern communities contemplating a Confederate monument's removal would be unmistakable and straightforward: whether to remove the monument from its current public space in order to terminate the community's sponsorship of symbolic speech that promotes racial bigotry. Even in the current period of American history that is witnessing a rise in White nationalism and the spread of far-right White extremist ideology, one could reasonably predict, certainly hope, that most Americans would applaud efforts by communities to dissociate themselves from appeals to anti-Black racial bias by removing their Confederate monuments.[3]

But the current imbroglio over what to do with the South's Confederate monuments is not so easily resolved. The reality is that objections to proposals to relocate Confederate monuments from public spaces also are couched in terms wholly unrelated to support for White supremacy. Indeed, many Confederate monument supporters state that they find White supremacist views anathema to them. A recurring theme is that altering or removing a Confederate statue amounts to an erasure of history and a disrespect for White Southern heritage, tradition, military valor, and pride.[4] Confederate monument supporters have perfected a "dual heritage" rationale that assumes the moral equivalency of White and Black heritage: Blacks have a right to their heritage and "we [Whites] have a right to ours." Monument defenders argue that heritage, "is the possession of a particular group of people who define its content and cling to it as a part of their identity [and their definition of heritage] cannot be challenged but must be respected at all costs."[5] Cloaking support for Confederate monuments in demands that Southern heritage be respected dissociates monument defenders from any charge of racial animus.[6] Moreover, through reliance on the "innocuously positive value of heritage," Confederate monument supporters have largely been successful in evading the need to justify, or even acknowledge, the consequences for contemporary civil society of their choice to exalt Confederate individuals or groups by means of monuments.[7]

Some may be scornful of these Southern heritage claims, believing that anti-Black racism, conscious or subconscious, lies at the core of all support for Confederate memorialization such as Confederate battle flags and Confederate monuments. Given the widespread appropriation of Confederate memorialization by anti-Black hate groups and the calculated disregard for historical accuracy that permeates much of Confederate memorialization, such skepticism has a degree of rational grounding.[8] But it is at least plausible that not all support for Southern heritage, such as celebrating the valor of the Confederate soldier, is rooted in anti-Black racism. Any who have difficulty dissociating the celebration of a Confederate soldier's valor from the racist cause for which he fought might want to consider the Vietnam Veterans Memorial in Washington, DC. The wide-ranging respect for the

Vietnam Veterans Memorial among most Americans demonstrates the capacity to commemorate the Vietnam War veterans' valor, steadfastness, and commitment while simultaneously opposing the war in which Vietnam veterans fought. It is well within our culture to commemorate the warrior but not the war.[9]

In any event, a productive conversation with respect to Confederate monuments is not possible if opponents of Confederate monuments persist in accusing all monument supporters of being motivated solely by racial bigotry. Alleging that Southern heritage claims are no more than pretext cloaking anti-Black racial bias guarantees that the Confederate monument removal discussion will devolve into reciprocal acrimonious exchanges that preclude any hope that the monument removal question can proceed to a reasoned conclusion. A productive evaluation of the merits of claims that something should be done with respect to a community's Confederate monument needs to begin with the assumption, if only for sake of argument, that opposition to Confederate monument removal can be advocated by honorable persons advancing non-racist-based views associated with the need to preserve their understanding of Southern heritage.

When the motives of Confederate monument supporters are so fixed, the question to be resolved then becomes whether a defensible case can be made for removing/relocating a Confederate monument from its current public space *even if* the opposition to removal is based on a good-faith claim that Confederate monument removal disrespects a version of Southern heritage that is dissociated from anti-Black racial bias. This book is written to answer *that* question.

An overarching principle in democratic political theory is that no right is absolute. For example, embedded in our constitutional liberties is the freedom of expression but also the principle that free speech gives no person the right to falsely shout fire in a crowded theater, thereby causing a clear and present risk of panic.[10] By further example, there is a strong presumption of the unconstitutionality of prior restraints on speech—halting publication of speech, usually by judicial injunction, as opposed to punishment after publication.[11] Yet it is widely agreed that there would be no constitutional bar to enjoining the publication of the sailing dates and times of troop ships during time of war due to the clear and present danger that such publication poses to national security.[12] And finally, the free exercise of religion guaranteed to all by the First Amendment does not protect the practice of human sacrifice even if some religion requires it.[13] Nor does the constitutional guarantee of the free exercise of religion preclude the government from banning the ingestion of a hallucinogenic drug for sacramental purposes, when such ingestion is prohibited by laws of general application regulating drug use.[14] The point is that even constitutional liberties sometimes need to be accommodated to competing and compelling societal interests.

By analogy, Southern heritage claims, even if *bona fide* and not motivated by racial bigotry, do not alone control the outcome of controversies over the removal of a Confederate monument. Southern heritage claims should be understood as but one consideration. Heritage claims must yield *if* maintaining Confederate monuments in their traditional public spaces causes a clear and present danger of creating an overriding societal harm, some pressing public necessity justifying the removal of these monuments.

The burden of the argument in this book is to demonstrate that Confederate monuments do foist material harm on contemporary American life of such a severe magnitude that ending the harm by removing these monuments from public spaces represents a pressing public necessity. My thesis is that Confederate monuments harm contemporary American society by perpetuating anti-Black racial stereotyping and systemic racism. This societal harm overrides even good faith claims to leave Confederate monuments undisturbed in order to preserve Southern heritage.

To fully comprehend the scope and seriousness of the deleterious impact of Confederate monuments, it is necessary to begin with an examination of late-nineteenth and early-twentieth century Southern history, politics, culture, and race relations, in other words the South during Jim Crow. This is the period during which most Confederate monuments were constructed. Jim Crow racial discrimination is the antecedent to today's systemic anti-Black racism and Confederate monuments were essential to "The Strange Career of Jim Crow."[15] Not only can Confederate monuments not escape the racist history of their creation, but the symbolic racist messaging and stereotyping contained in Confederate monuments continues into the present to reinforce attitudes that sustain racial bigotry.

In short, my claim is that debating the motives of Confederate monument supporters is a dead-end street. Focusing on motives pivots the monument debate into the realm of the unprovable and simply invites ill-will and resentment. It is unproductive for disputants to debate motives. The solution to the bickering over Confederate monuments is to focus on the deleterious implications of Confederate monuments for contemporary civil society by delineating as clearly as possible the harm that Confederate monuments foist on American society today. The removal/relocation debate can proceed more sensibly once the societal harms that Confederate monuments exact are exposed and better understood.

Acknowledgments

I am indebted to many people who assisted in this book's conception and completion. The traditional understanding of the cause and consequences of the Civil War in general, and the role of Confederate monuments in particular, changed most dramatically during a roughly twenty-year period of extraordinary scholarship that began in the late twentieth century. This body of work more clearly described a White-supremacy world during Reconstruction and in the post-Reconstruction South and provides valuable insights into who raised Confederate monuments and why. This scholarship provided a historical grounding that has permitted me to better understand the relationships between Gilded-Age Confederate monuments, the disfranchisement and lynching of African Americans, Jim Crow racial segregation, and the advocacy of a cult of White Anglo-Saxonism. I am indebted to this remarkable group of scholars who taught me through their books and scholarly articles. I dare not list their names here for fear that I might inadvertently fail to include one of these pioneers.

Of course, Isaac Newton was correct when he famously said, "If I have seen further than others, it is by standing upon the shoulders of giants." This is true of the breakthrough scholarship of the late-twentieth and early twenty-first century to which I refer. These scholars certainly benefitted enormously from giants who previously had published important foundational work. Perhaps the most influential of this groundbreaking scholarship was that of C. Vann Woodward and John Hope Franklin. And, of course, George W. Cable's innovative work at the end of the nineteenth century has withstood the test of time, providing for all who came thereafter a clearer understanding of segregation and White supremacy. All of this scholarship makes it more feasible now to trace roughly a century of Confederate monument construction (1865–1965) and knit together an accurate picture and understanding of the relationship between Confederate monuments and White supremacy's journey through America's twentieth and early twenty-first centuries. I am indebted to all of these scholars.

On a more personal note, I want to thank the many friends and colleagues who offered encouragement over the past several years of research and writing. My colleague George Smith's constancy has been remarkable.

It seemed that every week or so George emailed me with a bright idea for the book or attached a relevant newspaper article or reference to a recently published article in an academic journal. Professor Kathryn Kelly is one of those supportive colleagues who periodically checks in with a much-appreciated "how's it going." Daniel Attridge, former Dean at the Catholic University Law School, arranged for me to present an early version of my conclusions at a faculty-alumni conclave, which generated many useful insights. Countless friends and colleagues have encouraged me along the way. They include Bill Osborne (and the entire Osborne/McArdle family), Beth Darrough, Warren (Rusty) Rawson, Scott Shelley, Frank McDonald, Dos Hatfield, and Dr. Patrick Bailey. I ask indulgence and understanding of any who have been supportive but whom I inadvertently have failed to list. Upon reading the initial manuscript, Dr. Ehren Foley, Acquisitions Editor at the University of South Carolina Press, appreciated immediately the relevance and importance of my thesis that Confederate monuments' political potency is best understood not only from the perspective of their past impact on Southern society but also in terms of their contemporary contribution to systemic racism. Dr. Foley was extraordinarily helpful in moving this project expeditiously to completion. And finally, as has been true for more than a quarter century, my work has benefitted immeasurably from the patience and encouragement of my wife, Catherine Mack, to whom this book is dedicated.

"When we look at a work of art, especially when 'we' [Black people] look at one in which Black Folk appear—or do not appear when they should—we should ask: what does it mean? What does it suggest? What impression is it likely to make on those who view it? What will be the effect on present-day problems, of its obvious and also of its insidious teachings? In short, we should endeavor to 'interpret' it; and should try to interpret it from our own particular viewpoint."

 F. Morris Murray, *Emancipation and the Freed in American Sculpture: A Study in Interpretation* [Freeport, NY: Books for Libraries Press, (1916), 1972], xix.

Introduction

Overview of the Confederate Memorial Removal Controversy

The wrangling over a proposed removal of a Confederate monument normally proceeds through three phases. The first is reaching consensus on whether anything needs to be done with a community's Confederate monument. Several approaches to this threshold question dominate: doing something because a Confederate monument distorts history; doing something because the monument was raised as part of a larger effort to suppress racial justice during the time of Jim Crow; and doing something because African Americans today are harmed by the continued presence of Confederate monuments. Each of these approaches is built on assumptions that seldom are tested. This book uncovers and evaluates these assumptions. If the decision is that something should be done with a Confederate monument, the next phase is deciding what actions are appropriate— destroy the structure; contextualize it, for example, by adding clarifying explanatory signage or perhaps a countermemorial; or relocate it? Here too, the choices rest on various assumptions, usually unarticulated, that need to be clarified and tested. The third phase is deciding who ought to have the final say regarding the fate of a Confederate monument, the citizens of the community where the monument currently is located or a third-party, normally an organ of state government that is controlled by state officials who are elected by a majority-White, statewide constituency. Monument removal decisions often are ensnared in a complex legal framework that limits (or precludes) a local community from removing its Confederate monument. In endeavoring to understand more fully the specifics of the Confederate monument debate, readers also will benefit from understanding the number of Confederate monuments that proliferate in the South, the time period in which they were constructed, the White South's several attacks on Southern African Americans' civil rights and liberties that were contemporaneous with the time period when most Confederate monuments were constructed, and the goals of the contemporary social movement to remove Confederate monuments.

The Confederate Monument Debate in Three Acts

History shows that it is easier to erect, than to remove, a Confederate monument that is located in a public space. That became clear on a quiet midsummer Saturday afternoon in 2017 when Rockville, Maryland, the county seat of Montgomery County, Maryland (near Washington, DC), removed a thirteen-ton statue of a Confederate soldier from the lawn of the county courthouse. Without advance notice or fanfare, the quiet weekend afternoon was chosen for the statue's removal to avoid protests or backlash. The United Daughters of the Confederacy donated the statue of a Confederate cavalryman to the city of Rockville on June 3, 1913 (Confederate Memorial Day, in Maryland, a date chosen to coincide with Jefferson Davis's Birthday). The inscription on the statue reads: "To Our Heroes of Montgomery Co. Maryland That We Through Life May Not Forget to Love The Thin Gray Line."

Rockville's six-feet-tall standing soldier statue on an eight-foot pedestal became the subject of contentious deliberations in 2015 as its fate was debated. The wrangling over the Rockville Confederate statue unmasked the three phases that nearly all Confederate monument removal efforts must navigate. Initially, a community wrestles with the foundational question of whether *anything* needs to be done with its Confederate monument. Absent a good reason for changing the status quo, why not simply maintain a Confederate monument where it is and where it most likely has been for a century or more? If the decision is that something should be done, phase two entails deciding what actions are appropriate—destroy the structure; contextualize it, for example, by adding clarifying explanatory signage or perhaps a countermemorial; or relocate it? The final phase of the Confederate monument drama involves controversy over who ought to have the *final say* regarding the fate of a Confederate monument, the citizens of the community where the monument currently is located or a third-party, normally an organ of state government that is controlled by state officials who are elected by a majority-White, statewide constituency?

During each phase of the deliberation over the fate of a Confederate monument, both sides typically advance claims based on assumptions regarding who raised Confederate monuments, why, and with what effect, both when these monuments were raised and up to the present. Untangling the claims and counterclaims that dominate contemporary Confederate monument disputes requires illuminating, and then testing, the validity of these numerous assumptions.

Phase I: The Threshold Question—Should Anything Be Done

Montgomery County, Maryland's political leadership concluded that the county's participation in the Civil War should be told, but must told fully from all perspectives, Union, Confederate, free Blacks, and slaves. Making no change to the Rockville Confederate statue was rejected as an option since that choice did not result in a comprehensive recounting of the County's Civil War history. The statue recalled the actions of those who supported the Confederacy but not the struggle of those county residents who fought for the Union or the perspective of those who otherwise opposed the Confederate South's aspiration to break up the Union and maintain the enslavement of nearly four million African Americans. For example, the Rockville monument masks the fact that Maryland sent 63,000 to the U.S. army and navy during the Civil War and only roughly 24,000—less than 40% as many—to the Confederate side.[1]

By framing the issue as the community's insistence on a fair and complete rendering of history, Rockville chose a politically safe characterization of the question of whether anything needs to be done with respect to its Confederate statue. Rockville's framing does not shame by accusing either ex-Confederates or their contemporary supporters of any racist motive or pernicious behavior. Moreover, the Rockville city government could reasonably assume that most citizens would favor pursuit of an authentic and comprehensive rendering of history. Yet, lurking behind Rockville's *complete-history* approach are several controversial, albeit unstated, assumptions. The most important is that Confederate statues and monuments are inherently ill-suited to capture history accurately or comprehensively. Indeed, recounting history accurately is not the purpose of a Confederate monument, certainly not its central purpose. This is because, as is true of all monuments and other expressions of public interpretation, the function of Confederate monuments is to shape memory. Monuments to the Confederacy and its leaders do this by symbolically communicating certain attitudes regarding the Civil War from the Confederate South's point of view, attitudes that focus on glorification. The United Daughters of the Confederacy arranged to have hundreds of Confederate monuments built throughout the South in an attempt to vindicate, not just remember, the war that the South waged in order to create a separate slaveholding republic. Through the erection of Confederate monuments, the United Daughters of the Confederacy intended to persuade us how to *think* about the Civil War by urging us to revere the Confederate side. The inscription the UDC placed on the Rockville standing soldier statue strikingly illuminates this glorification motivation—"To Our Heroes . . . That We Through Life May

Not Forget to Love The Thin Gray Line." Lionizing Confederate soldiers as "heroes" and urging undying love for the Confederacy is one perspective on the Civil War, indeed the only perspective that Confederate monuments communicate. There are contrasting viewpoints that challenge whether the Confederacy was worthy of glorification and whether its adherents ought to be lauded as "heroes." In other words, an underlying, unarticulated assumption built into the *complete-history* framing of the argument for doing something with a community's Confederate monument is that something needs to be done because Confederate monuments, by their nature, provide incomplete history and thereby provide false history. Built into the *complete-history* approach to deciding that something needs to be done with a Confederate monument is the unstated view that the history of other groups, including free and enslaved African Americans, have competing viewpoints from those who raised Confederate monuments a century ago, viewpoints that the White South during Jim Crow endeavored to erase. The following chapters in this book clarify and evaluate these assumptions that undergird the *complete-history* rationale for taking action with respect to a Confederate monument.

Other opponents of Confederate monuments have chosen somewhat more contentious approaches to resolving the question of whether something needs to be done to modify a Confederate monument located in a public space. I call the first the *warping-of-history* approach. This framing of the question is self-consciously accusatory. Like Rockville's *complete-history* approach, the *warping-of-history* strategy insists on an honest and comprehensive rendering of history. The difference is that the *warping-of-history* approach overtly scrutinizes the racist motives that animated building Confederate monuments in the first place. Specifically, Confederate monument opponents assemble evidence that local political and cultural elites erected Confederate monuments with the explicit motive to promote the ideology of White supremacy. For example, when New Orleans removed several of its Confederate monuments, local officials explained that monuments the city removed did not accurately represent history, nor the soul, of New Orleans. Instead they were "the product of a warped political movement by wealthy people supporting a mayor who was determined to regain power for White people, to reduce Blacks to second-class status, and to control how history was seen, read, and accepted by Whites: these [monuments] were symbols of White supremacy put up for a particular [political] reason."[2]

Confederate monument opponents often raise the White supremacist motivation that animated raising Confederate monuments as a compelling reason why a community must do something with its Confederate monument now. But, *warping-of-history* advocates mostly assert, and too seldom attempt to document, their core claim that the hundreds of Confederate monuments erected throughout the South were raised to broaden and deepen attitudes of White supremacy. Such a racist motive is not apparent simply by examining almost any Confederate monument: inscriptions, for example, virtually never mention race or slavery. How, for example, does an innocent-looking statue of a standing Confederate soldier promote White supremacy? The answer is not self-evident yet is critical to the *warping-of-history* approach to the Confederate monument removal/relocation debate. For the Confederate monument debate to proceed rationally, the racist motive for raising Confederate monuments needs to be demonstrated and not just asserted.

Nor do *warping-of-history* proponents typically demonstrate why Confederate monuments forfeit any claim for a prideful space in a twenty-first century public space due to the fact that the motive for raising them, probably a century ago, was to promote White supremacy?

In short, the underlying assumptions on which the *warping-of-history* claims are based may be true, indeed may seem obvious to some. But monument supporters argue that Confederate monuments are not racist. Southern traditionalists assert that Confederate monuments were raised to celebrate the valor of the Confederate soldier, not to intimidate African Americans nor to reaffirm White supremacy and today they simply represent Southern heritage, unassociated with any racism. The persuasiveness of the *warping-of-history* justification for doing something now with a Confederate monument depends first on evidence of who raised these monuments and why and second requires close scrutiny of the *warping-of-history* claimants' assertion that a White supremacist motivation for raising these monuments a century ago warrants taking some responsive action now because these monuments have caused and continue to cause societal harm. The following pages clarify and evaluate the claims and counterclaims surrounding the *warping-of-history* approach to the Confederate monument debate.

I describe a third strategy to determine whether to remove or otherwise alter a Confederate monument as the *racial-reckoning* approach. This inquiry into Confederate monuments directly focuses on impact by raising objections to Confederate monuments based on the reality that a community's Black citizens have been forced to live in the shadow of a particular Confederate monument all of their lives and are harmed by the experience.

One rendition of this frame is the view that Confederate monuments matter because "monuments illustrate to citizens who is privileged in the public sphere [and who is not]. To literally put the Confederacy [and its White supporters] on a pedestal in our most prominent places of honor is an . . . affront to our present, and is a bad prescription for our future."[3] The *racial-reckoning* claim is that Jim Crow-era Confederate monuments that glorify the White men who fought to keep in bondage the ancestors of present-day African Americans not only harmed African Americans when these monuments were erected, by helping to secure the grip of Jim Crow racial segregation, but these monuments *continue* to cause harm today. The charge is that a community demeans and disparages—insults—its African American citizens, indeed all of its citizens, when it chooses to provide its imprimatur to the celebration of the Confederacy's effort to perpetuate African American bondage. Adherents of the *racial-reckoning* view insist that a community has a moral obligation to make a conscious decision whether it desires to exalt men who led the fight to achieve the twin goals of the Confederacy—destruction of the Union and perpetuation of slavery.

In addition, it is argued that a community that genuinely supports diversity needs to consider seriously whether continuing to permit Confederate monuments to occupy the community's most revered public spaces misrepresents the community's current racial attitudes. Confederate monuments located in a prominent public space can regrettably misrepresent a Southern city's present identity as a community that is inclusive and welcomes diversity. New Orleans is an example. In 2017, when New Orleans removed four Confederate monuments, its political leadership concluded that these monuments misrepresented and undermined the city's goal of projecting itself as a community that welcomes and promotes racial diversity.[4] In addition, the *racial-reckoning* approach to reconsidering the placement of Confederate monuments raises the question whether the community's citizens believe that institutional racism represents a contemporary national crisis that is exasperated by Southern municipalities continuing to provide their imprimatur to Confederate monuments and the racial stereotyping and bias that these monuments transmit. The following chapters address all of these questions surrounding the *racial-reckoning* framing of the Confederate monument debate.

Phase II: What Should Be Done with a Confederate Monument?

A decision not to remain quiescent but rather to do something with respect to a community's Confederate monument, catapults the Confederate monument debate into its next politically and culturally charged phase: determining what ought to be done with the monument. In Rockville, Maryland, for example, the issue became whether to destroy its Confederate statue, relocate it, or retain the statue at its current location but add context that further interprets the statue. In order to consider these options, the Rockville County government convened a community group representing a broad spectrum of views, some diametrically conflicting. This advisory group recommended that the statue be removed. The statue was relocated in 2017 to a location on private property near White's Ferry, a privately-run Potomac River car ferry named the "Jubal Early," honoring a Confederate general who until his death defended slavery as appropriate status for African Americans. This new home for Rockville's Confederate statue is located in a portion of the county that was the epicenter of Confederate sympathy during the Civil War.

Although destroying the statue was rejected, destruction proponents vigorously argued that the Rockville statue needed to be destroyed because it was implicitly racist: it represents a symbol of resistance to African Americans' civil rights and symbolically expresses support for slavery and the view of African Americans' inferiority. Destruction adherents urged that only eradication of the symbol would eliminate the harm it causes. Removal to a different location merely relocates the venue of the ongoing harm that the statue causes through transmission of its racist message. Others strongly opposed destruction. They advanced on two fronts. First, they argued that the statue evidenced a particular time in our history and destroying the statue would preclude the ability to use the statue to teach, interpret, and learn from the past. Second, some destruction opponents argued that the statue is a unique work of art relating specifically to Rockville and Montgomery County, Maryland, and destroying it would be interpreted as vandalism that would further polarize the community.

One alternative to destruction of the Rockville Confederate statue was to keep the statue in place but augment it by adding interpretive elements. Rockville rejected that option. Proponents of reinterpretation believed that adding context to the statue, by adding signage or interpretive plaques for example, could serve to educate the public and convey a more complete account of Montgomery County's Civil War history and the history of slavery in the county in general. The added context could include the viewpoints of free Blacks and slaves and could also provide a history of the statue itself. Opponents of reinterpretation successfully countered that placing the statue on prime public land in 1903 demonstrated White supremacists' grip on political power in the county during the period of Jim Crow racial segregation. Opponents of adding context at the present site of the statue argued that leaving the statue in place now, even with the addition of contextualization, implies that racists still have much influence within the county's government. In addition, contextualization opponents considered it problematic that new historical context could counterbalance to any significant degree the negative emotions the statue elicits, particularly among the county's African American residents. Finally, the location of the statue on the courthouse lawn symbolically implied that the courthouse does not represent justice for all and no amount of contextualization added to the statue can change that perception. Only removal of the statue, contextualization opponents argued, would convey that those in the community had been heard when they assert that the statue symbolizes Black suffering rather than communicating the unity and progress reflective of the present-day Montgomery County. There is no record that size and scale were raised at this community meeting, but that also is relevant. The monument will always dominate the landscape vis-à-vis an interpretive marker or plaque. Unless the countermarker was truly a countermonument of a scale to compete with, perhaps dominant, even change the meaning of, the original monument, then it will always be the secondary element.

The third option, relocation, was strongly opposed by some. They advanced two arguments. First, relocation opponents asserted that changing the statue's historical placement changes its meaning by denying the statue the historical context of the place in which it was erected. Second, relocation opponents believed that relocation of long-standing historical artifacts sets a dangerous precedent. These objects were created in a very different historical and cultural context and ought not be judged on the basis of contemporary standards and political climate. Banishing historical artifacts, relocation opponents argued, denies the existence of the past and is grounded in the belief that somehow contemporary society can change the past to better suit present perspectives. By contrast, those who supported relocation of the Rockville statue believed that a decision to remove the statue constituted a teachable moment: removal (banishment) added the most profound and appropriate interpretive context possible to the statue and its ideological projection of anti-Black racism. It was argued, moreover, that relocation is a reasonable compromise: relocation preserves the statue itself and permits interested individuals to learn about it in a more appropriate environment. At the same time, removal symbolically rejects the Confederate statue's implied racial bias and terminates all approving association between the community and the message that the Confederate statue transmits. Relocation also allows the creation of a new historical context for the statue in a new venue and invites adding a historical marker at the statue's previous location stating that a statue that had glorified the Confederacy had once been located there, when it was erected and by whom, and when and why it was removed.[5]

These arguments and counterarguments over what should be done with a Confederate monument are formulated around sets of assumptions grounded in Southern history, politics, culture, and race relations—such as the motives for initially raising these monuments, the harm these monuments have caused the African American community over the years, and the emotional anguish that they continue to inflict. The claim of present emotional harm caused by Confederate monuments is a powerful consideration. That harm is described in different ways: a feeling of degradation among African Americans resulting from their having to live with and everyday confront these monuments, which remind them of past, and present, injustices directed at African Americans; a sense of exclusion felt by African Americans arising from the fact that their city or town continues to choose to advertise White supremacy on a daily basis by continuing to sponsor Confederate monuments; and the view that adding context cannot erase the emotional damage these monuments have caused and do cause. Too seldom is evidence advanced to substantiate these recitations of emotional harm, perhaps because the harm seems so self-evident to many.

Confederate monument *supporters,* in turn, often build their case on unsupported assertions: the educational potential of Confederate monuments if they are left in place; exactly how Confederate monuments and their pro-Confederate message can possibly support a view of contemporary Southern (White Southern) heritage in a non-racist manner; how unique and valuable *are* these monuments from an artistic point of view; how exactly monument opponents are understood to be subjecting early-twentieth century objects to twenty-first century sentimentality (or more unkindly, allegations of yielding to political correctness); and why it can be fairly claimed that those urging removal of Confederate monuments are, like the Taliban, seeking to destroy symbols in an effort to deny and rewrite the past.

Confronting what to do with a community's Confederate monument has taken center stage and has caused bitter clashes. Comprehending and evaluating accurately the associated claims and counterclaims calls for a stout dose of calming rationality through the process of unearthing the facts relevant to each side's assertions. The following chapters provide those facts.

Phase III: Who Should Control the Fate of a Confederate Monument?

Montgomery County owns the Rockville Confederate statue. But the statue stood on the grounds of the county courthouse, which was listed in 1986 in the National Register of Historic Places. Accordingly, under state law, before the county could lawfully relocate the statue it was required to file an application to relocate with the Rockville Historic District Commission. A hearing before the Historic District Commission provided additional opportunities for relocation opponents to make their case, in particular to argue that moving the Rockville Confederate statue is akin to removing a significant piece of history from the site that for decades had been used to inform citizens about the Civil War. At the hearing before the Historic

District Commission, removal opponents attempted to characterize the county's efforts to relocate the statue as a "Talibanic"-type effort to "erase our history" and argued that even post-World-War-II Germany had not attempted to dismantle all reference to the past. In the end, the Historic District Commission granted the county's application to relocate the Rockville Confederate statue.[6] But it requires little imagination to recognize that a historic district commission controlled by members who strongly support "Southern heritage" (White Southern heritage), and thus support maintaining the *status quo* for Confederate memorialization, could have thwarted the decision by Rockville's citizens to remove the statue from the courthouse green. In other words, the commission could have appropriated the decision-making process to itself and thereby deny the community a preference that evolved following a democratic deliberative process.

Maryland is not among the states that have enacted laws that prohibit the removal or alteration of Confederate monuments. Seven states, all formerly part of the Confederacy, currently have legislation banning or severely restricting monument removal. Some local jurisdictions have identified unintended loopholes in such legislation that have permitted these jurisdictions to remove their Confederate monument. But state legislatures quickly amend statutes to remove the loophole. There is a plausible constitutional argument that state statutes that bar removal of Confederate monuments violate the free speech rights of residents of municipalities whose governments have voted to remove their Confederate monuments, if they could. Courts have not resolved these constitutional questions. The legal framework within which the Confederate monument controversy occurs requires close examination due to its significant influence on the outcome of monument removal disputes. This book provides that examination.

The Relationship Between Jim Crow Racial Segregation and Confederate Monument Mania

The Rockville statue relocation debate was but one of dozens that have flared up throughout the South. In April 2016, the Southern Poverty Law Center (SPLC) published its findings from a year-long study cataloging Confederate iconography in the United States. The SPLC database identified 718 Confederate monuments and statues on public property, nearly all (92 percent) located in the eleven states comprising the Confederacy and the two border states of Kentucky and Missouri.[7]

Confederate monuments predominately are found in four types of public landscapes: 1) battlefields (mainly commemorating individual units or troops from a particular state); 2) cemeteries (memorializing Confederate dead); 3) courthouse squares and urban streets and parks (commemorating the Confederacy itself and/or those who fought for the Confederacy); and 4) "large, impressive monuments" found on statehouse grounds throughout the South and often dedicated to Confederate soldiers from a particular state. By far, most Confederate monuments were erected either in cemeteries or in urban areas such as courthouse squares, streets, or parks.[8]

In 1983, John Winberry analyzed 666 Confederate monuments located in cemeteries and in urban areas (streets, parks and courthouse squares). Fifty-five percent of these monuments consisted of a lone Confederate soldier standing atop a column, with his weapon either at parade rest, in front of him between his legs, or (a small number) with his weapon at the ready. Most of these "standing soldier" monuments were oriented toward the North, as if the heroic White granite soldier were protecting the community from an anticipated invasion from that direction. In Winberry's study, the standing soldier monument represented nearly two-thirds of the monuments located on courthouse squares. The second type of monument observed in the study was the obelisk. This monument consisted of "a single shaft with a peaked top, covered with a shroud or flag, or supporting an urn, cannon balls, or other objects." Obelisks were the most prevalent type of the Confederate monument found in cemeteries.[9]

Immediately following the Civil War, scattered groups in the South raised some cemetery obelisks but otherwise Confederate monuments erected prior to 1870 are a rarity.[10] By the mid-1880s, the pace of Confederate monument construction slowly increased and monuments began to move to urban streets and parks and courthouse squares. By the end of the nineteenth century, the pace of construction of Confederate monuments increased dramatically, ushering in a period of Confederate "monument mania." The SPLC's 2016 study revealed that Confederate monument construction spiked during the early twentieth century, the most active period being between 1901 and 1912.[11] As Table 1 below shows, 354 of the 718 Confederate monuments identified by SPLC in 2016 (49.3 percent) were dedicated during the two decades between 1901 and 1920.

Gaines Foster's early study is consistent with the SPLC findings. Foster studied the Confederate monuments raised as of 1913 and found that approximately 60 percent of all of them were unveiled between 1900 and 1912.[12] During the first decade of the twentieth century alone (1900 to 1909), as many Confederate monuments were erected as in all previous decades combined.[13] John Winberry's research provides similar evidence of the concentration of Confederate monument construction in the first decades of the twentieth century.

Table 1: Number of Confederate Monuments, 1861–2010 by Decade

YEARS	TOTAL MONUMENTS	MONUMENTS ON COURTHOUSE GROUNDS	MONUMENTS IN OTHER LOCATIONS
1861–1870	21	2	19
1871–1880	25	7	18
1881–1890	31	6	25
1891–1900	46	12	34
1901–1910	208	91	117
1911–1920	146	82	64
1921–1930	56	18	38
1931–1940	45	11	34
1941–1950	14	1	13
1951–1960	18	6	12
1961–1970	36	9	27
1971–1980	14	1	13
1981–1990	13	5	8
1991–2000	23	7	16
2001–2010	22	6	16
TOTAL	718	264	454

Source: Southern Poverty Law Center, "Whose Heritage?" (2016).

Winberry concluded that 80 percent of all standing soldier Confederate monuments were raised after 1900 and 93 percent of *all* courthouse monuments were raised after 1895, more than half of these being raised in the ten-year period of 1903 to 1912.[14]

This "monument mania" that began in the late 1890s coincided in time with the South's sweeping onslaught of repression against the African American community. For example, Confederate mania began in earnest just as the Supreme Court decided its landmark *Plessy v. Ferguson* "separate but equal" decision of 1896, which upheld the legality of Jim Crow racial segregation.[15] Confederate monument mania also coincided with the Southern Democratic Party's race-baiting of the biracial Southern agrarian revolt, which doomed the Populist effort to bring economic justice to the South's poor White and Black farmers. The peak construction of Confederate monuments arose as the Whites in the South disfranchised millions of African Americans, entrenched Jim Crow racial segregation, and began to flood Southern public schools with school textbooks teaching White supremacy and the inferiority of African Americans to both the White and Black children in the South. In addition, the apogee in Confederate

Aerial photograph of Confederate Memorial on Stone Mountain, October 2017.
Carol M. Highsmith's America Project in the Carol M. Highsmith Archive, Library of Congress, Prints and Photographs Division.

monument construction paralleled in time the lynching of hundreds of African Americans, many of whom were victims of "spectacle lynching" where thousands of Southern Whites, often arriving on specially chartered excursion trains, attended the prearranged and advertised torture and lynching of (mostly young) Black males.[16] This turn-of-the century Confederate monument mania during the height of Jim Crow racial segregation also coincided with the unprecedented popularity of the racist film *Birth of a Nation* and the election of President Woodrow Wilson, the Southern racist who screened the *Birth of a Nation* in the White House and ordered the segregation of federal offices in Washington, DC. And "monument mania" accompanied the rebirth of the Ku Klux Klan at a late-night ceremony atop Stone Mountain, Georgia, where the Klan thereafter continued to hold ceremonies and meetings at what became one of the South's most famous Confederate monuments.[17]

A second spike in constructing Confederate monuments occurred during the South's "Massive Resistance" to the Supreme Court's 1954 school desegregation decision in *Brown v. Board of Education*.[18] As Table 1 shows, cities and towns raised more than twice as many Confederate monuments in the decade of 1961–1970 than during either of the previous two decades. The Stone Mountain Confederate monument, dedicated in 1970, falls in this "Massive Resistance" monument category.

The Social Movement to Remove Confederate Monuments

In 2018, the SPLC updated its 2016 report on Confederate monuments, adding a listing of Confederate monuments that were removed following Dylann Roof's 2015 massacre of nine African American worshipers at the Mother Emanuel A.M.E. Church in Charleston, South Carolina. Roof, a twenty-one-year-old White supremacist, was famously pictured on social media brandishing a handgun while holding a Confederate battle flag. That association between the Charleston massacre and the Confederate battle flag thrust into the forefront the "whole issue of Confederate ideology [which] had been percolating in the South for generations."[19] Opposition to Confederate iconography thereafter intensified and culminated in the August 2017 race riot in Charlottesville, Virginia, that left a young woman dead and many people injured.[20] Some White supremacists taking part in the rally wore red Make America Great Again hats. And David Duke, a former grand wizard of the Ku Klux Klan, expressed the view that the Charlottesville White supremacist protests were a fulfillment of the vision for America held by those who promise "to take our country back."[21]

The SPLC's 2018 report lists forty-seven Confederate statues and monuments removed from public spaces, many that had been in place for more than 100 years. By June 2020, following the May 2020 police killing of George Floyd, the total of removed monuments reached at least 55. Other proposed removals were embroiled in litigation.[22] In July 2018, a ten-member commission established by the mayor of Richmond, Virginia, recommended the removal of the memorial to Jefferson Davis, the president of the Confederacy, that has occupied space in Richmond's fabled Monument Avenue since 1907 when the United Daughters of the Confederacy arranged for its construction. On June 10, 2020, protesters toppled that statute of Davis.[23] Moreover, in the summer of 2018, a group of protestors toppled the divisive, century-old, "Silent Sam" standing soldier statue located at a prominent entrance to the campus of the University of North Carolina at Chapel Hill.[24] The statue, which had occupied this choice location for more than 100 years, subsequently was donated to a Confederate heritage group and relocated to an off-campus site. As of early 2020, in North Carolina alone, four Confederate monuments have been removed since the August 2017 race riot in Charlottesville, Virginia.[25]

A large proportion of the monuments listed in the SPLC database are located in cemeteries, adjacent to graves of former Confederate soldiers. These cemetery memorials are not the target of the movement seeking the removal/relocation of Confederate monuments.[26] Leaders in the removal movement, such as the SPLC, state that their objection is that by maintaining Confederate monuments on public property state and local governments add their imprimatur, their endorsement, to the ideology of the Confederate government, an ideology that the SPLC contends was grounded in and dedicated to advancing the ideology of White supremacy. As the SPLC stated in 2018, "The Civil War ended 153 years ago. The Confederacy . . . was on the wrong side of humanity. Our public entities should no longer play a role in distorting history by honoring a *secessionist government* that waged war against the United States to preserve White supremacy and the enslavement of four million people."[27] There is a meaningful difference between a cemetery memorial and a civic monument located on a courthouse square or an urban park that glorifies the Confederate cause. Location matters. "A public position [for a civic monument] serve[s] clearly to identify the community with [the] monument."[28] The central concern is that the state has "the ability to legitimate certain arguments merely by virtue of its being the state that is offering them [with the result that opposing views] will be denied legitimacy [and] marginalized."[29] The funereal memorials adjacent to the graves of thousands of former Confederate soldiers were generally not erected, are not understood, and are not maintained as a means to propagate the anti-Black racist ideology of the Confederate government.[30] The battleground is the confederate monument located in urban streets and parks and on courthouse grounds.

PHASE I
Act or Leave the Monuments Undisturbed?

1
History and Memory Distinguished

A commonly advanced argument for doing something with a local community's Confederate monument centers on Confederate monuments' distortion of history. Criticizing monuments due to their inadequate portrayal of history to some degree misses the mark. No town wants to sponsor distorted history. But Confederate monuments were not erected primarily to portray history accurately—notwithstanding claims to the contrary by monument supporters. The United Daughters of the Confederacy (UDC) raised hundreds of Confederate monuments out of a desire to influence attitudes and construct a "collective memory" of the Civil War that glorifies the Confederacy. Understanding the difference between history and memory is essential to untangling the competing claims dominating the Confederate monument controversy. History reflects what is objectively provable from the record of past events. Memory consists of subjective representations, constructions, of reality created by those with the power and cultural authority to do so in order to influence how we think about some historic event. Confederate monuments were erected to transmit collective memory: originally to transmit the tenets of what is referred to as the "Cult of the Lost Cause;" later, to communicate attitudes of White supremacy as Jim Crow segregation took hold at the turn of the twentieth century; and then, most recently, to help construct a Southern collective memory supportive of the "massive resistance" to the forced ending of Jim Crow racial segregation and the emergence of the civil rights movement. Understanding the Confederate monument controversy begins with an appreciation of the difference between history and memory and the role of Confederate monuments in transmitting collective memory.

WHEN A CONFEDERATE MONUMENT has stood for over a century in a town square or courthouse lawn, its presence represents the *status quo*. Rightly or wrongly, the expectation is that Confederate monument opponents should carry the burden to come forward with sound reasons why the monument should be disturbed after all these years. A common contention is finding fault with a Confederate monument's incomplete and inaccurate portrayal of history.

A monument's failure to communicate history fully is a recurring, but not entirely convincing, reason to disturb a Confederate monument. All monuments provide an incomplete portrayal of the person or event that they commemorate. Case in point: Americans "are not quite ready to raze the Jefferson Memorial or chip [Jefferson's] face off Mount Rushmore" notwithstanding that Jefferson owned hundreds of slaves or even given the relatively recent disclosure of Jefferson's sexual improprieties with his slave Sally Hemings.[1] This memorial celebrates Thomas Jefferson's extraordinary contributions to his country: a member of the Virginia Colonial Assembly, draftsman of the Declaration of Independence, delegate to the 1st Continental Congress, governor of Virginia, the country's first secretary of state, its second vice president, and our third president. We accept that the Jefferson Memorial celebrates Jefferson's strengths and we forgive that it ignores to mention of his flaws. That is the nature of a commemorative monument. By further example, the Lincoln Memorial celebrates a president who did as much as any other person in history to help free the South's slaves. But the Lincoln Memorial makes no reference to the fact that when Lincoln ran for the Senate in 1858, he was anti-slavery but not an abolitionist. Lincoln, raised in Kentucky, could not then imagine an interracial future for the United States and thus did not then urge granting equal citizenship to slaves once they were freed.[2] Moreover, even after Lincoln advocated freeing the slaves, he did not subscribe to social equality between the races and in fact advocated returning the freed slaves to Liberia.[3] The Lincoln Memorial is appropriately admired, notwithstanding its incomplete history with respect to Lincoln's racial attitudes. Unlike a written biography or the work product of academic historians, commemorative monuments are not expected to provide a warts-and-all rendition of history. There are compelling reasons for removing Confederate monuments from their currently occupied public spaces, but their failure to provide a complete history of the events that they symbolically celebrate cannot alone carry the argument for removal. No monument provides a complete history.

Distorting history is a different matter. A community may understandably recoil at lending its imprimatur to a monument that disseminates counterfeit history and for that reason may decide to remove the monument. Confederate monuments do distort history, and badly, as is documented in the next chapter. But one overlooks what is most interesting, and important, about Confederate monuments by fixating on Confederate monuments' failure to transmit history accurately. Notwithstanding claims by those who raised Confederate monuments, and some current admirers, these monuments were never intended to teach history scrupulously. Those who built Confederate monuments did so in an attempt to vindicate, not just remember, the war the South waged to create a separate slaveholding republic. Confederate monument builders raised monuments not primarily that we should know about the Civil War but rather to persuade us how to *think* about the South's participation in the Civil War. Postwar ex-Confederates invented a particular rendition of history in a calculated attempt to persuade us to develop memories that revere the Confederate side. Comprehending the difference between history (what actually occurred) and memory (how we think about what occurred) is essential in order to grasp the true nature of the Confederate monument controversy.

Gary Gallagher, history professor *emeritus* at the University of Virginia, is in a unique position to know, when he observes that among the most difficult things for students of history to fathom is the difference between history and memory.[4] Confederate monuments were erected to shape memory. They do this by symbolically communicating certain attitudes regarding the Civil War from the Confederate South's point of view, attitudes that focus on glorification of the Confederate cause and those who fought in behalf of that cause. By implication, a function of a Confederate monument is to denigrate, at least attempt to erase and marginalize, African Americans' alternative attitudes and memories of the Civil War and its consequences.

It is useful to recognize that both sides in the monument removal/relocation controversy begin at a common point of departure: that monuments are expressive, they possess robust communicative power. Monuments are not simply inanimate hunks of stone, marble, and bronze. Though constructed of bronze and stone, monuments "are messengers from the past" transmitting the perspectives and attitudes of those possessing the political and cultural authority to erect them.[5] For some, a Confederate monument is offensive and humiliating since it conveys a message supporting racial oppression and exclusion. For others, a Confederate monument evokes pride in Confederate heritage, a celebration of past heroic and patriotic activity, and perhaps a desire to return to a time of White supremacy. But the point of agreement is important: when a community converts a public space into a ritual site by adding a Confederate monument to a town square or courthouse lawn, for example, that community expresses its understanding of the essentials in its past, its identity, or what sociologists refer to as its collective memory.[6]

It is well established, and has been for nearly one hundred years, that in order to maintain cohesion, every social group needs to construct and maintain an identity that unites its members. To accomplish this, humans construct memories. Our memories are not generated simply by calling up sets of objective recollections drawn from the historical record. Rather, our memories consist of subjective representations—constructions—of reality.[7] As a member of a group, we adopt the group's collective memory of the past, not a recollection of what has "actually been preserved in popular memory, but what has been selected, written, pictured, popularized, and institutionalized by those whose function it is to do so."[8] Those with power and cultural authority are the ones who select events, dates, and persons to interpret the past. What is not selected is thus eliminated, erased from the collective memory. The process of silencing representations of the past that others would have chosen for inclusion in a social group's collective memory is termed "collective amnesia."[9]

Brian Black and Bryn Varley have explained the relationship between collective memory and monuments as follows: Humans construct memories built around myths, legends, and science, and in this process the details of certain places can take on significance and stir emotional reactions. We can generate an emotional response, for example, when we revisit a church, a classroom, a trail hiked many times, or, yes, a previously visited historic monument. We assemble stories of place that become part of our collective memory and often mature into legends and myths. Over time, we create "layers of meaning" for certain locales. These layers of meaning generate "such emotional force that groups or individuals strive to preserve these sites or try to change them."[10]

Eric Hobsbawm's and Terence Ranger's notion of "invented tradition" expands the concept of collective memory in ways that are particularly useful to the study of Confederate monuments. Hobsbawm and Ranger observed that a dynamic modern world creates social changes that destroy customs used to maintain authority, social control, and group solidarity. In other words, modernity creates a void in structures used to unite and animate modern society. Those with the greatest interest in maintaining power and status respond by inventing replacement traditions that promote certain beliefs and behavior that suggest "a continuity with [a fabricated] past." A core function of "invented tradition" is to camouflage new rules as simply a continuation of old rules.[11]

The post-Civil War decades were punctuated by enormous social and economic disruptions as the South recovered from losing the war, was pressured to integrate its African American population into the South's civic, economic, and political life, and was transformed from an agrarian society to a more urban and industrialized "New South." Southern social and political elites responded initially by raising Confederate monuments to advance their version of collective memory of the Civil War through the invented tradition called the *Cult of the Lost Cause.* Later, in the late-nineteenth and early-twentieth centuries, during the height of Jim Crow racial segregation, the United Daughters of the Confederacy gained nearly complete control over the erection of Confederate monuments. The UDC's self-conscious motive for erecting Confederate monuments shifted to a more aggressive and overt promotion of certain beliefs regarding a preferred racial hierarchy for the New South. This hierarchy represented continuity with a fabricated and romanticized vision of the Old South punctuated by White supremacy and Black inferiority. In the mid-twentieth century, with the dismantling of the Jim Crow system of *de jure* racial segregation following the school desegregation decision in *Brown v. Board of Education,* and with the coming of the civil rights movement, many in the White South joined the "massive resistance" and deployed Confederate memorialization (including raising Confederate monuments) as one means to resist racial equality by mounting a last-ditch effort to retain *de facto* White supremacy.

Deciding whether *anything* needs to be done with a Confederate monument, and if so what, thus begins with a recognition that while Confederate monuments purport to recite history, they principally are designed to construct attitudes, to condition how we think about the Civil War and its consequences. Confederate monuments symbolically encourage the formation of attitudes that glorify of the Confederate cause by transmitting an invented historical viewpoint called "The Cult of the Lost Cause" also referred to as the Lost Cause myth. Imparting the tenets of the Lost Cause myth has been an objective of every Confederate monument.

To comprehend the contemporary harm Confederate monuments cause, it is necessary to understand several things about the relationship between Confederate monuments and the Lost Cause myth: the many ways that the Lost Cause myth distorts history; how that distortion promotes an ideology of White supremacy and Black inferiority; and how the imagery in Confederate monuments symbolically transmits the tenets of the Lost Cause and thus contributes to the creation of attitudes of White supremacy and Black inferiority that undermine contemporary aspirations for racial equality.

2
The Distortion-of-History Approach

The Cult of the Lost Cause

Confederate monuments were raised to transmit the tenets of what is referred to as the Cult of the Lost Cause, the term given to a romanticized recounting of Confederate history. In order to assuage ex-Confederate leaders' anxieties that history would view them as murderers and traitors who had engaged in a rebellion, the Southern elite after the Civil War assembled a fabricated justification of the Confederate cause that depicts ex-Confederates as having acted honorably at every turn. The Lost Cause narrative denies any significant role for slavery in the South's decision to secede from the Union; the narrative justifies secession as a noble choice to protect Southern liberties and characterizes secession as an option reserved for every state by the United States Constitution; and the Lost Cause Myth claims that slavery was a benign institution overseen by caring masters and populated by happy and faithful, albeit innately inferior, Southern African Americans who were held in servitude. The Lost Cause Myth denies that the Civil War was prosecuted, even in part, to provide political equality for the former slaves. In short, the Lost Cause narrative glorifies Whites whose fate it was to fight steadfastly and valiantly for a noble cause they were not able to attain and excludes from its celebration of human effort and self-sacrifice any achievements of Southern African Americans. The Lost Cause Myth distorts history and Confederate monuments transmit the tenets of the Lost Cause Myth, so Confederate monuments also distort history. But more fundamentally than just distorting history, the Lost Cause Myth and Confederate monuments that communicate it promote White supremacy by lauding a constructed view of antebellum Southern life with its racial hierarchy intact. Surviving histories of Confederate monuments' dedication ceremonies provide excellent evidence of how Confederate monuments were instrumental in transmitting the tenets of the Lost Cause Myth.

THE CIVIL WAR CREATED the worst carnage in American history up to that time. The conventional estimate is that 647,000 soldiers, North and South, died during that four-year conflict. That number of deaths represented two percent of the United States' population, one out of every 50 persons. In recent years, the death toll has been revised upward and the current estimate of Civil War deaths is 750,000.[1] In the North, 6.1 percent of its White military age males (ages 13–43) died in the Civil War and in the South more than twice that figure (nearly 13 percent) died. African Americans served in the Union military (army and navy), 134,000 out of a total of 180,000 coming from slave states. Twenty percent of these African American soldiers perished.[2] The Civil War was a slaughter that visited grief on nearly every family and every town and village in the South. It is estimated that one in every three Southern households lost at least one family member. One in thirteen surviving Northern and Southern Civil War soldiers returned home missing one or more limbs.[3] Neither the North nor the South was prepared for this "all but unfathomable cost of the war."[4]

Anxiety Over Posterity's Opinion of Confederate Veterans

Some portions of the South escaped the Civil War's physical devastation, but most of the region did not. The majority of the Confederate veterans returned to bereaving communities that were physically in shambles. The South's ex-Confederate leaders needed to justify the catastrophe of the war to the Southern people. Not only had secession caused the South to be invaded and conquered, and not only had the war cost hundreds of thousands of lives, but the war destroyed much of the South physically and economically. The war cost the South two-thirds of its assessed wealth, 40 percent of its livestock, more than 50 percent destruction of its farm machinery, and incalculable damage to its rail and industrial infrastructure.[5] Based on the prices for slaves quoted at the time of the Civil War, the nearly four million emancipated slaves were worth more than the value of all of the farmland in the South at that time and three times the construction cost of all of the railroads that operated in the United States. Added to the significant financial loss caused by emancipation was emancipation's cost to the South in lost labor. Prior to the Civil War, slave labor had produced half of the South's tobacco, nearly all of its sugar, rice, and hemp, and 90 percent of its cotton.[6] Historian Richard White writes that the Civil War left the South defeated, broken, and battered. "The heartland of the Confederacy [had dissolved] into a snarling mix of rumor, resentment, self-recrimination, blame, rage, and self-pity [after having] gambled virtually everything on the attempt to create a slave state [and having lost the gamble]."[7]

The roads in the South could be repaired and the fields replanted. Livestock could be replenished. Factories could be rebuilt and farm machinery could be repurchased. The Southern economy could be reinvigorated. The class conflicts that emerged in the South during the Civil War could be healed. However, returning Confederate veterans, and in particular their elite planter-class leaders, feared one incalculable loss that would be irretrievable: the loss of their honor. The concern was that history would view Confederate loyalists as murderers and traitors who had engaged in a rebellion and required a pardon from the North for their transgressions.[8]

Ex-Confederates had reason to be anxious. Following Appomattox, some Southerners questioned the righteousness of the Confederate cause and therefore questioned the honor of those who brought on the war. These Southerners were concerned that perhaps the South lost the War because God had abandoned the South. Perhaps Southerners had invited God's wrath due to their act of secession and the "sin of slavery." Southerners overwhelmingly concluded that their cause had been righteous. Yet the anxiety was that if the South, believing it was right, was in fact wrong in 1861, then the South must hang its head in shame for eternity because its blunder and crime had persisted for four years and caused such a prodigious loss of life and property. Following the Civil War, some Southerners publicly accused the former Confederate leadership of such dishonorable behavior.[9]

In addition to post-war criticism from their own citizens, former Confederate leaders' anxiety was heightened by the treason indictments lodged against them immediately following the end of hostilities. Viewing the ex-Confederate leadership as a of gang of traitors, the United States government obtained treason indictments against nearly forty former leaders of the Confederacy, including Robert E. Lee and Jefferson Davis. For various reasons treason trials were not conducted, but some of these men ultimately had to be pardoned "for the offense of treason against the United States."[10]

In addition to treason, there remained continuing wonderment among many Union veterans why Confederate military figures deserved any honor since so many, such as Robert E. Lee, took up arms against the United States in breach of the oath taken upon being commissioned a United States Army officer following receiving a West Point education at taxpayer expense.[11]

But accusations of treason and oath-breaking were not the only concerns. In addition, ex-Confederates required affirmation that they had not brought dishonor upon themselves and their generation by being defeated in the war. Personal honor began with personal bravery. But defeat challenged the Confederates' self-confidence that they had acquitted themselves honorably and with dignity during the war, that they had lived up to expectations of personal honor and bravery.

Finally, returning Confederate veterans also needed encouragement regarding preservation of their manhood in defeat—the ability to return from war defeated yet able to reinstate traditional roles of masculinity and femininity. In this regard it became necessary for Southern women to sustain despairing Southern males and to assure them that, though defeated, they had discharged their responsibilities in a manly manner.[12]

In short, vanquished ex-Confederates longed to be viewed, both at home in the South and by the North, as noble warriors who had fought for a just cause (as they saw it) and yearned that posterity would provide them heroic recognition. But they well understood the forces that might deprive them this quest. History might well view them negatively: impulsive men who had attempted illegally to overthrow the Union, men who would be scorned for having seceded and having caused monstrous suffering and shedding of blood simply to preserve their slave property.[13]

The Cult of the Lost Cause became a vehicle that was calculated to rescue ex-Confederates from history's opprobrium and acquit them from history's verdict of treason and rebellion. The Lost Cause myth praised the Confederate fallen and emphasized their valor, steadfastness, sacrifice, loyalty, nobility of their motives, and dedication to a noble cause. By implication this praise for the Confederate dead applied equally to the survivors.[14]

Tenets of the Lost Cause Myth and Distortions of History

Each death of a Southern son, brother, husband, or other loved one during the Civil War was an occasion for bereavement. Soon after Appomattox, in 1865, groups of women in the South, primarily members of the Ladies' Memorial Associations (LMAs), began collecting Confederate dead, constructing cemeteries for their interment in the South, and organizing annual Confederate Memorial Day observances eulogizing the fallen. With the death of Robert E. Lee in 1870, LMA-sponsored Confederate Memorial Day observances began to place less emphasis on mourning the dead and more on providing opportunities for speakers to stress the nobility of the Confederate Lost Cause and the surviving ex-Confederates who had fought to achieve it.[15]

But the key development in maturation of the Lost Cause myth was formation of the Southern Historical Society (SHS), organized in 1869, originally headquartered in New Orleans, and then moved to Richmond in 1873. In Richmond, former Virginia Confederate officers led by ex-Confederate

General Jubal Early assumed control of the SHS. They began publication of the Southern Historical Society Papers (SHSP) in 1876. The SHSP was a periodical expressing the Confederate view of the War. The takeover of the SHS by Jubal Early and the so-called "Virginia coalition" and publication of the 52 volumes of the SHSP represented a self-conscious effort to take control of and to shape the Confederate tradition.[16]

Jubal Early "loathed Yankees and Blacks" and was "prickly" regarding Southern honor and manhood. He and the Virginia coalition insisted on acknowledgment from the North that the South had acted honorably in seceding and in defending slavery and had acted with martial valor during the Civil War. The SHSP published accounts of the war that were proactive efforts to counter anticipated humiliations resulting from Northern accounts that had begun to characterize Confederates as rebels and traitors rather than as Southern patriots. *But Early and his group did more,* and this becomes critical for understanding the racist implications of Confederate monuments. Early and his followers also tried to construct in postwar Southern consciousness, an imaged narrative of the Old South as a glorious era.[17] Early and his group at the SHS "supported an aristocratic social order resting on deference to leaders and duty to society. Indirectly it supported White supremacy as well."[18]

The Lost Cause myth, symbolically transmitted through Confederate monuments, contained many historical distortions. They fall into four categories: The South's constitutional right to secede; slavery as not constituting the cause of the war; the nature of antebellum race relations; and the explanation of the South's defeat.[19]

The Myth That Secession Was Justified

A bedrock tenet of the Cult of the Lost Cause, and a claim made implicitly or explicitly by every Confederate monument, is that secession may have been unwise and inexpedient, but it was not wrong. The United States Constitution, the argument goes, incorporated a compact theory of government that permitted every state to retain its sovereignty. A fundamental prerogative of such retained sovereignly was the right of each state to secede from the compact at will. Secession by the South was thus legally and morally justified, Confederate apologists argued, and the North abandoned and violated this compact theory of government when it invaded the South simply because Southern states had peaceably withdrawn from the Union in order to create an independent slaveholding republic. The Lost Cause myth stated that defeat may have been humiliating, but the South acted honorably, morally and legally, and was on the side of right and justice by seceding. Accordingly, Southerners had not committed treason by seceding but rather were patriots exercising and defending their reserved constitutional liberties.

It was imperative for ex-Confederates to uphold the legitimacy of secession. Otherwise the verdict of history would be that Confederates were brave but were rebels who behaved dishonorably.[20] By glorifying the Confederacy, Confederate monuments proclaim, at least implicitly, this sanitized view of secession and portray ex-Confederates as dignified White Southern patriots fighting in defense of their inalienable constitutional rights against an oppressive Northern regime. This defense-of-liberty mystique is the foundation of the White Southern heritage that Confederate monuments supporters state they wish to preserve.

Lincoln once addressed the South's definition of liberty as the right of each state to go its own way in order to create its own government in order to keep other men in bondage. Lincoln told the parable of the wolf and the sheep to explain these differences in notions of liberty. In Lincoln's parable, the wolf claims the liberty to attack the sheep's throat and the sheep praises as a liberator the shepherd who drives the wolf away and saves the sheep's life, and the wolf denounces the shepherd as the destroyer of its liberty.[21] By praising the Confederacy, Confederate monuments symbolically eulogize a bygone period of White Southern heritage that incorporates this wolf and sheep definition of liberty that Lincoln spelled out. At a minimum, by maintaining in place today a hundred-year-old Confederate monument, Southern communities choose to add their imprimatur to a view of liberty that entails the right of each state to go its own way to form independent governments that are free to define the limits of human rights and constitutional liberties as they wish.

The South's unique definition of liberty aside, the inconvenient truth for the South was, and is, that the states' rights constitutional interpretation that it manufactured for its own benefit to justify secession contravened not only the constitutional traditions of the North but also core principles embedded in sixty years of antebellum United States Supreme Court constitutional law precedent.[22] That precedent, *most of it developed by Supreme Court Justices who came from the South,* supported the polar opposite understanding of American constitutional law from the South's self-serving states' rights version. Prior to the outbreak of the Civil War, the Court consistently had held that states lack the "states' right" to go their own way and disregard decisions of the central government. This view of United States constitutional law has continued into the modern era.[23] Explicitly, in the *Prize Cases,*[24] the Supreme Court ruled that secession was never a constitutional right. There the Court ruled that because the seceding states never possessed the constitutional right or legal authority to secede, the Confederate states had never become a sovereign power independent from the United States and, therefore, the Civil War could only be legally understood as a "domestic insurrection." In its 1869 decision in *Texas v. White*,[25] the Supreme Court confirmed the embedded constitutional principle that no state ever possessed the option to lawfully secede from the United States. The court reasoned that prewar constitutional law precedent had never supported the claim that each state had merely created a compact with the other states from which any state could simply withdraw at will. Rather, as the court made plain in *Texas v. White*, from the beginning of our constitutional form of government, in order to create "a more perfect Union" than the one that had been created by the Articles of Confederation, each state had agreed to incorporate itself with finality into an indissoluble political body. Today, we acknowledge that fact when we recite the Pledge of Allegiance and pledge our allegiance to "one nation, under God, *indivisible,* with liberty and justice for all."

After the Civil War, some Confederate leaders continued to assert that there was a legitimate debate regarding the right to secede. Robert E. Lee advanced this claim in an April 1865 interview, after the surrender at Appomattox.[26] But there never was a *legitimate* debate regarding a state's right to secede—not in 1861 and not in 1865. The war had *finally* resolved the question of the right to secede, but Supreme Court constitutional interpretation had settled that question well before the war began.[27] A Confederate monument's explicit or symbolic message that secession was a constitutionally valid and irreproachable act, and that the Confederate soldier died in defense of a protected constitutional liberty to secede from the Union, represents an ongoing effort to promote distorted beliefs and attitudes that run counter to both antebellum and post-bellum constitutional law.

The Myth That Slavery Was Not the Cause of the War

Ex-Confederates were adamant that the Civil War was a violent confrontation fought among honorable White men, not over the moral principle of slavery but rather over high principles of states' rights and "to protect from Northern aggression a chivalrous antebellum way of life."[28] It was essential that the myth underlying the Cult of the Lost Cause hold that slavery was not the cause of the war. Slavery, always morally indefensible notwithstanding arguments to the contrary by Confederate proponents, was widely and increasingly viewed as indefensible in the postwar years.[29] Most Confederate veterans, however, considered neither secession nor slavery as morally wrong so there was no reason to confess any guilt.[30] Yet, ex-Confederates well understood the widespread Northern opprobrium directed at the institution of slavery and the growing weight of international condemnation of slavery. Thus, anxiety over how posterity would view secessionists increasingly motivated the aging Confederate veteran population to deny vehemently that slavery was a root cause of the Civil War. Ex-Confederates wanted to be remembered by posterity as having fought for a more noble cause and feared that their children would view them as unworthy of honor because they had fought a war causing unprecedented destruction for "no higher motive than the desire to retain the money value of slave property."[31] It thus became an article of faith among ex-Confederates that future generations should conclude that Confederates fought in defense of the noble political principle of local self-government and for protection of hearth and home, not in defense of slavery.[32]

Of the various misrepresentations and historical distortions contained in the Cult of the Lost Cause, the most implausible, the easiest to debunk, and the most completely rebuffed in the historical record, is the claim that the preservation of the social and economic system based on slavery was not an underlying cause of the Civil War.[33] The original seven Confederate states seceded to protest the outcome of the 1860 presidential election of Abraham Lincoln. The single greatest issue in the campaign of 1860, nearly the sole issue, was the Republican opposition to extension of slavery into the Western territories.[34] Certainly, the North understood that slavery was the war's precipitating cause.[35]

But, the best evidence of why the South seceded is what secessionists themselves stated. In 1861, Alexander Stephens, the vice-president of the Confederacy, publicly announced that the "*cornerstone* [of the new Confederate government] rests upon the great truth that the negro is not equal to the White man; that slavery, subordination to the superior race, is his natural and normal condition."[36] In addition, Georgia placed three conditions on not seceding, all having to do with slavery's protection.[37] Moreover, following Lincoln's issuance of the Emancipation Proclamation in September 1862, Jefferson Davis, president of the Confederacy, declared before a session of the Confederate Congress that "a restoration of the Union has been rendered forever impossible by the adoption of [the Emancipation Proclamation] which from its very nature neither admits of retraction nor can *coexist with union.*"[38] The Confederate press understood that the Civil War was waged by the South to defend slavery. During the Civil War, planters became reluctant to lend or lease their slaves to the Confederate army and the *Richmond Examiner* found that conduct to be contemptible. As this Southern newspaper stated, "the war originated and is carried on in great part for the defence (sic) of the slaveholder in his property rights, and the perpetuation of the institution [of slavery]."[39] Further evidence of slavery's central role in secession are the various articles of secession that

Confederate states drafted, which expressed in great detail the justifications for seceding. These documents make plain that the states "left the Union to preserve the institution of slavery."[40] In addition, five of the seven states that first seceded sent a total of fifty-two official commissioners to speak to the legislatures of the Southern slave states that had not yet seceded but had scheduled conventions that would consider secession. These commissioners' arguments in support of secession are a matter of public record and uniformly support the view that "the only states' right they were interested in was the right to maintain slavery."[41]

The demographics of slavery constitute additional evidence of the centrality of slavery as a precipitating cause of secession: the more slaves and slaveholding families in a state, the greater the likelihood of the state seceding. Likewise, "soldiers who owned slaves—or lived with family members who did—turned out in greater numbers to fight on behalf of [the Confederacy]; they incurred higher casualties, [and] deserted less frequently . . . than the troops who did not own slaves and were otherwise unconnected to the peculiar institution."[42]

After the war, most Confederate veterans viewed slavery "as central to the [Confederate] cause."[43] Indeed, many applications for pardon after the war that ex-Confederates filed termed slavery "the paramount cause of the Civil War." Postwar letters and writings and statements of the Southern participants affirm the view of slavery's essential role in states seceding.[44] Indeed, in 1868 Edward Alfred Pollard, the "father" of the Myth of the Lost Cause, described White supremacy as the "true cause of the war" and the "true hope of the South."[45]

As historian Kirk Savage has concluded, secessionist leaders "'cited slavery as the most compelling reason for Southern independence' . . . and the same reasoning was repeated in press, pulpit, and school . . . until virtually the end of the war. 'Negro slavery is the South,' wrote one Georgia editor in 1862, and the South is negro slavery.'"[46]

The central strut of the argument that the South did *not* fight the war to defend slavery is the incontrovertible fact that only roughly one-fourth of the Confederate soldiers lived in slave-owning families and as few as five percent of the Confederate soldiers personally owned slaves. Thus, the argument goes, how could the Civil War have been fought in defense of slavery?[47] One answer is what is referred to as the "social value of slavery." Being White during the time of slavery meant being free in relation to enslaved Blacks. "As a boundary marked by both race and class, 'Whiteness' was thus both unifying and exclusive."[48] With slavery, Whites, especially poor Whites who were not slave owners, had the psychological satisfaction of being able to embrace their superiority to Blacks in Southern society and enjoy the economic advantages associated with racial discrimination that provided Whites superior economic opportunities over Blacks.[49] The long history of racial exploitation and oppression that occurred in the antebellum South created for ordinary Whites opportunities, wealth, and privileges not available to Blacks. Most Whites, whether or not slaveholders, would not want to forego the privileges gained from their Whiteness. Non-slaveholders had a stake in preserving slavery because it provided them generous benefits.[50] As one Confederate veteran from Georgia stated in 1890, "We fought . . . for the supremacy of the White race in America."[51]

Today, but for a few Confederate nationalist historians, the consensus in the academic community is that slavery was the fundamental cause of secession. Slavery might well not have been the Confederate soldier's *primary* motivation for fighting, but virtually all Whites in the South believed that they had a stake in the slave system and were fighting to preserve the slave system.[52] Southern Whites were dedicated to White supremacy and the social control over Blacks it provided. Keeping Blacks under strict control and thereby maintaining domestic tranquility, was essential to maintain White supremacy. "White supremacy . . . served as a powerful glue binding [non-slaveholders] to the slaveholders' republic." All who defended the South defended slavery because "few . . . defenders of the South could imagine the beloved South without slavery at the center."[53]

The motivation of the common soldier aside, the evidence is overwhelming that the defense of slavery was the primary motive for the Confederate officials who orchestrated secession and managed the war. Following an exhaustive review of the evidence, Edward Bonekemper has concluded that no amount of "postwar backing and filling" by Jefferson Davis or Alexander Stevens can "cover their slavery tracks" notwithstanding the revisionist efforts by each after the war alleging that states' rights and the opposition to centralized federal governance, and not slavery, were the causes of the war.[54]

Implicit in every Confederate monument, and often explicitly stated in a monument's inscription, is the politically-charged message that ex-Confederates were patriots who fought for the noble goals of states' rights and preservation of constitutional liberties.[55] The symbolic sub-text of every Confederate monument is that the fight was not to perpetuate the institution of slavery. An evaluation of the societal harm that Confederate monuments inflict on contemporary American life needs to address the implications of this distortion of the causes of the Civil War.

First, since the Confederate states seceded, and brought on the Civil War to preserve slavery, Confederate monuments that glorify the Confederacy and its cause necessarily glorify an effort to perpetuate African American human bondage. That messaging constitutes transmission of White supremacy and anti-Black racism, hate speech pure and simple.

Second, and perhaps less obvious, the Lost Cause view that slavery was not a cause of the Civil War conveniently excuses Confederate supporters, when constructing their vision of "Southern heritage," from any need to consider either the history of the pre-war slave communities or the postwar interests of freedmen and freedwomen. The Lost Cause view would have us understand the Civil War was a squabble between two groups of honorable White men whose disagreement was over a political issue, not a moral issue, with each side advancing a respectable position, from its point of view. Other than acknowledging that one consequence of the Civil War was the freeing of the slaves, there thus was no need for the corpus of Southern Civil War history and heritage to even mention Southern African Americans. Nor would there be any reason to incorporate as part of Southern heritage slaves' collective memory of the Civil War or African Americans' understanding that the Civil War was fought to secure both their physical freedom and their political equality. Under the Lost Cause version of history, Southern heritage is almost exclusively the heritage of White people, not Black people. Accordingly, without apology, Southern heritage could, and did, and does, focus exclusively on the White Confederate soldier's valor and the glorious Confederate states' rights cause, except where a passing reference is made of the faithful slave who is represented as also supporting the White Confederate cause. In short, postwar Southern Whites adopted a version of Southern heritage that was consistent with the view that four million freedmen and freedwomen who occupied the South immediately following the end of the Civil War in effect did not exist, certainly were not integral to the spirit or substance of Southern heritage. Confederate monuments raised throughout the South perpetuated the distorted vision of Southern civic life as something exclusive to Whites, a constructed White collective memory that erased the Southern Black experience, attempted to render the Black experience invisible. Southern communities that today keep Confederate monuments in their public spaces choose, at least implicitly, to lend their imprimatur to a Confederate monument's symbolic emphasis on White supremacy and erasure of Black history and culture.

The Benign Nature of Antebellum Race Relations; or, the Myth of the Happy and Loyal Slave

Slavery was not a benign institution. It was cruel, enforced through a combination of the whip, intimidation, exploitation of Black labor, and murder. It separated Black families. Once freed, many former slaves spent years in an effort to locate lost family members.[56] Rape of slave women by their masters produced offspring that then could be sold for a profit. The effect, if not the intention, was the breeding of Black slaves. Whites maintained well-armed militias to repel feared slave revolts. Workdays often were extremely long—sixteen hours per day and seven days a week in the sugar plantations during harvesting season was not unusual. Sunstroke killed many. The working conditions of agricultural gang labor could be harsh, food and clothing minimal, and housing abominable. Evidence of slaves' dissatisfaction with their condition includes the fact that prior to the Civil War, tens of thousands of slaves ran away, so many that it was necessary to maintain slave patrols—slave catchers—who roamed the South to locate and return runaway slaves and who entered the North to reclaim runaway slaves. Constant coercion often was needed to keep slaves working. During the Civil War, hundreds of thousands of slaves crossed over into the Union lines to escape slavery.[57] Most states had slave codes that created, in effect, a police state to control the several million humans in bondage.

The master's ultimate control was violence. Short of murder or cruel punishment such as maiming and castration, the universal legal rule in Southern jurisdictions was that "courts affirmed the right of masters to treat a slave however they wished."[58] In his book, *Mind of the South*, W. J. Cash detailed many of the brutalities of the lash, chains, dogs, and pistols needed to maintain order. Cash concluded that slavery brutalized not only the slaves but also their White masters, due to the sadism and cruelty slavery released in Whites. Poor Whites, enraged by being required to endure the planters' epithets of "White trash," developed a "savage and ignoble hate for [Blacks] which required only opportunity to break forth in relentless ferocity."[59] Immediately following the end of the Civil War, Southern Whites were haunted by the fear of ex-slaves' vengeance ("retaliatory violence against a system sustained by the lash and the gun") that never materialized but which puts in perspective the postwar claims that slavery was a benign institution, that relations between slaves and masters were mutually beneficial, and that the slaves were happy and faithful.[60]

Postwar Southerners, of course, knew these facts. Yet, the cornerstone of the Cult of the Lost Cause rests on the myth, the outright distortion and fabrication, of happy, loyal slaves who were content in their condition and who lived harmoniously and in close communion with a humane and caring master who viewed his slaves as part of his family, with slave and master each caring for the other and contributing to the other's welfare.[61] Historian Grace Elizabeth Hale has referred to this distortion of reality as the imagined "plantation pastorale of racial harmony."[62]

The plantation pastorale contains several interrelated components. First was the proposition that slavery was good for Africans since it brought

Christianity to the "heathens" who might revert back to heathenism if freed and thus were better off as slaves.[63] Moreover, well after the end of the Civil War, slavery apologists continued to argue that the status of being a slave elevates the African. Not only is the slave guaranteed lifetime employment and protected from starvation or any need to become a beggar, but slaves "are happy, content, unaspiring, and utterly incapable, from intellectual weakness, ever to give [the South] any trouble by their aspirations."[64]

The Lost Cause Myth's historical distortions also maintained that the happy slave also was a "faithful slave." The Cult of the Lost Cause advanced the fanciful image of an enslaved people who, acting contrary to their own self-interests, resisted freedom that became available to them during the Civil War. Instead, they preferred to remain nobly faithful to, and risk their lives for, their White masters and mistresses—both in battle as they joined their masters on the front lines and when devotedly protecting the family's White women and children at home in the face of Yankee invasion. The "faithful slave" portrayal was designed to demonstrate the mutual affection, perhaps even selfless love, that Confederate apologists asserted was the foundation of these cross-race slavery-based relationships in the South. At the same time, the myth of the happy/faithful slave masked the brutality and coercion of chattel slavery.[65]

The myth of the happy/faithful slave deprives enslaved African Americans of any independent identity. Under the Lost Cause myth of the happy/faithful slave, Black people had no role other than as White constructions of simple, happy, loyal slaves "frozen in time" and defined as extensions of the White people who dominated them.[66] This "plantation pastorale" represented the racial hierarchy that post-bellum Southern Whites strove to maintain in the "New South" even in the absence of slavery. That aspiration, that African Americans respect Whites, "know their place," and otherwise have no independent identity is a symbolic message of every Confederate monument transmits as it symbolically proclaims the "truths" of the Lost Cause myth and glorifies those who fought for the Confederacy in an effort to maintain the "plantation pastorale."

The Myth That the South Was Overwhelmed but Never Defeated

By the 1880s, the Cult of the Lost Cause had widely adopted the overwhelming-disparity-in-numbers-and-resources argument for explaining the Confederate defeat in the Civil War. The Cult of the Lost Cause held that there was no shame in the South's failure to prevail in the war. The South had made no martial mistakes during the course of the war; its troops did not lack heroism, dedication, lack of self-sacrifice, or manliness; Confederate forces had not been beaten in battle; and there had been no internal dissension and collapse within the Confederate armies. Indeed, Southern soldiers were superior to those in the North, as were their leaders. The war was lost because the North was able to amass overwhelming numbers, resources, technologies, and industrial might against the South whose starving army fought heroically and nobly until, finally overwhelmed, it was unable to continue. The outcome of the war was thus not attributable to the Union soldier's heroism or superior martial skills or the superiority of the Union army's leadership.[67]

The overwhelming-numbers-and-resources argument had distinct advantages for Confederate apologists, then and now: it vindicated the Confederate army by explaining defeat and permitted the South to claim that the soldiers of the Confederate armies were the better fighting men in proportion to their numbers and the resources available to them. But most important, the overwhelming-numbers-and-resources argument permitted the White South to adulate and celebrate Confederate leaders, even in defeat, for their noble character, devotion to duty, heroic accomplishments, and military prowess and facilitated raising the money needed to construct monuments to these Southern war heroes and the men the led in battle.[68]

Except for the faithful slave myth, every glorification found in the Lost Cause myth, and thus every glorification found in a Confederate monument today, is White. And, of course, even the faithful-slave myth works only when one assumes a benevolent White master race that earned the faithful allegiance of its slaves. Confederate monuments symbolically trumpet the theme that White is valorous, and pure, and noble. The Confederate monument erases Black people from these exalted character categories. The unarticulated symbolic message of Confederate monuments then is that White is where one finds the nobility of the human race—White supremacy.

In sum: The Lost Cause myth constructs a romanticized memory of the Confederacy and those who fought in its defense. Most of the myth contradicts the irrefutable historical record. The purpose of the Confederate monument is to glorify, not elucidate. A good example is the Confederate statue that was located on the courthouse lawn in Rockville, Maryland, until 2017 and discussed in the preface to this book. Its inscription described the Confederate soldier as a "hero" and enjoined those observing the statue to never forget and to "love [forever] the thin gray line." Similar sentiments, variously expressed, are found in hundreds of inscriptions on other Confederate monuments. The sub-text is a plea to those viewing these monuments: they should conclude that the Confederacy was comprised of a group of noble Southern patriots, "heroes," exercising their constitutional right to secede from the Union and that victory by this "thin gray line" would have been good for Southern African Americans because it would have continued the wholesome relationship of a benign master and happy and faithful African Americans in servitude who worked together for a common good. Yet, so the myth goes, it was the fate of this "thin gray line" to be overwhelmed, but never defeated, by the industrial might of an aggressive and oppressive North. That is the message of the Cult of the Lost Cause and thus also is the collective memory of the Civil War that every Confederate monument was built to communicate and still endeavors to communicate.

Confederate monuments do distort history, and yes, it is eminently reasonable for any community to resist sponsoring counterfeit history. Some communities may wish to remove their Confederate monument for that reason alone. But Confederate monuments' principal failings are lodged in the distorted *memory* of the Civil War and contrived *attitudes* regarding the Confederacy that these monuments attempt to inculcate. Confederate monuments are intended to encourage the formation of positive attitudes of the White ex-Confederates who prosecuted the Civil War and to erase from notions of Southern heritage the heritage of the four million Freedmen and Freedwomen whom the White South resisted incorporating politically, civilly, or socially into the New South. Otherwise stated, Confederate monuments contributed, and still contribute, to efforts to relegate Freedmen and Freedwomen to a status of inferiority in postwar Southern civil and political life.

Linking Confederate Monuments to the Lost Cause Myth: Evidence from Monument Dedication Ceremonies

Confederate monuments built before the late 1870s were mostly erected in cemeteries, "crowned with funerary urns." These cemetery memorials commemorated the nobility of the fight far more than the virtue of the cause. In order to effectively propagate the myths surrounding the Cult of the Lost Cause, Confederate apologists needed monuments that celebrated the Confederacy itself and its cause—monuments that "reinforced a social, racial, and political structure rooted in the past."[69] Following the death of Robert E. Lee in 1870, monument erection efforts slowly began to move beyond the cemetery walls and into "courthouse squares and other prominent public places [such as] parks." The pace of that shift from cemeteries to courthouse lawns and town squares accelerated in the decade from 1885 to 1895 and peaked in the years 1895 to 1915.[70] As with all Confederate memorialization, politics seeped in. The story of Confederate monuments, and Confederate memorialization in general, is inextricably bound up with the efforts by the leaders of the South's Democratic Party to deploy memorialization, built around the Cult of the Lost Cause, to impart the political message of White supremacy, in part to combat forces that would split the White vote. This motivation for erecting Confederate monuments continued well into the twentieth century. This was the finding, for example, of the Blue Ribbon Commission on Race, Memorials, and Public Spaces empaneled by Charlottesville City council in 2016. The commission concluded that "the Lee and Jackson statues [erected in Charlottesville, Virginia, in the 1920s] embodied the Lost Cause interpretation of the Civil War, which romanticized the Confederate past and suppressed the horrors of slavery and slavery's role as the fundamental cause of the war while affirming the enduring role of White supremacy."[71] This political message of White supremacy surrounding the erection and dedication of Confederate monuments warrants close attention.

Confederate veterans running for office on the Democratic Party ticket called upon citizens to stand by them as they had stood by the South at Gettysburg. It was particularly useful if the candidate had lost an arm ("the empty sleeve") or, perhaps even better, had lost a leg. Appeals to White voters to remember the Confederacy was code for voters to remember and maintain White supremacy. Moving beyond mourning the dead, orators at monument dedication ceremonies routinely celebrated the surviving veterans crippled in service to the Confederate cause. Here too, speakers deployed the metaphor of the "empty sleeve or the empty pant leg." Speakers, normally themselves members of the ruling political class, argued that White political factionalism dishonors the Confederate dead and the surviving crippled veteran because discord among Whites elevates the Black man. Standing as a permanent symbol of Confederate soldier sacrifice, the Confederate monument functioned as an image, a symbol, of the empty sleeve and pant leg "to prevent disgruntled White men from breaking party ranks [and also to] drive a wedge between White and Black people who were finding common political ground."[72]

Some of the best evidence of how Confederate monuments were deployed to transmit the tenets of the Cult of the Lost Cause and the ideology of White supremacy can be found in the ceremonies accompanying the dedication of Confederate monuments in city squares and courthouse lawns throughout the South.

The 1875 Dedication of Richmond's Monument Commemorating Confederate General Stonewall Jackson

The days set aside for the unveiling of Confederate monuments assumed great ritualistic significance, even more than Confederate Memorial Day observances. The Stonewall Jackson monument in Richmond was the first

Stonewall Jackson monument (1875), Richmond, VA. Detroit Publishing Photograph Collection, Library of Congress, Prints and Photographs Division.

Confederate monument in a public space commemorating an individual. It was funded by a group of British citizens and unveiled in Richmond on October 26, 1875. Nearly 50,000 people attended the unveiling ceremony and the accompanying parade and related festivities. It was the first mass assembly of Confederate veterans since the end of the war. By this time, Virginia had been "redeemed," that is, the gains of Reconstruction had been erased when White supremacist Democrats recaptured political control from interracial alliances of Republicans. Wounded former Confederate General James L. Kemper was Virginia's governor. Historian David Blight has described the day as a "celebratory funeral."[73]

The unveiling parade and ceremony took on great political significance as a public statement of Southern revival following defeat. Governor Kemper, a Democrat who was facing a stiff reelection challenge from Republicans, gave a speech at the unveiling. In it, he made clear to the North that ex-Confederates were again in political control in the South and that they did not intend to repent and be forgiven by the North since they had done nothing requiring forgiveness. Instead, as a condition for reunion with the North, the South insisted on "equal honor and equal liberties of each section" of the country, North and South.[74]

This unveiling event also made it abundantly clear that the White South did not intend to welcome freedmen into its civic circle. During Congressional Reconstruction, Black militia units had been authorized. In an act of racial accommodation (and in an effort to provide Republicans no space to challenge Democrats' conciliatory posture) Kemper, the Democratic-Redeemer governor, had authorized Black militia units and a group of Black ministers to participate in the parade. Former Confederate General Jubal Early protested most strongly, calling Kemper a Judas and arguing that Black participation would dishonor Jackson and insult Confederates. As a compromise, and to avoid the appearance of racial mixing, Kemper placed the African Americans at the extreme rear of the several-mile-long parade. "Perhaps anticipating their humiliation" the Black militia units and most other Black groups chose not to march.

Anyone who attended the 1875 unveiling of the Stonewall Jackson monument in downtown Richmond and listened to all of the speeches would not have known that the slaves had been emancipated, that the Constitution had been amended with the ratification of the Thirteenth, Fourteenth, and Fifteenth Amendments, or that Lincoln's Gettysburg Address had announced a "new birth of freedom." The unveiling of the Jackson memorial was a White pride event through and through. The bickering over racial ordering at the parade accompanying the unveiling of a monument lionizing a Confederate general illustrates how Confederate memorialization events were awash with political symbolism. These events were designed to keep the White voter faithful to White supremacy and the Democratic Party.[75]

Monument dedication events at three additional Confederate monuments that were raised between 1885–1895 additionally illuminate how Confederate monuments helped disseminate the myths embedded in the Cult of the Lost Cause and promoted attitudes of White supremacy. These three events were the unveiling in 1890 of the Robert E. Lee monument located on Richmond's Monument Avenue, the unveiling of Richmond's Soldiers' and Sailors' Monument in 1894, and the 1895 unveiling of the Confederate Monument at Raleigh, North Carolina.

Promoting the Cult of the Lost Cause Through Richmond's 1890 Lee Monument

Prior to the mid-1890s, Ladies' Memorial Associations continued as the primary promoters of Confederate memorialization. The Confederate heritage groups that assumed responsibility for Confederate memorialization after 1895 were just getting organized, groups such as the United Confederate Veterans (UCV), which was formed in 1889, and most importantly, the

United Daughters of the Confederacy (UDC), which was not formed into a national organization until 1894.[76]

Robert E. Lee died on October 12, 1870. Lee's death inspired renewed introspection regarding the Confederate past and aroused ex-Confederates' desire to lionize Confederate war heroes. During his life, Lee himself had avoided attending memorial events and "refused to support publicly the erection of monuments because of the inflammatory feelings they could provoke among Northerners." In a letter to a former general, Lee presciently explained that "a monument, no matter how welcome for Confederate sentiment, would have the effect on continuing, if not adding to, the difficulties under which the Southern people labor."[77]

After some bickering, it was decided to construct two Lee monuments: the Richmond monument and a recumbent sculpture, dedicated in 1883, located at the Memorial Chapel of Washington College in Lexington, Virginia, where Lee had been president and now was interred.[78] The Richmond monument was delayed due to a rivalry between a female-led group and a male-led group. There was no disagreement, however, that the Lee monument's function was to celebrate Confederate nationalism by propagating the tenets of the Cult of the Lost Cause, but "the women resisted ceding their authority over public representations of the Lost Cause [and] control over Confederate traditions."[79] By 1886, disputes between the competing groups had been resolved and by 1890 the impressive Lee equestrian statue and monument was completed. It was unveiled in a magnificent celebration in a Richmond suburb at a location that today is known as Richmond's famed Monument Avenue.[80]

Between 100,000 and 150,000 people from across the South attended the dedication of Richmond's Lee monument. The parade and procession of veterans alone included 20,000 participants, was four miles long, and required two hours to pass. Ex-Confederate general, and Virginia governor, Fitzhugh Lee led the procession, followed by forty ex-Confederate generals, other renowned ex-Confederate military leaders, and the governors of every former Confederate state.

Again, this was overwhelmingly a Whites-only civic event. Few Blacks participated or were invited to participate. One African American observing the festivities famously blurted out, "The Southern White folks is on top—the Southern White folks is on top." That clearly was the intended message of the monument and its elaborate dedication and unveiling ceremony—to "vindicate the Old South and its slaveholding class."[81] By lionizing Lee, a military leader, rather than Jefferson Davis, a political leader, ex-Confederates attempted to de-politicize the Confederacy, disassociate the Confederate narrative from its slavery past, and shape its portrayal as a valorous

Distortion-of-History Approach 43

Robert E. Lee monument (1890), Monument Avenue, Richmond, VA. Jean Antonin Mercie, sculptor. Historic American Buildings Survey, Library of Congress, Prints and Photographs Division.

White military effort conducted by Southern patriots in defense of their constitutional liberties. Historian Kirk Savage described the Southern strategy this way: "With the equation of canonical Whiteness and moral virtue so deeply embedded in the consciousness of race, Lee's [handsome] outward appearance was easily read as a reflection of inner superiority [viewed by some as] the realized King Arthur."[82] The Civil War had pitted White men against White men and had aligned Northern Whites with Southern Blacks. The goal of the ex-Confederates was to drive a wedge between Northern Whites and Southern Blacks and the Lee monument was a step in that direction. The magnificence of Lee as portrayed in the Richmond monument was designed to move Northern Whites away from viewing Lee (and other Southern leaders) as traitors and to begin viewing Lee and the others who attempted to destroy the Union and maintain slavery as true American heroes, courageous Christian White men worthy of respect by all White men, North and South. The narrative was straightforward: Lee loved the Union, followed his state of Virginia into war out of a reluctant sense of duty, and afterward immediately resumed his loyal support of the Union. The Lee monument was intended to resuscitate Lee's postwar image in the eyes of the North, in the process help legitimate all who had fought for the South, and restore traditional bonds of racial sympathy between Northern and Southern Whites.

African Americans were the net losers in this reconciliation gala. They, of course, could not lionize Lee who had worked to keep them enslaved, and thus African Americans were marginalized by the Lee hero worship jointly engaged in by Northern and Southern Whites. In short, the erection of the Lee monument helped remove Lee from the ignominious status of a traitor but, in turn, caused African Americans to suffer increased ignominy due to their inability, at least unwillingness, to join the all-White celebration of Lee the valorous Christian gentleman, and national hero.[83] Gradually, Lee came to represent, symbolically, the White moral authority of the postwar Southern government—a proud, powerful, morally upright, former adversary who, once defeated, warmly and loyally reunited with his former countrymen and racial peers.[84]

The African American press in Richmond resoundingly condemned the Lee monument dedication festivities, lamenting that the frenzy of Confederate glorification evidenced Whites clinging to racial theories that many thought the Civil War had buried for all time—that the South was right to have attempted to continue "dealing in human beings, selling children from their parents, wives from husbands, [and separating] sisters from brothers."[85] The Black press attempted to expose the 1890 dedication of the Lee Monument for what it was: a vehicle ex-Confederates deployed to promote the factual distortions inherent in the Lost Cause Myth, to celebrate the Confederate independence movement and its White supremacist goals, and to forge positive attitudes of the Confederacy and the White men who fought for its cause. At least one group of Union veterans that had been invited to march in the Lee monument dedication procession refused the invitation, not desiring to march under, and implicitly in support of, the Confederate flag. For similar reasons, the secretary of the Navy refused to permit the United States Marine Band to participate.[86]

Historians widely agree that the 1890 dedication and unveiling of the Richmond Lee monument marked the beginning of a new phase of Confederate memorialization. Ex-Confederates and a supportive Southern press used the Lee monument dedication to transform the myths surrounding the Cult of the Lost Cause "into national reunion on Southern terms."[87] The speeches during the Lee monument dedication implicitly insisted that formulation of Southern racial policy must be left to Southerners, who, after all, knew "their Negroes" better than anyone else. Dedication speakers used the dedication to urge upon the entire nation the South's interpretation of the Civil War based on the tenets of the Cult of the Lost Cause. As historian David Blight has concluded, "the unveiling of the Lee monument incorporated unabashed worship of the Confederate past."[88] Blight further writes that "a new, more dynamic Lost Cause was thrown into bold relief" by the Richmond unveiling of 1890.[89] In short, the Lee monument dedication was integral to a "larger political campaign to legitimate Southern White supremacy in the national consciousness."[90]

Monument Avenue in Richmond became the situs for a two-mile Confederate monument row after four more Confederate monuments were added in the early twentieth century. By the 1990s, if not before, Monument Avenue prompted among African Americans vivid memories of racial oppression and exclusion. After the Lee Monument was raised, Monument Avenue became a beautifully landscaped boulevard, Richmond's most fashionable address. Developers cleared land and built impressive homes for Richmond's White elite—lawyers, merchants, and other professionals. Property deeds excluded African Americans from either purchasing or renting a home on Monument Avenue. Nor were African Americans welcome to visit the Avenue, and, therefore, few did. To keep the African American "help" from showing themselves on Monument Avenue, developers constructed back alleys so that African American servants could come and go to work at the magnificent homes along the Boulevard without being seen walking on Monument Avenue.[91]

As contemporary controversies over Confederate monuments build, it is useful to consider the Lee Monument in Richmond as clear evidence that Confederate monuments do not represent an all-inclusive "Southern history;" at best they represent *White* Southern history, more specifically, the collective memory of the South's role in the Civil War that the White South constructed and promulgated—and the desire to expunge the Black countermemory from Southern history. The Black South never ceased to express its opposition to such attempted White hegemony over the South's collective memory of the Civil War. John Mitchell, the editor of the Black newspaper, the *Richmond Planet,* provided the most famous, and perhaps prophetic, observation emanating from that May 1890 dedication of the Lee Monument. Mitchell warned that "He [the African American] put up the Lee Monument and should the time come, will be there to take it down."[92]

Richmond's Soldiers' and Sailors' Monument and Reinforcement of Racial Hierarchy

The May 30, 1894 dedication of the Richmond Soldiers' and Sailors' Monument is another good example of a Confederate monument dedication promoting well-worn racial hierarchies implicit in the Cult of the Lost Cause. The remarks by the principal dedication orator, Confederate veteran the Rev. Robert C. Cave, were widely denounced—at least across the North and West. Some Northern newspapers called Cave's remarks treasonous. A few Southern newspapers called the remarks "ill-gotten" and not representative of Southern sentiments, but most expressed no criticism.

One hundred thousand spectators gathered to watch a parade of 10,000 marchers and to listen to speeches celebrating the Confederacy and its cause. One thousand children carried Confederate battle flags.[93] Cave began his remarks with the boilerplate tribute to the bravery of the Confederate war veteran and his devotion to duty as was standard among monument dedication speakers intending to appropriate the valor of the Confederate soldier for the political ends of their elite social class. Cave quickly moved to the gravamen of his remarks, what one historian has referred to as "a eulogy for the Confederacy."[94] The essence of Cave's presentation at the Richmond Soldiers' and Sailors' Monument dedication was that Appomattox represented only a verdict of "brute force" asserted against an overwhelmed South. But the defeat at Appomattox had not resolved any of the moral issues around which the Civil War had been fought, did not "settle questions of right and wrong." Cave argued that "the South was right [and] the cause was just" and those who fought for the Confederacy were "patriots." But Cave then insulted those who fought for the North. Cave denounced the character and moral fitness of the Northern soldier, adding that the North was the aggressor that had orchestrated an armed invasion of the South to "trample upon the rights of [Southerners] to effect its own ends." Cave's verbal assault and protest were code for an accusation that the North had trampled Southerners' "states' rights" to maintain and expand the institution of slavery. The overarching states' rights dispute, the transcending feud, between the North and the South was the North's opposition to the expansion of slavery into the new territories.[95]

Confederate Soldiers' and Sailors' Monument, Libby Hill [Park], Richmond, VA. Image ca. 1908. Detroit Publishing Company photograph collection, Library of Congress, Prints and Photographs Division.

Newspapers reported that following Cave's remarks, those in attendance rose "in thunderous applause." Northern veterans who had worked diligently to put aside the "bloody shirt," and to acknowledge the valor of the Confederate soldiers, were outraged. The last two decades of the nineteenth century constituted the era of increased reconciliation between North and South when many Union veterans were prepared to excuse the rank-and-file Confederate soldier from the moral complicity of fighting for the cause being advanced by the slave oligarchy. The rank-and-file Confederate soldier, it was argued, was brave, reliable, and self-sacrificing, but had been exploited, misled, and duped by the slave holding Southern elite.[96] But Cave's remarks and the audience's strongly positive response to them, made the "duped" rationalization seem particularly problematic. Moreover, during the weeks following the dedication, Confederate groups expressed agreement with Cave's memorial dedication remarks, thereby affirming Cave's core assertion that the war had not settled the Civil War's underlying question of the morality of the Confederate cause to keep millions of human beings in bondage.

Cave's remarks at the dedication of the Richmond Soldiers' and Sailors' Monument encouraged White Southern resistance to racial justice. But there was more. Cave's remarks are a prime example of how Confederate monuments created opportunities for the Southern elites to appropriate the valor of the rank-and-file Confederate soldier to advance political views helpful to their class. Cave's racist reaffirmation of the Confederate cause at the 1894 dedication of the Richmond Soldiers' and Sailors' Monument coincided in time with the advent of Southern Populism. Southern Populists endeavored to develop coalitions of poor farmers and to frame political and social controversy not as a struggle between races but rather as a class struggle. Framing Southern farmers' disaffection with the *status quo* as a class issue was contrary to the interest of the White supremacist Southern Democratic Party of the 1890s. Encouraging class solidarity over White racial solidarity promoted factionalism—formation of biracial coalitions of farmers and other poor Southerners that challenged the established upper-middle class and upper-class White elite leadership of the Democratic Party in the South. From the point of view of maintaining traditional Democratic Party control of the South, it was better to keep White and Black Southerners divided. The Lost Cause helped accomplish this goal by encouraging White solidarity built around the Lost Cause ideals of the Old South and its established social and racial hierarchies. Cave's racist remarks at the 1894 dedication of Richmond's Soldiers' and Sailors' Monument well-served the goal of the South's political ruling class to drive a racial wedge between poor Whites and poor Blacks by reaffirming the righteousness of the Confederacy's racist objectives.[97]

Promoting the Lost Cause Myth Through
Raleigh's Confederate Monument

On May 20, 1895, North Carolina's Democratic ruling class orchestrated the dedication of the seventy-five-foot-tall North Carolina "Confederate Monument" in Raleigh, the state capital. Like the Lee monument in Richmond and Richmond's Soldiers' and Sailors' Monument, the Raleigh Confederate Monument transmitted the Lost Cause canon and thus also its White supremacist creed. In addition, the Raleigh monument exposed the strong opposition within the Southern African American community to the funding and erection of Confederate monuments.

In 1892, Democrats worried that the interracial coalitions of Populists were threatening White unity among the electorate in North Carolina. Thus, prominent Democrats formed the North Carolina Monumental Association (NCMA) and with the assistance of elite women in the Raleigh Ladies' Memorial Association began a campaign to raise funds for a North Carolina Confederate Memorial. Private fundraising proved inadequate to meet the monument's ongoing construction costs, due in large part to the national economic depression of 1893. Accordingly, the NCMA sought an appropriation of $10,000 from the North Carolina legislature, then controlled by conservative White elites. In 1893, both houses of the North Carolina legislature approved the appropriation with little dissent, on the condition that the Confederate Monument be placed on the statehouse grounds, confirming "the official identification of the state with the NCMA's cause."[98]

Changing political fortunes temporarily thwarted the monument campaign. In 1894, a biracial coalition of Republicans and Populists in North Carolina joined forces as "Fusionists," defeated Democrats in statewide elections, and in 1895 took control of the North Carolina legislature. The all-White, mostly Democratic, NCMA concluded that to meet contractual obligations incurred in building the North Carolina Confederate Monument, it immediately required a $10,000 loan from the Fusionist-controlled legislature. The bill authorizing the loan was defeated by nearly a 4:1 ratio. This biracial North Carolina legislature chose not to become enablers of the toxic behavior of those who were propagating a White supremacist message and creating "sectional bitterness" within the state through the financing and construction of Confederate monuments.

Two days before this defeat of the monument loan request, the North Carolina House of Representatives had voted to adjourn for a day to pay tribute to ex-slave, American social reformer, abolitionist, writer, and statesman Frederick Douglass who had recently died. The Democratic press pounced on this and race-baited. The Democrats immediately labeled Frederick Douglass an "apostle of miscegenation" and the North Carolina House of Representatives the "Miscegenation Legislature." These were references to the fact that Frederick Douglass had been married to a White woman and had thereby, in the view of White supremacist Democrats, promoted social equality and interracial sexual relationships. The Democratic press intoned that White men in North Carolina needed to unite to preserve Anglo-Saxon civilization. The Raleigh Democratic newspaper, the *News and Observer*, published a cartoon showing a group of White women, one kneeling, alongside a partially-completed Confederate monument pleading to an unconcerned racially-mixed group of North Carolina legislators for a loan to complete the monument. In the cartoon, the legislators were depicted as unmoved by the Ladies' loan request as they mourned the death of Douglass. The cartoon implied African American dominance of the North Carolina state government meant White servitude and an utter disregard for Southern heritage. Whites in the North Carolina Fusionist legislature were subjected to a fusillade of protest from their White constituents. Soon the previously-rejected Monument Bill requesting a loan was reconfigured as an appropriation, not a loan, and passed in the state senate by a single vote and passed in the house by a comfortable margin, but only after rancorous debate.

This vignette outlining the political maneuvering to obtain funds to build the Confederate Monument in Raleigh provides a rare glimpse into the racial motivations animating efforts to build Confederate monuments and the racially-charged opposition to their construction. To be able to finance Confederate monuments and place them in prime public spaces, those proposing Confederate monuments required the support of the normally-White-controlled Southern governments.[99]

Thirty-thousand people attended the unveiling of the Raleigh Confederate monument. Just two weeks prior to the monument's dedication, conservative Democrats defeated interracial Fusionists in local elections in Raleigh. The local Democratic newspaper proclaimed a triumph of "pure White Democracy—The City Still Ours . . . No Negro Rule in Raleigh." A theme at the unveiling of the Raleigh Confederate Monument was unity (White unity). The advertising for the upcoming monument dedication urged those in attendance to make all of the Confederate veterans attending feel welcome, the goal being to promote the Confederate cause as a people's cause that enjoyed the support of all true (White) Southerners. The decision to top the memorial with the statue in bronze of a ten-foot tall common soldier, rather than a high-ranking Confederate officer, was designed to advance this goal of White unity. Historian Catherine Bishir has written that "the symbolic reversal of hierarchy stressed the shared experience of war and served the purposes of the organizers by promoting social unity across [White] classes." In some parts of the South, including western North Carolina hill country, there had been bitter resistance to secession and the South's prosecution of the Civil War. And, as explained above, during the period of a biracial Fusionist state government in North Carolina, there had been much opposition to public financial support for Confederate monuments. Those organizing the dedication festivities of the North Carolina Confederate monument thus endeavored to affirm "social stability and race loyalty despite widening class divisions" by attracting a statewide attendance at the unveiling. By emphasizing a "*shared* Confederate tradition," the dedication sponsors strove to urge abandonment of

An infantryman depicted on the Confederate monument on the state capitol grounds in Raleigh, NC (Image June 2017). Leopold Von Miller II (sculptor).
Carol M. Highsmith's America Project in the Carol M. Highsmith Archive, Library of Congress, Prints and Photographs Division.

Fusion politics and encourage Populists to return to the fold by again embracing the Democratic White man's party.[100]

The lure to attend these monument dedication festivities was enhanced by offers to attend social events such as luncheons, the opportunity to meet famous Confederate generals at receptions, concerts, a parade leading to the memorial site that included Confederate veterans carrying their battle-scarred regimental flags, and topped off by late-night balls following the monument's dedication and unveiling. Dedication speeches were very important for they articulated the Lost Cause narrative that idealized the qualities of the antebellum Southern life populated with noble men and genteel women, the righteousness of the Confederate cause, the heroic, valorous, self-sacrificing, and patriotic devotion of the White Confederate soldiers, the denial that slavery was a root cause of the war, and the assurance that slavery was a benign institution as evidenced by the image of the happy and loyal slave.[101]

There is no reported mention of any Black presence at the dedication of the North Carolina Confederate Monument. The organizers' intent was the marginalization of African Americans and the goal that they remain invisible. This was a White event for the benefit of Whites, promoting White solidarity, and advancing the White South's Lost Cause ideology. On the day of the unveiling there was a special edition of the local newspaper that included reminisces by older White members of the community remembering past Confederate heroics, the villainous acts of both Blacks and the conquering Yankees, and the tyranny of Reconstruction. The reminisces contributed to a construction of an altered memory of the war and its consequences. The dedication and unveiling festivities of Raleigh's Confederate monument facilitated myth creation and cultivation of a Confederate cult.[102]

In sum, the Lost Cause myth began as an apology for the Confederate cause, dignifying it in order to acquit ex-Confederates from history's verdict that they were brave but rash men who were traitors and who had caused unfathomable harm in their quest to establish an independent slaveholding republic. From its inception, the Cult of the Lost Cause was thus grounded on "passionate interest in how the future would judge the Confederacy"[103] But, from its inception, the Lost Cause myth also had a robust political component: promoting support for White supremacy. From the earliest Confederate monuments, those erected prior to 1895, these monuments were deployed to symbolically transmit the tenets of the Lost Cause myth and thus indirectly the ideology of White supremacy.[104]

Once the United Daughters of the Confederacy (UDC) took control of Confederate memorialization and, by the mid-1890s, began to erect hundreds of Confederate monuments throughout the South, the motive for erecting Confederate monuments shifted. The UDC self-consciously erected Confederate monuments to advance what has been referred to as a Cult of Anglo-Saxonism. The *warping-of-history* approach, relied on by many today to urge that something needs to be done with a community's Confederate monument, is rooted in the UDC's motivation to deploy Confederate monuments instrumentally to advance this Cult of Anglo-Saxonism.

3
The Warping-of-History Approach

The Rise of Monument Mania

Many who oppose Confederate monuments rely on the racist motivation for erecting them in the first place—a desire to promote White supremacy. This racist pedigree, it is argued, provides a strong case for a community to conclude that it must do something about its Confederate monument. Confederate "monument mania" began in 1895 and continued until roughly 1915. It was during this twenty-year period that the United Daughters of the Confederacy (UDC) arranged for the construction of most of the monuments that are subject to criticism today. The UDC leadership was dedicated to the promotion of White supremacy—the Cult of Anglo-Saxonism. The period of Confederate monument mania coincided with an array of other racist developments in the South: the disfranchisement of most Southern African Americans, the lynching of hundreds of Black men, the hardening of Jim Crow racial segregation, and the indoctrination of Southern children at school through textbooks that taught them invented history, White supremacy, and the inferiority of African Americans as a racial group. The "Daughters" were determined that the next generation would be taught the "correct" view of the Civil War, its consequences, and the "proper" racial hierarchy upon which Southern civic and political life was to be built. The Confederate monument was integral to the UDC's strategy of creating a racial hierarchy of White superiority and Black inferiority. Recognizing Confederate monuments' role in perpetuating institutional racism today begins with understanding how Confederate monuments were inextricably intertwined with Jim Crow racial segregation, disfranchisement, lynching, and the UDC school textbook initiative.

ON MARCH 25, 1965, near the Montgomery, Alabama, state capitol grounds, Martin Luther King Jr. delivered his famous "Our God is Marching On" speech following the historic fifty-four-mile march from Selma to

Montgomery.[1] Dr. King presented his audience a short history lesson on segregation in the South. He said:

> Racial segregation as a way of life ... did not come about as a natural result of the hatred between the races immediately after the Civil War. ... As the noted historian, C. Vann Woodward, in his book, *The Strange Career of Jim Crow,* clearly points out, the segregation of the races was really a political stratagem by the emerging Bourbon interests in the South to keep the Southern masses divided ....

Dr. King then explained what Woodward's academic research had proved. The biracial Southern agrarian reform movements of the late-nineteenth and early-twentieth centuries had held great promise for racial accommodation and cooperation but, as King explained:

> Through their control of mass media, the [Southern aristocracy] revised the doctrine of White supremacy. They saturated the thinking of the poor White masses with it, thus clouding their minds to the real issue involved in the Populist Movement. They then directed the placement on the books of the South of laws that made it a crime for Negroes and Whites to come together as equals at any level. And that did it. That crippled and eventually destroyed the Populist Movement of the nineteenth century.

In the fall of 1954, C. Vann Woodward, a Southerner and perhaps his generation's leading historian of the American South, delivered the annual James W. Richard lectures at the University of Virginia, just months after the Supreme Court's May 17th *Brown v. Board of Education* decision. It has been suggested that Woodward's lectures "changed ... the life of the nation."[2] Woodward demonstrated that racism existed in the South during and following Reconstruction, to be sure. But the aggressive Jim Crow system imposing humiliating and overarching racial segregation, American Apartheid, was a relatively recent phenomenon. Jim Crow segregation arrived in the South in a tidal wave at the end of the 1890s as a political construction by operatives in the Democratic Party.

Southern African Americans pushed back as best they could. But as Dr. King stated, "through their control of mass media, the [Southern aristocracy] ... saturated the thinking of the poor White masses with [the ideology of White supremacy]." Confederate monuments were integral to that "mass media" saturation that Southern elites deployed to maintain the Jim Crow system. Particularly for Whites and Blacks who were illiterate, monuments were far more effective than books in transmitting the ideology of White supremacy.

Jim Crow Segregation and the Construction of Southern Racism

This era of Jim Crow ascendancy (1895–1915), coincided in time and motive with the work of the United Daughters of the Confederacy (UDC), a Southern heritage group that aggressively promoted White supremacy by, among other initiatives, erecting hundreds of the Confederate monuments that dominate prime public spaces in the South today. Many contemporary critics of Confederate monuments describe this White supremacist motivation for constructing Confederate monuments as a sufficient reason to do something with these monuments today. To understand this objection to Confederate monuments, it is beneficial to fathom the nexus, both in time and in motive, between Confederate monuments and the systemic assault directed at the Southern African American community at the turn of the twentieth century: disfranchisement, spectacle lynching, Jim Crow racial segregation laws, and the flooding of Southern public schools with textbooks teaching White supremacy and the inferiority of African Americans. Confederate monuments were part of a unified strategy, an onslaught, that was designed to advance the ideology of White supremacy and relegate Southern African Americans to a position of "otherness" in Southern civic and political life.[3]

As one travels through this portion of Southern history, it is useful to keep in mind that many of the ex-Confederates who are celebrated through Confederate monuments may well have been personally honorable, as surely was true of the hundreds of thousands of young men who fought for the Confederacy—men who are the ancestors of some who today oppose removal of Confederate monuments from prime public spaces. However, the *warping-of-history* view for why a community needs to do something with its Confederate monument does not focus on the merits of individual soldiers. The growing opposition to Confederate monuments is not a referendum on the valor of the Confederate soldier. Nor is opposition to Confederate monuments intended in any way to shame those who fought for the Confederacy. The valor of the rank-and-file Confederate soldier is intact: it predates erection of monuments glorifying the Confederacy and respect for that valor will continue whether or not a Confederate monument is relocated from its current public space. The *warping-of-history* view rather claims that the Southern ruling class that dominated the membership rolls of the United Daughters of the Confederacy commandeered soldiers' valor for their own purposes: as a means to promote racial bias during the late-nineteenth and early-twentieth centuries in order to secure their own political power and cultural authority. The *warping-of-history* view is that the Confederate monument removal/relocation debate is incomplete, indeed deficient, in the absence of facts demonstrating and explaining the close nexus between Confederate monuments and other actions by the South's ruling class that inflicted physical, economic, psychological, and political harm on African Americans during the period of Jim Crow and continuing to the present.

Disfranchisement of Southern African Americans

Southern Populism threatened Bourbon political control in the 1890s and Bourbons responded by unleashing a counterattack that included the successful deployment of race-baiting against the Populists. This race-baiting strategy successfully denied Populists White voter support by equating Populism with the threat of a rise in the political power of Southern African Americans, what was referred to as the threat of "Negro domination."[4] The irony is that Black voters in the South provided Populists little electoral support, both because so many Black voters retained a political allegiance to the Republican Party and because either through intimidation and coercion, voter fraud, or by purchasing votes, the Democrats were successful in controlling most of the Black votes that Republicans were unable to capture.[5]

Bourbon Democrats, nevertheless, perceived several advantages for themselves from Black disfranchisement.[6] First, suppression of the Black vote through Black disfranchisement rewarded the South with disproportionate representation of White votes in the electoral college and in choosing members of the House of Representatives. A state's representation in the electoral college and the number of congressional seats a state is allocated in the House of Representatives are based on its entire population, Black and White, including all eligible voters whether they vote or not. In states where Blacks were effectively disfranchised, the Black population contributed to the number of a state's presidential electors and the congressional seats allocated to a state, but for the most part, only the votes cast by White voters determined election outcomes.[7] Second, vote-buying became expensive and the Democrats desired to eliminate the cost. Third, Democrats concluded that with the elimination of Black voting, the threat of factionalism among Southern Whites would subside as there would be few Black voters with whom insurgent White groups could form voting coalitions, and in any event the removal of Black voters as the arbiter between White factions would permit Whites alone to resolve their differences if White factionalism did develop. Fourth, voting fraud soiled all who engaged in it and created a disillusioned Southern electorate. Southern Whites wanted to suppress the Black vote and Black political power but also felt repugnance and popular disgust over the corrupt and fraudulent election practices required to achieve that end. With Black disfranchisement there would be no need for the political parties to corrupt the electoral process by purchasing Black votes or engaging in election fraud in order to manipulate the Black vote in favor of Democrats who controlled the voting apparatus.[8] Of course, the irony was that the White South chose to address its own voting corruption, born of a desire to maintain Black subjugation, by punishing Blacks, the object of that subjugation, with disfranchisement.[9]

The Fifteenth Amendment to the United States Constitution posed an obstacle to the South's ambition to disfranchise Blacks. The Fifteenth Amendment provides that "The right of citizens of the United States to vote shall not be denied or abridged by the United States or by any State on account of race, color, or previous condition of servitude." Thus, in order to suppress Black voting power, the South's Democratic establishment was required to construct subterfuges masking the assault on Black voting rights.

The template used throughout the South to deny Southern African Americans voting power became known as the "Second Mississippi Plan."[10] In 1890, the Democrat-controlled legislature in Mississippi approved a revised constitution. As amended, it effectively disfranchised most Blacks by erecting various barriers to voter eligibility, primarily through adoption of a poll tax and requiring literacy as a prerequisite to voting. The avowed motive for amending the Mississippi constitution was to deny the state's African Americans the right to vote.[11] Most Blacks in Mississippi subsequently stopped trying to register or vote. In 1898, the United States Supreme Court in *Williams v. Mississippi*[12] upheld the constitutionality of Mississippi's poll tax. The *Williams* decision opened the way for other Southern states to follow Mississippi's lead. By 1910, all of the states in the Old Confederacy had effectively disfranchised African Americans by means of a poll tax, literacy tests, or other devices.[13] Virginia, for example, held a special constitutional convention in 1901. One of the convention's chief objects, openly avowed by racists who dominated the constitutional convention, was to disfranchise Black voters in Virginia and thereby eliminate them as a force in Virginia politics.[14]

The poll tax was a tax levied on every registered voter at every election and was to be paid whether or not one voted. The poor bore most of the burden of disfranchisement resulting from the inability to pay the poll tax. Voter participation often was less than 5 percent among African-Americans in states with a poll tax.[15] The poll tax also disfranchised many poor Whites; in some states in the 1890s, the poll tax disfranchised a majority of Whites. Where this occurred, the Southern states accepted disfranchisement of some poor Whites as a reasonable cost for disfranchising nearly all Blacks.[16] Decades of opposition to the poll tax finally eliminated it as a voter suppression device, first through adoption of the Twenty-fourth Amendment to the United States Constitution, which barred the poll tax in federal elections, and then in 1966 when the Supreme Court ruled that enforcement of a poll tax in any election constituted a violation of the Fourteenth Amendment's Equal Protection Clause.[17]

Black disfranchisement and Confederate monuments are closely linked. Both supported a joint venture designed to deny racial justice by marginalizing and stigmatizing the South's African American community, a harm that continues into the present. Both disfranchisement and Confederate monuments were integral to what historian Henry Louis Gates Jr. explains was a "desperate effort to reassert White supremacy and decimate the gains in Black equality promised by Reconstruction [a "desperate effort" that] led to the effective disenfranchisement of Black male voters in the former Confederate states [and then to] 'continued decline in recognition of [their] political and legal rights.'"[18] Disfranchisement and Confederate monuments each symbolically declare that only White skin mattered in the New South. Disfranchisement asserted that only White skin mattered in voting. Confederate monuments memorializing the White Confederate soldier symbolically communicated that only White skin was to be associated with the valorous, self-sacrificing, and patriotic devotion to the South's well-being. Frederick Douglass recognized the stigmatizing effects of these efforts to marginalize Southern African Americans. Douglass explained:

> By depriving [African Americans] of suffrage, [the White community] affirm[s] [African Americans'] incapacity to form an intelligent judgment respecting public men and public business [declaring] before the world that [African Americans] are unfit to exercise the elective franchise, and by this means lead [African Americans] to undervalue [them]selves, to put a low estimate upon [them]selves, [and] *brand [African Americans] with the stigma of inferiority* . . . .[19]

In other words, Confederate monuments and disfranchisement were mutually reinforcing sources of stigmatization based on skin color. Each, in different ways, celebrated the virtues of White culture while simultaneously dismissing Southern African Americans as an underclass lacking the virtues associated with White skin. Historian Henry Louis Gates Jr. has succinctly stated the relationship of White supremacy and Black disparagement: "The privileging of White culture and White people was directly tied to the denigration of Black culture and Black people in a mutually reinforcing relationship."[20] In sum, one misses what is most socially and culturally important about Confederate monuments if these monuments' linkage to White supremacy, and thus their linkage to the racial denigration of African Americans, is ignored. This is the crux of the argument of the *warping-of-history* argument for why communities need to do something with their Confederate monuments.

Confederate Monuments and Lynching

Historian Grace Elizabeth Hale has explained that "the culture of segregation was always a process, never a finished product." White Southerners established racial lines in an effort to maintain in the New South the romanticized "pastoral utopia" of slavery that they imagined existed in the Old South. As we have seen, this yearning among post-bellum Whites for the resumption of their imagined antebellum racial harmony built on the Old South's racial hierarchy was the ethos that animated the Lost Cause themes that Confederate monuments transmit.[21] The South used color to fix strict social boundaries. But these color lines were always contingent and often blurred in the 1890s, particularly with the emergence of a rising Black middle class. There was much jockeying back and forth as Southern Whites presumed authority and prerogative to enforce limits on Southern Black freedom and autonomy and as Black Southerners resisted economic, political, and social racial separation and exclusion. The color lines that Southern Whites erected occasionally gave way. The resulting boundary disputes spawned conflict. The White Southerners' most notorious act of reactive violence was lynching.[22]

Lynching is the mob execution of one or more persons by extrajudicial means, death often arising from hanging but also by other means, such as burning or shooting.[23] Lynching in the South was not an unusual, aberrational activity, not just "the work of crazed fiends and psychopaths." One database documents that there were 4,742 lynchings in the United States between 1882 and 1968 of which an estimated 3,445 of the victims were Black. Undoubtedly there were many more unreported cases.[24] Lynching increased dramatically in the mid-1880s and became an epidemic that peaked in the 1890s, just as most Confederate monuments in existence today were being built. The lynching epidemic consisted of "ritualized spectacles of racial terrorism" that occurred as often as every other day in the United States. By one account, during the 1890s, mobs killed between 78 and 161 Black men and boys every year.[25]

Lynching somewhat declined following its mid-1890s peak, even in the South. However, the *percentage* of lynchings that occurred in the South increased from about 82 percent of the total in the decade 1889 to 1899 to 92 percent of the total in the next decade. Moreover, the percentage of lynching victims who were White *decreased* from 32.2 percent in the decade from 1889 to 1899 to 11.4 percent from 1900 to 1909. In other words, lynching decreased overall as the twentieth century progressed, but at a slower pace in the South and lynching increasingly became more a Southern crime of racial brutality.[26]

Lynching in the Southern way was different from lynching that most have in mind with respect to the "justice" meted out to a horse thief or a cattle rustler in the old West when there was an absence of readily available courts and law enforcement officers. Lynching is a horrific act, no matter the circumstances. But lynching of cattle rustlers in the West typically entailed a "quiet form of vigilante 'justice'" consisting of simply hanging the miscreant. There was not also the mutilation and torture of the victim over many hours in the presence of thousands of spectators as occurred so often in the South where observers traveled many miles to view the lynching, which became a ritualistic and sadistic act of racial violence. English philosopher and statesman Edmund Burke once stated "An event has happened upon which it is difficult to speak and impossible to remain silent."[27] That is an apt description of the late-nineteenth century South's "odious social ritual" of spectacle lynching of Southern African Americans. As the Jim Crow South was building hundreds of Confederate monuments between 1895 and 1915, it was simultaneously acting out an obsession with viewing lynching's ritualistic burning, cutting, and finally death.[28]

Four peculiarities stand out with respect to Southern spectacle lynching: the type and number of persons who attended the lynching; the sadistic and ritualized nature of the torture and mutilation to which the (mostly) Black victims of spectacle lynching were subjected; the White participants' obsession with being photographed while posing next to the dead Black victims; and the compulsion to acquire relics, souvenirs, mementos, and photographs related to the lynching event.

Southern lynching was predominantly, though not exclusively, a rural activity in the cotton-growing counties of the deep South, and thus often a small-to-medium-size town phenomenon. The victims mostly were young Black men who were relatively new to the area as they were moving across the South, often in search of work. The lynching victims' alleged transgressions most often consisted of murder, assault, arson, and theft, not rape or other sexual acts, though an unsubstantiated rape charge might be added *post hoc* to a murder charge in order to inflame a mob.[29] The lynch mob consisted of church-going folks from the community, neighbors and friends who knew one another, truly ordinary people. While strangers often came to observe, the lynch mob, those orchestrating the lynching, typically were not strangers from neighboring communities, as often was claimed after the event by those who had participated in the lynching. Southern African Americans seldom attended a lynching. Otherwise, the lynch mob represented a cross-section of classes. As the *Atlanta Constitution* reported in 1899, when discussing the apprehension and lynching of Sam Hose, the mob was comprised of community leaders, the best men, "lawyers, doctors, [and] merchant farmers."[30] Southern lynching developed into a "modern viewing phenomenon" providing an opportunity for local citizens to watch a neighbor torture a victim without fear of criminal sanction.[31] The "cultural power of spectacle lynching was in the looking."[32]

Even as the overall incidence of lynching in the United States decreased following its 1890s peak, Southern racial lynching thereafter increasingly became an elaborate spectacle that conformed to set ritualistic patterns of torture and murder. As the nation moved into the early decades of the twentieth century, a time period when Confederate monuments increasingly were constructed, lynching in the South progressively morphed into larger, more widely publicized open-air events that drew large crowds. Newspapers, and later radio and telegraph, advertised the upcoming time and location of a planned "lynch party," specifically communicating that "all Whites" were invited. Thousands of people assembled to view spectacle lynchings, sometimes by specially chartered excursion trains.[33]

A famous photograph was taken of those attending the 1893 lynching of Henry Smith in Paris, Texas. This photograph shows the mass of spectators who assembled to view this lynching. Taken from an elevated vantage point hundreds of yards from a six-feet square, ten-feet high scaffold where the lynching took place, the photograph shows thousands of people packed together in a massive circle surrounding the scaffold. A contemporary newspaper account estimated that "a surging mass of humanity 10,000 strong" had assembled to view the torturing and burning death of Henry Smith.[34]

In 1899, Sam Hose was tortured and lynched by being burned at the stake by a White mob in Coweta County, Georgia. The railroad scheduled special excursion trains to transport 1,500 to the execution site to satisfy their curiosity and to take part in the lynching. In addition, many others arrived by other conveyances.

Historian Dora Apel reports that "[f]ifteen thousand men, women, and children crowded into City Hall Square in Waco, Texas to witness the burning of seventeen-year old Jesse Washington, a boy who had allegedly confessed to the killing of a White woman for whom he worked." After he was arrested, a charge of rape was added to the allegation against Washington, although the doctor who examined the dead woman had made no mention

Crowd assembled at Paris, TX, fairgrounds to witness the lynching of Henry Smith (Feb. 1, 1893). Prints and postcards of the event, such as this one, were later sold as souvenirs. Library of Congress, Prints and Photographs Division.

of sexual assault or rape. But the added rape charge inflamed the community. Following four minutes of deliberation, a jury convicted Washington, and a mob immediately seized him and lynched him. Well-documented evidence substantiates that attendance by hundreds or thousands of people, drawn from the community or brought in by a special excursion train, was typical of spectacle lynching.[35]

Lynching of Blacks in this Southern way increasingly evolved into a horrendous spectacle of torture and grievous suffering prior to death, all designed to "turn human beings into horribly shamed objects." Southern lynching revealed White supremacists as "vicious, rapacious, envious, and depraved." The torturers inflicted pain on the lynched victims and prolonged the suffering as long as possible. In one case, one hundred White men reportedly took turns torturing a lynching victim for ten hours. Southern lynching increasingly became a ritualized process that often began with the public "severing of toes, fingers, ears, or genitals" and included beating, whipping, clubbing, stomping, and stabbing. In almost all cases, clothes were torn off the person. The torture culminated with the naked victim's death from hanging, burning—or in the case of Jesse Washington, both.[36] Documentary film maker Gode Davis recounted the exploits of Captain Jeremiah Pratt, "a mysterious figure claiming to have served the Confederacy who became renowned for tutoring Southerners in the art of ritualistic burnings. Like a socially sanctioned serial killer, Pratt earned his livelihood by helping to choreograph spectacle lynchings in at least five states."[37]

Many onlookers at spectacle lynchings had an obsession with being photographed while posing next to the dead Black victims. These lynching photographs preserve evidence of men and women manifesting attitudes of pleasure and smug self-satisfaction. Amateur snapshot photography was all the rage at the turn of the century. In 1900, Kodak sold more than 150,000 of its affordable one-dollar cameras. Consequently, there exists today considerable visual documentation of this turn-of-the-century racial violence. For example, one report stated that at the lynching of Thomas Brooks, spectators took hundreds of amateur snapshots.[38] In addition, enterprising professional photographers brought their professional-quality photography equipment and a portable printing plant to lynchings, which they used to capture the event and convert lynching photographs into thousands of picture postcards that were sold as souvenirs to spectators, usually for ten cents each. Group photographs from this era capture the proud gazes of smiling, self-satisfied participants who are not ashamed to be seen, but who rather are jostling for position to ensure being included in photographs of executioners posing with their tortured and maimed Black human trophies dangling by a rope. These photographs include people of both genders and a broad range of ages, sometimes including young children.[39] In 2000, James Allen assembled nearly 100 lynching photographs and published them in a single volume with accompanying essays.[40] The images of the victims are gruesome, but the surviving images of the lynch mob are arguably even more revolting. These photographs reveal "sadistic voyeurism" reflecting attitudes of "self-righteous cruelty and gloating [and] lethal 'superiority' of the White community." Dora Apel has written that these photographs of "self-confident White killers or voyeuristic spectators who face the camera" juxtaposed with the dangling, lifeless, mutilated bodies of the victims "embod[y] the relationship of power to helplessness, citizen to outsider, privilege to oppression, subjecthood to objecthood, and community to outcast."[41] In viewing these photographs, one is struck by the obvious smugness and genuine pleasure on the faces of those who have been photographed, men and woman who had just participated in the lynching of these mostly young Black men and who had dehumanized them by transforming their young bodies into lifeless heaps of unrecognizable, charred flesh and bone.

Those attending a lynching engaged in compulsive souvenir gathering, both while the lynching was taking place and afterward. As clothing was stripped from the victim it was cut into pieces that were distributed as mementoes. The same was true of a lynching victim's body parts: ears, fingers, toes, and the penis that were publicly severed prior to the hanging or the fire while the victim was still alive. These body parts were fought over and then sometimes sold in a secondary market at inflated prices to persons who were not "fortunate" enough to secure a body part when it first became available. There is documented evidence that body parts of lynching victims were preserved in a jar and displayed at the local country store. This was another way to dehumanize lynching victims—reduce them to specimens in a bottle to be gawked over by store customers. Lynching spectators routinely cut the hanging rope into small pieces and distributed the pieces as mementoes, or they would disassemble the links of chain used to immobilize the lynching victim and share these with "lucky" participants. Souvenir hunters even gathered the burnt embers from the fire that burned the victim to death. Following death, souvenir seekers hacked the victim's body, retrieving the teeth, heart and internal organs, often fighting with others for the choicest parts. One contemporary newspaper account described the scene as "men scrambl[ing] and [falling] over each other in their mad haste to secure something that would be a memento to the horrible tragedy. And anything that had any bearing on the occasion was grabbed and pocketed, even the ashes were picked up in handkerchiefs and carried away in triumph [as well as] pieces of bone, and revolting bloody segments of skull."[42]

A popular book in the 1930s described spectacle lynching as "lynch carnivals." Indeed, racial terrorism through lynching became both a habit in the South and a form of leisure, a well-choreographed form of White Southern amusement and entertainment. For decades, scholars have pondered the root cause of this terrible epidemic of racial violence that provided Southern Whites such sadistic pleasure, amusement, and entertainment.[43] While unable to agree on any single cause of this legacy of terrorism, this shameful "memory stain" on our national history, the academic literature concurs that Southern lynching represented the culmination of White communities' struggle to "reestablish the [racial] boundaries that they believed were being traversed [by African Americans in the South], to crush the attacks and violations that [Whites] could associate with the weakening of their own leverage."[44] As Erika Doss has written, lynching "in modern America was the result of pervasive and oppressive racism . . . rooted in . . . affirmation of . . . a White supremacist national community."[45] As early as 1941, W. J. Cash explained that violence against an African American, such as by lynching, constituted "an act of patriotism" when done "to smash a Sassy Negro, to kill him, to do the same to a White 'nigger-lover' [for this] was to assert the White man's prerogative . . . toward getting the Black man back in his place."[46]

Spectacle lynching is closely linked in time with the erection of Confederate monuments. That linkage is more fully clarified from insights regarding lynching provided by historian Grace Elizabeth Hale. Hale agrees with others who have argued that lynching was an act of racial terrorism grounded in White supremacy, motivated to put and keep Blacks in their place, to maintain White control, and to chill Black political activity. But Hale advances an innovative, and more subtle and insightful, understanding of spectacle lynching. Hale's work does not focus on Confederate monuments. But her insights provide an opportunity to develop an uncommonly clear understanding of the linkage between spectacle lynching and raising Confederate monuments, an explanation that until now has not been described.

Hale argues that there was more at stake in lynching in a Southern way than asserting and maintaining White control over Blacks. That purpose alone cannot account for the open-air public nature of spectacle lynching, the attendance of thousands, the advance publicity in newspapers and radio, the prolonged torture, the photographic record that was produced and widely circulated after the fact, and the morbid fighting over souvenir body parts. Hale argues that spectacle lynching developed as a means *for Whites to maintain their own White identity*, what Steven Hahn refers to as Blacks providing Whites the ability to maintain a clarity of the significance of their own Whiteness by enforcing "the deference and ostensible submission that Whites relished."[47]

To maintain political hegemony, the ruling class in the South knew it must convert heterogeneous Southern Whites into a "new Southern order" populated by a homogenous White public. Achieving such a goal was challenging, a more demanding task than one might imagine, and required constructing, and retaining, *in the White imagination* vivid negative images of African Americans—an imagination of African Americans, as historian Henry Louis Gates Jr. explains, as the "'Old Negro' (rural, Southern, impoverished, illiterate, premodern, 'uncivilized,' even 'unwashed.')."[48] In the extreme, the goal of lynching, indeed the goal of all strategies to promote White supremacy, was to convince Whites to view African Americans as barely human, as was the established view during slavery. Spectacle lynching created the desired imagery that reinforced a White view of African American "otherness." Lynching removed from a Black male all semblance of his humanity, severing his body parts, even symbolically removing his manliness through castration, treating him worse than almost any of the lynching participants would treat a dog, prolonging his death as fiery torture was applied, and finally burning him into an unrecognizable "otherness," a mass of charred indistinguishable flesh and bone. W. E. B. Du Bois understood this linkage between lynching and constructing in the White imagination the image of White unity by reinforcing the perception of Black inferiority: "The cultural power of spectacle lynching lay . . . in the looking," DuBois explained, and that looking at an objectified and dehumanized Black man produced "the spectacle of African American otherness [that] created White unity and gave birth to the modern nation."[49]

It was not Hale's project to pair the mania to erect Confederate monuments with her thesis that spectacle lynching's goal was to create Jim Crow imagery of Black "otherness" in order to fortify the goal of instilling in Whites a sense of White identity. Yet Hale's thesis provides invaluable insights coupling monument mania and lynching. The image of African American "otherness" that lynching was designed to construct in the Southern White mind matched in critical ways the same myth-driven, objectified image of the loyal and happy slave at the core of the Lost Cause myth that those raising Confederate monuments intended to communicate. White compulsion to maintain in the present the imagined Old South African American "otherness" that existed during slavery was an important motivation for Southern elites who propagated the Lost Cause myth and also animated White Southerners to build Confederate monuments as a way to transmit that myth. Confederate monuments and spectacle lynching have as their common denominator the marginalizing and stereotyping of Southern African Americans by projecting an objectified image of them—reducing (eliminating) Blacks' humanity in the White imagination.[50] Hale writes that "spectacle lynchings brutally conjured up a collective, all-powerful Whiteness even as they made the color line seem modern, civilized, and sane." The same is true of Confederate monuments: they too "conjured up a collective, all-powerful Whiteness even as they made the color line seem modern, civilized, and sane."[51]

On nearly every Southern courthouse lawn and town square, Confederate sympathizers raised stone, marble, and bronze monuments glorifying some White Confederate hero or generic standing soldier. These monuments to a White South reinforced the stereotype of White supremacy and, concurrently, Black inferiority, exclusion, and separation. By conflating civilization with "Whiteness," these monuments symbolically communicated that all heroes are White and that these town squares and courthouse lawn spaces dominated by Confederate monuments thus constitute shrines to White supremacy in a White man's country. The core function of both Confederate monuments and spectacle lynching was to solidify the ideology of racial difference and separation—bringing into the present, and maintaining, the racial hierarchy of the antebellum past. Referring to lynching, Hale argues that "racial violence was modern."[52] So was Confederate monument mania. Both perpetuated an emerging twentieth-century ideology of a cult of White Anglo-Saxonism in the New South.

Those who raised Confederate monuments may never have touched a Black man in anger or attended a lynching, but the Confederate monuments they raised were complicit in the lynching death of thousands of young Black men in the late-nineteenth and early-twentieth centuries who died violent deaths so that a Southern culture of White supremacy could flourish. Confederate monuments and lynching were partners in the perverse crime of racial debasement.

Confederate Monuments and Jim Crow Segregation

Jim Crow had a "strange career," as C. Vann Woodward first explained more than sixty years ago in his slim 1955 volume, *The Strange Career of Jim Crow*. Woodward's core thesis in *Strange Career* was that following Reconstruction it was unclear to Southerners what the status of Southern African Americans ought to be in the New South. Currents of interracial cooperation and harmony competed for acceptance with segregation and racial animus.[53] Woodward explained how there "remained a considerable range of flexibility and tolerance in relations between the races . . . between 1870 and 1900."[54] For example, it was more than a decade after Redemption in the early- to mid-1870s before any Southern state enacted a Jim Crow segregation statute. There was extra-legal discrimination and segregation to be sure. But prior to the last decade of the nineteenth century, the time when Confederate monument mania began, there was little, and then only sporadic, legislation mandating near-total separation of the races through segregation and ostracism and the "needless humiliation [of Southern African Americans] by a thousand reminders of their subordination."[55]

Things changed abruptly in the mid-to-late 1890s, however. These years are generally considered to be the beginning of a complete capitulation to racism in the states of the Old Confederacy and also constitute the exact time period when Confederate monument mania took hold. At this time, as the dark cloud of disfranchisement and apartheid descended on the South and spectacle lynching as a Southern specialty became rampant, Southern African Americans were ostracized in nearly every aspect of civil, religious, political, and cultural existence.[56]

This attack on Southern African Americans was nothing less than a "process of dehumanization."[57] One manifestation of this ostracization was subjecting African Americans to a pattern of dehumanizing group libel. Newspapers published false stories of Negro crime, fabricated charges of rape, and falsified allegations of arrogance, impertinence, insufficient servility, and Black atrocities. This reported falsely in newspapers was designed to promote White unity. Roving gangs were permitted to indiscriminately and freely loot and murder Blacks in their own communities as occurred frequently in the South in the final years of the 1890s, years when Jim Crow was being launched in earnest and Confederate monument mania was reaching its apogee.[58]

The Supreme Court also added its weight to the group libel of Southern African Americans when, in *Plessy v. Ferguson*, the Court upheld the legality of separation of the races based on one's "proportion of colored blood." In *Plessy*, the Court concluded that "distinctions based on physical differences" were sufficiently rational indicators of African Americans' otherness to justify dissimilar treatment from Whites.[59]

These incidents of group libel of African Americans coincided with "a scientific, intellectual, and artistic hardening of anti-Black concepts of 'race.'"[60] Much falsity was contained in racist literature published in the disciplines of sociology, anthropology, and history, sometimes referred to as the "Yellow Peril" school of literature and the "cult of Nordicism." This literature portrayed all African Americans as inferior to Whites, thus libeling an entire race. Racist accounts of Reconstruction in academic publications shaped the public's understanding of the Civil War and its consequences for three generations, reaching popular audiences through early-twentieth century films such as *Birth of a Nation* and *Gone with the Wind*. At academic conferences during this period many intellectuals promoted racial stereotypes portraying African Americans as a race of people who were "rapidly deteriorating in morals and manners, in health, and efficiency [and] incapable of self-government, unworthy of the franchise, and impossible to educate beyond the rudiments." The intellectual world of the early 1900s assembled arguments that paralleled antebellum pro-slavery arguments that Blacks are non-educable and thus predestined to serfdom. These views of inherent Black inferiority and White superiority *exactly* encapsulated the core messages implicitly conveyed by the Cult of the Lost Cause and transmitted by Confederate monuments. All of these manifestations of group libel were part of a White supremacy movement.[61]

It was in this turn-of-the-century environment of growing racial intolerance, prejudice, hatred, and racial antagonism that Southern communities erected nearly half of all Confederate monuments in existence today and concurrently adopted and expanded Jim Crow laws that imposed second-class citizenship on Southern African Americans. These laws denied most

Southern African Americans civil and political equality and the economic opportunities needed for entry into the middle and upper classes. State-sanctioned segregation and exclusion provided the mechanisms for maintaining Black subjugation. The Jim Crow laws provided *de jure* limits on the physical, civic, political, educational, and economic spaces that African Americans could occupy in the New South: seating on trolleys, trains, steamboats, and theaters; access to public accommodations such as restaurants and hotels, and sporting events; the communities where African Americans could and could not live; and the interactions with Whites that were legally permissible and impermissible. But beyond these *de jure*, legally enforced, separations between the races, Jim Crow laws provided public symbols, constant humiliating reminders to Blacks, *and to Whites*, of African Americans' inferior, second-class, "otherness" status and African Americans' "proper role" in Southern society.[62]

As the South's "final solution" to its race problem, Jim Crow laws provided legal sanction to "racial ostracism in virtually every aspect of life." The South had decided to "tak[e] its stand." The "cardinal test" of a true Southerner was a commitment to the idea that the South "shall be and remain a White man's country." By 1915, the mania to construct Confederate monuments had begun to recede. But by then, Jim Crow had matured, hardened, and invaded Southern economic and social life to such an extent that the level of economic subordination of Southern African Americans and the separation of the races approximated the apartheid system in South Africa.[63] W. E. B. Du Bois's oft-cited observation was that "The slave went free; stood for a brief moment in the sun; then moved back again toward slavery."[64]

The critical insight about Jim Crow—and what most persuasively links Jim Crow and Confederate monuments—is that the structure of racial oppression and humiliation that Jim Crow laws created was not designed to protect society from some perceived peril. That is to say, Jim Crow laws were not defensive. To the contrary, these laws were "assertive and combative." But toward what end? Crucial to understanding the link between Jim Crow segregation and Confederate monuments is an appreciation that Jim Crow segregation existed primarily to fashion, "in the imagination of the White man, an absolute identification of the stronger race with the very being of the state."[65] Segregationists deployed the twin ideologies of White superiority and Black inferiority to construct within the White imagination this image of Whiteness as constituting the essence of civilized life. What ties Jim Crow segregation to Confederate monuments, what most persuasively connects the two (in addition to the conspicuous congruence of their timing), is that forging such an "absolute identification" of the White race "with the very being of the state" was also an aim of Confederate monuments.

To appreciate why segregationists needed Confederate monuments to help maintain White supremacy, consider the challenges confronting segregationists who were intent on convincing Whites to whole-heartedly support an apartheid society. The threshold problem for extreme racists who promoted segregation, separation of the races, was persuading Southern Whites to commit to a culture where Whites would view Southern African Americans as "theirs to define" and control, as had been the case during in slavery. There were many centrifugal, disunifying, forces that impeded achieving such complete White control over Southern African Americans.[66] Steven Hahn has written, for example, that "the formulas and constituencies of support for Jim Crow were not easily or quickly found."[67] Grace Elizabeth Hale concurs when she writes that by the beginning of the twentieth century Whites discovered that a mass culture of racial otherness constructed on the idea of Whiteness "was always continent, always fragile, always uncertain. . . . Segregation remained vulnerable." White supremacists were thus forced to confront the hard reality that "the culture of segregation was always a process, never a finished product."[68]

The metaphor of herding cats comes to mind as an apt summary of the challenge of creating and sustaining the level of White unity necessary to maintain a culture of racial segregation built upon a nearly complete separation of the races. The struggles and conflicts *among Southern White men* from 1860 to 1900 provide insight into some of the obstacles to creating the necessary White unity: the serious White-on-White class struggles among Southern men that occurred during the Civil War;[69] political conflict in the South among White men during the early years of Redemption (e.g., conflicts between White Republicans and White Democrats and the early Readjuster Movement in Virginia);[70] and White disunity during the Southern agrarian revolt (e.g., the challenges posed by the White Farmers' Alliance, the fusionist revolt in North Carolina, and the Populist movement).[71] The White unity that Democratic Party leaders desperately needed to maintain political control proved elusive when the agrarian revolt during the late-1880s and early-1890s challenged the Democratic Party's political hegemony. To overwhelm the factionalism that split the "solid South" White vote during the Southern agrarian revolt, Democratic Party elites inundated the political process with race-baiting built around the "ghost dance of Negro domination."[72]

The dawn of the twentieth century made it no easier for White supremacist leaders to maintain White solidarity. First, Black communities pushed back against Jim Crow by remaining politically mobilized. Southern African

Americans sought alliances with White groups where they could.[73] Moreover, Southern African Americans opposed absolute color bars in employment, leisure and travel. Such Black resistance denied Whites the ability to simply assume their own superiority and African Americans' concomitant inferiority.[74]

A rising Black middle class unhinged the maintenance of strict color lines when, for example, African American consumers in the South were able to dress themselves and their children better than many Whites, or were able to obtain university educations that Whites did not possess and could not afford, or could purchase first-class coach tickets on trains or seating on steamboats beyond the financial reach of poor Whites, or were able to purchase any number of other consumer goods unattainable by poorer Whites. The development of a small but growing Black middle class shaped class lines that threatened to transcend color lines, raising the serious question of whether "a Whiteness founded in a culture of segregation [would] be able to hold White Southerners together."[75]

Whites, of course, were not willing to forego the profits from Black middle-class consumer spending and thus could not, or would not, attempt to stem the Black consumerism that created stunning class differences that could arise between middle-class Blacks and working-class Whites. So, White supremacists' responsive strategy was to structure a culture of segregation and exclusion that assured that race always trumped class and, most critically, that *Whites* never lost sight of that truth.[76] Jim Crow turned the South into a living seminar that constantly reinforced to Whites the lessons of racial difference, its importance, and the *need for Whites* to maintain the "otherness" of Blacks. As much as Jim Crow was designed to delimit Black autonomy, its more significant contribution to White supremacy was that, in effect, it created one giant minstrel show portraying at every turn of civic and political life the inferiority—near inhumanity—of Blacks and the concomitant superiority of Whites.

Jim Crow segregation was used to indoctrinate Whites, to advertise to them—and of course to Blacks—this idea of Black "otherness." Take, for example, the dilapidated Jim Crow railroad car to which Southern African Americans were relegated irrespective of wealth, education, or class. The cultural power of that Jim Crow car arose not from its second-rate accommodations, its soiled and tattered upholstery, its soot-laden air, or its fetid toilets. Rather, the power of the Jim Crow rail car resided in the humiliation African Americans suffered from being relegated to seating in such an unkempt, run-down car simply by virtue of their color. Whites received a powerful message of superiority from the disparity between the quality of rail cars available to White passengers as compared to the sordid conditions available to their neighbors based entirely on the color of their skin. White persons walking through the Jim Crow rail car, no matter their own low social station, were instantly reminded of their own superiority and of the inferiority, the "otherness," of being Black. The inferior Black rest rooms and waiting rooms at train stations similarly were part of the Southern social seminar designed to create stereotyping that reinforced *to Whites* the fact of their own superiority and Black inferiority. The logic of Black inferiority, Black otherness, and White superiority was communicated by every "colored" drinking fountain, every theater's inferior "colored" seating area, every low-level job to which Blacks were relegated, the South's substandard Black schools, and every city park that barred Blacks. Architects designed back alleys in Richmond, Virginia's Monument Avenue's residential district so that the Black "help" could leave for home at the end of the workday and remain invisible on Monument Avenue, considered White man's territory.[77]

In sum, understanding the social and cultural significance of Confederate monuments begins with appreciating Confederate monuments functional relationship with Jim Crow segregation, disfranchisement, and lynching. All of these efforts by the White ruling class highlighted *to Whites* the critical lesson of the "otherness" resulting from having Black skin. These efforts were integral to a strategy for achieving the elusive goal of White's imagining unity with other Whites at a sufficiently intense level that they would identify their Whiteness with the very existence of civilization.[78]

Confederate monuments, all of which celebrated White soldiers and a White world view, reinforced to Whites this lesson of White centrality and Black "otherness." The *warping-of-history* view that maintains that contemporary communities must do something with their Confederate monuments is grounded in the clarity that Confederate monuments have operated as a tool of Black subjugation, no less than did Black disfranchisement, Black lynching, and Jim Crow segregation. *Warping-of-history* advocates are able to proffer a powerful case supporting their viewpoint.

The UDC and the White Supremacist Motive in Raising Confederate Monuments

The *warping-of-history* approach to deciding whether a community should do something with its Confederate monument examines not only the *effect* of Confederate monuments but drills more deeply to unearth evidence of the *motives* of those who raised these monuments. All monuments communicate. They communicate literally through their inscriptions but also symbolically through their sculpture and design. Monuments attempt to convey the messages and ideologies preferred by those who build them.

The *warping-of-history* charge leveled today against Confederate monuments is that these monuments, especially those raised in the early twentieth century (which is most of them) contained a slant on Southern history that tracked the well-documented racial prejudices and ideologies of the United Daughters of the Confederacy (UDC).

The UDC was formed in 1894 and beginning in 1895 assumed the primary responsibility for generating the funding for, and then erection of, hundreds of Confederate monuments.[79] UDC membership steadily increased, growing from 17,000 members in 1900, to "an army of 100,000 women" by World War I, and then falling to 68,000 members in 1920.[80] Like their mothers in Ladies Memorial Associations (LMAs), the Daughters in the UDC continued memorial work honoring the Confederate dead but increasingly "pursued a broader social and political agenda." The UDC endeavored to "mass-market a nostalgic mood [for return of an antebellum White controlled society], a mood made respectable because southern matrons cultivated it."[81]

Like other heritage groups at the time, such as the Daughters of the American Revolution (DAR), the UDC limited its membership to "Anglo-Saxon" women. These women gravitated enthusiastically to the work of the UDC in order to give meaning to the past by bolstering the historical vision of the role of their class in America's nation building. The UDC accelerated the celebration of White supremacy and advanced a more racist memory of the Civil War and Reconstruction than had their mothers in the LMAs. At monument dedications, a common UDC tactic was to pay tribute to faithful slaves and mammies because they "'understood' their proper role" in Southern society. Beginning around the mid-1890s Confederate hereditary societies like the UDC espoused the romantic ideology of a contemporary cult of Anglo-Saxonism, the view that civilization was a White Anglo-Saxon racial trait. One recurring theme of Confederate monuments, always implicit, was that White Western civilization manifested "the highest achievement of social evolution." By implication, other cultures (read as African) constituted a lower level of evolutionary achievement. White racial privilege inevitably flowed from this presumed superiority of White civilization. The average White Southerner well understood that Confederate monuments were designed to advance a view of Southern history that reinforced a Southern racial order built on the superiority of Anglo-Saxon civilization over the inferiority of Black culture.[82] By the turn of the twentieth century, as Jim Crow took ever greater hold on Southern race relations, some monument dedication speakers overtly added White supremacist racial references to their monument dedication presentations. One example is the November 30, 1899 address by J. H. Henderson at the dedication of the

Confederate monument at Franklin, Tennessee. Henderson said that Confederate veterans "are the men we desire to honor [today]. *It is an honor to belong to the race that could produce them.* Our children should know them, and the richest heritage we have to leave them is that their blood flows through their veins. Such is the sentiment that built this monument and located it where it is."[83] Those who have most carefully examined the UDC's activities at the turn of the twentieth century conclude that the Confederate monuments the UDC raised were intended to advance an idealized "White supremacy as an Old South custom that should remain intact [in the New South]."[84]

The official records of the UDC, its annual reports, and its chapter archives overflow with the transcending commitment to this racialized conception of nationhood, or as one UDC report put it in 1902, preservation of the "Anglo-Saxon race [as] the master work of the creation." The UDC "took up the banner of White supremacy" with a vengeance, stridently asserting the privileges of race and class as "natural" concomitants of Southern culture. Mildred Lewis Rutherford, among the most widely known early-twentieth century leaders of the UDC, was the UDC's chief historian from 1911 to 1916, the period when the UDC was most actively engaged in raising Confederate monuments. Rutherford held racial views typical of the generation of the UDC "Daughters" who championed the construction of hundreds of Confederate monuments. A life-long resident of Athens, Georgia, Rutherford was an unapologetic proponent of White supremacy and held strong pro-slavery views, a true believer. Fifty years after the end of the Civil War, Rutherford argued, in effect, that Africans were fortunate to have been slaves because Southern slavery brought them from savage Africa to civilized America, had Christianized them, and had "made them the happiest set of people on the face of the globe." If slavery had a defect, Rutherford argued, it was "the great burden the institution placed upon Whites." Rutherford admonished postwar Southern African Americans to accept White supremacy in all things, to remain faithful and deferential to their former masters, and to prove themselves as faithful and loyal "servants" even as their ancestors had during slavery. Rutherford insisted that harmonious race relations in the New South depended on this.[85] David Blight writes: "In all of their efforts, the UDC planted a White supremacist vision of the Lost Cause deeper into the nation's historical imagination than perhaps any other association."[86]

A vivid example of this linkage between the UDC commitment to advancing a Cult of Anglo-Saxonism and their erection of Confederate monuments can be found in the Confederate monument located at Arlington National Cemetery.

The Confederate Monument at Arlington National Cemetery

By America's entry into World War I in the spring of 1917, Confederate monument mania was subsiding. Many Confederate monuments were yet to be built across the South, but fewer and fewer Southern towns and hamlets were erecting monuments during this period, in part because so many Confederate monuments already had been raised during the previous twenty years.[87] But it was near the end of the monument mania era that the UDC had one of its greatest achievements: the unveiling on June 4, 1914 of the Confederate monument located in Arlington National Cemetery. This monument was the UDC's most defiant pantheon to White supremacy.

In the growing spirit of sectional reconciliation following the Spanish-American War, in which many Southerners had fought heroically for the United States, President McKinley announced that the time had arrived for the United States government to care for the graves of Confederate soldiers. Accordingly, in 1900, arrangements were made for the remains of 128 Confederate soldiers buried in the North in scattered graves to be transferred to a Confederate section of Arlington National Cemetery for re-interment. And in 1906, Congress enacted legislation providing for the care of Confederate graves at many other locations in the North, mostly the more than 30,000 southern soldiers who had died in Northern hospitals and prison camps. While Congress was considering an appropriation to care for Confederate graves in the North, Congress voted to return captured Confederate battle flags to their regiments. These developments salved the wounded egos of Southerners who for many years had sought the return of their regimental battle flags. And the change in the federal government's policy, to appropriate funds for the care of Confederate graves, softened the resentment that festered since the end of the Civil War over the federal government's policy to create national cemeteries for Union dead but not for Confederate dead.[88] But the UDC was not satisfied.

UDC leaders initially opposed the transfer of the remains of Southern soldiers to Arlington, in part because the United States government had refused to permit the UDC to raise a Confederate monument in Arlington National Cemetery. Once re-interment of Confederate dead in Arlington began, the UDC insisted that the federal government permit it to erect a Confederate monument there, and in 1906, Secretary of War William Howard Taft gave permission.[89] Fundraising and construction of the monument took eight years, but the UDC's Confederate Monument at Arlington was finally unveiled in 1914. It remains there today.

Many viewed the Arlington Confederate Monument as a shining emblem of sectional reconciliation, and it was. But this monument also was,

Dedication of the Confederate Monument in Arlington National Cemetery, June 4, 1914. National Photo Company Collection, Library of Congress, Prints and Photographs Division.

and is, an enduring emblem of White supremacy. It is a restatement of the essential themes of the Cult of the Lost Cause. A bronze figure of a woman adorns the top of this thirty-two-foot-high monument. One hand rests on a plow and sickle, a symbol of the South's agrarian past. The monument's circular pedestal contains a frieze featuring thirty-two life-size figures interpreting the war directly from the pages of the Cult of the Lost Cause. One historian has described the frieze as "A Textbook in Bronze." The monument is defiantly pro-Confederate. Some of the life-size figures portray the "proper" racial hierarchy. For example, one relief depicts a faithful slave as a stoic body servant joining his benevolent master as the two go off to war. The image is of a Black slave willingly volunteering to lay down his life, if necessary, to protect a White master whom he loves. Another is of a departing Confederate soldier placing his baby for safe keeping into the protective arms of a faithful Black mammy as another young White child, seeking reassurance, clings to the mammy's dress and buries her apparently sobbing face into the protection of the mammy's body. These two reliefs adorning the Arlington Confederate Monument portray the kind, indeed loving, relationships that Confederate apologists wanted to convey existed between master and slave. Some reliefs depict appropriate gender roles, such as one depicting a young (apparently unmarried) Southern woman tying a sash around the waist of her dashing Southern gentlemen as she bids him farewell on his way to war conveying that meanwhile she will persevere, stay faithful, and "keep the home fires burning." Another shows a wife providing approbation to her powerfully built blacksmith husband who has forged his own sword and is readying his departure for war—apparently to protect hearth and home from aggressive and oppressive Yankees. Another depicts a minister and his wife bidding farewell to their young, school-age son, showing the sacrifices made by all in the South for a worthy cause, even the sacrifice of a man-child. These are noble people performing noble acts, without reference to the dreadful ramifications to the future of the United States if their prosecution of the Civil War had been successful: destruction of the Union and creation of an independent slaveholding republic and perpetuation of the institution of chattel slavery. One of the inscriptions (in Latin) praises the Confederate cause. Other inscriptions speak to heroic sacrifice by men who "dared all" in "simple obedience to duty." One could teach a seminar on the Cult of the Lost Cause just by using the Arlington Confederate Monument and its friezes as the classroom. The monument's sculptor stated that the monument encouraged peace, even as it symbolically reiterated the standard claims that the White South fought for its constitutional rights and not for the perpetuation of the institution of slavery. At the dedication, UDC President General and Mississippian Daisy McLaurin Stevens, surrounded by Confederate battle flags, emphasized the homage that the memorial intended to extend to the Confederate soldier. She then quickly shifted the emphasis of her dedication remarks to "the theme of self-government" and states' rights, well-understood code words then for White supremacy. Historian Karen Cox has asked: "how can the Confederate monument at Arlington be viewed as a monument either to 'peace' or 'reconciliation'" since the monument's aim was to defend the South's claim that the war was fought to uphold the South's Constitutional liberties (to destroy the Union and to expand slavery) and since the monument's supporters continued to deny that the war was prosecuted, even in part, to perpetuate the institution of slavery?[90]

The UDC's monument at Arlington National Cemetery is a useful reminder of the need to be clear with respect to who raised Confederate monuments and why and also the need to remain focused on the misdirection inherent in all Confederate monuments. Every Confederate monument has several faces, some more obvious than others. One face commemorates the Confederate soldier, his valor and sacrifice. Other faces, usually less pronounced and more often symbolic than explicit, celebrate the racist values of the political class in the South whose members made the monument possible.

The women of the UDC, mostly local White elites, "shared a conviction that it was both their place and their right to nurture the memories of their class and their people," memories constructed around the ideology of Anglo-Saxonism, the superiority of the White "race" and its destiny to rule the world. The UDC carried out its mission by assuming responsibility as a self-appointed body controlling the fund-raising, design approval, inscriptions, and construction of hundreds of Confederate monuments that dot the Southern landscape today.

During the era of Confederate monument mania, the Daughters of the UDC self-consciously marketed themselves as representing a spontaneous public will, even when they did not. Harnessing a public mandate to support its monument-building efforts permitted the UDC to advance its racist version of the Southern collective memory of the Civil War in the name of the "public" when, ironically, the UDC was among the least democratic of Gilded Age organizations in the South. The misdirection was effective, in large part, because of the deep affection Southerners felt after the Civil War toward the rank and file soldier who had sacrificed and given so much. The Southern ruling class took advantage of, hijacked, the Southern people's genuine and heartfelt affection for the Confederate veteran. The women of the UDC were extraordinarily successful at colonizing Southern public spaces with monuments that mirrored their racist ideology, promoted White unity, and thereby solidified political control for their class at a time when many forces operated to undermine it.

Once the monuments were built and unveiled, the origins of the monuments' creation faded from historical memory and these monuments soon defined their community's self-image. Confederate monuments operated, and continue to operate, as bronze and stone textbooks teaching each succeeding generation in the South the lessons of racial orthodoxy that the UDC deemed essential for a harmonious and prosperous New South. It is difficult to disagree with Fitzhugh Brundage's conclusion that the UDC placed a "stamp on civic life in the New South [that] was both conspicuous and subtle. . . . More often than not it was White women's fund-raising acumen that determined what in the South's White past was commemorated."[91]

The UDC and the Effort to Raise the Mammy Monument

An excellent example of the UDC's use of Confederate monuments to project its understanding of "proper" racial hierarchy can be seen in the failed attempt to erect a "Mammy Monument" in the nation's capital. In 1922, the Washington, DC, chapter of the United Daughters of the Confederacy proposed to Congress that it be permitted to raise a memorial on public land in Washington, DC, to the "Faithful Slave Mammies of the South." The UDC stated that the memorial was to recognize the supposed loyalty during the Civil War of enslaved women to their masters. This 1922 proposal by the UDC for a so-called mammy monument coincided closely in time with the 1922 dedication of the Lincoln Memorial, which segregationists resolutely despised and which "incited Confederate veterans to action."[92]

On February 28, 1923, the United States Senate passed Bill S4119 that allocated public land in Washington, DC, for the erection of a monument to the "faithful colored mammies of the South." The growing, and increasingly influential, African American press immediately swung into action to oppose the proposed legislation, arguing that such a monument "can only be a symbol of [Blacks'] servitude to remind White and Black alike that the menial callings are [the Negro's] place." African American newspapers, including the *Chicago Defender*, viewed the proposal to erect a mammy monument as insulting to African Americans, especially given the Southern filibuster in the Senate just a few weeks earlier to defeat an anti-lynching bill. An avalanche of protests followed. In the House of Representatives, the Mammy Monument bill died in Committee and thus never reached the floor of the House for consideration. This so-called "mammy controversy" is an important chapter in the history of the production of public memory and provides further valuable insights into the motives of the UDC in placing sculpture in public spaces to infuse in the public mind certain formations of racial identities and categories.[93]

The "faithful slave" fiction and the glorification of the loyal and loving Black mammy held a special place in the mythology on which the UDC based its Cult of Anglo-Saxonism.[94] Debate among Southern leaders over the value of raising a monument to the faithful mammy began during the early years of the twentieth century (1904–1907). Historian Micki McElya has written that from the beginning, White Southerners' ambivalence regarding slavery permeated the mammy statue movement. In the imagined Southern past, the "faithful slave" was to be commended for staying loyal to the family when he or she could have claimed freedom. But this reasoning was flawed as McElya has explained. If the slave's life was as pleasant and rewarding as the Lost Cause fiction colored it, then it should have not been surprising, or particularly commendable, that the slave would have remained in service. Moreover, the inscription on the proposed mammy memorial referred not to the devotion of "faithful slaves" but rather to commemoration of the loyalty of "former servants." If slavery was as just and benevolent an institution as the Lost Cause myth portrayed it, then there would have been no reason to shy away from naming these Black workers slaves rather than renaming them as "servants."[95]

Perhaps the most revealing, and in many ways stunning, Southern argument favoring a mammy monument was the claim that such a monument held promise for promoting positive race relations. Advocates of the monument argued that the monument could demonstrate the value of slaves' devotion and loyalty. As one Southern congressman asserted in support of the monument, "The traveler, as he passes by, will recall that epoch of southern civilization" when "fidelity and loyalty" prevailed. "No class of any race of people held in bondage could be found anywhere who lived more free from care or distress." This reasoning was intended to promote a view of the mammy slave as a symbolic role model to shape the current behavior of the descendants of slaves into "acceptable" patterns of behavior toward Whites.[96]

Another strong motive for wanting to raise a mammy monument on public land in Washington, DC, in the early 1920s was the mounting post-World War I Black activism confronting segregationists combined with an unwanted increased migration of Blacks from the South to the North. By the end of World War I, Black opposition to racism became more intense and militant. Black soldiers returning from serving their country in World War I were still denied full citizenship and correspondingly resisted segregation with unprecedented vigor. The war that was supposed to make the world "safe for democracy" energized arguments for political and social equality among African Americans. The NAACP was organized in 1909 in large measure to mobilize Black political power and to provide legal expertise to resist lynching. Black migration from the South to the North and Midwest intensified immediately after World War I, resulting in a loss to the South of much of its subservient Black labor force. And the summer of 1919 was referred to as "Red summer," in reference to the bloodshed in twenty-five race riots that broke out throughout the United States in the latter half of 1919.[97]

The racial discord manifested by these developments reinvigorated the UDC to push for a mammy monument in 1922–23. The UDC perceived that it needed to strengthen White racial homogeneity, solidarity, and resolve by energizing the organization's White supremacist base through increased advocacy for White supremacy. The UDC seized upon a Black mammy monument as a vehicle to symbolically transmit to Whites its ideology of White supremacy and elite privilege. A related consideration was that in addition to strengthening solidarity among Whites to resist emerging Black militancy, a mammy monument would advance the UDC's invented vision of racial harmony. As with the other monuments the UDC had built over the previous twenty years, a stone and bronze mammy sculpture would add permanence to the UDC's message expressing the "appropriate" societal

Ulric Stonewall Jackson Dunbar working on a model of a statue titled "Mammy" that came close to being built in Washington in 1923. National Photo Company Collection, Library of Congress, Prints and Photographs Division.

role for those who were Black: doing the servile work of a mammy for a White master class was a laudable activity.[98]

The mammy image was a good candidate for energizing the UDC's White supremacist base and projecting the UDC's point of view of appropriate interracial relations. The Black mammy was chosen as the archetypical "faithful slave" because by the 1920s the mammy image connoted beloved, asexual, motherly (grandmotherly) "tenderness and domestic labor [so] central to the [UDC's] notion of affectionate segregation." Many Southerners had mythologized and venerated the mammy image, associating it with the perception of the mammy who was servile, loyal, and "content in her servitude." Thus, among Whites, a mammy monument would reinforce White superiority. Among Blacks, a mammy monument, it was hoped, would encourage Blacks to see the world the same way as Southern Whites imagined the happy mammy did—a social order where Blacks were inferior to Whites but nevertheless held genuine affection for White masters.[99]

Black journalists led the effort to dissemble the romanticized mythic image of the affectionate interracial relations during slavery by exposing the reality of slave life for mammies. These exposés in the Black press detailed how, under slavery, Black women were abused and sexually exploited by predatory White men. The Black press argued that White men invented the mammy image, and initiated the movement to commemorate the mammy, as a self-conscious effort to deny the prevalence of cross-racial sexual partnering in the South and to shield and deflect criticism, centered on historical evidence, of Southern male rape and other sexual depravity directed at African American domestic servants—both slave and free.[100] White men hyped the mammy image in an effort to re-characterize and legitimate the White male/Black female relationship from one that was sexual to that of a nurturing maternal relationship. The mammy image became that of an asexual, aged, rotund figure who loved her White family and was respected in return. She abided no backtalk from the White children whom she guided affectionately, if sometimes gruffly, into adulthood. Occasionally, she could be crotchety when confronted with the vicissitudes of her mistress, but at all times she was fiercely protective of her White family.

Clarifying the reality of a mammy's life, the Black press demonstrated that mammies often were "tragic figures," unable to provide their own children the tender care they provided White children, due to being coerced into long days of domestic duties and caring for the master's family. The Black press contended that the proposed mammy statue movement represented an effort to advance a distorted, White supremacist, view of Black freedom and political equality.[101]

In addition, the mammy image that White segregationists promoted suggested the appropriateness of disenfranchising Black women and by extension all African Americans. It is useful to recall that in 1920 women had just obtained voting rights through the Nineteenth Amendment. One way to discourage Black women's participation in the political process through voting was to relegate Black women symbolically to the servile role of domestic servants performing menial work and perpetuate the image of Black woman as best suited to serving as surrogate mothers for White children and their families. To Southerners philosophically bent toward an ideology of White supremacy, the mammy image suggested the proper natural order: the appropriateness of segregation—the legally enforced separation of the races—as well as of the disenfranchisement of Black citizens. The proposed mammy monument advanced both goals by symbolically suggesting who ought, and who ought not, to be regarded as a full-fledged citizen in the South and indeed throughout the nation. The mammy monument effort answered that question by excluding Black women, indeed all African Americans, by perpetuating a view that African Americans as a group are destined to serve Whites who were in the better position to lead the nation politically. Historian Micki McElya has summarized this aspect of the mammy movement as follows: "Though African Americans were not to share in the rights of full citizenship, . . . they nevertheless had a civic duty to labor for, support, and love those who did." The racist goal of the mammy monument was that the children and grandchildren of slaves, although living under apartheid regimes of segregation and disenfranchisement, the violence of lynching, and White privilege, nevertheless would learn to "measure up" to the high standards of behavior of their mothers and grandmothers who had been mammies, measure up in terms of the replicating mammies' "mythical traits" of character, dependability, industry, and acceptance of their role in the social order.[102]

The mammy monument movement orchestrated by the UDC and its supporters was, therefore, yet another example of the effort to use memorialization to promote Black "otherness"—by portraying Southern African Americans within a framing of menial labor that White segregationists had constructed for Blacks. So understood, the proposed mammy monument, and indeed all of the Confederate monuments, were not simply built to celebrate a past that never actually existed but more importantly were raised to fix the future at a time of uncertainty. Both supporters and detractors of the mammy monument well understood the powerful symbolic communicative power of monuments.[103]

The UDC Textbook Initiative and Confederate Monuments

To supplement and reinforce its efforts to promote the ideology of White supremacy through the erection of Confederate monuments, the UDC took control of the textbooks used in Southern schools to ensure that children received a "proper" Confederate education. This textbook initiative enhanced the ability of Confederate monuments to promote White supremacy.

By the end of World War I, 85 percent of Civil War survivors had died—the 15 percent still alive were quite aged (most over the age of 75). The South's goal of creating a segregated society had largely been accomplished, and the women of the UDC could justly claim a large share of the credit. Their many Confederate monuments, raised in nearly every Southern city, town, and village square, had helped solidify support for a segregated society among a broad cross-section of White citizens. With the Confederate generation quickly passing from the scene, Southern women continued to raise Confederate monuments although fewer of them than during the previous two decades. The challenge now for committed segregationists was determining the best strategies for *maintaining* the segregated society they had worked so hard to create. This was accomplished by promoting "a more explicitly racist memory" of the Civil War and Reconstruction, one that erased as completely as possible the roles of slavery and emancipation.[104]

What has been largely lost in the twenty-first century public mind is the reality that by 1920 racial segregation was a fragile ideal.[105] Many forces threatened its maintenance. A "national network of committed segregationists" was needed to resist racial equality, administer the system of racial segregation, and sustain the political support required for segregation's perpetuation. Here again, the women of the South stepped up. As had their grandmothers in LMAs immediately following Appomattox and their mothers in the UDC at the turn of the century, Southern women of the post–World War I generation took the lead. As Elizabeth Gillespie McRae has written, to preserve and nurture racial segregation in the roughly four decades from the end of World War I through the end of the post-*Brown* "Massive Resistance" of the early-1960s, "it was often White women who shaped and sustained supremacist politics." These everyday women at the local level worked prodigiously to resist equality and assure that racial segregation "seeped into the nooks and crannies of public life and private matters [in the South], of congressional campaigns . . . and of textbook debates." To women of the South, being a good woman and mother entailed "teaching and enforcing racial distance" both at home and within the larger community. It was a woman's role to teach children to love and believe in the sanctity of "our White skin" and urge neighbors to vigilantly "maintain the color line." Perceptive White women understood that the reproduction of racial hierarchies, which formed the core of White supremacy, required constant gardeners who would work to protect against public apathy that would erode an appreciation of the benefits of racial segregation, primarily White privilege.

The school was an essential venue for teaching the ongoing importance of maintaining racial segregation. When properly structured, public education could provide generations of children a formalized citizenship education "centered on the politics of White supremacy [taught to children of the South through] lessons on the benefits of racial segregation and the work needed to keep it going." Thereby segregationist politics could be replenished and remade decade after decade. The burden was on dedicated segregationists to assure that school curricula and textbooks provided the necessary "correct" education.[106]

As early as 1919, aging former UDC historian-general, Mildred Rutherford, a committed segregationist, argued that the school textbooks from which most Southern children studied American history failed to provide a "correct" teaching of White supremacy and the values of Confederate culture. Among other things, these textbooks were deficient, in Rutherford's view, by placing an insufficient emphasis on states' rights, by positioning slavery as a cause of the Civil War, by failing to teach that the South had the right to secede, and by overstating the brutality of slavery. Rutherford insisted that school texts used in the South should indoctrinate Southern children in the tenets of the Cult of the Lost Cause. Such a "proper" education would supplement other cultural forces that transmitted White supremacy values to children such as their attendance at Confederate monument dedication ceremonies, annual Confederate Memorial Day events conducted at the local Confederate monument, rallies held at the monument to promote the ideology of White supremacy,[107] and simply children's everyday comings and goings that required them to pass by Confederate monuments.[108] Confederate monuments and school indoctrination would then have the desired reciprocal effect: indoctrination at school regarding the Cult of the Lost Cause would reinforce the monuments' symbolic celebration of White supremacy and monuments would reinforce the White supremacy lessons children were taught at school.[109]

The UDC, perhaps more than any other group in the South, understood that using schools to promote the Lost Cause ideology as the dominant collective memory of the Civil War was, like the raising of Confederate monuments, "nothing less than a political movement, a quest for thought control aimed at shaping regional and national memory of the war."[110] In other words, Southern schools should teach political correctness—Southern style.

The UDC was the perfect group to lead an effort of White supremacy indoctrination in Southern schools because the UDC membership's "loyalty to White supremacy was implicit," as a UDC historian once explained. For example, an organizational history of the UDC touts that its past efforts to construct Confederate monuments had brought the UDC acclaim by making visible the UDC's invisible efforts to communicate to ensuing generations Southern pride in White achievements and elite privilege.[111] As one speaker at a Confederate monument dedication stated, Confederate monuments are built in town squares so that they can operate as visible ongoing reminders to successive generations of the grandeur of the Confederate past. This speaker explained: "We build for our children [and] the public square [is] the place [to build the monument so] that our children ... by daily observation of this monument, [will understand that their parents] regarded the Confederate soldier as the grandest character in all history."[112] Yet, after World War I, the UDC leadership gradually came to agree with their former historian-general, Mildred Rutherford, that the hundreds of stone and bronze monuments to the Confederacy throughout the South were necessary but insufficient to perpetuate the Lost Cause myth of White supremacy into the indefinite future. The South required a new strategy to supplement the Confederate monuments' White supremacy message. The centerpiece of the UDC's new strategy entailed recruiting in their schools the grandchildren and great-grandchildren of Confederate veterans to serve as "living monuments," who would remember the heroic deeds of their forebears and the goals of the Confederacy and who would defend their ancestors' Civil War actions well after the last Confederate veteran had died.

The UDC determined it would need to assume primary responsibility for shaping attitudes among Confederate prodigy through their public education in order to amplify and reinforce Confederate monuments' ability to communicate symbolic messages of White unity and the "otherness" of Southern African Americans.[113] To accomplish this goal, the UDC made the conscious decision to shape the content of textbooks used in Southern schools. The UDC textbook crusade was especially effective for it assured indoctrination at school when children were a captive audience.

By 1910 there was a scramble among Southern school districts to purchase high school history textbooks in order to meet the need of an increasing high school enrollment throughout the South. But almost all existing history books were "Yankee textbooks"—published in the North and tending "to reflect the triumphant nationalism growing out of Union victory in the Civil War" rather than a "true" Southern account of what had occurred in the Civil War. The fear among the South's ruling elite was that if the textbooks were permitted to associate the Confederate cause with "the stigma of slavery" the Confederate soldier would be dishonored by future generations. It was necessary to defend the reputation of the South by reinventing the cause of the Civil War through purging from textbooks any suggestion that the Civil War arose out of a desire to preserve chattel slavery.[114]

Accordingly, throughout the South, UDC chapters formed so-called Rutherford committees that created "measuring rods" for evaluating whether textbooks provided students a proper Jim Crow education, one centered on racial hierarchy. For a textbook to be acceptable, at a minimum it must champion the myth that slavery was an institution beneficial to Blacks because it rescued them from barbarity and introduced them to civilization and Christianity. Moreover, the textbook must expound the "truth" that Blacks were, and continue to be, unfit emotionally and intellectually for participation in the political system that the Fifteenth Amendment of the United States Constitution guarantees them.[115]

These Rutherford committees took it upon themselves to review the textbooks that their local school districts had adopted. James McPherson has described these Rutherford committees as "censorship committees." When these self-appointed review committee members discovered that a school district had adopted texts wanting in "proper" instruction, the UDC historical committee would meet with the local school board to persuade it to adopt approved U.S. history textbooks, ones that were stripped of Yankee lies. In some states the UDC successfully pushed for legislation that in effect required the use of only such approved textbooks in all of the state's public schools, sometimes through the creation of state textbook selection commissions that prescribed the books that every public school must adopt.[116] To be "approved," Southern textbooks needed to erase the brutality of slavery, omit the glorious valor of Black troops during the Civil War, and make no mention of the indomitable commitment of slaves to escape slavery and reach Union lines during the Civil War at great risk to their own lives and those of their children and other family members. The only narratives that survived in these sanitized textbooks were those "that suited the political program of White supremacy."[117]

The UDC historical committees not only supervised the content of what must be included in an approved textbook for use in a Southern school but also what a textbook must omit, what it must erase from the historical record. Textbooks perpetuating the Confederate narrative would need to erase from history certain inconvenient historical facts such as any discussion of the April 12, 1864 Fort Pillow massacre of Black Union Troops by Confederate troops, which had been a staple of textbooks until the UDC historical committees were able to censor textbook content.[118] In her study of the UDC textbook campaign, Karen Cox concludes that "the Lost Cause narrative [that was communicated] to a younger generation ... was replete with racial stereotypes, emphasized the inferiority of Blacks, and exaggerated the benevolence of slave ownership."[119] A typical White child could go through elementary and secondary public school and never confront evidence challenging the truism that a White supremacist racial order was natural and unchangeable, that secession was right morally, legally, and constitutionally, that the Southern cause in the Civil War was noble, that slavery was a benign institution, and that the North generally, and Lincoln in particular, were singularly responsible for the war.[120] UDC representatives were eventually able to announce with much self-satisfaction that due to the efforts of the UDC textbook campaign, every Southern state now had adopted textbooks that taught the tenets of the Lost Cause.[121]

In Mississippi, the adoption list included a primer titled *The KKK* written by Laura Rose, Rutherford's successor as UDC Historian-General. This book glorified the KKK as a savior of the South during Reconstruction and an antidote to the racial strife and oppression suffered by Southern Whites at the hands of African Americans and organizations from the North that supported them. Children learned that the "best citizens" in the South joined the KKK and among the various "oppressions" Whites were made to suffer during Reconstruction, which the KKK repulsed, was "the impulse among Black men to take White wives." Children learned that moderation and persuasion were the KKK's chief tactics and violence was used only as a last resort to preserve "the purity and domination of the Anglo-Saxon race."[122]

The UDC textbook campaign was enormously successful, not only in the South but nationally. The myth of the Lost Cause dominated the content of the U.S. history textbooks used throughout the South and much of the North for nearly half a century. And it bears repeating that these textbooks amplified the same White supremacy messages that Confederate monuments symbolically transmitted. Voluntary associations such as the UDC "became the arbiters of public opinion . . . with regard to the Confederate tradition."[123] For example, a North Carolina–educated scholar, who rose to become the dean of the Yale Divinity School, reflected during the 1920s on his grammar school and high school education in the North Carolina public schools. "I never could understand," he exclaimed, "how our Confederate troops could have won every battle in the war so decisively and have lost the war itself."[124]

Southern White children were not the only recipients of the lessons of White supremacy assured by the UDC textbook campaign. African American children also were taught reinvented history from these UDC-approved textbooks, including lessons regarding their own Black inferiority. Black schools in the South received recycled textbooks previously used in White schools. These hand-me-down textbooks that Black children were required to use subjected Black students to the Rutherford-approved, White supremacy centric, distorted history contained in textbooks previously used in White schools.[125] Black schools thus exposed their students to a version of history that was destructive of Southern African American children's sense of self-worth.

For example, one report from an African American teacher in 1891 stated that from White history books used by Black students, the Black students would learn that "they belong to the most inferior race on earth and also fail to learn one single great thing done by a Negro." A 1937 survey reviewed fourteen history textbooks widely used in Southern schools. That study concluded that half failed to teach students anything suggesting that the South confronted challenges with respect to race relations, only four made any mention of the subject of Southern race relations, and the remaining three reinforced Southern racial prejudice. A 1941 study of textbooks used in the South during Jim Crow found that African Americans were virtually absent from these books, that there were no pictures of African Americans in most of the eighty-six books reviewed, and that they "justified the South's treatment and attitude toward Black Americans." An audit by the Mississippi Education Association concluded that "a student who mastered all the textbooks provided in Mississippi from elementary through secondary school could in all likelihood never meet in his or her reading one Black person who had contributed in a significant way to the nation's development." In another study of the literature lessons provided Mississippi's students, "'there were no readings from Negro authors, no readings about Negroes, no references to Negro poets, short story writers, novelists, or artists.' There was almost complete erasure of Black history and Black Americans." As always, Reconstruction was portrayed as the period when the South was governed by recently freed people lacking fitness to govern or to participate in governance and their having been corrupted and exploited by their so-called friends. Southern textbooks continued the myth that "slave life was pleasant for master and slave."[126]

Among the most harmful of the racist lessons contained in the hand-me-down racist textbooks that Black children were required to use was the message that Confederate monuments symbolically transmit: the ideology that slavery was beneficial to slaves because slavery civilized the savage African. Karen Cox has shown that White-controlled Southern school districts self-consciously directed such racist historical materials to Black schools in the hope that Black students assigned these pro-Confederate materials would accept the UDC version of proper race relations as they existed in the Old South, more robustly accept "the necessity of maintaining the status quo [of White supremacy and racial segregation] in the Jim Crow South . . . [and] be persuaded of the benefits of White supremacy."[127] Elizabeth McRae writes that during Jim Crow, African Americans were virtually ignored and their history was erased from Southern White children's education or "decidedly warped." White Southerners only provided students in the South (Black and White) instruction that "upheld a natural order of White over Black."[128]

Well into the 1970s, school textbooks and curricula in Southern schools did not "veer far from Lost Cause interpretations." Historian John Dittmer found that as recently as the 1990s "most Whites in [Mississippi] still believed in the Lost Cause myths of Reconstruction, which he attributed to 'an interpretation drilled into the minds of generations of schoolchildren.'" Children were taught in school a reverence for Robert E. Lee and the validity of states' rights and White supremacy.[129] Even today, many who were educated in the South prior to 1970 continue to harbor the view that slavery was not a cause of the Civil War.[130]

The erasure of Black achievement and Black heroes from Southern children's education may have created lasting damage. White women across the South bear much responsibility for "rendering Black lives invisible in the school curriculum." An effective way to teach White supremacy was to teach the inferiority of African Americans, something history textbooks effectively accomplished by erasing Southern African Americans from history and thus converting them to an invisible otherness unworthy of historical mention. The Jim Crow lessons transmitted in textbooks over decades of teaching in both Black and White Southern public schools "reinforc[ed] the 'naturalness' of White over Black."[131]

One can only imagine the psychic harm done to generations of Black children—many of whom are still alive—who were taught through these "corrected" Jim Crow textbooks that the UDC textbook campaign placed in Southern schools. Historian Fitzhugh Brundage relates a poignant incident in 1936 at a Black school in Hampton, Virginia, at what appears to be a parents' night event. There a third-grade boy recited in front of assembled classmates and parents verses from a poem he had written entitled "Poem of Great-Grandfather." In the poem this young boy recounted that "they" would whip to death his great-grandfather "if he didn't behave," kept his great-grandfather illiterate, and shipped off his great-grandfather's children. The lad ended the poem asking whether it was "right" "To whip poor great-grandfather with all their might."[132] On the one hand, this young boy—a third-grader, thus probably less than ten years of age—had teachers who had taught him some of the truths regarding the evils of slavery. On the other hand, seventy years after the end of the Civil War, this young boy had developed such strong negative mental images of his great-grandfather being viscously whipped that he cried out through his poem asking whether such whipping was "right." One wonders what thoughts went through this young lad's mind as he was taught his own inferiority from hand-me-down textbooks containing the UDC-imposed version of Southern history. Moreover, what did he think as he passed by the local Confederate monument located in his town's square that celebrated and lionized White men who had fought for the right to continue to "whip poor great-grandfather with all their might." Black children continue today to pass such monuments in hundreds of Southern communities.

The *warping-of-history* approach to the Confederate monument debate evaluates Confederate monuments by investigating the historical and cultural context that begat these monuments and that has surrounded their presence throughout the South for more than a century. *Warping-of-history* proponents argue that Confederate monuments need to be placed in context in order to understand and appreciate the harm they cause: how they worked in tandem with such contemporaneous events as Black disfranchisement, lynching, Jim Crow racial segregation, the hardening of anti-Black concepts of "race" through the group libel of African Americans, and finally the UDC textbook initiative. Additional useful evidence of harm can be gleaned from the speeches and other events accompanying the dedication of Confederate monuments because these speeches often disclose the White supremacist motives of those erecting these monuments. Since the UDC raised most of these monuments, the UDC's own internal documents also are relevant to evaluating the intended political role of Confederate monuments. These internal documents demonstrate the UDC's commitment to a Cult of Anglo-Saxonism. The UDC-sponsored Confederate monument at Arlington National Cemetery is a caricature of all other Confederate monuments. Its friezes make explicit what is implicit in all Confederate monuments: the distortions of the Lost Cause myth and in particular a view of the proper racial hierarchy for the South. The Mammy Monument effort failed but the attempt to raise the Mammy Monument exposes the UDC's ongoing attempts to marginalize the African American community and channel White imagination of African Americans as a people best suited for menial work and serving Whites. And, finally, it is appropriate that the *warping-of-history* approach for evaluating Confederate monuments also investigate the linkage between Confederate monuments and the UDC textbook initiatives. Confederate monuments and the textbook initiative were reciprocal: indoctrination of Southern children at school regarding the racist tenets of the Lost Cause myth reinforced the monuments' symbolic celebration of the supremacy of White valor. Meanwhile, daily encounters with Confederate monuments located in a town's most revered public space reinforced the White supremacy lessons children were taught at school. In short, understanding Confederate monuments within the cultural context of their construction and location illuminates their decades-long role in promoting the ideology of White supremacy.

4
The Racial-Reckoning Approach
The Stereotyping and Erasure Functions of Confederate Monuments

The racial-reckoning approach to determining whether anything should be done with respect to a community's Confederate monument focuses on impact, the societal harm inflicted by Confederate monuments, in particular the harm that Confederate monuments unleash on the African American community. Such harm exists, but isolating it and proving its existence to skeptics can be challenging. One challenge to demonstrating this harm is that on their face Confederate monuments seem benign: Confederate monuments never make reference to slavery, for example, and in the rare instance when a Confederate monument makes any reference to race, through an inscription or in a monument's sculpture, the reference is to the happy and faithful slave. Confederate monuments cause harm by perpetuating stereotypes. The political and social elite in the South, who possessed cultural authority to decide what to commemorate through erecting Confederate monuments, deployed monuments to create a positive image of Whiteness and, implicitly, negative stereotypical images of Blackness. The Confederate monuments they erected filled the South at the turn of the twentieth century with hundreds of heroic White images and no positive Black images. When all the Confederate monuments are of White persons and thus lionize Whiteness in various ways, then White skin becomes indelibly associated with valor, sacrifice, and steadfast commitment to the community's well-being. If White skin represents these commendable human qualities, then what does Black skin represent? A second way that seemingly benign Confederate monuments promote racial stereotyping is through the process of "erasure." Confederate monuments were constructed to promote a variety of pro-Confederate attitudes and beliefs concerning an "appropriate" racial hierarchy and concomitantly to silence the more historically accurate Black historical narrative of slavery, the Civil War, its goals, and its consequences. Confederate monuments have contributed to the development of a Southern myopia that has precluded recognition, understanding, and appreciation of African American *institutions and history, a blindness that has impeded many Southerners' ability to fathom any Southern racial order other than the one dominated by White supremacy and privilege.*

THE PREVIOUS CHAPTER has demonstrated *motive:* that Confederate monuments were raised, in conjunction with other assaults on the African American community, to instill, and reinforce, in Whites a sense of their own superiority and the inferiority of Blacks. By contrast, the *racial-reckoning* approach to determining whether anything should be done with respect to a community's Confederate monument focuses on *impact,* the harm inflicted by Confederate monuments, in particular the harm that Confederate monuments unleash on African Americans, and on all of us today. Such harm exists, but isolating and proving that harm to skeptics can be challenging.

Unlike disfranchisement, lynching, Jim Crow segregation, and the UDC textbook initiative, Confederate monuments tend to conceal their ideological projection of anti-Black bias. Misdirection is a core function of every Confederate monument—to direct the viewer's attention to Confederate soldiers' valor and sacrifice while diverting attention from the monument's more subtle symbolic message of glorifying the Confederacy's racist cause or lauding the various tenets of the Cult of the Lost Cause, which promote the ideology of White supremacy.[1]

Confederate monuments never make reference to slavery, for example. In the rare instance when a Confederate monument makes any reference to race, through an inscription or in a monument's sculpture, the reference is to the happy and faithful slave. The Confederate monument at Arlington National Cemetery, discussed above, is a good example. It portrays a male slave accompanying his benevolent master to war, happily serving as the master's faithful body servant. The Arlington monument also depicts a slaveholding family's loyal mammy. Rather than claiming her own freedom, and that of her children, by escaping to the Union lines, the mammy willingly remains on the plantation to assist the mistress of the homestead until the return of the master who is serving at the front defending the South from Yankee aggression. The classic movie *Gone with the Wind* deploys this plot line: loyal, and sometimes childish, slaves choosing to serve a White family faithfully rather than fleeing to the protection of Union troops who are close by. Monuments portraying Southern African Americans as servile and happy and faithful in their enslavement are the easy targets for criticism due to their self-evident distortion of the horrors of slavery. But most Confederate monuments make no reference to slavery or race.

Unveiling of the Confederate Monument, later known as "Silent Sam," June 2, 1913. From Orange County, North Carolina Postcard Collection (P052), North Carolina Collection Photographic Archives, Wilson Library, University of North Carolina–Chapel Hill.

Occasionally, the historic record exposes a White supremacist motivation for raising and maintaining a Confederate monument. One such example is the "Silent Sam" Confederate monument that until 2019 had, for over one-hundred years, been located in a prominent location on the campus of the University of North Carolina. In his 1913 dedication speech of the "Silent Sam" monument, Julian S. Carr, a Ku Klux Klan member, clarified the symbolism of the statue and unmasked the motives for raising it. Praising the soldiers that the statue lionized, Carr explained "what the Confederate soldier meant to the welfare of the Anglo-Saxon race" by crediting Confederate soldiers with saving "the very life of the Anglo-Saxon race in the South." Carr added that "to-day, as a consequence the purest strain of the Anglo Saxon is to be found in the 13 Southern States—Praise God." Nor was Carr able to resist bragging about his own act of racial violence on the very ground where the "Silent Sam" monument was placed. Carr told those attending the dedication that "[o]ne hundred yards from where we stand, less than ninety days perhaps after my return from Appomattox, I horse-whipped a negro wench until her skirts hung in shreds, because upon the streets of this quiet village she had publicly insulted and maligned a Southern lady."[2]

Unlike the Arlington Confederate Monument, most Confederate monuments do not reference slavery. And it is rare that a "smoking gun" revealing racist motives has survived in the historic record of a Confederate monument's dedication speech, such as the Carr dedication speech of the "Silent Sam" Confederate monument. Accordingly, an apologist for a Confederate monument typically is able to mount a seemingly formidable claim that Confederate monuments cause no harm: they contain no overt derogatory references to African Americans, nor do they typically contain any explicit evidence disclosing a motive to use the monument to disrespect African Americans or promote the ideology of White supremacy. Confederate monuments do glorify the Confederacy but apologists can argue that the Civil War was fought over states' rights not slavery so lauding the Confederacy is celebrating Southern patriots' efforts to claim their constitutional liberties. At that point, the debate is at risk of devolving into a never-ending shouting match over the role of preserving slavery as a cause of the Civil War or a debate over some of the finer points of political and constitutional theory regarding states' rights.

In other words, the most formidable obstacle to demonstrating the efficacy of the *racial-reckoning* approach for determining if something needs to be done with a Confederate monument is demonstrating how a benign-looking, ostensibly harmless, Confederate monument causes contemporary societal harm. The racist motives of those who originally raised these monuments is a start. The previous chapter documented those racist motives. But that was one-hundred years ago. What harm do these monuments cause today? Answering that question is fundamental to resolving the Confederate monument imbroglio.

Confederate Monuments' Imagery—The Symbolic Message of White Superiority

Kirk Savage's ground-breaking book, *Standing Soldiers, Kneeling Slaves*, provides a powerful rejoinder to claims that Confederate monuments are unjustifiably accused when charged with causing racial harm.[3] Without becoming bogged down in disputes over whether slavery was a cause of the Civil War, Savage explains how seemingly benign, and often artistically appealing, Confederate monuments operate to dehumanize and ostracize Southern African Americans from Southern civic life and inspire Southern Whites to self-consciously identify their Whiteness with the very existence of a civilized society. Savage thus provides essential insights for understanding the linkage between Confederate monuments and harm suffered by African American communities throughout the nation up to the present.

His focus is the Confederate monuments' imagery—the symbolic message of White superiority that emanates from the proliferation of the hundreds of White faces, and the absence of Black faces, in the nineteenth- and early-twentieth-century Confederate monuments. Savage begins with the sound premise that a public monument is intended to mold history through certain visual patterns and to provide closure by condensing public history into a series of "heroic accomplishments." When a group erects a public monument in an effort to construct a particular version of public history, the aspiration is that the patterns of historical understanding projected by the monument will be fixed for all time. The goal of those erecting monuments is that what is not included in the memory communicated by the monument will be considered not worth remembering and is to be discarded.[4]

The Confederate monuments erected during the era of Confederate monument mania, between 1895 to 1915, were not primarily great-man hero monuments, but rather mainly were monuments commemorating the common soldier and his traditional virtues of heroism, sacrifice, and steadfastness. State and local governments controlled the prime civic spaces where these monuments were erected—town squares, parks, and courthouse lawns—but did not typically fund and erect these monuments. Instead, local civic groups hosted the effort to erect Confederate monuments.[5]

Slavery could not be mentioned in these monuments for that would acknowledge a massive Black-White divide, wrecking the illusion of an undivided postwar Southern citizenry. Unable to ignore slavery as a fact, the postwar South adopted a strategy that both excised slavery from the war's cause and romanticized it, as we have seen in the Cult of the Lost Cause. But there remained the reality that slaveholders and slaves had competing histories that needed somehow to be integrated into one history. The solution adopted by the Southern ruling class was to choose Whites as the people portrayed in the "people's memory" that Confederate monuments would represent and simply to ignore, even erase if possible, any other historical memory of the Civil War. One important consequence of choosing White people as those whose memory constituted the "people's memory" of the Civil War was that those who raised these monuments were able to, and did, commandeer for their own political purposes the high esteem in which the Southern public held the Confederate soldier. These monuments to the memory of White Confederate soldiers implicitly nominated who was to be considered worthy to become a member of the community. All others were relegated to "otherness," essentially were treated as outcasts.[6] In this way, the standing soldier monuments reinforced and reminded the community of the Southern racial and social hierarchy that was to be maintained— White was superior, as symbolized in the White standing soldier who nobly defended his community and whose heroism was being celebrated. That common soldier, in turn, knew his place and knew it was his duty to follow the commands of his superior officers—those promoted as his social betters.[7]

In any given community, there is only so much prime public space. Control of it can be contested, converting it into what Savage calls a "representational battlefield." Although monuments constructed in the nineteenth and early twentieth centuries were erected on public space with the consent of the local governments, it was certain self-appointed, "public-spirited," citizen groups that organized the funding, the design, and the erection of these monuments. What gave these monuments cultural power was their democratic appeal, arising from the fact that, ostensibly, those promoting the construction of a Confederate monument *did not* represent the authority and viewpoints of the ruling class. Instead, these monuments were retailed as mirroring the spontaneous will of civic-minded people who funded them through public subscription and subsequently donated them to the government for safekeeping.[8] In fact, as has been earlier noted, it was local elites, those with access to local governing power, who dominated the voluntary associations that controlled monument construction. For example, the United Daughters of the Confederacy (UDC) always erected Confederate monuments in the name of the "public," although its membership was limited to women drawn from the South's social and economic elite, often women who were decedents of planter families and whose fathers had been Confederate officers.[9]

In an effort to maintain the myth that the monuments reflected the shared public memory and that they, the project sponsors, were merely submissive agents of the popular will, the UDC widely advertised cornerstone laying ceremonies and monument dedications. People from far and wide were encouraged to attend to demonstrate popular enthusiasm for the "people's monument." One important reason that the UDC focused its monuments on the past valor and sacrifice of the common Confederate soldier, rather than constructing hero monuments to Confederate generals and leaders, was to gain for the monument effort the imprimatur of a popular mandate to commemorate the common soldier.[10]

The UDC well understood that the memory that these monuments would help construct was a *White* collective memory, as communicated through the *White* history, values and memories that the UDC chose to emphasize in the monuments.[11] Accordingly, the history, values and memories of the Southern African American community were ignored and thus lost, forgotten, and erased, except to the extent that the Black community itself was able keep these matters alive by other means.

Savage argues that those Southern elites who possessed the cultural authority to decide what to commemorate through erecting Confederate monuments were able to shape the beliefs and ideologies of the citizenry throughout the South and helped harden an ongoing White version of the collective memory of the Civil War, its causes and consequences. Think of a Confederate monument as a school textbook.[12] Students are taught only what is included in that text and never learn what is excluded. Soon, what the textbook contains becomes the "truth" of what occurred. In the public mind, it is as if the textbook's factual omissions never occurred. Monuments are powerful memory-creating devices that provide history lessons, especially for the young and for those who are unable to read.[13] Therefore, if a monument implicitly or explicitly proclaims that the Civil War was not fought to preserve the horrific institution of slavery but rather some unrelated notion of states' rights and constitutional liberties, professes that the war was fought by White men who were all heroic in their failed attempt to protect the community from Yankee aggression, and declares that slaveholders were benevolent masters whose slaves were happy and loyal and actually benefitted from the civilizing effects of slavery, then that becomes historical truth. Once this "truth" is sufficiently lodged in a community's collective memory, it is difficult for any amount of counterevidence to dislodge it.

Savage's argument, perhaps his greatest contribution to understanding the cultural and political power of Confederate monuments, is that when all the Confederate monuments are of White persons and thus lionize Whiteness in various ways, then White skin becomes indelibly associated with valor, sacrifice, and steadfast commitment to the community's well-being. If White skin represents these commendable human qualities, then what does Black skin represent? Black skin represents the antithesis: a lack of such valor, sacrifice, and steadfast commitment to the community's well-being. Once that distorted association of color and the presence or absence of admirable human qualities is embedded in collective consciousness, contrary evidence may be unavailing to alter the resulting misperceptions. Every day that the monument stands, the racial stereotypes contained in its symbolic narrative become ever more ingrained. That was the reality when these monuments were first constructed and is the reality into the present time when communities continue to add their imprimatur to Confederate monuments by maintaining them in public spaces.[14]

Savage advances a second thesis: he argues that the *standardization* of virtually identical standing soldier monuments in nearly every small town in the South affixed yet another layer of White unity and Black otherness to the South's White supremacist culture. An aggressive monument industry developed after the Civil War to meet the high demand for standing soldier monuments at affordable prices. Granite and metal companies dispatched sales representatives throughout the South who, along with retail cemetery-monument dealers in local communities, distributed catalogs of ready-made, mass-produced standing soldier statues with minimal variations. These nearly indistinguishable off-the-rack monuments used a standardized generic White form. Accordingly, at the peak of Confederate monument mania, virtually identical White forms proliferated in one town after another on courthouse lawns, town squares, and village greens. Together, these generic White standing soldiers created a chain of interconnected White images with each becoming "one member of a much larger group, [a] collective [White] army in stone and bronze." Each town's decision to adopt for *its* Confederate monument the same standardized commemorative type that had been chosen by other towns and villages contributed to the construction of a region-wide White unity built around identical symbols of the White common soldier. In the process, these virtually interchangeable White standing soldier monuments that mushroomed across the South bolstered racial division by fostering a *region-wide* association of the White body with civic allegiance and moral worthiness, meanwhile erasing all reference to the struggles and accomplishments of Southern African Americans during slavery and the Civil War. The chain of near-matching standing soldier monuments in the South promoted racial formation: they reinforced the image of White male nobility and, by implication, reinforced the stigma, and otherness, of being Black. This region-wide chain of standardized standing soldier monuments also reinforced the White political and cultural authority of the class responsible for raising them.[15]

Savage's insights expose how, from their initial construction and still today, the Confederate monument is a brilliant and inspired misdirection. On its face the monument purports to do no more than represent the people's memory of the Civil War and the valor of the Confederate soldier when in fact the local aristocracy symbolically added to every Confederate monument the theme of White superiority. What can be so confusing about Confederate monuments is that from the day of their dedications, Confederate monuments have always had more than one purpose, more than one face: one that toasts valor and one that exalts White supremacy. The several faces of Confederate monuments contribute to the confusion that often besets proposals to remove/relocate the monument. The face one observes when viewing a Confederate monument will influence one's view with respect to whether these monuments should stay undisturbed or be removed/relocated. The "valor face" is easy to recognize. But for most persons, a Confederate monument's "White supremacy face" is obscured until a monument's political and cultural history and functions have been decoded and clarified. The *racial-reckoning approach* to evaluating whether anything needs to be done with a particular Confederate monument needs to acknowledge in its presentation the presence of these two faces in Confederate monuments. Because the average observer is not likely to see any face other than the valor face, careful guidance is needed to illuminate in the simplest terms possible a Confederate monument's White supremacy face and the racial stereotyping created as a result of the many Confederate monuments proliferating positive White images to the exclusion of any positive Black images. The racial stereotyping that results from the proliferation of White faces in Confederate monuments that are located in public spaces represents a serious harm undercutting aspirations of racial equality.

Confederate Monuments' Erasure of Black Presence from the "Southern Past"

Within a decade following the publication of *Standing Soldiers,* historian Fitzhugh Brundage published *The Southern Past.* In this study, Brundage expanded upon Savage's principal conclusions in *Standing Soldiers,* added important additional insights, and invited the reader to shift focus. Savage had emphasized primarily the adverse impact on the African American community from the proliferation of White heroic images throughout the South and the absence of positive Black images. Brundage focused on Confederate monuments' contribution to the erroneous view that "White heritage and Southern identity are synonymous" and that Southern African Americans' heritage merits little recognition. As a consequence of Southern Whites concluding that Southern heritage is theirs exclusively to define, Southern Black heritage has had a limited influence on the region's definition of its heritage."[16] Brundage's project primarily entailed unearthing those things that Confederate monuments exorcize from the historical record and the effect of that purging on the development of Southern race relations and African American history. Brundage explained that there is the "willfully recalled and deliberately forgotten." The focus of *The Southern Past* is the harm Southern African Americans suffer from the "deliberately forgotten."[17]

Brundage initially clarified the "social permission" that some groups receive, and others are denied, to use public space to conduct political debate, to engage in social action, and to further a group's construction of historic memory. Being welcomed to share use of public space constitutes a marker of those with cultural authority and collective power. Those who are not so welcomed will be ignored. The outcome in contests over access to the public sphere determines whom a society's members deem worthy and unworthy, those having and those lacking cultural authority.[18]

In all societies, the elites normally are able to gain control of public space due to their dominant collective power. They may assert control over the most sacred public space to erect monuments commemorating their heroes while denying other groups that space for their commemorative use. In various ways, as a means of exercising power, elites are able to position themselves to control and thus communicate what is remembered and what is forgotten. All of this was true in the postwar South. Brundage argued that the current appearance of the Southern civic landscape is best understood as "inequality etched and erected in public spaces" by "self-appointed private groups" that were able to exploit their access to political power to promote their preferred construction of history.[19]

It makes sense that during the Jim Crow era of racial segregation monuments in public spaces reflected White supremacy, the Confederacy and its racist cause, Confederate heroes, and the common Confederate soldier. It is hardly surprising that Jim Crow-era White supremacist community leaders erected no monuments to Southern African Americans' heroes, men such as Frederick Douglass, Abraham Lincoln, Black inventors or writers, leaders of the several slave revolts in the South, Senator Hiram Revels, the first African American to serve in either house of Congress, any of the most prominent African Americans active in the antebellum abolition movement, or the tens of thousands of Black servicemen who served, and died, in the Union army and navy. What needs to be kept in mind, a key point Brundage advanced, is that just because the White Jim Crow historical version of the causes and consequences of the Civil War dominates Southern history, it does not follow that there was not, and is not, a rich, competing Black historical narrative that is far more accurate in terms of objectively provable historical fact but whose fate was to be silenced in the contest over control of the public sphere.[20]

Confederate monuments attempted to silence, and to an extent were successful in silencing, this other, more historically accurate, Black historical narrative. Due to a combination of illiteracy, inadequate financial resources, and denial of "social permission" to raise monuments in public spaces, Southern African Americans did not raise their own monuments.[21] Moreover, Southern Whites vigorously resisted Southern African Americans' efforts to tell their own history through other means, as this would entail a truthful portrayal of slavery's horror and former slaves' own agency in securing their freedom from slavery before and during the Civil War. White Southerners preferred to erase this portion of the historical record because it challenged their sanitized notions of a harmonious racial hierarchy and inherent Black inferiority. The Black counternarrative survived even as it was engulfed and somewhat overwhelmed by an overarching White-constructed memory that continues to dominate so much of the public understanding of the Civil War and its consequences. Southern Whites largely ignored this Black collective memory and made every effort to render it invisible to the White community.[22]

Brundage's central argument is that as Southern elites constructed public history, in part by raising Confederate monuments, they purged from recalled public memory those historical facts that did not conform with their preferred historical narrative. Confederate monuments have thus caused, or certainly have contributed to, the development of a Southern myopia that has precluded recognition, understanding, and appreciation, indeed even acknowledgment, of African American institutions and history. This blindness to that huge swath of the Southern past that is outside the Jim Crow perspective has impeded many White Southerners' ability to fathom any Southern racial order other than the one dominated by White supremacy. This myopia has been costly. Lack of recognition of African American contributions to the nation's history and progress assured that the African American community would be relegated to "the margins of American life."[23]

Black Memory in Southern Heritage

It is useful to pause and contemplate what the Southern civic landscape and collective memory might have contained if self-appointed White supremacist elites had not monopolized Southern public spaces with Confederate monuments transmitting the ideology of White supremacy. What if, for example, early twentieth-century Southern monuments had included commemorations of African American institutions, history, and achievements?

Good evidence of what post-bellum Southern African Americans would have commemorated through monuments can be found in what post-bellum Southern African Americans did in fact celebrate, albeit not through the permanency of marble, stone, and bronze. Public observances became the principal forum for developing, articulating, and propagating freed people's collective recalled past. Whites may have intended that no Black collective memory should survive their attempted erasure, but through their diligent work Southern African Americans kept their memory of the past alive.[24]

For example, the prewar slave culture incorporated a "wiliness and wisdom that assured [slaves'] survival and their sense of grace."[25] Freedmen did not permit the erasure of this rich heritage of survival during slavery.

For example, as early as April 3rd, 1866, and many April 3rds thereafter, Southern African Americans in Richmond celebrated Richmond Evacuation Day, the day when Confederate troops withdrew from their capitol in Richmond and the day when Confederate oppression of Blacks began to recede. Richmond Evacuation Day celebrated a Black history accented with an indomitable will to survive and overcome adversity.[26]

Freedmen also celebrated April 9th, the day Confederate troops of the Army of Northern Virginia surrendered at Appomattox. January 1st also became a sacred holiday for Southern African Americans. During the time of slavery, the first day of January was a day of great sorrow because that was the day when slaves were sold or transferred to new locations. Such sale or relocation dismantled slave families: slave owners permanently separated an estimated one-fourth of slave marriages and frequently separated young children from their siblings and their parents.[27] But after emancipation, freedmen and freedwomen chose January 1st to celebrate Emancipation Day, turning one of the year's most sorrowful days into one of the most festive, a day to remember both the pain of slavery and the joy of freedom.[28]

The African American community created other celebrations throughout the year that recalled memories, sad and joyous.[29] Juneteenth was an annual celebration by African Americans in Texas every June 19th during the last third of the nineteenth century and continuing even to today. Juneteenth commemorates the date of the first announcement to Texans that the Emancipation Proclamation had initiated the end of slavery in Texas.[30]

Emancipation Day events brought orators who recounted the years of slavery. Some speakers described the suffering of slavery in stark, vivid, bleak, and poignant terms causing grown men and women to sob and stream tears as they recalled their prior lives filled with "sorrow, anguish, and degradation." More often, African American lecturers tried to spare their audience the memory of the worst of the carnage of slavery and the trauma it visited upon the slave population while still arming the children of the slave generation with facts needed to refute the White romantic rendition of slavery. Speakers reminded former slaves, and explained to their children, that chattel slavery was an inhuman and debased institution, countering the White myth of the happy and loyal slave who lived in, and agreeably accepted, an essentially benign environment punctuated by mutual affection between slave and master.[31]

African American orators also presented a counternarrative to the White myth that the South's secession from the Union had nothing to do with slavery and its defense. It was important to these speakers that the Black collective memory be clear: The Civil War was fought by the South to preserve the institution of slavery. But for slavery, there would not have been a Civil War. Had the South won the war, those in the audience who had been slaves would still be slaves, as would their children. The plight of the slave had turned on the war's outcome.[32]

The Southern Black community also commemorated the sacrifices of African Americans who fought and died in the American Revolutionary War against Great Britain and celebrated other community heroes. Patriotic festivities commemorated the Fifteenth Amendment's ratification guaranteeing Black suffrage. These were communal events that could be staged without the need to expend substantial financial or political resources. Moreover, the entire Black community could participate and benefit—both the literate and the illiterate. Freed people well understood that through these celebrations and observances the Black community was redressing "historical exclusion" and adding to the corpus of Southern civic memory its version of historical memory, including yet-to-be-realized claims to political and civil equality.[33]

African Americans served in both the Union army and navy. By the end of the Civil War, African Americans comprised more than 10 percent of the Union military: 134,000 soldiers out of a total of 180,000 were from slave states. Twenty percent of the African American soldiers who served in the Union army and navy during the Civil War perished, a higher fatality rate than among White Union soldiers. Black Union troops exhibited a special type of valor: near the end of the Civil War, Confederate troops on several occasions specifically targeted Black Union troops, executing them as they were attempting to surrender and even after they had surrendered.[34] After the war's end, African American communities held public celebrations to mourn the African American Civil War dead who had fought for the Union. Fallen Black Union troops were commemorated through wreath-laying events held annually in numerous African American communities at Memorial Day observances in May.[35] The valor of Black Union troops was the source of great pride among African Americans, even as Southern Whites expunged the gallantry and intrepidity of Black Civil War soldiers from their portrayal of Southern heritage. There can be no mistake: the rendition of "Southern heritage" created by Southern Whites is distorted, truncated, and hopelessly incomplete when the memory of Southern military valor during the Civil War is limited to White valor.

Black militias enjoyed exceptional status within the Black community after the Civil War, and Black militias no doubt would have been the subject of postwar monuments if Blacks had been provided access to the Southern civic landscape. Black militia units' presence in parades and celebrations organized by African Americans during the postwar years was particularly important to the development of racial pride and historic memory. During Reconstruction, local biracial Republican governments inducted Blacks into previously all-White militia units. Prior to the Redemption in the early 1870s, many militia units became all-Black organizations that White political leaders opposed and Whites sometimes terrorized. Military service by Blacks in militia units had enormous symbolic significance. At a time when White racism characterized Blacks as racially inferior, lazy, and incompetent, the Black community felt a justified sense of pride in Black militia members' display of military prowess, precision parade-ground marching, military bearing and "correctness," and spit-and-polish. The Black community could, and did, hold Black members of militia units in high regard, celebrating them as a counterrepresentation to the depiction in Confederate monuments of the citizen-soldier as all White. In an era when Southern White women built monuments commemorating the heroism and valor of the common White Confederate soldier, while totally ignoring the similar heroism and valor of the nearly 200,000 Black troops who served in the Union army, the Black males in the local community's militia unit provided a powerful rejoinder. In the early 1900s, however, White officials abolished these Black militia units. But until this abolition, service in a Black militia unit was one way that Black males could demonstrate civic responsibility, develop a positive Black collective memory of the Civil War, and contribute to a community's contemporary civic culture.[36]

Post-emancipation memoirs written by former slaves, called "slave narratives," also were important to the preservation of Civil War memory from a Southern African American perspective. These slave narratives provide "an essential form of documentation for American slavery." Fifty or more such narratives were written after the Civil War. The purpose was not primarily to "catalog the horrors of slavery." While these narratives touch on the repugnance of slavery—the rape of enslaved women by masters and overseers, the separation of young children from their families, and the whippings—their focus was on racial uplift, ex-slaves' effort to tell their progeny with pride what their forebears had gone through to provide their children freedom.[37]

Southern political leaders were unwilling, or at least reluctant, to give Southern African Americans social permission for even occasional use of prominent public spaces to hold outdoor public observances. Often the public spaces Southern African Americans selected for outdoor programs, such as parks or particular neighborhoods, were places that had been off-limits to Southern African Americans during the era of slavery. Their use by freed Blacks after Emancipation irked Whites, who sometimes expressed their contempt at freed people's brazen arrogance in asserting racial pride and freedom by harassing, humiliating, or beating celebrants, staging violent racial clashes, denying parade or vendor permits, or attempting to ban these African American celebrations altogether.[38] For several years after the Civil War, for example, Blacks routinely attended Memorial Day observances at Andersonville, Georgia, the location of a national cemetery for Union dead at the Confederacy's most notorious prisoner-of-war camp. Railroad companies provided special excursion rates for those attending until White authorities applied pressure on the railroads to end such practices. Eventually, local White government officials effectively banned Blacks from conducting Memorial Day ceremonies at the Andersonville national cemetery.[39]

Confederate monuments were also deployed to impinge on Southern African Americans' celebration of their own collective memory. For example, in 1878, the "Women of Augusta, Georgia" took a leadership role in constructing a Confederate monument in the middle of Broad Street, one of the widest streets in the United States and "Augusta's busiest thoroughfare and the very 'soul' of the city," the street where African Americans celebrated Emancipation Day. This monument, which cost $20,000, consisted of a "marble image of a lone standing Confederate soldier atop a tall shaft" with heroic figures of four Confederate generals below. After erection of the monument, marchers using Broad Street on days of Black celebration were required to "thread their way around the soaring monument" and pass alongside figures of men who had fought to keep them enslaved. This physical impediment to the flow of the parade, and the psychological impact on the atmosphere of Black parades served as "indelible evidence of White residents' determination—and capacity—to shape the historical landscape of the city with substantial, not to mention costly, physical markers."[40]

Southern African Americans exercised much agency in securing their own freedom, acts requiring great heroism. Southern myopia effectively erased from White understanding and recognition the heroic initiatives slaves undertook to claim their own freedom. The brave efforts of African Americans to escape and overturn slavery would have become the subject of much Black commemorative activity if Southern African Americans had been able to raise monuments at the turn of the twentieth century that celebrated their admirable Civil War history.[41] For example, just escaping plantations to find and enter the safety of the Union lines during the Civil War was dangerous, life-threatening, and presented daunting obstacles. It is estimated that between 600,000 and 700,000 slaves fled from their masters to cross into Union military lines and settle in contraband camps. Many fled prior to the promulgation of the Emancipation Proclamation. An escape from slavery required great courage because of the risk of being caught by the ever-increasing numbers of mounted slave patrols, which

Confederate Monument, Augusta, GA. Image ca. 1903. Detroit Publishing Company photograph collection, Library of Congress, Prints and Photographs Division.

would result in being returned to slavery and made an example through severe punishment. Fleeing slaves were required to leave friends and family behind with no certainty of ever seeing them again. And those left behind might suffer the wrath of masters.[42] Such flight invited hunger, exposure to the elements, and death to many slaves who risked all to seize freedom. The Union army enlisted as laborers and soldiers many of the Black men who fled slavery. Their families who also escaped often were stranded in contraband camps where thousands of them died. James McPherson has endorsed the view first advanced by Vincent Harding, that through their "relentless movement," these self-liberated slaves "took their freedom into their own hands." The slaves themselves forced the Lincoln administration to confront the emancipation issue. The Emancipation Proclamation merely "gave ambiguous legal standing to the freedom which Black people had already claimed through their own surging, living proclamations."[43]

Although Black collective memory includes all of the above, and much more, all of it verifiable from the historical record, virtually none of it can be found in the rendition of "Southern heritage" that White segregationists incorporated into their Confederate monuments or in the Southern heritage contemporary Southern heritage advocates cite as a reason to not disturb Confederate monuments. One of the core lessons Savage taught in *Standing Soldiers* and Brundage emphasized in *Southern Past* is that Confederate monuments are instrumental in erasing, or attempting to erase, invaluable Black Civil War and post-Civil War history that is needed for a comprehensive understanding of Southern history and heritage.

In sum, racial-reckoning arguments for the need to change the status quo of Confederate monuments will encounter claims that Confederate monuments are harmless celebrations of apolitical valor, honor, duty, or service, and there is no evidence to the contrary that can be found on the face of most Confederate monuments, or even from the dedication speeches for many. Confederate monument supporters, citing the preservation of Southern heritage, claim that it is unfair to associate any racial animus with these monuments. The work of a generation of scholars who have carefully evaluated Southern history, politics, culture, and race relations has assembled considerable evidence to answer this claim. The challenge is to distill this extensive body of scholarship and present it in ways that those with an open mind can comprehend it and thereby begin to understand how inanimate, seemingly benign, hunks of stone, marble, and bronze possess enormous power to harm.

5
Confederate Monuments and Contemporary Institutional Racism

Racial framing is the most prevalent form of racial discrimination in the United States. Confederate monuments contribute to the perpetuation of racial framing. Racial framing is the persistence of assumptions of White superiority and privilege and an associated array of attitudes that together create negative racist stereotypes, all of this inherited from the past and constantly reiterated and reinforced in the present. These stereotypes shape our ideas about race and bias, our perceptions, and our actions. Numerous academic studies prove the existence of this implicit bias across a wide spectrum of American life. Implicit racism causes great societal harm and greatly impedes our quest for racial justice. Many forces contribute to racial framing. Among them is the presence of hundreds of Confederate monuments located across the South.

EVALUATING THE CONTEMPORARY SOCIAL HARM that Confederate monuments cause is incomplete without examining the persistence of racism in the United States, in particular the institutional and structural bases of racial discrimination and their linkage to Confederate monuments. We know, as demonstrated above, that early-twentieth century White Southerners created "a racial caste system" by constructing "a physical environment to support and reinforce Black inferiority." The elite "Daughters" of the United Daughters of the Confederacy contributed to that physical environment by building Confederate monuments that had the intent and effect of stigmatizing Black skin by creating "cultural associations that mark White as a sign of purity and Black as something else entirely."[1] Architectural historian Dell Upton has explained this caste-creating function of Confederate monuments. Upton writes:[2]

> In the memorial landscape commemorating the Civil War[,] Confederate monuments recast the war as a violent contest among White men over

> high principles having nothing to do with slavery [with the result that] implicitly African Americans . . . had no place in [the] debate [over the direction of the New South]. In the New South, Blacks would be relegated . . . to a permanent nonpolitical underclass, a compliant labor force for an industrialized urban region.

Confederate monuments' racist pedigree fairly raises the question of these monuments' *current* contribution to racism. Specifically, it is important to clarify Confederate monuments' role in White Americans' contemporary racial framing of African Americans, which accounts for most present-day racial discrimination.

Racial framing is the perpetuation of assumptions of White superiority and privilege and an "associated array of anti-Black attitudes, images, and emotions." Racial framing creates racial barriers. When Blacks and Whites interact, Blacks confront Whites' negative stereotypes and images with respect to Blacks' abilities, orientations, and values. Sociology professor Joe R. Feagin explains: "Research indicates that when most Whites interact with Black Americans [in everyday recurring contacts] they tend to think about [African Americans], consciously or unconsciously, in terms of racist stereotypes or other racial framing inherited from the past and constantly reiterated and reinforced in the present."[3] This phenomenon, also referred to as "implicit bias," is explained as "a kind of distorting lens that's a product of both the architecture of our brain and the disparities in our society, [that creates] ideas about race [that] are shaped by the stereotypes to which we are exposed on a daily basis [and] have the power to bias our perception, our attention, our memory, and our actions."[4] Such socially triggered anti-Black attitudes translate into actual discrimination. The cumulative effect is like death from a thousand cuts: "racial oppression is sustained by thousands of everyday acts of mistreatment."[5]

Just Get Over It

For many Whites, "just get over it" is the reflexive response to protests that Confederate monuments continue to project an ideology of White supremacy into contemporary American life. The view of many Whites is that "slavery was abolished more than 150 years ago—just get over it." The logic is that because emancipation occurred more than 150 years ago so also did its accompanying heritage of racism. If racism has ended, then it follows that the continued presence of Confederate monuments in public spaces can cause no ongoing racial harm.

Whites tend to downplay the persistence of racism. Repeated surveys show that the majority of White Americans see equality of opportunity as the social reality. Racial discrimination is thought by many Whites to be a thing of the past in the United States and any Blacks, or their White liberal friends, who see things differently are simply "wrongheaded." Most African Americans see things otherwise. For example, a Gallup poll asked: "Do you feel that racial minorities in this country have equal job opportunities as Whites, or not?" Among Whites, the answer was 55 percent yes and 43 percent no; the rest were undecided. Among Blacks, the answer was 17 percent yes and 81 percent no. White perceptions of America as a "post-racial society" seldom are rational reflections based on available evidence. Whites can be inclined to deny racism out of an emotional need to do so, a need motivated by a desire to resist substantial change in the racial status quo, which is awash in White privilege.[6] The Confederate monument removal/relocation issue cannot be intelligently understood without addressing these perception differences regarding the persistence of racial bigotry in the United States.

Ongoing White Racial Framing

Hundreds of research papers, reports, and investigations have established, beyond question or doubt, the continuing presence of significant racial discrimination in America. Some of it is the expression or acting out of openly racist or White supremacist views, but most is not.[7] Racial discrimination today is best understood as structural racism, racial barriers created by White racial framing—"a diverse assortment of racist practices [and] racialized relationships developed over many generations and imbedded in all major social institutions."[8] Contemporary racism has been described as "color-blind structural racism—a racism without overt racists." Such racism may acknowledge the accomplishments of individual African Americans while denying that "economic and political structures constrict most Americans of color and protect White dominance."[9]

Such racial framing is readily visible once one seeks out its tracings in modern culture. For example, racial framing is evident in national political campaigns where leaders "blatantly encourag[e] White supporters to buy into ugly, long-discredited racist stereotypes about African Americans" by, for example, characterizing accomplished Black candidates as intrinsically less qualified than Whites because of their asserted low I.Q., "shady past," and inherent lack of trustworthiness.[10] Hard evidence of racial bias against African Americans is easily accessible from published compilations of reported racial bias.[11] Listed below is a small sample of the abundant evidence of persistent White racial framing in contemporary America.[12]

Employment

Racial discrimination in job hiring often is uncovered through job screening experiments. This approach entails either sending written responses to help-wanted advertisements by simulated Black and White "applicants" or sending actual Black and White testers who "apply" for jobs to uncover any racially discriminatory responses by potential employers.

In one study, researchers at the University of Chicago and at the Massachusetts Institute of Technology (MIT) sent job applications in response to help-wanted advertisements in Chicago and Boston. The applicants had comparable credentials. Some applications carried names that an employer likely would identify as White, such as Greg Kelly or Emily Walsh and others that would be understood as African Americans such as Jamal Jackson or Lakisha Washington. In this study, White-identified applicants were 50 percent more likely to receive a callback for an interview than applications with names commonly associated with African Americans. As a variation, some African American applications added work experience as an ancillary credential. When this was done, Whites continued to receive a higher callback rate than Blacks. Not until the Black applications showed eight more years of job experience than White applications did Black applications generate a callback rate equal to White applications. In other words, putting a White-sounding name on an application equaled an extra eight years of work experience.[13]

In a Milwaukee study, a matched pair of young high-school graduates with similar job credentials and demeanor applied for 350 jobs as waiters, warehousemen or other low-skilled positions advertised in a Milwaukee newspaper. Thirty-four percent of the White applicants were called back but less than half that number (14 percent) of the equally-qualified Black applicants were called back. The study then added the variable of an added criminal record to the application. Under this variation, the White applicant admitted to having served eighteen months in prison for possession of cocaine with intent to distribute. The other applicant, an African American, showed no criminal record. Even with a serious drug conviction, the White applicant was more likely to be called back (17 percent) than the Black applicant (14 percent). One writer concluded, "the disadvantage carried by a young Black man applying for a job as a dishwasher or a driver is equivalent to ... a White man [carrying] an 18-month prison record on his back."[14]

In another study, 192 White sales professionals evaluated the credentials of two sets of applicants with virtually identical credentials for a sales professional job. Those with Anglo-sounding names received more favorable pre-interview evaluations than those with ethnic-sounding names. When the job sought was an outside-sales job rather than inside-sales job, that differential increased. Conclusion: "irrelevant factors or considerations associated with 'racial clues' can affect the employment prospects of Black applicants."[15]

One researcher reviewed sixteen studies using Black and White testers for employment. In each, White applicants were favored over Black and Latino applicants at a net rate of 20 percent of the time. When this preference for Whites over Blacks occurs over an entire career, the White applicant is more likely to acquire negotiable job skills unavailable to the Black applicants who were never hired in the first place. This discrimination creates a cumulative racial differential resulting in the Black applicants losing out over time on the basis of the legitimate factor of job experience. In other words, a young White person's earlier unjust advantage resulting from being White builds up over time.

In short, "research shows that in the hiring process African American workers are less likely to obtain jobs than Whites with equivalent credentials." Repeatedly in employment testing studies, those hiring (often Whites but not always) "view certain groups of workers as much more acceptable than others, and individual applicants are periodically judged by perceived racial characteristics." Employers state that they just "know" that Whites make better employees even when the Black workers who are rejected are as qualified or even better qualified than the White applicant who is chosen. Black parents also just "know" that their children are likely to confront employment discrimination as a result of White racial framing. Accordingly, in an attempt to protect their children, some savvy Black parents have gone so far as intentionally providing children White-sounding names. For example, African American author Austin Channing Brown has written that her parents told her that they "named her Austin . . . because they thought she'd get more job interviews if employers expected a White male."[16] Multiple studies support her parents' sense of reality with respect to White racial framing.

Housing

Since the late 1930s, surveys have shown that Whites believed that Blacks should be kept from White neighborhoods. As late as 1963, a national survey of White attitudes concluded that half expressed an objection to an African American family becoming their next-door neighbor. More recent data shows that the rate of residential segregation of Blacks and Whites in the North and the South in 2010 was about the same as in 1940.[17] Recent studies show that, fearing high crime rates and poorly maintained property, "more than half of Whites say that they would not move to an area that is more than 30 percent Black."[18]

Screening studies using Black and White testers demonstrate that a significant contributing factor explaining racially segregated housing is the continuing discrimination by owners of rental property, real estate managers, and sales staff. These studies show a persistent pattern of racial barriers both in rental housing and home purchasing. For example, apartment seekers after hurricane Katrina (2005) confronted racial discrimination. In 66 percent of the calls to obtain rental housing (43 out of 65 efforts), White callers received more beneficial treatment than African American callers with respect to "unit availability, . . . security deposit, rental rates, discounts for evacuees, and other rental terms."[19]

A 2013 report by the United States Department of Housing and Urban Development on housing discrimination concluded that in one large paired testing study in twenty-eight metropolitan areas, "Black, Latino, and Asian American homeseekers were more likely than similarly qualified White homeseekers" to be denied an appointment and were shown fewer rental units and houses.[20]

In a Los Angeles-based study, researchers sent out 1,115 email messages inquiring about the availability of rental property. Those emails from persons with distinctive African American names received significantly fewer positive responses than those emails from persons with distinctive White American names. This discrimination occurred before the landlords knew relevant information about the applicant such as education, credit, income, references, etc.

Lending Institutions and Insurance Companies

Studies also have documented discrimination by lending institutions against African Americans seeking mortgages and loans. One significant cause of the 2008–2010 recession was the tendency of White lending officials to channel African Americans into "subprime (high interest) home loans when they would have qualified for regular-interest, less risky loans."[21] Minority loan applicants were more than twice as likely as White home buyers to receive expensive subprime mortgages from lenders–even after loan amounts and household incomes were taken into account. Most of these borrowers had credit scores that would have qualified them for loans with more favorable rates of interest and other conditions.

Insurance companies also have engaged in racial discrimination creating barriers to home ownership. In one study, Black and White testers posed as homeowners seeking to purchase insurance. Researchers uncovered an overall 53 percent rate of racial discrimination with respect to coverage and insurance rate among insurance companies writing homeowners insurance in nine cities. "Being White increased insurance options and saved money."[22]

Voting and Representation

African Americans and other minorities suffer discrimination in voting and representation through a variety of different White "blocking strategies." Among the strategies are gerrymandering of voting districts, converting elective offices into appointive offices, appending new qualifications to existing eligibility prerequisites for elective office, purging voter-registration rolls to require renewed registration, unexpected changes in polling places, devising difficult registration procedures, contriving at-large electoral systems instead of providing election of representatives from districts with African Americans majorities, and so-called ballot security measures such as photo ID requirements that have been shown to disproportionately disqualify otherwise eligible minority voters.

Policing

There was a period in American history (1920–1932) when White police officers accounted for more than half of all Whites who had killed African Americans. And, White police officers often were implicated in lynching Blacks. Police discrimination against African Americans subsequently declined but the evidence shows that it continues.[23]

One example is the documented incidence of racial profiling that law enforcement agencies have engaged in to screen and stop motorists—often as part of a drug interdiction initiative. Such racial profiling has become so much the norm that in the African American community the practice is known as DWB—driving while Black. The American Civil Liberties Union has assembled extensive evidence of racial profiling throughout the United States.[24] Several examples from the vast body of evidence provide insight.

For example, in 2000, the Los Angeles Police Department (LAPD) was placed under a federal consent decree to reform the department by, among other things, eradicating the practice of racial profiling. In August 2008, Yale University Professor Ian Ayres analyzed data collected through the federal consent decree over the LAPD. Professor Ayres noted statistically significant disparities in the rates at which African Americans and Latinos in Los Angeles were stopped, frisked, searched and arrested, and found that these disparities were not justified by local crime rates or by any other legitimate policing rationales.[25]

In 1999, the State of New Jersey entered into a consent decree arising out of racial profiling on the New Jersey Turnpike. The consent decree provided for federal monitors to evaluate data on traffic stops in the state. A study of those highway patrol stops in New Jersey showed that while racial minorities represented only 15 percent of the drivers on the New Jersey Turnpike, Black motorists represented 42 percent of all stops and 73 percent of all arrests, "despite the fact that Blacks and Whites violated the traffic laws at almost exactly the same rate."[26] As the consent decree was about to end, the New Jersey legislature deemed the racial profiling problem sufficiently unresolved that it considered a bill that would permanently establish an independent monitor in the state executive branch to replace the federal monitor.[27]

In 2006, the Arizona Department of Public Safety (DPS) settled a class action lawsuit brought by the ACLU, requiring DPS, among other things, to collect and maintain traffic stop data. An analysis of the first year of that data revealed that African American and Latino drivers were 2.5 times more likely than White drivers to be searched after being stopped by the highway patrol, and Native American drivers were 3.25 times more likely to be searched, even though both groups were *less* likely to be found with contraband.[28]

The racial profiling by the Maryland State Police (MSP) along the Interstate 95 (I-95) corridor resulted in a landmark settlement in 2008. In that case, African Americans comprised 17 percent of the drivers on a portion of I-95 outside of Baltimore but constituted 70 percent of those stopped and searched. And while all racial minorities (Black, Latino and Asian) represented only 21 percent of the drivers, this group comprised 80 percent of those stopped and searched.[29] Litigation was initiated in 1998. One striking revelation in the 1998 litigation was evidence demonstrating a continuing pattern and practice of discrimination by troopers working for the MSP that violated an agreement reached in an earlier lawsuit in 1995. In addition to substantial monetary damages to the individual plaintiffs, the settlement in the 1998 suit against the MSP provided that the MSP retain an independent consultant to assess its progress toward eliminating the practice of racial profiling. The consent decree arising out of the 1998 litigation also required, among other things, ongoing data collection, the installation of video cameras on many patrol cars, a review of the training protocols, and enhanced supervision of troopers.[30]

Perhaps the most stunning finding from the New Jersey and Maryland litigation was that although state police stopped and searched minorities far more often than Whites, in each case these stops and searches did not find drugs on the minority drivers any more frequently than when searching Whites. *In fact, just the contrary:* in both the New Jersey and Maryland cases, a higher percentage of Whites than Blacks carried drugs or contraband in their cars, twice as many Whites than African Americans and five times as many Whites than Latinos in the New Jersey study.[31] A federal probe of the Ferguson, Missouri police department in 2015 unearthed the same pattern: a disproportionate number of African Americans stopped; twice as many searched; African Americans less likely than Whites to be found in possession of contraband; and no explanation other than "unlawful bias against and stereotypes about African Americans."[32] In short, Blacks were less guilty but more suspicious to the police officers making the discretionary decisions on whom to pull over.

Professor Michelle Alexander cites a New Jersey official who labeled this disjunction between suspicion and reality as the "circular illogic of racial profiling." As Alexander explains the disjunction: "Law enforcement officials . . . often point to the racial composition of our prisons and jails as a justification for targeting racial minorities, but the empirical evidence actually suggested the opposite conclusion was warranted. The disproportionate imprisonment of people of color was, in part, a product of racial profiling—not a justification for it."[33]

The ACLU report, "The Persistence of Racial and Ethnic Profiling in the United States," provides considerable additional evidence of racial profiling in twenty-two states throughout the United States.[34] Some of the more egregious additional examples of racial profiling are: 148 hours of video footage covering 1000 traffic stops in Volusia County, Florida where African Americans and Latino represented 5 percent of the drivers but 80 percent of the traffic stops and searches; targeting of Latino drivers in Illinois who comprised 8 percent of the Illinois population, accounted for only 3 percent of automobile trips, but represented 30 percent of highway stops by state police who stopped drivers on the pretext of slight traffic violations such as failure to signal a lane change, stops that resulted in Latinos being found to be *less likely* than Whites to have illegal contraband; and racial profiling in Oakland, California, in 2001 that resulted in African Americans being approximately twice as likely to be stopped and three times as likely to be searched than Whites.[35]

Racial Framing, Mass Incarceration of Black Youth, and the War on Drugs

The mass incarceration of African American males provides an additional window into how White racial framing operates. To understand the linkage between mass incarceration of African Americans males and White racial framing, the place to begin is the incarceration data for drug offenses.[36]

Since the early 1970s when the war on drugs was first announced, there has been a huge increase in the incarceration rate in the United States. In

1972, somewhat fewer than 350,000 persons were held in prisons and jails in the United States. By 2012, that total exceeded two million. That is more than a five-fold increase in 40 years. By the end of 2007, more than 7 million Americans—or one in every 31 adults—were behind bars, on probation, or on parole." The racial disparity of the American prison population is stark. "One in three young African American men will serve time in prison if the current trends continue, and in some cities more than half of all young adult Black men are currently under correctional control—in prison or jail, on probation, or parole."[37]

Drug offense convictions represent the single most significant cause of the rise in United States incarceration rates. Drug convictions accounted for two-thirds of the rise in the federal inmate population and more than half of the rise in state prisoners between 1985 and 2000. In 1980, an estimated 41,100 persons were behind bars for a drug offense. Thirty years later, 2010, the total number of persons incarcerated for drug offenses had reached an estimated half-million people, an 1,100 percent increase. Altogether, since the drug war began, more than 31 million people have been arrested for drug offenses. In many states, such as Colorado and Maryland, drug offenders represent the largest category of people incarcerated.[38] Professor Michelle Alexander writes that "there are more people in prisons and jails today just for drug offenses than were incarcerated for *all* reasons in 1980. Nothing has contributed more to the systematic mass incarceration of people of color in the United States than the War on Drugs."[39]

Throughout America, the rate of Black incarceration for drug offenses "dwarfs the rate for Whites." In seven states in 2000, African Americans represented 80 to 90 percent of all drug offenders incarcerated. In at least 15 states, African Americans are incarcerated for drug offenses at a rate from "twenty to fifty times greater than that of White men." Black incarcerations for drug offenses have skyrocketed since the 1980s. White drug offense incarcerations also have risen but at a far lower rate. The White rate of drug incarcerations is small compared to the rates for African Americans and Latinos: three-fourths of those imprisoned for drug offenses have been Black or Latino.[40]

The perception among most Whites is that illegal drug-users and drug-sellers are concentrated among poor, inner-city African Americans and this fact explains the glaring racial disparity in incarceration rates for drug offenses. That explanation is empirically unfounded and "simply wrong." Neither the rate nor the patterns of drug crime by African Americans account for the grossly disparate rate of Blacks' incarceration for drug crimes compared to such incarceration of Whites. Studies demonstrate that African Americans, Latinos, and Whites *use and sell* illegal drugs at remarkably similar rates and, if anything, the rate of White illegal drug use and distribution is higher. For example, one federal government study found that the use of cocaine among White students was seven times greater than the rate among Black students; crack cocaine use among White students was eight times greater than the rate among Black students; and White students' use of heroin was seven times the rate for Black students. The rates of use of marijuana by Black and White youth is about the same, with some studies showing greater use among Whites. Yet, throughout the United States, in small counties and large, urban and rural, counties with large Black populations and small, wealthy and poor, "a Black person is 3.73 times more likely to be arrested for marijuana possession than a White person." In Baltimore, for example, between 2015 and 2017 police enforced marijuana laws mostly against African Americans, who represented roughly two-thirds of the population but received more than 90 percent of marijuana citations.[41] In some counties where discrimination is most rampant, African Americans were "10, 15, even 30 times more likely to be arrested [for marijuana possession] than White residents of the same county."[42]

Nor are drug dealers mostly African American. If anything, "the surveys frequently suggest that Whites, particularly White youth, are more likely to engage in illegal drug dealing than people of color." A study in 2000 found that Whites aged 12–17 were at least 30 percent more likely to have sold illegal drugs compared to African Americans of the same age range. In short, drug use and distribution among Blacks simply is not a greater societal problem than drug use and distribution among Whites. Government data simply paint a different picture than the stereotype of illegal drug use and distribution concentrated among poor, Black youth. Blacks and Whites violate the drug laws at roughly the same rates and in fact White youth are more likely than Black or brown youth to be guilty of drug use and distribution.[43] Yet Blacks are far more likely to be targeted by police and incarcerated for drug offenses.

In short, the police disproportionately target Black drug users and dealers even though "a majority of drug dealers are White and there is much drug-selling on predominantly White college campuses and in White suburban areas."[44]

Confederate Monuments, White Racial Framing, and Implicit Bias

The false stereotyping of African Americans in contemporary American society has its roots in slavery, Jim Crow segregation, and turn of the twentieth century White elite efforts to perpetuate a negative racial frame of African Americans, especially the libel of the inherent criminal inclinations of African American males. As the previous chapters have demonstrated, in the early twentieth century, and throughout the four decades of Jim Crow racial segregation, the combination of Confederate monuments, disfranchisement, spectacle lynching, biased school textbooks, and segregationist legislation operated in concert to contrive a negative racial framing of African Americans, creating a racial narrative of Black "otherness." Indeed, well into the second half of the twentieth century, Confederate monuments continued their role as progenitors of a societal frame of White supremacy as Southern Whites raised additional Confederate monuments as part of the South's "massive resistance" to racial change. For over a century, Confederate monuments have been the constant gardeners cultivating the preservation of an ideology supportive of Jim Crow segregation and the cult of White Anglo-Saxonism.

This legacy of Jim Crow-era negative stereotyping of African Americans, of which Confederate monuments have played an integral part, continues today and contributes to the contemporary racial framing and implicit bias demonstrated earlier in this chapter. The racial disparity in the incarceration of Black youth for drug offenses is an excellent example of the contemporary harm caused by the legacy of Black stereotyping we have inherited from the era of Jim Crow segregation and the associated mania to erect monuments to the Confederate past.

Police have great discretion in deciding where to concentrate drug surveillance and which neighborhoods to sweep for drugs. Of necessity, police need to choose where and how to enforce the nation's drug laws. In any given year, 1 in 10 Americans violate the drug laws, but resource limitations constrain law enforcement authorities to be able to arrest, convict and incarcerate only a small fraction of all offenders. For example, in 2002 there were an estimated 19.5 million persons unlawfully using drugs, 1.5 million drug arrests for various drug offenses, and 175,000 drug-related incarcerations. The war on drugs swept up only a small percentage of all drug violators. With illegal drug use normally constituting a victimless crime and with such wide-ranging acceptance of drug use across a broad spectrum of the American population, police were required to depend on their own proactive approach in order to enforce the drug laws. A slight percentage of offenders can be identified and arrested, so law enforcement officials need to make choices with respect to which groups to target.

Law enforcement officers' racial framing creates the stereotyped, but false, belief that drug use and drug dealing are behaviors that are concentrated among poor Blacks and Latinos living in communities of color. As a result of that erroneous belief, it makes sense that law enforcement would focus enforcement efforts on poor, inner-city African American neighborhoods. For it is in these neighborhoods where police believe that their efforts will have the greatest impact, where they can make more arrests per unit of effort, and, they believe correctly, where there will be the least White backlash over a police drug-sweep of a neighborhood. In short, the policing approach has been to catch Black drug criminals operating in inner-city Black neighborhoods because that is where almost all Whites imagine that the drug problem primarily resides. Concomitantly police under-enforce the drug laws among White drug users and dealers notwithstanding the above-cited empirical evidence demonstrating that most drug dealers and users are White and their illegal activity mostly occurs in White suburbs and on predominantly White college campuses. Not surprisingly, more Blacks and Latinos than Whites are arrested, convicted, and incarcerated for drug offenses.[45]

Racial framing distracts law enforcement officers and deprives them of the benefits that could be gained from following the facts of illicit drug use, facts demonstrating that there are many drug markets in White neighborhoods where police could efficiently sweep for drug offenses. Far fewer Whites than generally is imagined obtain their drugs by traveling to a ghetto drug market for their purchases. In fact, the data show that for the most part, "Whites tend to sell to Whites: Blacks to Blacks." University students purchase drugs from others at the university. It makes no sense for rural Whites to travel some distance to an inner-city ghetto neighborhood to purchase drugs when they can, and do, purchase what they need from a local White distributer who lives nearby. Similarly, White high school students purchase marijuana and other drugs from White classmates and sometimes from other White associates and relatives. "The notion that most illegal drug use and sales happen in the ghetto is pure fiction. Drug trafficking . . . occurs everywhere else in America as well." Yet, in state prisons, Black males are incarcerated on drug charges at a rate thirteen times greater than Whites. Racial bias accounts for the fact that in 2006, 1 in every 14 Black men was incarcerated compared to 1 in 106 White men.[46]

Biases and stereotypes of the Black male as inherently criminally-inclined are ingrained in many Whites. These stereotypes arise directly from the libeling of Black males during the period of Jim Crow and Confederate monument mania.[47] These false perceptions are part of a strongly-held belief systems formed early in life.[48] Cognitive bias research demonstrates the conscious and unconscious racial bias that leads to discriminatory actions.[49] For example, in 1995 a survey was conducted that asked the participants to close their eyes and imagine a drug user and describe that person. "Ninety-five percent of the respondents pictured a Black drug user, while only 5 percent imagined other racial groups." In 1995, African Americans constituted but 15 percent of drug users; then, as now, Whites constituted the overwhelming majority of drug users. Yet, almost none of the respondents could imagine a drug user as anyone other than an African American. In that same study, the vast majority also inaccurately imagined drug *dealers* as typically Black. One assumes that had police officers and prosecutors taken the same test the outcomes would have been similar. As Jennifer Eberhardt has written, "It is implausible to believe that [police] officers . . . can be immersed in an environment that repetitively exposes them to the categorical pairing of Blacks and crime and not have that affect how they think, feel, or behave."[50]

In another study participants read a standard news account of a crime. The account contained no images. Nor did it indicate the race of the perpetrator. Readers were so racialized that 60 percent falsely remembered that the story contained an image and of that group 70 percent recalled that the perpetrator in the image was Black.

We are all exposed to external inputs that arise from political rhetoric, imaging of various sorts, and otherwise. Most learn from inputs during early childhood to associate race with certain impressions and depictions that influence thinking and attitudes. Among many Whites, the dominant racist framing generates the mental image of White superiority—overestimation of White moral virtue, intellectual capacity, and ambition—paired with distorted negative images of African Americans and other minorities. These negative racial stereotypes assail us throughout our adult lives through newspapers and magazines, television, internet, movies, radio talk shows, etc. The negative racial frame to which we are subjected everyday can advance false perceptions of African Americans as lazy, dangerous, criminally inclined, immoral, or intellectually inferior. Even the Uncle Ben and Aunt Jemima product packaging contribute to negative racial imaging—though in recent years these racist images on product packaging have been altered to be less stereotyping.[51] The influences we obtain from White racial framing collectively condition and transmit to each new generation overly positive images of valorous Whites and overly negative racial images and perceptions of African Americans and other Americans of color. These mental images and impressions of reality operate at a level of conscious, rational deliberations but also influence perceptions and behaviors not animated by conscious awareness or intent.[52]

An excellent illustration of the negative, subconscious, racial stereotyping that arises from the dominant White racial frame in contemporary America can be found in a study where respondents were shown a video game of Black and White persons holding various objects, some dangerous such as a gun and some innocuous such as a soda can or cell phone.

The pictures were rapidly flashed across the screen and the respondents were asked to decide quickly whether or not to shoot the target because it was armed. Consistently the respondents mistakenly shot images of Blacks concluding that they were armed when they were not, and did not shoot Whites although they were armed. The researchers' conclusion was that the results demonstrated evidence of implicit bias—the presence of a reflective, unconscious racial bias painting Blacks as dangerous and Whites as not dangerous. Even Black respondents exhibited some of the same "shooter bias" against Blacks that Whites had exhibited.[53] Other studies measuring hostility and punitiveness consistently demonstrate that respondents "become increasingly harsh when an alleged criminal is darker and more 'stereotypically Black' [and tend to be] more lenient when the accused is lighter and appears more stereotypically White."[54]

Social science literature has demonstrated that "even among persons who hold a sincere belief in race blindness" their thinking is influenced by "images and depictions of members of racial groups learned beginning in childhood." Implicit association tests have uncovered built-in racial biases and negative racial stereotypes arising from an often-subconscious White racial frame. For example, when presented with a Black face, most Whites promptly will link the Black face with negative words and traits and will experience greater difficulty associating photos of Black faces with pleasant words and positive traits than they do for White faces. "Analyses of thousands of such facial-response tests at psychology websites have shown that the overwhelming majority of Whites signal an anti-Black, pro-White bias in such face reaction tests." Brain scans confirm the presence of racial bias. Research studies have shown that when Whites view Black faces, even for milliseconds, "key areas of their brains that respond to perceived threats have tended to light up automatically [indicating] racialized emotions." Implicit association tests, even among children, show implicit racial attitudes about Black Americans. In one experiment, White children were shown White and Black faces and asked to associate the images with good and bad words. The children showed a pro-White and anti-Black bias when matching the color of faces to good and bad words.[55]

Confederate monuments contribute to the tenacity of contemporary implicit racial bias because such monuments contribute to the White racial framing that accounts for most racial discrimination today. Obviously, thousands of inputs from early childhood lead Whites to create a model of themselves that overvalues their own virtue, merit, high moral standards, and superior intelligence and concurrently creates an "'anti-model' of Black deficiency, pathology, and threat. Both are part of the dominant White racial frame in [American] society."[56]

Confederate monuments are one of many inputs that contribute to society's White racial frame. First, Confederate monuments are a paradigmatic example of "sincere fictions about the White self." Such fictions about White virtue comprise one part of White racial framing. The virtuous valor and sacrifice of many common Confederate soldiers are matters of historical fact. These are not fictions! Yet Confederate monuments *otherwise* perpetuate an overstated and indeed fictional account of White virtue. Confederate monuments distort history in an effort to glorify an odious cause that the Whites depicted in Confederate monuments orchestrated. The preceding chapters have demonstrated that slaves were not happy and loyal to benign masters as Confederate monuments would have us believe. Slaves were whipped, raped, bound, and robbed of the bounty of their labor. Moreover, secession was not constitutional, notwithstanding contrary explicit and implicit assertions in hundreds of Confederate monuments. Rebel leaders were separatists at best and at worst were traitors against the United States, men who met the United States Constitution's definition of treason: those who "lev[ied] war" against the United States and/or "adher[ed] to their enemies, giving them aid or comfort."[57] Nothing in nearly one-hundred years of antebellum constitutional law provided any rational basis for leaders of the rebellion to conclude that the United States Constitution had been adopted with the intent to reserve for every state the option to secede from the Union at its whim. Every Supreme Court decision, before the war and after, rejected the Confederacy's claim that built into our constitutional form of government was a reserved right for any state to undermine the Constitution's quest to create an indivisible Union of States in order to form a "more perfect Union" than had been created by the abandoned Article of Confederation. And finally, no matter how vociferously a Confederate monument may symbolically balk at the truth, the historical record overwhelmingly demonstrates that the Civil War *was* fought to preserve the deplorable institution of slavery. In short, Confederate monuments were raised to symbolically transmit the historical perversions that underlay the Lost Cause myth. There is no White "virtue" in such attempted historical deception; nor is there virtue in raising monuments to transmit the warping of truth. Whole forests have been felled providing the paper consumed by scores of historians demonstrating that the goal of the Confederate cause was the perpetuation of the horrors of slavery and those who seceded attempted to unconstitutionally deprive the people of the United States of the "more perfect union" that our constitutional form of government endeavors to provide. And slavery was not a benign institution populated by happy and loyal slaves who loved their caring masters and mistresses. It is all a lie! Raising Confederate monuments at the turn of the twentieth century, and retaining them on public property today, was, and is, an attempt to add White virtue where none exists. Such deceitful representation of White virtue through Confederate monuments is one face of racist White framing.

The other face of White racist framing is perpetuation of a negative framing of African Americans. The above chapters have demonstrated that Confederate monuments were instrumental in the desperate efforts of the Southern aristocracy to maintain a system of Jim Crow segregation, which prevailed in the South for four decades, and ultimately to preserve White elites' own political hegemony. By transmitting the tenets of the Lost Cause myth, Confederate monuments helped create the negative Black anti-model of the lazy, criminal, immoral, intellectually inferior, and cheating African American. Monuments symbolically helped create this anti-model by perpetuating the image of Black "otherness" in the minds of Whites, as has been documented throughout this book. Confederate monuments perpetuated the image of the African American as the outcast, one who was in, but not part of, Southern society. Southern society was for Whites, not for the Black sub-caste. As one historian has summarized: Confederate monuments advanced values that "all rested on the White realm. There was no room for African Americans in this universe. The Civil War was a White affair, and . . . Blacks were neither citizens nor members of Southern society in the view of most ex-Confederates."[58] The Black "otherness" communicated by the Confederate monument was different only in degree from the images of Black otherness transmitted by disfranchisement, Jim Crow racial segregation, spectacle lynching, and contrived textbooks used in Southern schools, often until the 1970s. Negative stereotyping of the Southern African American is the subliminal message of every Confederate monument that glorifies the cause of the White Southerner who fought to maintain the racial subordination of slavery and later the system of Jim Crow.

Many studies, some of which are detailed in this chapter, demonstrate that Whites today are socialized at an early age to accept the racist framing of White superiority and the inferiority of non-Whites. This racial hierarchical learning comes from informal lessons at home, church, synagogue, etc., but also from images that surround children everyday as they mature. It is beyond dispute that one of the images that acculturates children in the South is the ubiquitous White standing soldier Confederate monument found in hundreds of Southern communities. Confederate monuments regularly reinforce White framing by "speak[ing] glowingly of the 'lily White,' which often is defined and affirmed through the defined inferiority of the non-White Other.'"[59] The young learn White racist framing through intergenerational transmissions, which in the South is facilitated by a history of four decades of Jim Crow. Jim Crow as a system of *de jure* segregation has finally been buried. But the Confederate monuments that transmitted the historical perversions of the Cult of the Lost Cause remain with us in literally hundreds of cities, towns, and hamlets in the South that continue to host Confederate monuments. It is fair to conclude that Confederate monuments that continue to lionize a cause to keep in perpetual slavery nearly four million human beings are complicit in contributing to attitudes that dehumanize the prodigy of those viewed as proper subjects of such enslavement. Moreover, Confederate monuments' complicity in efforts to dehumanize the ancestors of slaves is exacerbated by the recurring use of Confederate monuments by White extremists today who deploy Confederate monuments to "fire up their base [and] inflame their fellow extremists."[60] Henry Louis Gates has eloquently explained that "it was in this period [of Jim Crow] that White supremacist ideology, especially as it was transmuted into powerful new forms of media, poisoned the American imagination in ways that have long outlasted the circumstances of its origin. You might say that [Jim Crow] anti-Black racism . . . long became part of our country's cultural DNA."[61] Clarifying the role that Confederate monuments have played, and still play, in perpetuating White supremacy and Black inferiority is not intended to end the conversation regarding what should be done with Confederate monuments. Many factors need to be considered as is discussed in Part II of this book. The *racial-reckoning approach* to deciding if something needs to be done with a Confederate monument simply insists that the role of the Confederate monument as a wellspring of the ideology of White supremacy be acknowledged and that the resulting contemporary societal harm this causes be recognized. Racial-reckoning proponents argue that the role of Confederate monuments in perpetuating implicit racism deserves to be a central part of the discussion when the question of what to do with Confederate monuments is evaluated.

PHASE II The Disposition

Destroy, Contexualize, or Relocate the Confederate Monument?

6
The Case Against Monument Destruction

Iconoclasm, the shattering of images, is an ancient tradition. In modern times, there are many examples of destroying monuments as a way to purge a society of an image's negative ideological projections. Following World War II, for example, the Allied Control Authority, in May of 1946, ordered, with few exceptions, that all memorials commemorating the Nazi party were to be completely destroyed. The July 1776 toppling of the equestrian statue of King George III, at Bowling Green, New York is well known, and widely applauded still. A cultural universal is that nothing signals emergence into a new and brilliant future quite as defiantly and eloquently as smashing into pieces the likeness of one who has caused another great emotional pain. Destruction of the symbol helps one live with the pain. However, destruction of Confederate monuments is an inappropriate response to the harm Confederate monuments have caused and continue to cause. First, some Confederate monuments, certainly not all, are of great artistic value and for that reason alone should be preserved. Second, Confederate monuments should be preserved for what they have to teach: providing opportunities for us to confront unpleasant things about the past and deal with them; to reflect that we once had a society that raised monuments to those who sought to keep others enslaved or to intimidate Black citizens; and to revisit these monuments' invaluable testimony to racist traditions that, we hope, have been banished but ought not be forgotten.

APPLYING PRINCIPLED CRITERIA to decide whether it is appropriate to do *something* with respect to a Confederate monument is difficult enough. But deciding *what should be done* requires additional rigorous inquiry. The three most likely choices are destruction, contextualization of the monument, for example, by adding clarifying explanatory signage, or removal/relocation of the monument.

There is a certain logic to the choice to destroy a Confederate monument once it has been decided that a Confederate monument's ideological projection contributes to the societal harm of contributing to systemic racism. As detailed above, just by celebrating the Confederacy, Confederate monuments transmit an implicitly racist message and become a symbol of resistance to African Americans' civil rights and aspirations for racial justice. Accordingly, as historian Cynthia Mills has explained, Confederate monuments "place a stigma on the South, . . . they offend or, at the least, represent an indifference to the oppression of Blacks in antebellum years."[1] But Confederate monuments harm in additional ways: Confederate monuments' false history that describes a superior White race communicates the message that African Americans are members of an inferior and untouchable caste who are unworthy to participate in the larger community. Like segregation itself, Confederate monuments become the means for "conveying an idea [that] stamps a badge of inferiority upon Blacks, and this badge transmits an [injurious] message to others in the community, as well as to Blacks wearing the badge.[2] Destruction adherents advance the logic that only eradication of the symbol can eliminate these harms that Confederate monuments cause. Removing the monument to a different location does not purge the monument of its toxic propensities. Relocation merely relocates the venue of the damage.[3]

Case in point: The Confederate statue that was removed from the Rockville, Maryland, county courthouse lawn, discussed in the preface, was relocated to privately-owned land at White's Ferry, in a relatively remote part of Montgomery County, Maryland. At its new location, the statue's inscription continues to implore onlookers to adopt a favorable attitude toward the Confederacy. That attitude views ex-Confederates as "heroes" and enjoins the observer "Not [To] Forget to Love The Thin Gray Line" and all it stood for. White's Ferry is a car ferry. Once loaded with cars, the ferry follows a wire cable that crosses the Potomac River, one end anchored in Maryland and the other in Virginia. The ferry can hold 24 cars, takes two minutes to load and five minutes to cross the river. Thus it carries thousands of cars a year and many thousands of individuals, all of whom now have an occasion to view the Rockville Confederate statue.[4] Ironically, many more persons may now annually view the Rockville Confederate statue than ever did when it was located in a quiet grove of trees on the lawn of the Montgomery County, Maryland, courthouse. And that is the core of the argument of those who urge destruction: the only way to end the harm the monument causes through is overt and symbolic racist messaging is to eliminate the source by destroying the monument.

Destruction advocates certainly have history on their side. Iconoclasm (breaking images) is as old as time. There is much historical precedent for destroying monuments deemed offensive and harmful to society. For example, recognizing monuments' symbolic authority, power, and influence, the United States military routinely destroys the monuments and memorials of another country it invades or occupies in order to eliminate them from the "social and political landscape."[5] This explains the denazification Directive 30, jointly issued by the Allied Control Authority in May of 1946, entitled "Legislation Dealing with the Liquidation of German Military and Nazi Memorials and Museums." Directive 30 ordered that except for "an object of exceptional artistic value," all memorials commemorating the Nazi party were to be "completely destroyed and liquidated" within eighteen months.[6] By further example, much of the world viewed, with wide-ranging approval, the iconic picture of the destruction of the forty-foot statue of Saddam Hussain in Firdos Square in Baghdad on April 9, 2003 shortly after the United States invasion of Iraq.[7] One of the earliest, and most famous examples of monument destruction in American history occurred just 5 days after the signing of the Declaration of Independence. On July 9, 1776, immediately following George Washington's reading the Declaration of Independence to his assembled troops of the Continental Army, "a rambunctious crowd . . . worked its way South on Broadway" and toppled the equestrian statue of King George III, at Bowling Green, New York. The lead in the statue was later melted down to make musket balls for use by troops of the American Continental Army in the Revolutionary War against Greater Britain.[8] Perhaps the most celebrated recording we have of monument destruction is the photograph of Hungarians in Budapest standing over the toppled likeness of Joseph Stalin on October 23, 1956.[9] As historian Harold Holzer has written, iconoclasm is not new. "The desire to destroy effigies . . . has been part of the human experience ever since Moses destroyed the golden calf."[10] For example, Medieval Christians smashed sculptures of Ancient Rome. Spanish conquerors destroyed temples of the Aztecs and the Incas. Germans destroyed images of a reviled Adolph Hitler and Libyan protesters in Tripoli dismantled the head of a statue of Muammar el-Qaddafi and toppled an "iconic statue of [Qaddafi's] golden fist crushing a fighter plane." In 2015, in Cape Town, South Africa, protesters dismantled a statue of the imperialist businessman Cecil John Rhodes. After the demise of the Soviet Union, many statues of Vladimir Lenin were destroyed.[11]

Destruction can represent a symbolic act of retribution, like symbolic capital punishment of certain offenders. Destruction, moreover, can operate as a cathartic act that rids the mind of negative memories—"out of sight out of mind." The 1949 Richard Rodgers and Oscar Hammerstein II melody "I'm gonna wash that man right outa my hair . . . and send him on his way" became an iconic song among the post–World War II generation because it accurately captured the cultural universal that nothing signals emergence into a new and brilliant future as defiantly and eloquently as smashing into pieces the likeness of one who has caused another great emotional pain. Destruction of the symbol helps one live with the pain.[12] In addition, it has been argued that destruction of an image represents, in the most dramatic way, "vengeful truth telling, . . . a way of unmasking the secrets that lie at the core of power [and] unveiling and destabilizing fundamental narratives of . . . power."[13] That is one side of the argument.

There is a strongly held contrary view holding that destruction of monuments is not an acceptable or efficacious option for expressing discontent with a disgraced monument. First of all, some monuments, including some Confederate monuments, deserve to be judged not just by their ideological projections but also as legitimate works of art that deserve to be preserved as such.[14] It is a mistake to flatten-out all Confederate monuments and treat them all the same in terms of their artistic value. The range of artistic expressions among Confederate monuments varies widely. As one observer has noted, many "are not Bernini sculptures." For example, the off-the-rack, mass produced, store-bought standing soldier monuments found in many Southern towns lack "aesthetic significance and [are] underwhelming." Other Confederate monuments are grandiose.[15]

The artistic argument for protecting Confederate monuments from being smashed into rubble has much to recommend it, but it has two major deficiencies. First, few Confederate monuments are so grandiose and so clearly "ambitiously aesthetic" that there is easy consensus with respect to which monuments deserve preservation as genuine works of art. Much dispute can be expected especially since beauty is, after all, in the eye of the beholder.

Second, the artistic argument is under-inclusive. For even the run-of-the-mill, off-the-shelf, standing soldier monuments may have much to teach and can do so only if preserved. This argument is grounded in the view that a Confederate monument can be instrumental by providing opportunities for us to learn and reflect. These monuments can be "used as tools for education, deliberation, and even protest" as historian James Broomall has argued.[16] Monuments teach in different ways. Monuments may compel us to look back and "confront unpleasant things about the past and deal with them." In addition, a Confederate monument that was raised to glorify the vile ideologies of the Confederacy or was erected with the self-conscious motive of advancing the ideology or the Lost Cause myth and its White supremacy foundation, or was built to intimidate Black citizens may be worth preserving because it provides invaluable testimony to traditions that, we hope, have been banished but ought not be forgotten. Ironically, destruction of a Confederate monument may harm the goal of racial justice by obscuring the legacy of slavery rather than addressing it. Monument destruction risks hiding the past, "downplaying the lasting effects of slavery, and substituting a false and misleading narrative" that "might allow us to feel complacent or, even, self-congratulatory."[17] Confederate monuments can usefully serve as cultural markers reminding us of where we have been and where must never return.[18] If it is possible to learn from the past, then the Confederate monument can serve an instructional function.

In addition, if the goal of doing something with a community's Confederate monument is to eliminate the hate in a Confederate monument's hate speech, destruction of the monument will not well serve that objective. If hate could be eliminated by banning hate speech, we might choose to ban such speech, and maybe also endorse burning books that are hateful. But we don't do either. Banning the expression of ideas does not extirpate the idea and censorship of ideas is antithetical to our culture.[19] Our constitutional culture, for example, dictates freedom of conscience even when that freedom entails the expression of ideas we find abhorrent.[20] We protect speech we loathe in part because we recognize that both verbal and non-verbal expression "serves a dual communicative function: it conveys not only ideas capable of relatively precise, detached explication, but otherwise inexpressible emotions as well. In fact, [expression is] often chosen as much for [its] emotive as [its] cognitive force." Our constitutional traditions are solicitous of both "the cognitive content of individual speech [and] the emotive function which, practically speaking, may often be the more important element of the overall message sought to be communicated"[21] To be clear: of course government has the *constitutional right* to destroy a Confederate monument located on its public space if it wants to. Local governments own most of these monuments. A local government has the reserved right to decide to maintain or remove its imprimatur from any monument located on its public space. When a decision is made to remove its imprimatur from a Confederate monument, there is no constitutional bar to government deciding to destroy a monument it owns. Such destruction does not thereby infringe on the free speech rights of its citizens. Through destruction, government is regulating its own speech.

The question is *should* government destroy a Confederate monument—is that a wise decision? In reaching that answer, government needs to recognize that for some a Confederate monument represents expressions possessing enormous emotive power associated with Southern heritage. White Southerners have unique dialect, customs, culture, etiquette, and ethics. Moreover, there are certain values unrelated to racial bigotry that are highly associated with the South and comprise the South's heritage, such as fierce independence, resistance to the authority of a strong central government, suspicion of labor unions, highly honed sense of patriotism, fundamentalist or evangelical Christianity, a mystical faith in agrarianism, and an unabashed appreciation of home and family.²² It is irrational to assume, *a priori*, that anyone who advances an argument supportive of Confederate monuments based on respect for Southern heritage necessarily does so as a pretext for racism.²³ Destruction opponents argue that destroying Confederate monuments would be interpreted as vandalism that would further polarize the community. This is a plausible argument.

Nearly three decades ago, a noted Yale historian, the late Robin Winks, eloquently advanced a compelling case for not destroying Confederate monuments, a view that has withstood the test of time and is widely accepted. Winks clarified the difference between defensible and indefensible alterations of historical monuments based on "two different concepts of history." History consists of those things that actually occurred and should not be forgotten. "It is wrong to purge the record" by removing any item from the historical record. Winks cited the justly disparaged "Great Soviet Encyclopedia" as a paradigmatic example of unjustifiable removals from the historical record. Additions and deletions from that encyclopedia reflected as "history" the shifting ideological preferences of the ruling Party leaders then in charge of the Soviet Union at any given time.²⁴

But Wicks identified a second conception of history. It is *that portion* of the historic record that those with sufficient cultural power and authority choose to *commemorate and memorialize*. Memorialization, especially through the erecting of monuments glorifying certain individuals, groups, or events, represents an ideological projection, an effort by cultural elites to transmit a favorable view of certain preferred values. "A change in the way a community memorializes [glorifies] its past offers a way to recognize important alterations in the community's values."²⁵ Wicks argued that each conception of history deserves to be respected. A community ought not erase the objective facts from the historical record, for example, the fact that there was a Confederacy whose goal was to perpetuate chattel slavery, that after the Civil War the defeated South attempted to maintain White supremacy by stereotyping African Americans as inferior, and used Confederate monuments as a vehicle to accomplish these ends. These are facts that should be preserved. But, over time a community will rightly decide which portions of the historical record it wishes to commemorate and what groups and events it wishes to honor. Each generation is privileged to make *those* decisions for itself, "subject always to the obligation not to efface the history that informs the world in which we live."²⁶

When destruction is eliminated as an option, a community is left with the choices of contextualizing its Confederate monument or removing/relocating it.

7
The Trouble with Contextualization

Of the several options available to those attempting to decide what to do with a community's Confederate monument, contextualization, initially, seems appealing. It is a compromise in the sense that contextualization leaves the Confederate monument in place but augments it, through signage or interpretive plaques for example, providing opportunities to add clarity and context to the past and argue a viewpoint challenging the ideological projection of the Confederate monument. The political and cultural realities in the contemporary South disqualify contextualization as a viable option. Two related forces uniformly work to undermine the ability of contextualization to convey an efficacious countermessage to a Confederate monument. The first reality is the democratization of modern monument building and the impact of Southern urban politics. The elites who raised Confederate monuments were not required to negotiate the monuments' content with the larger community. Today, such negotiation and accommodation are required. The White Southern business community demands meaningful input and its goal is to project a post-racial Southern society, one where a Southern city has acknowledged its past racial mistakes, corrected them, and now has created an environment that stresses racial justice and is a good place for business investment. The White community, whose views must be accommodated, insists that racial uplift, triumph effected through law, African American self-help, and the "unfettered possibilities" in America dominate contextualization. Contextualization seldom is approved if it proposes to depict or describe the fundamental ongoing role of race in American society or otherwise seeks acknowledgment of the painful history of race in the United States—before and after emancipation. The second force mitigating contextualization as a preferred choice is the impact of the dual heritage ideology. The dual heritage ideology states that Whites and Blacks have different heritages but each heritage is honorable. The corollary is that each heritage, therefore, deserves to be respected, and adherents of each heritage should abstain from reproaching or otherwise condemning or criticizing the other. In particular, Blacks must respect the "delicacy of White sensibilities" by complying with demands to not offend Whites. Accordingly, context added to a Jim Crow Confederate monument may not disparage the Confederacy, its cause to maintain chattel slavery, its leaders, or the White Southerners who oppressed slaves. Even where mention of the racial oppression intrinsic to slavery is permitted in contextualization, the oppressors must remain invisible. Because these forces cause contextualization to be limited to a rosy assessment of the future, many find that contextualization does not adequately counter the negative ideological projections of a Confederate monument.

ON FIRST IMPRESSION, contextualization might strike one as a prudent approach to the question of what to do with a Confederate monument. Contextualization leaves the Confederate monument in place but augments the monument, through signage or interpretive plaques, for example. Or a Confederate monument might be left undisturbed but a countermonument is raised in close proximity to it—such as a civil rights or a Black history memorial. Such a countermonument potentially can serve as a didactic tool to add clarity and context to the past and argue a viewpoint challenging the ideological projection of the Confederate monument.[1]

Advocates of contextualization argue that the contextualization option serves to educate the public and conveys a more complete account of a community's Civil War history. The added context could include the viewpoints of a wide array of the citizenry and could also provide a history of the statue itself. Moreover, contextualization as an alternative to removal/relocation of the Confederate monument shows respect for the sensibilities of those who define their Southern heritage through Confederate monuments and encourages mutual respect. In addition, monument supporters argue that contextualization rather than removal/relocation avoids the "Taliban error" of attempting to "erase history," reasoning that Confederate monuments express demonstrably accurate historical facts, that is, they "embody history, defined as objective reality [and not just memory]." Accordingly, altering or removing a Confederate monument attempts to deny historical truth as proclaimed by a Confederate monument, akin to destroying a fossil that exists in the natural world without human agency.[2]

Opponents of reinterpretation of Confederate monuments through contextualization, in lieu of removal/relocation of a Confederate monument, advance on several fronts. First, Confederate monuments transmit false history; they distort history. Thus, altering a Confederate monument is not akin to altering objective historical "truth." Nothing is part of history if it deceitfully represents that history and much of the historical representations symbolically transmitted by a Confederate monument is deceitful.

Second, when the location of a Confederate monument is a courthouse lawn, that location symbolically implies that the courthouse does not represent justice for all and no amount of contextualization added to the statue can change that perception. Only removal of the statue, contextualization opponents argue, conveys that those in the community have been heard when they assert that a Confederate monument symbolizes Black suffering rather than a message of unity and progress reflective of the community's current views.

Third, contextualization opponents have successfully argued that placing a Confederate monument on prime public land, probably sometime in the early decades of the twentieth century, demonstrated White supremacists' hold on political power during the period of Jim Crow racial segregation. Leaving the statue in place now, even with the addition of contextualization, implies that racists still have influence within the community's government.

In addition, contextualization opponents consider it problematic that adding additional historical context to a Confederate monument could counterbalance to any significant degree the negative emotions that the Confederate monument elicits, particularly among the community's African American residents. For example, by adding a plaque, New Orleans added context to its 1891 Liberty Monument, which celebrates the 1874 takeover by the White League of a bi-racial government in New Orleans. The plaque plainly stated that the White supremacist sentiments and suppression of African Americans rights expressed by the memorial are contrary to community beliefs and feeling and are contrary to present New Orleans policy. Yet, the NAACP persuasively argued, and the New Orleans *Times-Picayune* newspaper agreed, that in light of the contemporary resilience of racism, it is understandable, notwithstanding the addition of context by the addition of the plaque, that the Black community would consider the monument "as a public affront that preserves or promotes the sentiments of an earlier time." The *Times-Picayune* called for the monument's removal and placement either in storage or in a museum to make plain the "fossil character" of the monument.[3]

Finally, relatively recent scholarship has identified an additional powerful objection to contextualization: its political impracticality in most cases. Professor Dell Upton has most forcefully and persuasively assembled evidence demonstrating how political forces set limiting parameters of what can and cannot be said when adding contextualization to existing

Confederate monuments. Upton describes these limiting political forces as "political censorship, or at least squeamishness."[4]

As Upton explains, contextualization seldom is approved if it proposes to depict or describe the fundamental role of race in American society or otherwise seeks any acknowledgment of the "long bloody history of race in the United States before and after emancipation."[5] Instead, political reality dictates that contextualization must suppress any reference to racial conflict or White domination. Contextualization usually is limited to positive thinking and an idealized imagery of racial uplift and triumph effected through law, African American self-help, and the "unfettered possibilities" in America.[6] The obligatory uplift theme imposed on most contextualization means that struggle can only be shown as an "endless, conflict-free [march of] progress . . . toward Black liberation" in America. The implication is that the Black struggle on the road to racial justice is now at an end: liberation has been achieved. Insistence that contextualization be upbeat and emphasize uplift often is justified by the importance to "have the children in mind:" use contextualization of a Confederate monument to memorialize Black accomplishments for the benefit of coming generations.[7] One White critic who strongly opposed depicting the Black struggle in America in the context of ongoing racism very efficiently summarized the political reality that limits the content of contextualization. This Confederate monument supporter argued that it is permissible to "talk about Black endurance in the face of oppression, [but] not about who was doing the oppressing."[8]

To the extent that depiction of the Black experience in America is permitted at all, only a generic historical narrative "rooted in the specifics" of that experience is permitted: that slaves arrived at a certain time, that emancipation occurred, that *de jure* racial discrimination developed, that there was resistance to racial injustice, that the civil rights movement followed, and that success on the road to racial justice has largely been achieved. What is silenced and censored are renditions of things such as the horrors of slavery, the Middle Passage, the slave auction, the destruction of the Black family during slavery, and the harsh and harmful realities of post-emancipation Jim Crow existence. Also barred are references to slaves' own agency on the road to freedom, the centrality of African Americans to the development of American society and culture, depiction of historic figures in Black history whom Whites find controversial, such as Denmark Vesey, who led slave revolts, any reference to slave rebellions, any hint of those who oppressed African Americans, the ongoing resistance to racial justice, or the continuing "struggle for freedom and power." [9]

Two related realities contribute to the censorship that so limits the content of contextualization and renders it an ineffective option to removing

Confederate monuments: first the "democratization of monument building" combined with the reality of day-to-day local and state politics in the contemporary urban South and second "a convoluted ideology [of] dual heritage."[10]

Democratization of Modern Monument Building and the Impact of Southern Urban Politics

When Jim Crow Confederate monuments were constructed, local political and economic elites were able to commandeer public space and funding to erect monuments honoring the Confederacy. There was no need to share control of the monument project with representatives from the broader community and, therefore, no need to negotiate the monument's specifics with non-elites. Today, that is not the case. Contemporary monument construction is a negotiated activity. Potent opposition from throughout the community must be addressed and accommodated. This is the reality when groups propose to construct countermonuments to Confederate monuments or initiate other efforts to augment Confederate monuments with contextualization such as plaques or interpretive materials. All such contextualization initiatives are closely scrutinized and criticized. Before a countermonument can be constructed on public space or other contextualization added to an existing Confederate monument, African American organizations must negotiate the content of contextualization with Whites and reach consensus.

Various groups of Southern Whites claim a stake in the content of the contextualization that is proposed to augment Confederate monuments. These White organizations demand a seat at the table where contextualization content is determined. One powerful group is the White business community in Southern urban areas. Politics at the state and local level operate through the formation of coalitions of public and private parties. Powerful business interests have a stake in how these coalitions govern and insist that local politics focus on economic development. In the urban South today Blacks often possess the political power and Whites the economic power. Coalition success requires that local government agendas delicately accommodate the needs of each group, and the developmental agendas of the White business establishment in the South have become an influential force in determining the content of contextualization.

Southern business interests insist that contextualization decisions not threaten economic development by adding, or even creating the risk of adding, the appearance of any racial conflict within the community. Indeed, the business community's incentive is to assure that contextualization communicates the message of a deracialized Southern community, one where changes have occurred that have served to rehabilitate the community's past racist reputation. The White business community in Southern urban centers wants to promulgate the message that the Southern community is a good place for corporate relocation and other business investment. The Southern White business community is thus highly motivated to assert its influence to assure that contextualization that augments a Confederate monument always projects the comfortable view of the community being one that has engaged in reform "that righted imperfections in a fundamentally just system through peaceful political action leading to legislative and judicial reforms." Whites prefer communication of the view that the South has paid the price for its past mistakes and now "the civil rights movement is a 'won cause.'" Such a claim depends on framing the civil rights movement as limited to achieving political rights, something many African Americans dispute. Dell Upton has described the goal of White groups as assuring that new memorials operate as "tombstones of racial strife and heralds of a rebirth."[11]

The Impact of the Dual Heritage Ideology on the Content of Contextualization

The dual heritage ideology also constricts the content of contextualization. The dual heritage ideology has two components. The first is that Whites and Blacks have traveled parallel paths but each have their own heritage and each heritage is independent from the other. The second component is that each heritage is honorable, each therefore deserves to be respected, and adherents of each heritage should abstain from reproaching or otherwise condemning or criticizing the other. In particular, Blacks must respect the "delicacy of White sensibilities" by complying with demands to not offend Whites.[12] This dual heritage ideology is reinforced by a cultural norm that dictates that in the public sphere, monuments should not express opinions offensive to another person. The dual heritage ideology, packaged as late-twentieth-century multiculturalism, calls for mutual respect of Blacks and Whites and is calculated to permit Whites to set the terms of political and social engagement.

To Confederate monument supporters, the Confederacy belongs to the White heritage portion of the South's dual heritage ideology. Thus, the dictum is that Blacks are enjoined from criticizing or otherwise disparaging the Confederacy, including when adding context to a Jim Crow-era Confederate monument. An attack on the Confederacy or a disparagement of a Confederate monument is spun by many Whites in the South as an attack on Whites who deserve as much respect and recognition as any other racial group and the "freedom to be ourselves as any other minority in the country." Properly understood, according to this view, an attack on a Confederate monument is an unjustifiable act of racial bigotry and ethnic cleansing and thus a civil rights violation. Neo-Confederates' deploy the pluralist language of "tolerance and ethnic victimization" to advance their objection of any disparagement of the Confederacy or of the White Southerners who oppressed slaves. The primacy of Whiteness thus implicitly pervades the defense of Confederate heritage.[13] When what can and cannot be said in contextualization that augments Confederate monuments is constricted by the facially innocuous ideology of dual heritage, Whites end up largely controlling contextualization for they claim unilateral authority to determine when proposed content disparages Whites as a race. Accordingly, what has occurred in the South, with very few exceptions, is that the content of contextualization has devolved into a "rosy assessment of the present" rather than a description of the ongoing struggle for racial justice.[14]

Sometimes Southern heritage groups and Black civil rights groups spar for years over the wording of interpretive signs and never are able to agree. This occurred, for example, over the effort to add context to the Heyward Shepherd Monument, known as the "Faithful Slave Memorial," raised by the UDC and the SCV in 1931 at Harpers Ferry, the site of the 1859 John Brown raid that was intended to encourage a slave uprising. Shepherd was an African American who was killed during the John Brown raid by an unknown assailant and whom Southern traditionalists lauded as a "faithful slave" although he actually was a free man when killed. Objection to the Harpers Ferry memorial to "faithful slaves" arose immediately following the memorial's dedication and reached a climax in 1981 when the United States Park Service, then the custodian of the memorial, proposed adding interpretive signage. Southern heritage groups rejected the wording on the proposed signage and compromise efforts over the next fifteen years were unsuccessful. Each side objected to the others' attempt to control the memory of the death of Heyward Shepherd. Finally, in 1995 the Park Service installed two interpretive signs—one supportive of the views of Southern heritage groups and one supportive of the efforts of John Brown and commemorating the 200,000 African Americans who fought on the side of the Union forces during the Civil War. The Harpers Ferry "Faithful Slaves" Monument controversy is a good example of the hazards of attempting contextualization, since the effort so often devolves into a political process of negotiation that satisfies no one.[15]

Erika Doss has assembled considerable evidence demonstrating that an upbeat assessment of contemporary Black life usually is the fate of proposed countermonuments once their design proposals have undergone the required negotiation and accommodation process. Doss shows how the content of monuments that are raised to counter the racist projections in Confederate monuments are constricted by the well-developed cultural norm that monuments need to advance social unity and erase from memory things that might distance groups from one another.[16] These cultural forces that tend to purge references to social conflict from countermemorials collide with the need of under-represented and previously silenced social and political groups to use memorialization for their *affective* value, that is to deploy monuments in order to claim a voice, seek representation in the public square, and use memorialization to revive and then put to rest past painful memories. These marginalized groups view counter memorials as one way to reckon with the silenced historical traumas of the past by "posit[ing] new ways of thinking about memory and history." Counter memorials such as a Black history monument hold the potential promise to shift from a "worshipful focus on [some historical figure] to the consequences of [that historical figure's actions]" and thereby encourage informed conversations about past and present racial conflicts and economic relations in America.[17]

But contemporary civil rights or Black history monuments seldom satisfy these needs. They mostly ignore discussion of slavery's trauma and instead, tend to depict Black slaves in heroic terms and "slavery itself as a narrative of endurance and overcoming." Through many examples, Doss demonstrates that contemporary civil rights and Black history monuments tend to follow a narrative of racial uplift that celebrates Black survival in the face of adversity that is integral to "a progressive upward reach of the nation's destiny." These memorials depict "only those to whom shameful things were done, rather than those who did shameful things (or the shameful things that were done), such as wrecking and ripping apart slave families." Memorials to slavery leave invisible the slave owners who "violated human rights and profited from slavery's obscene violence" and thus end up excluding the slaveholders from local and national histories of slavery. In short, countermonuments tend to erase an important portion of the narrative that African Americans wish to air. Doss's conclusion is that a "litmus test" of a society's commitment to address the historical degradations of slavery and racial segregation is the willingness to confront the institutional underpinnings of slavery as well as slavery's "political and social resonance today in terms of abiding national assumptions about racial difference." Contextualization seldom meets this litmus test given its "banal representation[s]" of uplift and middle-class social success.[18]

To be clear, the case against contextualization as a viable alternative to removing/relocating a Confederate monument is not that contextualization can never serve as an effective augmentation to counter a Confederate monument's racist projections but rather that contextualization seldom can serve that function. It is, of course, possible to construct countermonuments that can serve as effective counterstatements to the racist messaging transmitted by Confederate monuments. A good example is the 2019 addition to the public landscape in Richmond, Virginia, by Kehinde Wiley's towering, twenty-seven-foot tall bronze equestrian statue named "Rumors of War." The statue is located near the entrance to the Virginia Museum of Fine Arts on a broad boulevard that intersects Richmond's Monument Avenue. This location places "Rumors of War" only a few blocks from the two-mile long collection of monuments that, for more than one-hundred years, had commemorated Confederate generals along Monument Avenue. "Rumors of War" is designed to mock what one observer has called "the reflective deference [that Confederate] statues have commanded for decades."[19] Wiley's creation was inspired, and to a degree imitates, the majestic equestrian statue of Confederate General J. E. B. Stuart, unveiled on Monument Avenue in 1907. The horse in the "Rumors of War" statue mirrors the design of the horse in the Stuart monument. But rather than a noble Southern gentleman, the "Rumors of War" rider is a triumphant and heroic young African American man wearing Nike shoes, a hoodie, ripped jeans, and sporting a knot of short deadlocks gathered atop his head. The horse, on three legs with one leg extended and its tail swept parallel to the ground by the wind, seems symbolically ready to take flight. The young African American rider astride the horse is looking over his shoulder "as if about to turn and re-engage with a battle raging behind him," just as J. E. B. Stuart is depicted in the memorial that was the inspiration for "Rumors of War." The "Rumors of War" imagery is intended as an intellectual rejoinder to the legacy of Confederate imagery found in hundreds of Confederate monuments, and especially those located for many years on Richmond's Monument Avenue. But more broadly "Rumors of War" invites the viewer to ponder "the urgency of the cultural moment" with respect to the devaluation and subjugation of Black bodies. "Rumors of War" is powerful because the sculptor was provided the freedom to create art that is subversive, indeed scornful of Confederate symbolism with the goal of thereby "destabilizing [Richmond's] stultifying landscape of racist imagery."[20]

The Virginia Museum of Fine Arts commissioned the "Rumors of War" statue and that funding source, perhaps, insulated the design from powerful voices insisting that the statue exclude the mocking aspersions to

Confederate imagery that are implicit in the statue. The evidence assembled by many scholars demonstrates that such artistic freedom is the exception, however. More typically, contextualization that is intended to augment a Confederate monument, such as a countermonument, must accommodate and satisfy the demands of Southern Whites who demand what the contextualization not bruise the sensibilities of Whites. The dual heritage claims are designed to preclude imagery in a countermonument that Whites interpret as criticism of Confederate memorialization or anything else Whites might choose to annex and include in their definition of "Southern heritage." Contextualization can be, but seldom is, a viable alternative to removing/relocating a Confederate monument.[21]

8
Relocation and Its Critics

Relocating a Confederate monument from a revered public space to a museum, a memorial park, or to private land, severs the association in the public mind between the monument's message and the local community and does nothing to destroy the structure itself. Opponents of relocation argue that relocation represents an attempt to rewrite history, needlessly causes racial strife, disrespects Southern heritage, and begins a slippery slope toward a policy of banishing from public spaces all memorials to any who owned slaves. Relocation does not literally rewrite history since the monument merely is relocated. Relocation could be understood to "rewrite history" in the sense that relocation could cause a loss of the historical fact that once a particular public space contained a particular monument over the course of certain years and that the monument was constructed by a certain group for a particular purpose. These historical facts need not be lost, however. In the public space that once contained a Confederate monument a local community could add a plaque or other reference material collecting all of the data needed to provide an accurate account of the presence of the now-removed moment. Nor does removal needlessly cause racial strife: indeed, honestly confronting the racial injustices of the past may provide the best hope for healing. Local communities need to be clear that monument removal reflects the local jurisdiction's decision that it no longer will lend its imprimatur to the Confederate monument's pro-Confederate message. There is no need to shame those for whom a pro-Confederate message remains valuable or shame their ancestors. Every generation of citizens is entitled to decide for itself what message it wishes for its community to project to the public. Nor are monuments to Washington, Jefferson, Jackson, etc. in jeopardy by the removal of a Confederate monument. A municipality chooses to remove a Confederate monument not because the person or persons honored in the monument owned slaves but rather because the citizenry has chosen to disassociate themselves from the pro-Confederate messaging, and its racist implications of White superiority, that the Confederate monument transmits. Unlike Confederate

> monuments, monuments to the nation's founders do not exist because they owned slaves; they exist despite that they owned slaves in order to celebrate matters disassociated from slave ownership.

A PROPOSAL TO REMOVE a Confederate monument can precipitate a salvo of bitter responses, many grounded in the ideology of dual heritage: the accusation that removal constitutes an act of discrimination against Whites. This discrimination claim often is paired with complaints that removal of any Confederate memorialization diminishes the worth of those who value Southern heritage by sending the message "that they are not important."[1] To those who claim such an attachment to Southern heritage, those portions of the public landscape containing Confederate memorialization can take on the status of "sacred places" that become sites of controversy when their original designation is contested and new groups with enhanced cultural and political authority seek to have the site redefined.[2]

Proposals to remove/relocate a Confederate monument typically are met with what might be termed the "Confederate trifecta:" a run of three arguments that are most often advanced for not removing a Confederate monument.[3] The three trifecta claims are: 1) the history claim—one cannot rewrite history, slavery and the Civil War happened, monuments were raised, those are historical facts, and these historical facts cannot and should not be erased; 2) the "let sleeping dogs lie" argument—efforts to remove/relocate Confederate monuments needlessly provoke racial strife and inflame race prejudice at a time when we should be working to heal and promote racial harmony; and 3) the heritage argument—White Southerners have as much right to their heritage as do African Americans to theirs and removing monuments demeans Southern heritage.

The Rewriting/Erasing History Claim

If one were to catalog the most commonly advanced arguments for retaining Confederate monuments on public land, that list surely would include the claim that removing a Confederate monument is tantamount to an effort to rewrite history, an attempt to erase history. Monument removal, it is argued, is akin to book burning. Southern heritage preservation groups argue that "history isn't for sissies. If you made statues only of saints, you'd have no statues."[4] It is argued by supporters of the Confederacy (mostly, though not entirely, Southern Whites) that while it may be a painful reminder for some African Americans, the Confederacy and the Civil War are part of the Southern past for African Americans and White Southerners alike. History cannot be erased by banning flags, removing monuments, renaming buildings and streets, or substituting new pages into history books. Heritage groups sometimes express this argument as an accusation that efforts to remove Confederate symbols and other reminders of White Southern heritage represent little more than a "totalitarian impulse [that] should be resisted" sometimes expressed as "historical revisionism and political correctness" or "radically politicized affront to [White Southerners'] canonical histories."[5]

Initially, it is useful to keep in mind that those proposing the removal/relocation of Confederate monuments from the public spaces they now occupy make no demand for relocation from private spaces. Moreover, relocation proponents do not urge the destruction of monuments, thereby destroying the physical historical record of their past placement at a certain time, by a certain group, at a certain place, and for a certain purpose. In other words, there is no attempt to purge from history the fact that a community once made the decision to erect a particular Confederate monument on certain public land.

Nor do opponents of Confederate monuments endeavor to destroy or erase the messages the Confederate monument transmitted while it was located in a prideful public space within the community. Removal proponents urge a change of venue for transmittal of a Confederate monument's message.[6] The Confederate monument debate is not over proposals to destroy monuments or their message.

The controversy centers on an insistence that public entities modify a Confederate monument's placement in order to sever the community's association with the monument's message. The objection to Confederate monuments is that maintaining their placement in public spaces has the effect of local governments adding their imprimatur, their endorsement, to the monument's message. It is the government imprimatur that opponents find objectionable. Relocating the monument from space that the community controls protects a community from being associated with a viewpoint that it finds objectionable.

A group that funds a private monument and donates it to government to be placed on public land does so with the intent to convey to the public that government endorses the monument's message. If not, the monument's sponsoring organization could simply erect the monument on private land. Sponsors prefer that the monument be erected in a public space rather than on private land because location in a public space imparts a local community's agreement with the message the monument communicates. Indeed, gaining the benefit of government endorsement of the monument's message is the whole point of securing a public space for the monument's location.[7] The central concern of Confederate monument opponents is that the state has "the ability to legitimate certain arguments merely by virtue of its being the state that is offering them [with the result that opposing views] will be denied legitimacy [and] marginalized."[8]

For its part, every government insists, and has the constitutional right to insist, that it retain control over how it presents itself to its constituency and to the outside world. In other words, as the Supreme Court has made plain, by erecting a monument on public land, "the State is speaking on its own behalf" and has the right to limit the content of its own speech.[9] "Governments have always used public monuments to express a government message [of its own choosing], and members of the public understand this."[10] The public associates government with a monument's message whether the monument is government-commissioned or is a "privately financed and donated monument that the government accepts and displays to the public on government land."[11] In either case, in the public mind a monument's message represents the government's viewpoint when government permits a monument to be placed on land it controls. Confederate monument opponents object to a local government extending its endorsement to the symbolic messages that a Confederate monument transmits. That objection, not a desire to rewrite history or erase the monument's message, is why opponents seek removal/relocation of Confederate monuments from public spaces.

For example, in 2018, the Southern Poverty Law Center, a highly visible advocate for removal/relocation of Confederate monuments, argued that "The Confederacy . . . was on the wrong side of humanity. Our public entities should no longer play a role in distorting history by honoring a *secessionist government* that waged war against the United States to preserve White supremacy and the enslavement of four million people."[12] The thrust of this claim is a plea to end public entities' role in "honoring" the Confederate government and its cause "to preserve White supremacy and [slavery]" by retaining Confederate monuments in public spaces. There is no intent here to destroy or erase history, only to end local governments' approval (affirmation) of the Lost Cause version of Confederate history, and the racist ideology underlying that history, that monuments transmit.

Nobody can reasonably charge that removing a Confederate monument from a public space to, for example, a museum, private land, or a Confederate memorial park constitutes "historical rape," or "intellectual vandalism," or otherwise is tantamount to the city's attempt to rewrite or erase history, or that the monument removal was akin to book burning. National values remain fundamentally fluid. The fact that Southern cities and towns once chose to glorify the false ideology of White supremacy by choosing to sponsor Confederate monuments is an important event in the evolution Southern culture. The past glorification of White supremacy by the raising of Confederate monuments is a fact that needs to be retained as part of a community's historic record. Each generation profits from being taught this stain on Southern public life. But Confederate monuments that are removed to a museum, to private land, or to a memorial park containing many Confederate monuments do not cease to exist: they remain an important artifact for the study of racial hostility in the South and the South's retreat from the ideology of White supremacy. Confederate monuments should be preserved and studied for the clarity they provide with respect to how racism was once able to gain such cultural authority in the South. White supremacy is an important historical fact that ought to not be lost to history and the legacy of White supremacy as evidenced in Confederate monuments is not lost as a result of removing and relocating a Confederate monument from its previous situs in the city's town square. At its new venue, a museum for example, or a monument park, the monument remains intact for all to see, contemplate, and derive whatever benefit anyone desires to gain from viewing it. All that has occurred is a relocation and the concomitant decision by local government to end lending the community's assistance in any way to the *celebration or glorification* of a Confederate monument's racist messaging by hosting the monument on its public land.

Just because one group controlling city government in 1920 possessed the political and cultural authority to make "politically motivated decisions regarding the placement of monuments in sacred public spaces," it does not follow that their viewpoints retain a permanent claim to retain possession of those spaces for all time. Because one city administration chose to permit a particular Confederate monument to be located on its public land, and thereby chose to lend its endorsement to the monument's message of White supremacy, it does not follow that all subsequent city governments have surrendered their autonomy to withdraw the city's affirmation of White supremacy a century later by removing the monument. There is no justification in accusing the city of engaging in efforts to erase history, or rewrite it, simply because it has decided to remove a Confederate monument from a town square and thereby disassociate itself from the monument's racist messaging. No community is bound to endorse viewpoints simply because those governing in a prior generation chose those viewpoints as praiseworthy. It surely is true, as Sanford Levinson has written, that "to commemorate is to take a stand, to declare the reality of heroes (or heroic events) worthy of emulation."[13] Each generation has the right to insist on the autonomy to speak for itself and decide for itself what is and is not praiseworthy.

For example, a community may conclude that it has unique needs to strive for racial inclusiveness and that continued association with a Confederate monument's pro-Confederate message undermines that goal in a particular way because public opinion associates the community with racism due to its continued sponsorship of a Confederate monument.[14] Claiming that the monument's removal is tantamount to an effort to erase history or rewrite it is a transparent distraction, one that is calculated to divert attention from the real issues that a community presented with a demand to remove/relocate a Confederate monument must confront: what message does its Confederate monument transmit and does the public entity on whose land the monument is located wish to be associated with that message?[15] Southern communities cannot escape these questions, for the local government's grant of its imprimatur makes it an "active participant in the molding of the general culture." As Kirk Savage has shown, a "public monument represents a kind of collective recognition—in short, legitimacy—for the memory deposited there."[16] Every community reserves the right to decide what legitimacy it wishes to bestow. Accusations that a proposal to remove/relocate a Confederate monument is tantamount to rewriting history diverts the debate from this core insight.

The removal/relocation of a Confederate monument does create the risk of expunging history in one sense. The presence of the Confederate monument at a certain place, during a certain period of time, and constructed by a certain group for a certain reason is itself history. Removal without more can erase the historical fact of a Confederate monument's previous placement on a certain public space. This concern is easily addressed by adding appropriate signage at the former location of the Confederate monument explaining the facts of the now-eliminated presence of the Confederate monument in particular public space, including who raised the monument and why and the reasons why the community chose to remove the monument.

The Avoid Needless Provocations of Racial Strife Claim

The second of the Confederate trifecta arguments to resist the removal/relocation of Confederate monuments states that efforts to remove/relocate Confederate monuments should end because such efforts in the name of "racial justice" needlessly provoke racial strife and inflame race prejudice. In other words, the *status quo* of race relations should not be tinkered with—leave sleeping dogs lie.

The racial *status quo* may be satisfactory to some Whites, but African Americans have little reason to be content with the current state of race relations given the structural racism that is so prevalent in America, as has been detailed earlier in this book. Whites may resist substantial change in the racial status quo and assert that Blacks who seek change are making "illegitimate demand for societal change." But for many Whites the real source of their anxiety is that granting Black demands for social change (such as removing/relocating Confederate monuments), is that Whites lose power and/or status, and perhaps also privilege.[17]

A variation of the avoid-needless-provocation argument accepts that race relations might benefit from a greater degree of racial justice but contends that the removal/relocation of Confederate monuments is an excessive remedy, simply political correctness and "multiculturalism run amok."[18] Those holding this view might conclude that structural racism is not a serious enough problem to justify risking increasing the racial strife already present in American life or it may be premised on the assumption that Confederate monuments do not contribute substantially to current levels of structural racism. In either case, proposals to remove/relocate Confederate monuments are viewed as an overreaction.

The discussion above has documented the dark shadow of contemporary structural racism, the bountiful evidence that such racism is real and substantial, and that Confederate monuments cannot escape the legacy of their creation. Southern elites such as the United Daughter of the Confederacy deployed these monuments to advance a cult of Anglo-Saxon superiority and Black "otherness." To many, these monuments are reminders of the humiliation and exclusion suffered by African Americans. Removal/relocation will not cure racism or satisfactorily atone for its harm. But addressing racism one step at a time surely represents more than a vacuous exercise in political correctness. There is efficacy in dismantling all aspects of the house of Jim Crow, if only brick by brick.

The avoid-needless-provocation argument thus reduces to the plea simply to avoid disputation. To such a plea, a community might wish to agree with Fitzhugh Brundage who has argued that we ought not lament the contentiousness that can develop over efforts to resolve questions regarding how Confederate memorialization has marginalized African Americans and their history and heritage. It is honorable for a community to initiate a "process by which inequities are acknowledged and the [Southern] region's civic live energized." It is quixotic to hope that "a pluralistic public culture will [magically] emerge in the South." The South will develop a multiracial shared memory of its history "only through the strenuous expression and airing of public differences." Contestation, the airing of different views, will provide opportunities for localities to learn more about their history and provide a forum for advancing Black historical memory.[19] The alternative to *not* revisiting and reevaluating the distorted constructed memories and myths that comprise so much of the received Southern past is a continuing distortion of history that fosters unresolved problems, unaddressed emotions, and damaging legacies.[20]

The Respect for Southern Heritage Claim

Those opposing a Confederate monument's removal/relocation possess the ability, if they choose, to inform themselves of Confederate monuments' heritage of racism and the linkage between Confederate monuments and White supremacy detailed in the above pages. This book has amassed compelling evidence that racism was integral to Confederate monuments when they were raised, during decades thereafter as they resided in courthouse lawns and town squares, and to the present. Only the disingenuous or the tragically ill-informed can deny the historic association between Confederate monuments, racial segregation, and White supremacy.[21]

Historian Ulruch B. Phillips claimed that "the determination to maintain White supremacy 'is the cardinal test of a Southerner and the central theme of Southern history.'" Phillips wrote this in 1928. Political scientist V. O. Key concluded in 1949 that "the key to understanding Southern politics is 'the position of the Negro.'" Key concluded that many Southerners are not racist, yet "Southern political development after the Civil War revolved around issues of race."[22] For at least the first roughly three-quarters of the twentieth century, Southern history was the history of a campaign by constant gardeners of White supremacy to secure White unity built on an ideology of White racial superiority. Traditionalists who oppose removing/relocating Confederate monuments undercut their own credibility if they exhibit an unwillingness to acknowledge that race and racism have played a pivotal role in the South's history and traditions including the raising of Confederate monuments. "One cannot in good faith discuss the noble traditions of the South without mentioning the region's less favorable aspects as well." The appropriation of Confederate symbols by extremist hate groups further perpetuates and associates Confederate symbols with ideas of bigotry, hatred, and racial intolerance.[23] In short, Southern heritage, White Southern heritage, is inextricably bound up with oppression of Southern African Americans.

By the same token, a genuine desire for productive dialogue with respect to proposals to remove/relocate Confederate monuments requires acknowledgment by monument opponents that pride in Southern heritage can exist today in the absence of racial prejudice and hostility. That is to say, Confederate monument opponents bear some responsibility for a breakdown in communication if they find themselves unable to accept that one need not be a racist to support maintaining a Confederate monument's present location in the name of preserving Southern heritage.

To be sure, some claimed respect for Southern heritage is a pretext for bigotry, hatred, and White supremacy. But it is unhelpful with respect to efforts to find common ground to assume *a priori* that *all* argument in support of respect for Southern heritage is a cloak for racism. There are certain values unrelated to racial bigotry that are highly associated with the South and comprise the South's heritage.[24] Nothing is gained but intransigence from assuming that anyone who advances an argument supportive of Confederate monuments based on respect for Southern heritage necessarily does so as a pretext for racism.[25]

But a community that is open to the possibility that a Southern heritage defense of Confederate monuments can be severed from racial bigotry, might still justifiably decide to remove/relocate its Confederate monument. The decision whether to remove/relocate a Confederate monument must consider all competing legitimate interests, of which respect for Southern heritage is but one. A Southern heritage defense to retain a Confederate monument on public land is somewhat a misnomer. The Southern heritage referred to in a defense of a Confederate monument is an interest in preserving a *White* version of Southern heritage because Confederate monuments do not remotely transmit any of the wealth of Black Southern heritage. The interest in preserving White Southern heritage needs to be balanced against competing claims raised by African Americans and others.

For example, Confederate monuments are understood by many as "offensive reminders of the worst aspects of Southern culture: a degrading, paternalistic view of African Americans as racially inferior people and a belief that slavery was necessary, and appropriate, to the economic and cultural interests of the antebellum South." It is particularly offensive to the decedents of slaves, and to many others, when, for example, Confederate symbols such as monuments are associated with the denigrating argument advanced by the Lost Cause movement that plantation life was a benign institution that in fact benefitted those held in bondage. In addition, Confederate symbols, such as the Confederate battle flag, are particularly egregious when one understands that they were deployed in the South in relatively recent memory, during the 1950s and 1960s, as a symbol of defiance to court-ordered school desegregation and other court-ordered racial integration.[26]

Even if some members of the community (White members) honestly do not see connotations of crippling, demeaning images of African Americans as a class in Confederate monuments, and even if a defense of Confederate monuments is not motivated by racial hostility, many African Americans continue to genuinely, and reasonably, view Confederate monuments as oppressive symbols of racial inferiority and proclamations of White superiority. One needs only remember the old "colored" man who, when viewing the unveiling of the Lee monument in Richmond in 1890, blurted out, "The Southern White folks is on top—the Southern White folks is on top." That was perceptive. Part of White "Southern heritage" entails a heritage of intent to deploy Confederate monuments to "vindicate the Old South and its slaveholding class."[27] Moreover, abundant evidence assembled in previous chapters of this book substantiates that Confederate monuments are closely linked with the ideology of the Cult of Anglo-Saxonism, the Ku Klux Klan, and other variants of White supremacy.[28]

Negative emotional responses by African Americans to Confederate monuments are real and are well-documented. Those whose ancestors were slaves have expressed great pain and have explained the humiliation caused by their communities' decisions to praise Confederate generals and the Confederate cause that attempted to keep their ancestors in human bondage. For example, at a hearing before the Richmond City Counsel to discuss adding a monument honoring African American tennis star Arthur Ashe to Richmond's fabled Monument Avenue, "Blacks could hardly contain the rage they felt about Monument Avenue and the decades of Confederacy-worship they'd suffered through before the civil rights struggle. For them, putting Ashe on Monument Avenue represented . . . [a] gesture that would salve some of the insult Blacks had so long endured."[29]

Likewise, American jazz trumpeter, composer, and music educator Terence Blanchard encountered New Orleans's Confederate monuments as a teenager. His reaction was that these statues of Confederate generals left a feeling that denied his humanity. "Blanchard *felt* the weight of history. [He] knew that every day, to get to his high school . . . he had to pass by a mounted warrior, a symbol of the war to preserve slavery. Terence got the message promoted by the United Daughters of the Confederacy, politicians, and city officials associated with the Lost Cause [that] the South had fought a noble war . . . and it would rise from defeat to rule by White supremacy. Terence got it, he swallowed it, and he hated it."[30]

In the median strip on the busiest street in Salisbury, North Carolina, stands a Confederate monument raised in 1909. It depicts in bronze an angel cradling a dying Confederate soldier and chiseled in the monument's stone base are the words *Deo Vindice*, which appear on the Great Seal of the Confederate States—"With God as Our Defender." The monument's symbolic message is that God was on the side of the slaveholding South and had dispatched an angel to escort a dying Confederate soldier to Heaven. An

African American minister, a life-long resident of Salisbury, objected to his community celebrating such a view: that God was on the side of the slaveholding class and was "involved with one race putting down another[;] [t]hat's going against the grain of a Christian nation. God ain't with racism or anything to do with subdividing people." This minister also recoiled to the reality that he was required to pass that monument every day on the way to work and confront it, particularly "every time I'm struck at a red light." This African American resident of Salisbury was unimpressed with the argument advanced by local traditionalists that the monument was not racial but rather was a "symbol" of ancestors of Whites who had "fought and died for their beliefs," to which he answered, "your great-grandfather fought and died because he believed my great-grandfather should stay a slave, I'm supposed to feel all warm inside about that?"[31]

Pulitzer-Prize-winning author and Yale law professor James Forman Jr. has relayed an event from his high school years that caused him anguish then and later into his adult years. Forman attended high school in Atlanta, Georgia, and in 1984 was in the twelfth grade. Atlanta was a mostly Black-populated city and Forman's high school had mostly Black teachers and Black students. In 1984, approximately 60 percent of the Georgia state flag consisted of the Confederate battle flag. As a protest to school desegregation, Georgia had integrated the Confederate emblem into its existing state flag in 1956. The state did not remove the Confederate reference from the flag until 2001. Every morning in the spring of 1984, Forman watched from his high school home room window as a Black groundskeeper pulled the cords to raise the Georgia state flag with its celebration of the Confederacy and symbolic demand for a return to Jim Crow racial segregation. Forman found he was unable to ignore this daily ritual although it pained him that his state government had chosen a flag design that called upon its citizens, Black and White, to honor the racist goals of the Confederacy. As an adult, Forman continued to feel the pain from those teenage years.[32]

Even more than the Confederate battle flag, Confederate monuments celebrate the Confederate cause and thus stigmatize—symbolically define African Americans as members of an inferior or dependent caste who are unworthy to participate in the larger White community. Fundamental to understanding Confederate monuments is that their celebration of the Confederacy is the celebration of an effort by White supremacists to create a slaveholding republic committed to maintaining the institution of slavery that would continue to hold in bondage the ancestors of millions of our fellow-citizens who are African American. If we have learned anything from the Supreme Court's decision in *Brown v. Board of Education*, it is that segregation generates a feeling of inferiority in its victims and the racism upon which all segregation is built amounts to a demeaning, caste-creating practice.³³ The core of the majority opinion in *Brown* is recognition that the "social meaning of racial segregation in the United States is the designation of a superior and an inferior caste, and "segregation proceeds on the ground that colored citizens are . . . inferior and degraded."³⁴ That degrading sense of exclusion was the cause of the pain felt by twelfth-grader James Forman Jr., which extended into his adult years. The message of humiliation and exclusion is what American jazz trumpeter Terence Blanchard was forced to "swallow" and learned to "hate." Indeed, a degrading sense of exclusion is the consequence of all of racism's demeaning cast-creating practices.

It would be a grave mistake to conclude that the horrific images that Confederate iconography forced upon our African Americans neighbors during Jim Crow resulted from racism that occurred in a bygone era of American history that has since been eradicated. One readily can find ample evidence of continuing virulent racism in the contemporary South and an ongoing association of Confederate monuments with overt expressions of racism.

In the late-1990s, Pulitzer-Prize-winning journalist Tony Horwitz took a ten-state journey mostly in the South, from Gettysburg, Pennsylvania, to Vicksburg, Mississippi, and from Charleston, South Carolina, to hamlets in Tennessee. His goal was to understand how the Lost Cause still resonates among many in the South. Horwitz wrote his book *Confederates in the Attic* to collect what he had learned.³⁵ Horwitz interviewed hundreds of local citizens.

In one summary, he reports a conversation with several men who were active in a local chapter of Sons of Confederate Veterans (SCV). In discussing why men who did not own slaves fought for the South, it was offered that men in 1861 objected to oppression of government control of their lives, at which point a SCV member chimed in, "Same as today . . . Government's letting the niggers run wild." Every week, at meetings of the Sons of Confederate Veterans, members pledge their allegiance to the Confederate battle flag by reciting, "I salute the Confederate flag with affection, reverence and undying devotion to the Cause for which it stands." Over breakfast with members of a group called the Council of Conservative Citizens (CCC), who had assembled to urge that South Carolina continue to fly the Confederate battle flag over the dome of the its capitol building, Horwitz was informed by one member of the all-White group that "I'm here to defend my race against the government and the Jewish-controlled media." And at the South Carolina Confederate memorial located on the statehouse grounds, a middle-aged CCC member who was an admirer of the memorial stated that "We may have lost the war, but at least we should have [Confederate battle flags and memorials] to look back on. . . . All my life it's been one thing after another. First, they integrated the schools. Then they integrated everything. . . . I feel like I've swallowed enough for one lifetime." Stating that things in the town where he lived would be better if the South were still racially segregated, this CCC member explained that during segregation "Blacks . . . knew they wasn't supposed to live with White people [but now] they're all around . . . . I'm here today to stand up for heritage." Another man in South Carolina told Horwitz that "I'm not an American, I'm a citizen of the Confederate States of America, which has been under military occupation for the past hundred thirty years." This same person told Horwitz that "Blacks are a primitive race, not as intelligent as we are. . . . They look human so you give them the benefit of the doubt, but really they're savages. They have bigger teeth than we do, for chewing things, but their brains are small. They need supervision to survive. . . . Black's natural overseers were Whites . . . ." At a saloon, located in Guthrie, Kentucky, near the Tennessee line, the customers recently had celebrated the Martin Luther King birthday by having a "Thank God for James Earl Ray Party." One patron told Horwitz, "We got a few people standing up for White rights. The rest are pussies who let niggers trample all over them." At Elkton, Kentucky, several roads intersect at the town square. On a Sunday after church, the KKK had set up what they called a "literature roadblock"—rebel-flag-toting trucks parked alongside the road and "a dozen people in jungle fatigues and combat boots standing at strategic points around the square handing out flyers to the afternoon traffic." The flyer was headlined: "The only Reason You are White! Today is Because Your Ancestors Practiced & Believed in Segregation YESTERDAY!" Below it the flyer stated: I WANT YOU FOR THE ALMIGHTY KU KLUX KLAN." It was signed—"Yours for White Victory and the name of a person identifying himself as "Grand Dragon for Christ, Race & Nation." Drivers returning from attending church stopped to take one of the KKK flyers, one "burly pedestrian in a farm cap [who] stopped . . . grouse[ing], 'I've had enough of niggers telling us what to do.'" The KKK members handing out the flyers discussed a cross burning they hoped to attend soon. At this literature roadblock, the Klan handed out 750 flyers and recruited ten new members.[36] Some who have researched Confederate monuments have noted that a town's local Confederate monument often is used as gathering places for groups desiring to memorialize the Confederate cause particularly as "Confederate monuments . . . became permanent symbols of devotion to patriotic principles as southerners understood them."[37]

Throughout the South, children today continue to be indoctrinated to accept the Confederate world view through participation in a group called Children of the Confederacy (C of C), which is an auxiliary of the United

Daughters of the Confederacy. The C of C prepares youngsters for Confederate citizenship and they move into either the UDC or the SCV chapters as they reach adulthood. At C of C meetings, after singing Dixie, the children recite the C of C Creed, which includes a pledge to "study and teach the truths of history," including the most important tenet, "that the War Between the States was not a Rebellion nor was its underlying cause to sustain slavery." Then the children are tested on their knowledge of the Confederate Catechism, "a sixteen-page pamphlet that serves as the children's guiding text." Arranged in a question-and-answer format, this catechism was published in 1954 in the wake of the Supreme Court's decision in *Brown v. Board of Education*. Some sample entries include the following:

> *Question:* What causes led to the War Between the States, from 1861 to 1865?
> *Answer:* The disregard of those in power for the rights of the Southern States.
> *Question:* What was the feeling of the slaves towards their masters?
> *Answer:* They were faithful and devoted and were always ready and willing to serve them."

C of Cs meetings include a Catechism Quiz that tests rote learning. A teenager, acting as the moderator, poses questions from the catechism to a group of children aged twelve and under who compete to be the first to provide the (often verbatim) answer the catechism provides. If, within fifteen seconds, none of the children is able to provide the correct answer, the moderator declares "Books," and all of the children pull out their Confederate Catechism and page through it to find the designated correct answer to the question.

At a meal at a restaurant with some local citizens who are active in the Confederate celebration movement, Horwitz was about to begin his meal when the family's four-year-old son was asked to say Grace. He said, "Lord, we thank thee for this meal and especially for the great and wonderful Confederacy." The four-year-old son was then asked by his mother to tell Horwitz whether "there [is] anything you hate more than Yankees." The four-year-old responded, "No sir! Nothing." Thereupon the child flung himself under the restaurant table yelling, "Someone told me there's Yankees around here. They hate little children."[38]

Parents enjoy the constitutional freedom to teach their child to hate Yankees, to thank God for the Confederacy, believe that the cause of the Civil War was unrelated to slavery, or bring up children to believe that slaves were treated well and loved their masters. And if one desires to travel to a Confederate monument and there express the view that his town was better off when segregated, we properly say that one has the right of free speech and association and freedom of conscience to hold and express these views, as do the patrons of the saloon who choose to celebrate the assassin of Dr. Martin Luther King and refer to African Americans by using the "N" word. To some, Southern heritage today continues to mean celebrating the heritage of hate, Jim Crow segregation, disfranchisement, lynching, school textbook distortion of history, and White supremacy. All of these things are integral to the historical development of Southern heritage as the previous pages document. African Americans (and others) thus can be excused when hearing White defenses of Confederate monuments in the name of "Southern heritage." Such heritage defenses evoke images of racial animus by Whites, teaching young children that slavery was a benign institution, and of Southerners advocating the view "The only Reason You are White! Today is Because Your Ancestors Practiced & Believed in Segregation YESTERDAY!" And a Southern community can thus also be excused if it chooses to reject "Southern heritage" as a sufficient reason to compel the community's continued association with the message of White supremacy that its Confederate monument continues to transmit.

A community may conclude, for a variety of reasons, that it now desires to sever itself from that portion of White "Southern heritage" that has caused such pain to so many over the years. Or it may conclude that its continued sponsorship of a Confederate monument is divisive—not well calculated to bring its citizens together. The point is that a demand to respect White Southern heritage cannot be the end game, even when the Southern-heritage claim is advanced by honorable people who themselves find racial bigotry anathema to them: there can be, and are, overriding competing interests that a Southern community may legitimately take into consideration. A community is privileged to conclude that no one group has the right to insist that its interests in preserving White Southern heritage are absolute just because they are pure, especially when those interests result is a clear and present danger of creating an overriding societal harm, some pressing public necessity justifying the removal of these monuments. An interest in preserving Southern heritage by maintaining a Confederate monument in a public space will need to yield when a community, through a democratic deliberative process, concludes that removing a Confederate monument is necessary as a step in ending the blight of racial bigotry.

The "What About George Washington and Thomas Jefferson" Claim

The previous three, "Confederate trifecta," arguments to retain Confederate monuments are the most often heard. But there is a fourth worth mentioning, though it is perhaps the easiest to refute. The claim is that once Confederate monuments are removed/relocated, there will be no principled way to resist the removal/relocation of monuments to other American heroes who were slave owners, such as George Washington and Thomas Jefferson. "It is a slippery slope!"—so goes the claim.

This argument misses the point. Confederate monuments are not removed/relocated because of the character traits of those depicted in the monuments, including whether or not the person honored by a monument owned slaves. A community is most likely to remove/relocate a Confederate monument located in its public space to dissociate itself from the monument's racist message. In other words, a community provides its imprimatur to the Confederacy and its cause of racial oppression by continuing to sponsor a Confederate monument in its town square. It follows that a community has the right to withhold that imprimatur by removing/relocating the monument. The decision to remove or not remove does not focus on the character of the individual[s] depicted in the monument. If a monument to Robert E. Lee or Jefferson Davis is to be removed/relocated, it is not because both owned slaves. It is a dead-end street to have the Confederate removal/relocation debate turn on shaming individuals by focusing on and debating their character. Plus, a decision to remove/relocate a generic standing soldier monument by definition can have nothing to do with slave ownership since most rank-and-file Confederate soldiers were not slave owners. In short, the debate over Confederate monuments has nothing to do with the slave ownership, or lack of ownership, by the figures depicted in statues incorporated into Confederate monuments. It is the glorification of the Confederacy and its cause by a local community that is at issue.

Unlike a Confederate monument, the Washington Monument, for example, is not a celebration of White supremacy. It never was built for that reason and is not understood today as a shrine to White supremacy. The same with the Jefferson Memorial in Washington, DC. There is no monument to George Washington or Thomas Jefferson in the United States that was raised to proclaim the "God-given right" of a White man to control the destiny of a Black man or otherwise was raised to symbolically transmit the message of a "proper" racial hierarchy for America. The Washington Monument and the Jefferson Memorial will be perfectly safe, even if (when) one day the equestrian statue of Robert E. Lee in Charlottesville, Virginia, is removed and relocated from a public park. If one day it is removed, the Charlottesville statue of Lee will suffer that fate not because Lee owned slaves but because the monument lionizes the actions of a man who directed his many talents to keeping other men in bondage and extolled a cause that the citizens of Charlottesville, Virginia, find offensive.

PHASE III
Who Decides?

9
The Legal Framework Protecting Confederate Monuments

The legal framework regulating the removal of Confederate monuments remains fluid since most of this regulation has developed in the past decade and continues to evolve. Legal controversy may take several forms. First, some citizens may assert a legal right to demand that a municipality remove a Confederate monument. But these claims are problematic because there is no First Amendment free speech right to insist that a municipality remove its Confederate monument from a public space. Individual constitutional rights, such as the right of free speech, exist to resist government regulation that substantially interferes with some liberty interest that the Constitution recognizes as a fundamental right. A municipality's decision to add or remove a monument from land it controls is an exercise of the municipality's own "government speech"— not an act of "regulation" of its citizens' speech. Thus, a citizen's free speech rights cannot interfere with a municipality's decisions to add or remove a monument from its public space. A different legal issue arises when a community, by vote of its governing officials, decides that it wants to remove a Confederate monument but state law prohibits such removal. For example, state historic preservation law may deprive a local community of the autonomy to remove its Confederate monument. More recently, states have enacted legislation specifically aimed at banning the removal of Confederate monuments, shifting removal authority from the local community where the Confederate monument is located to state government, or an administrative arm of state government, often controlled by state officials. There is a credible constitutional argument that state law banning removal of a Confederate monument violates the First Amendment free speech rights of residents of communities that have voted to remove their Confederate monument but cannot due to the restrictions of state law.

THE LEGAL FRAMEWORK protecting Confederate monuments can substantially influence the outcome of removal controversies. Federal, state, and local historic preservation laws can curb local initiatives to remove, alter, obscure, or contextualize a monument. In addition, many states have enacted monument-specific legislation that is designed to protect Confederate monuments. In addition, The United States Constitution sometimes also needs to be considered. This legal framework often precipitates protracted disputes and complicated proceedings, making removal efforts more difficult than many initially believe.[1]

As a threshold matter, any discussion of the legal framework surrounding monument removal must distinguish between claims that government is legally *required* to remove its Confederate monument from claims that law in some way *forbids* removing or otherwise altering a Confederate monument.

No Constitutional Right to Require Removal of Confederate Monuments

It is widely agreed that state or local governments do not violate individual constitutional rights by choosing to raise or maintain a Confederate monument on land that the government controls. In *Pleasant Grove City v. Summum,* the United States Supreme Court distinguished government speech from private speech and held that the placement of a permanent monument in a public park is a form of government speech that is not subject to scrutiny under the Constitution's Free Speech Clause. The Free Speech Clause restricts government regulation of private speech; it does not regulate a government's own speech.[2] The Court has made clear, for example, that no citizen can refuse to pay the portion of his or her taxes that are used to finance government speech. Thus, when engaged in government speech, government is permitted through taxation to force citizens to assist in transmitting views with which a citizen may disagree.[3]

Pleasant Grove City v. Summum arose out of a dispute over a town's refusal to add a monument to a public park. The Court upheld the constitutionality of the town's refusal, reasoning that "when a government entity arranges for the construction of a monument, it does so because it wishes to convey some thought or instill some feeling in those who see the structure." Indeed, "governments have long used monuments to speak to the public." Furthermore, a government entity "is entitled to say what it wishes" and "select the views that it wants to express."[4] While *Pleasant Grove* entailed a community's refusal to add a monument to a public park, the case has properly been interpreted as supporting the view that "the removal of . . . monuments [also] is a form of government speech and is exempt from First Amendment scrutiny."[5]

Exempting permanent monument displays on public property from the restrictions of the Constitution's Free Speech Clause does not provide government the right to violate the Constitution's other proscriptions, including restrictions found in the Constitution's Establishment and Equal Protection Clauses. Thus, for example, the Establishment Clause bars government from exercising its own speech to express a preference of one religion over another. In addition, communication of explicit racially offensive messages by government would call into question whether a state or local government has violated the Fourteenth Amendment's Equal Protection Clause.

In short, government speech generally is not regulated judicially. Instead, restraint on government speech primarily is to be accomplished by government advocacy being "accountable to the electorate and the political process." As the Court has stated: "If the citizenry objects, [to government speech] newly elected officials later could espouse some different or contrary position."[6]

As noted above, government may not express offensive speech violative of the Equal Protection Clause. Government speech potentially might violate the Equal Protection Clause in either of two ways, what the law describes as *de jure* and *de facto* discrimination. Neither constitutional limitation is likely to be a viable basis for forcing the removal of a Confederate monument, however.

De jure Equal Protection violations occur when government actions, on their face, treat two groups of citizens differently. For example, if a local community were to erect a billboard on public property that stated "Only Whites welcome in this town," that would constitute government speech violative of equal protection. In such a case, government action on its face draws an invidious distinction between two groups based on race. Racial discrimination by government is virtually *per se* unconstitutional. Confederate monuments, however, do not overtly proclaim such racial preference or otherwise, on their face, draw racial distinctions. Confederate monuments *overt* messaging typically proclaims a point of view regarding soldierly valor, the primacy of states' rights, and the celebration of a political movement, the Confederacy. None of this is explicitly derogatory of any race. A court is likely to find that Confederate monuments are *facially* neutral with respect to race.

The other form of equal protection violation, *de facto* discrimination, arises when on the face of government action all persons are treated equally but there is a disproportionate discriminatory impact on a particular class of persons. For example, in *Personnel Administrator v. Feeney*,[7] the Court adjudicated the constitutionality of a Massachusetts law that provided a lifetime preference to veterans for state civil service positions. On the face of the veterans' preference rule, men and women were treated equally—a veteran, male or female, received an identical lifetime preference. In operation, the preference operated overwhelmingly to the advantage of males because more males than females were military veterans. Women who were not military veterans challenged the constitutionality of the law because in operation it had a disparate impact harmful to women who applied for a civil service position. The Court held that *Feeney* was a case of *de facto* discrimination and that such cases follow a two-step inquiry. The initial inquiry is whether there is a plausible nondiscriminatory explanation for the law. If there is a plausible neutral explanation, the second inquiry is whether there is sufficient evidence that the discriminatory effect nevertheless was purposeful, that is that government officials enacted the seemingly neutral law with the intent to create the very discriminatory impact that the law in fact created. In *Feeney* there was a plausible legitimate explanation for the Massachusetts veterans' preference law—to reward veterans for their service. That answered the first question: whether the law plausibly could have been enacted to advance some legitimate governmental interest and not merely enacted as a pretext for preferring men over women. As to the second question—invidious motive—in *Feeney* there was no evidence proving a gender-based discriminatory purpose motivating adoption of the state's employment policies. Plaintiffs were not able to assemble evidence that the Massachusetts legislature in fact provided a veterans' preference for the purpose of discriminating against women who applied to the Massachusetts' civil service.

With respect to Confederate monuments, the previous chapters make a strong case that these monuments are facially neutral with respect to race but have an adverse discriminatory impact on racial minorities. Thus, an equal protection-based attack challenging a community's refusal to remove its Confederate monument would fall into the *de facto* equal protection category. Accordingly, the first question is whether there is any plausible explanation why a town would refuse to remove its Confederate monument other than to create the discriminatory effect on racial minorities that the monument in fact creates. Surely a court would find that there is a plausible neutral explanation—the desire to celebrate Southern history and heritage and honor the valor of the Confederate soldier. And, as with *Feeney*, it is highly unlikely that plaintiff could marshal sufficient credible evidence to demonstrate that notwithstanding the plausible neutral explanation for maintaining the Confederate monument, the true reason, the real motive, explaining local officials' current refusal to remove a Confederate monument was discriminatory, *i.e.,* the true purpose was to create the very discriminatory impact harmful to African Americans that the monument in fact has created. In short, there is little likelihood that a viable equal protection challenge could be lodged against a local governing body that chose to keep its Confederate monument undisturbed.[8]

Legal Restrictions on Removing a Confederate Monument—Historic Preservation Laws

Some Confederate monuments have been designated as historic structures under federal or local preservation laws. Once this designation attaches, there exist few options for removing the designation. Accordingly, two issues arise. First, can Confederate monuments normally be designated as historic under historic preservation laws and, if so, what is the legal effect of such designation with respect to thwarting a local government's decision to remove a Confederate monument from its current public space, altering it, or even adding contextualization?

The National Historic Preservation Act ("NHPA") is the primary federal historic preservation law. It requires a federal agency to conduct a so-called "section 106 review" before expending federal funds in order to determine whether such expenditures will cause adverse effects on historic properties. NHPA creates a mechanism for structures to be placed in the National Register of Historic Places.[9] State Historic Preservation Offices submit nominations for inclusion in the register; federal law sets criteria for such inclusion; and federal regulations state several exception categories that preclude inclusion of a structure in the register. Confederate monuments meet statutory inclusion criteria either because they are "associated with events that have made a significant contribution to the broad patterns of our history" or possess requisite architectural or artistic value. However, federal regulations "ordinarily" exclude from Register eligibility "properties primarily commemorative in nature." Notwithstanding that this commemorative-in-nature exclusion category would seem to exclude Confederate monuments from being added to the National Register of Historic Places, "there are in fact many listed monuments" in the National Register.[10]

Properties that are listed in the National Register, and those that are not listed but are qualified to be listed, are subject to certain requirements when *actions by federal agencies* could have an adverse impact on the structure.[11] In such cases, the federal agency must engage in a consultative process as provided by section 106 of the NHPA. That section 106 review must consider adverse impacts that a proposed agency action may have on a historic structure and requires consideration of measures that might mitigate any adverse impact that is identified. But, the NHPA is procedural not substantive. The NHPA does not impose any duty to cease federal funding for a project, even if such funding will cause an adverse impact on a historic structure.[12]

The NHPA can delay and complicate removal of a Confederate monument but, for three reasons, cannot prevent removal. First, a Confederate monument might be found excluded from NHPA coverage because the monument is a "propert[y] primarily commemorative in nature." Second, the NHPA does not forbid the destruction, removal, or alteration of historic sites by commanding their preservation since the NHPA is only procedural: it only requires that the federal government "take into account the effect any federal undertaking might have on them" by requiring a section 106 review.[13] Third, and most important for Confederate monument disputes, the NHPA applies only when there is some nexus between a local monument removal proposal and the expenditure of federal funds. Normally there would be no such nexus. A good example is the decision by New Orleans to remove several of its Confederate monuments. Removal opponents sued, claiming a violation of NHPA because New Orleans allegedly had failed to conduct a section 106 review. In *Monumental Task Committee, Inc. v. Foxx*, a federal court dismissed this NPHA claim, concluding that the monuments were not on federal land and the removal was not a "federally-assisted project"—there was no nexus between the removal project and the expenditure of federal funds. Thus, the NHPA was inapplicable.[14]

The federal Visual Artists Rights Act (VARA)[15] can in some cases prevent removal of a Confederate monument. This legislation provides a private right of action for creators of visual art (including statues) to block any "distortion, mutilation, or other modification of the work [that] would be prejudicial to [the creator's] honor or reputation." VARA creates a potential obstacle to removal only with respect to Confederate monuments constructed relatively recently because VARA rights extend only for the lifetime of the artist and this time period cannot be extended by the artist by assigning his or her VARA right to another.[16]

Many states have historic preservation or environmental protection laws that can delay, and in some cases prevent, relocation, alteration, or contextualization of a Confederate monument. Typically, these statutes apply to actions by state government, including funding, that have a significant adverse impact on historically significant structures, including monuments. While most of this legislation only provides for a review procedure, similar to the federal section 106 reviews, some state historic preservation legislation also is substantive. Some state historic preservation laws contain a substantive component requiring, for example, that, to the extent feasible, state agencies must mitigate significant adverse environmental effects, including adverse effects on cultural resources, as a condition to expending state funds. This duty to mitigate can ban actions that adversely change the historic significance of the historic structure and the mitigation duty has been interpreted to bar demolition of a historic structure.[17]

State Legislation Banning Removal or Alteration of Confederate Monuments

As of mid-2020, seven states had enacted legislation specifically aimed at protecting Confederate monuments.[18] This legislation adopts two distinct approaches.

In three states, Alabama, Georgia, and South Carolina, state legislation creates an absolute bar on disturbing in any way certain categories of war monuments. In each of these seven states, this legislation includes Confederate monuments within its protective sweep. For example, Alabama's Heritage Preservation Act of 2017 prohibits "the relocation, removal, alteration, renaming, or other disturbance of any . . . monument located on public property which has been in place for 40 or more years."[19] Eighty percent of Alabama's Confederate monuments were constructed more than 40 years ago and thus receive the Act's absolute protection.[20] By further example, Georgia law provides that "no publicly owned monument . . . erected . . . or maintained on the public property of this state . . . in honor of the military service of any past or present military personnel of this State . . . or the Confederate States of America . . . shall be relocated, removed, . . . or altered *in any fashion*.[21] In another example, in September, 2019, prior to the repeal of Virginia's monument removal ban, a Virginia court enjoined removal of the Confederate statues that sparked the August, 2017 "Unite the Right" rally in Charlottesville, Virginia. The court rejected the statutory argument that Virginia's memorial protection statute does not apply to Confederate monuments built in cities prior to 1997 and thus did not prevent the alteration or removal of the 1924 Lee Monument. The Court held that removal of the Lee monument, or any other Confederate monument, would contravene Virginia's historic preservation statute, which the Virginia legislature subsequently repealed.[22]

Other monument-specific legislation protecting Confederate monuments does not create an absolute bar to all modification of the states' monuments located on public land. Rather, this second category of monument-protection legislation provides a process for a local public entity to petition a state agency, such as a specially designated review commission, to waive statutory protection of a Confederate monument in order to permit a local government to remove or relocate its Confederate monument.

North Carolina, Tennessee, and Kentucky, for example, have enacted this type of heritage protection statute.[23] In Kentucky, the ban on removing or altering a Confederate monument only applies once the monument is designated as a "military heritage site" by the Kentucky Military Heritage Commission. Some Confederate monuments in Kentucky have been successfully removed or relocated from public land because they have not been so validly designated. If a Confederate monument in Kentucky is so designated, local governments in Kentucky may petition the Kentucky Military Heritage Commission to rescind that designation.[24]

State monument-specific laws that create review commissions may create a false impression that states have provided for *meaningful* local control over disposition of their Confederate monuments. Such an impression is false because the structure of the waiver process makes it highly unlikely that a local public entity's request for a waiver will ever be successful. For example, in Tennessee, waiver can be granted only upon a two-thirds vote of the commission members. In Kentucky, a monument's designation as a "Kentucky Military Heritage Site," cannot be rescinded without a unanimous vote of the Kentucky Military Heritage Commission. These super-majority voting requirements render the statutory waiver provisions a problematic source of meaningful reserved local control over the decision whether to remove a Confederate monument.

Mississippi is unique in its flexibility and commitment to the preservation of local autonomy to control Confederate monuments.[25] While Mississippi's legislation broadly defines the monuments it protects, it provides that the "governing body" responsible for the monument (normally a unit of local government) possesses the authority to remove a Confederate monument to an alternative location that the local entity deems is more appropriate to displaying the monument. It seems accurate to conclude, as one commentator has stated, that the Mississippi statute "may save [Confederate] monuments from destruction, [but] it does nothing to prevent local governments from moving such monuments to less prominent locations, or to locations where they can be placed in historical context and used as tools for education or reconciliation rather than as monuments to discrimination and intimidation."[26]

State monument protection legislation often contains a provision that the legislation does not ban efforts to "protect and preserve" a monument. It has been argued that when a monument is threatened with vandalism, a state court might be convinced that the only way to adequately "protect and preserve" the monument is to remove if to a safer location. Even commentators who support providing local governments greater autonomy to control their town's Confederate monuments have characterized this argument as "suspect."²⁷

Memphis, Tennessee, exploited a loophole, now filled, in the Tennessee monument protection statute. The statute applies only to monuments located on public property. The Memphis City Council thus deeded a park holding Confederate monuments to a private entity, which thereupon promptly removed the park's Confederate monuments. The courts upheld the legality of the deed of transfer that the Memphis city government had executed. But the Tennessee monument protection statute was subsequently amended to ban the transfer of property on which a monument is located. Other monument protection statutes are silent on deeding to private entities public land containing a Confederate monument. Thus, the option of deeding to a private party the public land on which a Confederate monument is located may remain available in some states as a way to avoid state legislative bans on removing monuments from public land.²⁸

North Carolina state legislation bars removal of most Confederate monuments that are owned by the state and located on public property. This language creates some leeway to remove Confederate monuments since some Confederate monuments located on public property are not owned by the state. Many North Carolina counties permitted the United Daughters of the Confederacy to erect monuments on public property but did not take ownership of the monument. For example, The United Daughters of the Confederacy retained ownership of a Confederate monument raised in 1906 and located on prime public property in Chatham County, North Carolina. The county executed a license that permitted the UDC to erect the monuments on public property but the license states that the monument is to "remain in the care and keeping of the UDC." In 2019, Chatham County claimed the right to terminate the license, rendering the monument a public trespass and thus subject to removal. Concluding that the county is likely to prevail on its asserted right to remove the monument, a lower court refused to enjoin Chatham County from proceeding with the removal.²⁹

Constitutional Challenges to State Legislation Banning Removal of Confederate Monuments

A municipality desiring to retain local autonomy to decide for itself whether to remove a Confederate monument might gain purchase by advancing a free speech claim challenging the constitutionality a state statute banning monument removal. There are two versions of such a free-speech-based claim. One asserts that a state's monument removal ban violates the municipality's own constitutionally protected right of free speech. The other version relies on an alleged violation of the free speech rights of a municipality's residents. The first version—relying on a local government's free speech rights—is highly problematic and not likely to be successful. The second approach—claiming that a state's monument removal ban violates the local residents' free speech rights—raises a credible constitutional claim, though one not without its difficulties.

The logic of a challenge to a state ban on monument removal that alleges a violation of a municipality's own constitutional right of free speech is grounded on the sound premise that a local government possesses a degree of autonomy to control the content of communications that it wants to transmit to the public—the choice of which views it wants to express or not express.[30] This principle is referred to as the government speech doctrine, which the Supreme Court fully endorsed in *Pleasant Grove City v. Summum*[31] and reaffirmed in *Walker v. Texas Division, Sons of Confederate Veterans*.[32] The liberty interest in free speech that is constitutionally guaranteed *to private individuals* includes the guarantee that government may not coerce any individual to communicate some government-approved message that the speaker considers offensive.[33] Some municipalities have argued that this same protection from coerced speech should apply also to local governments since they possess the right of government speech. It would follow, therefore, that a local government may raise a valid constitutional challenge to a state statute prohibiting it from removing its Confederate monument on the theory that the city's right to resist compelled speech includes the right to decide which monuments to place, or not place, on land it controls.[34] State law depriving a municipality of the autonomy to remove a Confederate monument that is located on its public space coerces the local government to support a Confederate monuments' pro-Confederate message, which is an "homage to the Confederacy" or some related message supporting the Confederacy and its purported goals. Such coercion, municipalities have argued, invades the municipality's "government speech."

Birmingham, Alabama, is a case in point. In a challenge to Alabama's Memorial Preservation Act of 2017, which prohibits local governments from removing their Confederate monuments, a lower Alabama state court found that "it is undisputed that an overwhelming majority of the body politic of the city [of Birmingham] is repulsed by the [city's Confederate] Monument." Accordingly, the court ruled that the Alabama Memorial Preservation Act violates the *city's rights guaranteed by the United States Constitution* to be protected from coerced speech and declared the entire Alabama

Memorial Preservation Act of 2017 null and void.³⁵ In November 2019, the Supreme Court of Alabama held that the Alabama Memorial Preservation Act does not violate Birmingham's free speech rights to be protected from coerced speech because the Constitution does not provide Birmingham, or any other unit of government, individual substantive constitutional rights such as a constitutional right of free speech.³⁶

The Supreme Court has not considered the validity of the above coerced-government-speech theory, centered on the proposition that a municipality possess its own constitutionally protected free speech rights. It is uncertain, and probably unlikely, that the Supreme Court will agree with any municipality that chooses to advance this argument, although legal scholars continue to argue that the courts should recognize that municipalities possess First Amendment protected free speech rights.³⁷

The Court has held that the government speech doctrine vests a municipality with the authority to resist attempts *by individuals* who assert their own free speech rights in an attempt to influence the content of a municipality's speech.³⁸ But the Court has never held that the Constitution clothes a local government with constitutionally recognized free speech rights that a municipality can deploy to challenge state legislation.³⁹ The simple reason is that the Court has never recognized that the United States Constitution provides fundamental constitutional rights and liberties, such as free speech, to any unit of government. The Constitution secures fundamental rights to *individuals* and federal law provides the means to remedy the deprivation of those rights by government.

The primary source of fundamental rights enforceable against the states is found in the Fourteenth Amendment. The Fourteenth Amendment does not secure First Amendment rights to the political subdivisions of a state to be used to compel the state to act or not act in certain ways. Section 1 of the Fourteenth Amendment provides that "No state shall make or enforce any law which shall abridge the privileges or immunities of *citizens of the United States;* nor shall any state deprive any *person* of life, liberty, or property, without due process of law; nor deny to any *person within its jurisdiction* the equal protection of the laws." Municipalities are legal entities but they are not "citizens of the United States" within the meaning of that term in the Fourteenth Amendment.⁴⁰ The "First Amendment protection does extend to business corporations."⁴¹ And while cities normally are structured as municipal corporations, the Supreme Court has refused to analogize municipal corporations to business corporations for free speech purposes.⁴² The consensus among the lower courts is that the Fourteenth Amendment does not provide constitutionally protected fundamental rights to a municipality or any other political subdivision of state government.⁴³

Nothing in *Pleasant Grove City v. Summum* provides a basis for a municipality to claim a right to challenge a state statute based on a municipality's alleged constitutional right of free speech. *Pleasant Grove* did not hold that the Fourteenth Amendment or any other constitutional provision vests the town of Pleasant Grove with any constitutionally protected free speech right of its own. The Court in *Pleasant Grove* simply held that the Constitution's guarantee of free speech rights that the Constitution vests in *individuals* does not include the right to force government to add a monument to a public park. The Court labeled the outcome in *Pleasant Grove* as an application of the "government speech" doctrine. But that characterization is misleading to the extent that it might suggest that the Constitution's Fourteenth Amendment vests free speech rights in a local government entity. The local government in *Pleasant Grove* prevailed, not because the Constitution provides it with free speech rights but because the free speech rights that the Constitution vests in individuals do not to privilege an individual to force government to express views other than those government wishes to express. The reason is, as the Court in *Pleasant Grove* made plain, that the free speech rights granted to individuals are limited to protecting individuals from government regulation. When government insists that it be free to speak in its own voice, for example, by choosing what monuments to add to its public property, government is not "regulating" anyone. The Court in *Pleasant Grove* could not have been clearer on this point when it stated, "the Free Speech Clause [of the Constitution] restricts *government regulation of private speech;* it does not regulate government speech."[44]

In 2009 the Court rejected the view that a municipality possesses its own constitutional rights that are enforceable against its own state. In *Ysursa v. Pocatello Education Association,* the court concluded that "a political subdivision, created by a state for the better ordering of government, has no privileges or immunities [of its own] *under the federal constitution* which it may invoke in opposition to the will of its creator.[45] *Ysursa* cited century-old precedent holding that local governments, being creatures of the state, lack legal capacity to sue the state alleging violation of any rights of its own.[46] *Ysursa v. Pocatello Education Association,* along with the precedent it cites with approval, strongly suggest that the Court would find that a municipality lacks a valid claim that the Constitution vests it with free speech rights that it can deploy to challenge a state ban on monument removal.

That said, local governments, along with local residents, might prevail in challenging a state statute banning monument removal if their constitutional claim is framed as protecting the free speech rights of a municipality's residents. Such a claim would assert that a state ban on removing

Confederate monuments unconstitutionally coerces individual residents of the municipality to support the pro-Confederate message of the Confederate monument located in their town.

The threshold hurdle for a municipality to assert such a claim is demonstrating that a municipality may gain standing to assert the free speech rights of its residents in these circumstances. Litigants who have suffered a concrete, redressable injury by government action may rest a claim for relief on the legal rights or interests of third parties if 1) the third party's legal rights are inextricably bound up with the activity that the litigant wishes to pursue and if 2) there is some "genuine obstacle" to the third party's ability to assert his or her own legal rights. This is referred to as the third-party standing doctrine.[47]

First, local governments suffer the requisite concrete injury necessary to be granted third-party standing. Monument protection statutes interfere with a municipality's ability to decide how to use its public spaces and how to allocate its financial resources. In addition, local governments that are prevented from removing a Confederate monument are harmed by being forced against their will to sponsor, and thus be associated with, Confederate monuments' pro-Confederate messages. Moreover, under most monument protection statutes, a municipality risks civil or criminal prosecution and fines were it to resist the state's coercion to support the racist messaging of the Confederate monument by "altering" or "disturbing" a monument's condition.

Second, the free speech rights of a local jurisdiction's residents are inextricably bound up with the activity that the litigant (a local-government) wishes to pursue. A local government seeks third-party standing to advance the argument that its residents' free speech rights bar a state from coercing residents to communicate the state's government-approved pro-Confederate message that the residents consider offensive. This legal right of the residents is inextricably bound up with the activity the municipality wishes to pursue, which is to be able to legally remove the offending Confederate monument.

Third, courts likely will find that the obstacle perquisite is satisfied. First, the Supreme Court has held that an obstacle to litigants vindicating their own legal rights is not always necessary.[48] Moreover, even where an obstacle requirement remains as a factor, the slightest hindrance satisfies the obstacle prerequisite to third-party standing. As the Supreme Court has explained, identifying some hindrance to the ability of the third party to litigate his or her own legal rights is a prudential, not a constitutional requirement. Even very modest hindrances are sufficient to meet the obstacle requirement. when, on balance, the adverse impact on third-party interests from the challenged government action is great and the litigant who is before the court will adequately represent the interests of the third-party who is not before the court.[49] The practical difficulty of a local resident financing and managing a free speech legal challenge to a state monument protection statute may qualify as the required obstacle. As a practical matter, local residents may have difficulty financing major litigation against a state, which has virtually unlimited legal resources to contest its claim. In most cases, the municipality on whose public space the Confederate monument rests is far better equipped than residents to fund the litigation. The municipality may also be well-positioned to provide the legal expertise needed to manage litigation centered on a constitutional claim that banning removal of a Confederate monument violates the free speech rights of the municipality's residents. In addition, the Court has found that the risk of mootness can constitute the requisite obstacle.[50] In cases such as this, the free speech rights of a municipality's residents are best vindicated by the municipality, rather than an individual resident of the municipality, because for a variety of reasons an individual resident may need to relocate his or her family from the jurisdiction, rendering that resident's free speech claim moot and risking dismissal of the case. In addition, there easily could be privacy concerns hindering residents' willingness to become a named plaintiff in litigation seeking authority for local government to remove a Confederate monument, especially given the current rise in White nationalism and the spread of far-right White extremist ideology.[51] The Court has found that concerns over the physical security of individuals who might need to come forward as named plaintiffs if third-party standing is denied an organization represents an obstacle justifying the granting of third-party standing.[52]

Satisfaction of the normal prerequisites for the grant of third-party standing should be sufficient to permit a municipality to raise the free speech rights of its residents to challenge a state monument removal ban. Nothing in *Ysursa v. Pocatello Educational Association,* or the precedent it cites,[53] should preclude granting a municipality standing to sue the state alleging the First Amendment free speech claims of its residents. For over half a century it has been clear that while a state has great authority to structure its relationships with its political subdivisions, states must exercise their power over their subdivisions in ways that do not violate the constitutional rights of the residents of those subdivisions. The classic example of this principle is *Gomillion v. Lightfoot.*[54] In *Gomillion,* African American residents of Tuskegee, Alabama, alleged that the Alabama legislature violated its constitutional rights when it redrew the city's boundaries in such a way as to deny plaintiffs the right to vote guaranteed by the Fifteenth Amendment. Finding that the boundary readjustment unconstitutionally denied plaintiffs the right to vote, the Court explained that while a state has plenary power to manipulate the affairs of its municipal corporations, the State's authority is restrained by the prohibitions of the Constitution. Courts are empowered to hear claims brought by a state's citizens alleging that a state's exercise of power over its municipalities has invaded constitutional rights guaranteed to the state's citizens. That is exactly what is involved when a state ban on monument removal is alleged to violate the free speech rights of a municipality's residents. The removal ban represents the exercise of state power over its municipalities (because most monuments are located on land controlled by towns and cities) but, as in *Gomillion v. Lightfoot*, that exercise of that state power is alleged to violate the constitutional rights of the municipality's residents because the monument removal ban coerces local residents to support pro-Confederate views that they find abhorrent. And as the Court held in *Gomillion*, "state power [to regulate a state's political subdivisions may not be] used as an instrument for circumventing a federally protected right."[55] Since a municipal resident could sue a state to challenge a state ban on monument removal on free speech grounds, there is no reason that a municipality that has satisfied the normal prerequisites for third-party standing may not raise this claim on behalf its residents.

The procedural posture of a suit against the state by a municipality to litigate the infringement of the First Amendment rights of the city's residents would be strengthened by adding several local residents as named plaintiffs, as was done in *Gomillion v. Lightfoot*. There is considerable precedent that a municipality may sue a state alleging infringement of the constitutional rights of its residents when residents themselves are parties to the litigation. This was the situation in *Washington v. Seattle School District No. 1*, a case where the Supreme Court held that a political subdivision of the state (a local school board) could raise the equal protection rights of minority students to challenge a state law banning busing to achieve racial integration of the state's schools.[56] Similarly, in *Romer v. Evans*, individuals and municipalities joined to challenge the constitutionality of state law discriminating against gays and lesbians and the Supreme Court held that the municipalities could assert the constitutional rights of their residents.[57]

Assuming that a municipality, alone or joined by some of its residents, is granted standing to assert the free speech rights of its residents to oppose state bans on removal of a Confederate monument, the question remains whether a state monument removal ban violates the municipal residents' free speech rights. The core of the residents' free speech claim is that a state cannot constitutionally require citizens to express a viewpoint that is offensive to their moral convictions and a state ban on removal of a municipality's

Confederate monument forces the local residents to continue to support, and be associated with, the pro-Confederate messaging transmitted by a Confederate monument located on public property of the plaintiff residents' city or town.[58]

No doubt, such an argument on behalf of a municipality's residents would be met with a state's counterargument that now that the state has enacted legislation banning monument removal, a Confederate monument located in a local park within the state represents the *state's own government speech*. A state may well argue that the monument removal ban has transferred the monument's message to the control of the state government, in the sense that state government now controls whether the monument can be removed. *If* the monument now constitutes the state's own government speech, the state has the right to choose whether or not to permit a monument's removal. The state's exercise of that monument removal authority does not unconstitutionally coerce the private speech of a municipality's residents. That is the teaching of *Pleasant Grove:* the decision whether or not to remove a monument is an exercise of the state government's own government speech, not the regulation of private speech, so the municipal residents' First Amendment free speech rights are not violated by the monument removal ban.[59]

In short, the focus of litigation that a municipally might bring asserting its residents' free speech claims to challenge a monument removal statute would be whether the state, by banning a local government from removing a Confederate monument located on its public space, may now claim that the expressive content of that Confederate monument represents the state's own government speech. The evolving government speech doctrine should reject a state's claim that a state monument removal ban transfers the locus of government speech from the local jurisdiction where the monument is located to the state that is now regulating the monument's removal.

In the context of a state ban on monument removal, the expressive content of the monuments that are covered by the ban does not become the government speech of the state unless onlookers will likely associate the monument's message with the state; that is, they will reasonably conclude that the state is lending its imprimatur to the monument's message. Onlookers will not likely connect the state to the expressive content of monuments whose removal is banned by state law but that are located within the boundaries of a town or city and situated on the public space owned, managed, and controlled by the municipality. As to such monuments, it is unlikely that onlookers will conclude that the state, rather than the municipality, is the entity that is deciding to keep the Confederate monument in place. The Supreme Court has explained that the public associates a monument's message with the municipality that owns and manages the space where the monument is located and links that message to the municipality's identity.

In *Pleasant Grove City v. Summum*, the Court held that "persons who observe . . . monuments routinely—and reasonably—interpret them as conveying some message on the property owner's behalf."[60] In *Pleasant Grove*, there was "little chance that observers will fail to appreciate the identity of the speaker [because] [p]ublic parks are often closely identified in the public mind with the government unit that owns the land. City parks . . . commonly play an important role in defining the identity that a city projects to its own residents and to the outside world." As the Court emphasized, "governments have long used monuments to speak to the public [through monuments]."[61]

For Confederate monuments that are subject to a state ban on removal, but that are located in a town's courthouse square, park, or street, it is likely that the public will misappropriate blame for why a Confederate monument has not been removed. The public will continue to hold local government accountable for the content of the speech transmitted by a monument located on land managed by a municipality notwithstanding that a local government would remove a monument if it lawfully could. "Persons observing the monument on city property would reasonably interpret it as conveying a message on the city's behalf."[62]

It is critical to the efficacy of the government speech doctrine that the state should not be permitted to claim a monument's expressive activity as its own government speech simply because the state has enacted legislation banning the locality from removing the monument. The public will misperceive that local government, and not the state, is the government entity that is accountable (responsible) for the keeping the Confederate monument in place. That misperception undermines the logic of the government speech doctrine. In *Pleasant Grove*, the Court emphasized the importance of accountability. Once government activity is denoted as "government speech," there is no valid free speech claim that a citizen can lodge to protest the content of government speech. Instead, restraint on government speech rests exclusively on government advocacy being "accountable to the electorate and the political process." As the Court explained, "if the citizenry objects, [to government speech] newly elected officials later could espouse some different or contrary position."[63] For the political process to operate effectively as a check on unwanted government speech, the public must have a reasonable ability to identify which government entity controls the content of speech that citizens find objectionable. This political remedy available to the citizenry to eliminate unwanted government speech malfunctions if citizens do not reasonably understand that the state now controls the content of monuments' expressive content by controlling whether the monuments can be removed. If the citizenry does not reasonably understand that the state, and not local government, is responsible for maintaining the objectionable pro-Confederate content of monuments' speech in some local public space, citizens necessarily will be confused with respect to knowing where in the political process to apply pressure for change. Without the ability to accurately gauge why local government is failing to remove an objectionable Confederate monument, it is unrealistic to expect that government speech that some find repugnant can be made "accountable to the electorate and the political process."

In short, a state monument removal ban may shift control of a Confederate monument's pro-Confederate message from local government where the monument is located to the state. But this shift in control does not result in the Confederate monument's expressive content becoming the state's own government speech because the public will continue to assign to local government the accountability for pro-Confederate message of any Confederate monument remaining on land that the local government controls. This failure of accurate accountability is fatal to any claim by the state that the Confederate monument's pro-Confederate message is now the state government's own government speech and, for that reason, the state is immune from citizens' free speech challenges to bans on monument removal. Therefore, citizens are free to challenge removal bans on the theory that such bans coerce local residents to support, and be associated with, these monuments' pro-Confederate messages.

Conclusion

WHEN I TEACH LAW STUDENTS the techniques of appellate court litigation, brief writing, and oral argument before panels of appellate court judges, I encourage them to skip conclusions, or at a minimum to keep them short. My reasoning is that if the advocate has not carried his or her argument during the main presentation, summing up by adding a conclusion will not save the effort. Those reading an appellate brief often simply skip the conclusion. In oral advocacy before a three-judge panel, the members of the appellate court seldom are interested in listening to the advocate's summing-up at the end of an argument; the judges typically have heard enough and are busy collecting their papers and getting ready to hear the next case. So why not dispense with conclusions altogether? A case can be made that this advice holds for book authors also—especially the part about the reader skipping over the conclusion unless convinced that it adds useful insights not already discussed in the book. So, I will spare you a recap here of the previous several hundred pages. I hope you do not need it and I suspect you would skip over it in any event.

Instead, permit me to conclude by inviting you to think about what you have just read in ways that you may not have considered. The previous chapters fill the interstices of the historical record with respect to the motives for constructing Confederate monuments and they expose the societal costs associated with Confederate monuments, in particular their contribution to the scourge of contemporary racism. From that perspective this is a book about history, race relations, and the social psychology of contemporary racism in America. Accordingly, one way to understand the previous chapters is to think of them as directed to scholars, students, the general reader, and all others who seek clarity regarding the role of Confederate monuments in contemporary America.

But consider that the arguments rehearsed in this book can also be understood in more utilitarian terms. They also speak to the functional needs of those who either currently are "in the arena," as President Theodore Roosevelt once described those who have chosen to thrust themselves into the vortex of public disputes in order to influence the outcome, or are now on the sidelines but are contemplating moving into the arena.[1] Who are these activists and potential activists?

First, there are those who currently labor as advocates urging their fellow citizens that a community's Confederate monument should be removed or relocated. Often such advocates are the ones who are approached for guidance by friends, family, colleagues, and others regarding the array of competing claims aired by those who propose and those who oppose the removal or relocation of Confederate monuments. The preceding chapters provide facts that are essential to focus the debate and sort out the competing interests at stake. This book provides the back-story of Confederate monuments: when most of them were raised, who raised them and why, and, in particular, the important political functions Confederate monuments have served, and continue to serve, in supporting and advancing the ideology of White supremacy. Those who advocate doing something with a community's Confederate monument inevitably confront claims that any change in a Confederate monument's *status quo* disrespects Southern heritage. The rejoinder to this claim is that the decision whether to remove or relocate a Confederate monument must consider all competing legitimate interests, of which respect for Southern heritage is but one. The interest in preserving White Southern heritage needs to be juxtaposed against competing claims raised by African Americans and others, and may well need to yield because maintaining a Confederate monument in its traditional public space creates a clear and present danger of causing an overriding societal harm. The burden of the argument in this book is that Confederate monuments foist material harm on contemporary American life of such a severe magnitude that ending the harm by removing these monuments from public spaces constitutes a pressing public necessity. Confederate monuments harm contemporary American society by perpetuating anti-Black racial stereotyping and systemic racism and inflict great harm on each of us and on hundreds of thousands of our neighbors, African Americans and others. This societal harm overrides even good faith claims to leave Confederate monuments undisturbed in order to respect Southern heritage. In short, the preceding chapters arm advocates for change with the tools needed to demonstrate the need, and justification, for a community to do something with its Confederate monument—probably remove or relocate it.

There is a second group of persons in the arena. They are related to the first but operate in a different venue. These are the social activists who are called upon to construct arguments leading to law reform with respect to laws that now deprive local communities the autonomy to decide for themselves whether to keep their Confederate monument undisturbed or to take action to remove or relocate it. The venue in which these activists work is not so much the city council meeting room, where the question is whether to do something with the town's Confederate monument, but rather in legislative chambers or the courts. Today, many states from the Old Confederacy, where most Confederate monuments are located, have enacted laws that deny local communities the democratically-derived choice to remove their Confederate monument. In many states, these laws are being re-examined. All of them should be. States historically have denied their municipalities much governing autonomy, often for good reasons, but there is no justification for a state to coerce residents of a municipality to financially or otherwise support and endorse political ideologies that they and their democratically elected local governments have concluded are an anathema. Reform of state law that denies a community the autonomy to decide what to do with its Confederate monument, difficult under the best of circumstances, can occur only through the force of an aroused public opinion exerted on state legislatures and the courts. For such public opinion to swell, it is necessary to clarify 1) the harm the community as a whole suffers, economically and otherwise, from being forced to extend its imprimatur to the racist messaging of the Confederate monument and 2) the cost to local residents individually (particularly to a municipality's African American residents) that Confederate monuments exact. Demonstrating to a state legislative body or a court how Confederate monuments create these harms and costs can be challenging. Twenty-first century casual observers of Confederate monuments might be excused if they do not readily grasp the racist messaging transmitted by the typical Confederate monument. The monuments look harmless, merely masses of stone, marble, and bronze that seem to do no more than commemorate the valor of Confederate soldiers. No racist, White supremacist, or other sinister motive is readily apparent from the figures that adorn these monuments or from the inscriptions most monuments carry. The monuments *seem* so benign: General Robert E. Lee grandly and gallantly riding a horse appears to do no harm. The popular mass-produced "standing soldier" statue of a lone rank-and-file Confederate soldier similarly appears inoffensive. Moreover, many of these monuments are grand, stunningly beautiful, and esthetically pleasing. For the law reformer, the challenge is to illuminate how these monuments contributed to the rise and maintenance of White supremacy when they were constructed and how they continue to nurture structural racism in contemporary America. Accomplishing this task requires careful explication of the motives of the organizations that raised these monuments and careful substantiation of how these monuments have served, and continue to serve, as instruments thwarting the cause of racial justice. The above chapters provide the detail needed to shape such arguments.

There is yet a third group—those who are not now in the arena, who are considering active involvement in this debate, but who remain uncertain whether to become involved. One reason for hesitancy is a lack of confidence in one's ability to support claims effectively with fact and reasoned argument. A second basis for hesitancy is uncertainty regarding the gravity of the underlying issues being contested, for example, whether those proposing to remove or relocate Confederate monuments are advancing compelling moral claims, thus warranting action by those still occupying the sidelines. The preceding pages arm the reader with facts sufficient to formulate well-supported positions regarding the controversy over the removal and relocation of Confederate monuments. With respect to the momentousness of the issue, its moral gravitas, this book shows how Confederate monuments are more than simply historically interesting masses of stone, marble, or bronze. For four generations, first during the reign of Jim Crow segregation, then during the subsequent "Massive Resistance" to racial desegregation, and finally into the present, these monuments have functioned for some as a catechism, a means to transmit doctrines of a civil religion grounded on a White supremacist view of a "proper" racial, social, and political order for America. The movement to remove and relocate these Confederate monuments is a reproach to the racist tenets of that civil religion. The movement to remove and relocate Confederate monuments shares time and space with other contemporary currents of protest. These include the "Black Lives Matter" movement protesting police brutality in communities of color; football players kneeling during the playing of the National Anthem in protest to police misconduct; opposition to the mounting evidence of "structural racism" in America; objections to White men masquerading in Blackface and calling it harmless "fun;" and the rising discontent over evidence that the current mass incarceration of African American males constitutes the "New Jim Crow."[2] The movement to remove and relocate Confederate monuments has joined this escalating cry for racial justice and presents opportunities to work for racial peace. Collectively, these renewed appeals for racial justice constitute a revived civil rights movement for the first third of the twenty-first century.[3] Readers who value the twin goals of racial peace and racial justice may well conclude that the preceding pages provide compelling reasons to step up and add their voice to the conversation.

Cases Cited

Ableman v. Booth, 62 U.S. 506 (1859).
Alabama v. City of Birmingham, (Ala. S.Ct),-So. 3d -. 2019 WL 6337424 (2019).
Alexander v. Sandoval, 532 U.S. 275 (2001).
Board of Education v. Barnette, 319 U.S. 624 (1943).
Board of Regents of University of Wisconsin System v. Southworth, 529 U.S. 217 (2000).
Brown v. Board of Education, 347 U.S. 483 (1954).
Brown v. Board of Education, 347 U.S. 483 (1954).
Bush v. Orleans Parish School Board, 364 U.S. 500 (1960).
Business & Residents Alliance of E. Harlem v. Jackson, 430 F.3d 584 (2d Cir. 2005).
Caplin & Drysdale, Chartered v. United States, 491 U.S. 617 (1989).
Citizens United v. Federal Election Comm'n, 558 U.S. 310 (2010).
City of Trenton v. New Jersey, 262 U.S. 182 (1923).
Cohen v. California, 403 U.S. 15 (1971).
Coliseum Square Association, Inc. v. Jackson, 465 F.3d 215 (5th Cir. 2006).
Cooper v. Aaron, 358 U.S. 1 (1958).
Craig v. Boren, 429 U.S. 190 (1976).
Eisenstadt v. Baird, 405 U.S. 438 (1972).
Employment Division v. Smith, 494 U.S. 872 (1990).
First National Bank of Boston v. Bellotti, 435 U.S. 765 (1978).
Gomillion v. Lightfoot, 364 U.S. 339 (1960).
Harper v. Virginia State Board of Elections, 383 U.S. 663 (1966).
Hunter v. City of Pittsburgh, 207 U.S. 161 (1907).
Johanns v. Livestock Marketing Association, 544 U.S. 550 (2005).
Keller v. State Bar of California, 496 U.S. 1 (1990).
League of Protection of Oakland's Architectural &Historic Resources v. City of Oakland, 60 Cal. Rptr. 2d 821, (Ct. App. 1997).
Monumental Task Committee, Inc. v. Foxx, 157 F.Supp.3d 573 (E.D. La. 2016), *affd. sub nom*, Monumental Task Committee, Inc. v. Chao, 678 Fed.Appx. 250 (Mem.) (5th Cir. 2017).
NAACP v. Alabama, 357 U.S. 449 (1958).
Nebraska Press Association v. Stuart, 427 U.S. 539 (1976).
New York Times Company v. United States, 403 U.S. 713 (1971).
Papasan v. Allain, 478 U.S. 265 (1986).
Personnel Administrator v. Feeney, 442 U.S. 256 (1979).
Pleasant Grove City v. Summum, 555 U.S. 460 (2009).
Plessy v. Ferguson, 163 U.S. 537 (1896).
Prize Cases, 67 U.S. (2 Black) 635 (1863).
Reynolds v. United States (1878).

Rogers v. Brockette, 588 F.2d 1057 (5th Cir. 1979).
Romer v. Evans, 517 U.S. 620 (1996).
Rust v. Sullivan, 500 U.S. 173 (1991).
Schenck v. United States, 249 U.S. 47 (1919).
Singleton v. Wulff, 428 U.S. 106 (1976).
Texas v. Johnson, 491 U.S. 397 (1989).
Texas v. White, 74 U.S. (7 Wall.) 700 (1869).
United States v. Peters, 9 U.S. (5 Cranch) 115 (1809).
United States v. State of Alabama, 791 F.2d 1450 (11th Cir. 1986).
Virginia v. Black, 538 U.S. 343 (1996).
Walker v. Texas Division, Sons of Confederate Veterans, Inc., 576 U.S. 200 (2015).
Washington v. Seattle School District No. 1, 458 U.S. 457 (1982).
Williams v. Mayor & City Council of Baltimore, 289 U.S. 36 (1933).
Williams v. Mississippi, 170 U.S. 313 (1898).
Wooley v. Maynard, 430 U.S.705 (1977).
Ysursa v. Pocatello Educational Association, 555 U.S. 353 (2009).

Notes

Preface

1. Associated Press, "Man in Charlottesville Car Attack Gets Life Sentence Plus 419 Years," *Huffington Post*, July 15, 2019, accessed at https://www.huffpost.com/entry/fields-sentence-charlottesville-rally_n_5d2cbce0e4b08938b09917fe. The Charlottesville protests also resulted in the deaths of Virginia state police troopers Jay Cullen and Berk Bates, whose helicopter crashed while they were observing and reporting on the riot.

2. For example, in October, 2019, Steven Reed was elected as the first African American mayor of Montgomery, Alabama, the state's capital and also the first capital of the Confederacy early in the Civil War. According to the U.S. Census, approximately 60 percent of Montgomery's 200,000 residents are Black or African American. Eric Levenson & Steve Almasy, "Montgomery, Alabama Elects its First Black Mayor," *CNN*, October 9, 2019, accessed at https://www.cnn.com/2019/10/08/us/montgomery-alabama-Black-mayor/index.html.

3. *See* Neil MacFarquhar, "Scrutiny for Extremist Symbols After Attacks in U.S.," *New York Times*, September 26, 2019 (discussing findings that "a more fluid use of [White extremist] symbols ha[s] accelerated since the 1980s"), accessed at https://wwww.nytimes.com/2019/09/26/us/White-supremacy-symbols.html.

4. See discussion at Dell Upton, *What Can and Can't Be Said: Race Uplift and Monument Building in the Confederate South* (New Haven, CT: Yale University Press, 2015), 33.

5. Upton, *What Can and Can't Be Said*, 48–50, 58.

6. *See, e.g.*, J. Michael Martinez, "Traditionalist Perspectives on Confederate Symbols," in J. Michael Martinez, William D. Richardson, and Ron McNinch-Su, eds., *Confederate Symbols in the Contemporary South* (Gainesville: University Press of Florida, 2000), 243–44, 271 (arguing that for "'traditionalists,' symbols of the Confederacy are inextricably linked to ideals of nobility, valor, and respect for Southern traditions and customs without regard to racism [and] White Southerners who cherish Confederate symbols are not necessarily racists . . ."). *See also* Robert Holmes and M. Christine Cagle, "The Great Debate: White Support for and Black Opposition to the Confederate Battle Flag," in Martinez, *et al., Confederate Symbols in the Contemporary South*, 281–82 (describing White Southerners' support for Confederate memorialization as based on versions of Southern pride, heritage, and tradition).

7. Upton, *What Can and Can't Be Said*, 58.

8. *See, e.g.*, Martinez, "Traditional Perspectives," 272 ("In some sense, racists have 'taken over' the meaning of Confederate symbols); John M. Coski, "The Confederate Battle Flag in Historical Perspective," in Martinez, *et al,, Confederate Symbols in the Contemporary South*, 118 & n.108 (arguing that during the life of the Confederacy and in the reaction against federal civil rights initiatives, 'states' rights' served to preserve

the White supremacist status quo). *See also* Karen L. Cox, "What Changed in Charlottesville?" *New York Times*, August 11, 2019 (rejecting that the monument debate was "ever simply about 'Southern heritage,'" and concluding that "Confederate monuments can no longer be debated solely as objects of history, when they have become rallying points for a violent [White nationalist] movement"), accessed at https://www.nytimes.com/2019/08/11/opinion/confederate-monuments-charlottesville.html; Erika Doss, *Memorial Mania: Public Feeling in America* (Chicago: The University of Chicago Press, 2010), 361–62 (arguing that "the 'creed of heritage' is a historical fiction that 'thrives on ignorance and error' and 'falsified legacies' [and] that [c]ontemporary neo-Confederates who argue that rebel memorials . . . represent 'heritage not hate,' and should be venerated as historically neutral symbols of southern cultural identity, deny the secessionist South's unforgivable defense of slavery: which is why these memorials were made and what they mean); Doss, *Memorial Mania*, 371 (showing that Southern heritage supporters assert a belief in the superiority of America and American culture, by which they mean "monocultural Anglo European identity").

9. *See, e.g.*, Doss, *Memorial Mania*, 251 (concluding that "more and more people understand that we can support the troops while condemning the war").

10. See Schenck v. United States, 249 U.S. 47 (1919).

11. Nebraska Press Assn v. Stuart, 427 U.S. 539, 559 (1976) (stating that "Prior restraints on speech and publication are the most serious and least tolerable infringement on First Amendment rights").

12. See discussion at *New York Times Co. v. United States*, 403 U.S. 713 (1971).

13. Reynolds v. United States, 98 U.S. 145 (1878).

14. Employment Division v. Smith, 494 U.S. 872 (1990) (burden on the free exercise of religion permissible if the unintended result of laws that are generally applicable).

15. See C. Vann Woodward, *The Strange Career of Jim Crow*, commemorative ed. (New York: Oxford University Press [1955] 2002).

Introduction

1. *See* Jim Loewen, "Rockville's Confederate Monument Belongs at White's Ferry," *History News Network*, May 22, 2017, accessed at https://historynewsnetwork.org/blog/153908. Nor did the Rockville monument make any reference to Confederate General J. E. B. Stuart enslaving many African Americans near the site of the Rockville monument. *See* Allen C. Guelzo, *Gettysburg: The Last Invasion* (New York: Alfred A. Knopf, 2013), 98 (explaining that on June 27, 1863, near Rockville, Maryland, Stuart captured a large Union wagon train whose teamsters were "most[ly] negroes," some of whom were claimed to be runaway slaves and the rest Stuart viewed as "prizes [who] could be converted into high-value slave property in Richmond").

2. Mitch Landrieu, *In the Shadow of Statues: A White Southerner Confronts History* (New York: Viking, 2018) 172, 182.

3. Shelley Puhak, "Confederate Monuments and Tributes in the United States, Explained," in Catherine Clinton, ed., *Confederate Statues and Memorialization* (Athens: The University of Georgia Press, 2019) 89, 90 (excerpt from *Teen Vogue*, September 6, 2017, quoting New Orleans' former mayor Mitch Landrieu).

4. *See* Landrieu, *In the Shadow of Statues*, 34 (stating that the Confederate monuments in New Orleans "never reflected what the true society of New Orleans, generations ago, actually felt when they were built. The structures reflected what the people

who erected them, mostly ex-Confederate soldiers or sympathizers, believed because they had the power to build them and because they wanted to send a particular political message. They cast a dark and repressive shadow over my city and, in a way, held us back.").

5. *See* Allan Browne, "The Confederate Monument in Rockville," *Landmarks,* March 26, 2017, accessed at http://allenbrowne.blogspot.com/2017/03/confederate-monument-in-rockville.html; Bill Turque, "Confederate Statue Moved from Rockville Courthouse Over the Weekend," *Washington Post,* July 24, 2017, accessed at https://www.washingtonpost.com/local/md-politics/confederate-statue-moved-from-rockville-courthouse-over-the-weekend/2017/07/24/cc80fae4-70a1-11e7-9eac-d56bd5568db8_story.html.

6. See discussion of the application before the Rockville Historic District Commission at Andrew Metcalf, "Rockville Historic District Commission Grants County's Request to Move Confederate Statue," *Bethesda Magazine,* September 18, 2015, accessed at https://bethesdamagazine.com/bethesda-beat/news/rockville-historic-district-commission-grants-countys-request-to-move-confederate-statue/.

7. Southern Poverty Law Center, "Whose Heritage?: Public Symbols of the Confederacy," 10 (2016), accessed at https://www.splcenter.org/20160421/whose-heritage-public-symbols-confederacy (hereinafter 2016 "Whose Heritage"). That total was revised upward to 772 in June 2018. See Southern Poverty Law Center, "Whose Heritage: Public Symbols of the Confederacy (June 4, 2018), accessed at https://www.splcenter.org/20180604/whose-heritage-public-symbols-confederacy#findings (hereinafter 2018 "Whose Heritage").

8. *See* John J. Winberry, "'Lest We Forget:' The Confederate Monument and the Southern Townscape," 23 *Southeastern Geographer* 107, 108 (1983).

9. Winberry, "Lest We Forget," 110. A third type of monument is the grand-scale "hero monument" consisting of statuary depicting the likeness of some military or civilian hero of the Confederacy. The "big three" choices for hero monuments are Robert E. Lee, Thomas (Stonewall) Jackson, and Jefferson Davis, though in South Carolina, Wade Hampton III was a favorite. Hero monuments are far less common than the standing soldier monument and the obelisk. *See* Gaines M. Foster, *Ghosts of the Confederacy: Defeat, the Lost Cause, and the Emergence of the New South* (New York: Oxford University Press, 1987), 120; Cynthia Mills, "Introduction," in Cynthia Mills & Pamela H. Simpson, eds., *Monuments to the Lost Cause: Women, Art, and the Landscapes of Southern Memory* (Knoxville: The University of Tennessee Press, 2003), xix.

10. Four obelisks were raised between 1867 and 1869, three in cemeteries and one on a courthouse square. Two standing soldier monuments were raised in 1870, one in a cemetery and one on a courthouse square. Winberry, "Lest We Forget," 110. There are some, but very few, monuments raised by Confederate veterans in the 1860s commemorating a fallen leader. See Caroline E. Janney, *Remembering the Civil War: Reunion and the Limits of Reconciliation* (Chapel Hill: The University of North Carolina Press, 2013), 134–35.

11. *See* Southern Poverty Law Center, *2016 "Whose Heritage?"* 11.

12. Foster, *Ghosts of the Confederacy,* 158 (also concluding that between 1900–1912 few Confederate monuments had any funeral aspect to them and more than 85 percent were placed on courthouse squares, downtown intersections, or other public places).

13. James M. McPherson, "Long-Legged Yankee Lies: The Southern Textbook Crusade," in Alice Fahs and Joan Waugh, eds., *The Memory of the Civil War in American Culture* (Chapel Hill: The University of North Carolina Press, 2004), 65.

14. *See* Winberry, "Lest We Forget," 110–11 (also stating that, by contrast, 60 percent of cemetery monuments are dated *before* 1900).

15. Plessy v. Ferguson, 163 U.S. 537 (1896).

16. See discussion at Grace Elizabeth Hale, *Making Whiteness: The Culture of Segregation in the South, 1890–1940* (New York: Pantheon Books, 1998), 201–39 (explaining spectacle lynching as "a modern spectacle of enduring [White] power").

17. Eric Foner, *Who Owns History: Rethinking the Past in a Changing World* (New York: Hill & Wang, 2003), 200; Jon Meacham, *The Soul of America: The Battle for Our Better Angels* (New York: Random House, 2018), 104–11. Stone Mountain, over one-half mile wide and today one the South's most famous Confederate monuments, is a huge bas-relief covering the northern face of the mountain that depicts three legendary leaders of the Confederacy—Robert E. Lee, Stonewall Jackson and Jefferson Davis—all astride horses, all holding a hat over their hearts. *See* Grace Elizabeth Hale, "Granite Stopped Time: Stone Mountain Memorial and the Representation of White Southern Identity," in Mills and Simpson, *Monuments to the Lost Cause*, 219–29.

18. Brown v. Board of Education, 347 U.S. 483 (1954).

19. Terry McAuliffe, *Beyond Charlottesville: Taking a Stand Against White Nationalism* (New York: St. Martin's Press, 2019), 48–49 (explaining that "all the publicity of [Roof] and his incoherent ranting put the spotlight on a virulent new mix of neo-Nazism, White supremacy, and identification with the Confederate cause").

20. In 2017, the Charlottesville, Virginia, City Counsel proposed removing the equestrian statue of Robert E. Lee, located in a formerly racially segregated city-owned park. White supremacist/neo-Nazi activists who opposed the removal of the Lee statue organized the "Unite the Right" rally scheduled for Saturday, August 12, 2017. Heavily armed, some outfitted with guns, clubs, and bats, the rally participants unfurled Confederate battle flags, brandished swastikas, adopted White supremacy, racist, and anti-Semitic rhetoric, openly displayed Nazi salutes and asserted "the right of White people to organize for our interest." Protestors chanted "Jews will not replace us!" and "Our blood and our soil," an English translation of a Nazi slogan. Matt Thompson, "The Hoods Are Off," *The Atlantic*, August 12, 2017, accessed at https://www.theatlantic.com/national/archive/2017/08/the-hoods-are-off/536694/. *See also* Stephen F. Hayes, "Where are Trump's 'Very Fine People'?," *The Weekly Standard*, August 17, 2017, accessed at http://www.weeklystandard.com/hayes-where-are-trumps-very-fine-people/article/2009330.

21. *See* Libby Nelson, "'Why We Voted for Donald Trump': David Duke Explains the White Supremacist Charlottesville Protests, *Vox*, August 12, 2017, accessed at https://www.vox.com/2017/8/12/16138358/charlottesville-protests-david-duke-kkk; Paul Duggan, "Four Alleged Members of Hate Group Charged in 2017 'Unite the Right' Rally in Charlottesville," *Washington Post*, October 3, 2018, accessed at https://www.washingtonpost.com/local/public-safety/federal-officials-to-announce-additional-charges-in-2017-unite-the-right-rally-in-charlottesville/2018/10/02/60881262-c651-11e8-9b1c-a90f1daae309_story.html?utm_term=.d6bdoccb2f80.

22. Southern Poverty Law Center, *2018 "Whose Heritage."* Other investigators have verified many of these removals. *See, e.g.*, Christopher Carbone, "Which Confederate Statues Were Removed? A Running List," accessed at http://www.foxnews.com/us/2018/03/11/which-confederate-statues-were-removed-running-list.html. *See* Scott Bomboy, "Confederate Monuments Debate Heads to the Courts," *Constitution Daily*, January 30, 2018, accessed at https://constitutioncenter.org/blog/confederate-monuments

-debate-heads-to-the-courts (discussing state and federal court litigation involving alleged conflicts with state and local laws that protect war memorials).

23. *See* Gregory S. Schneider, "Richmond Monument Panel Urges Removing Jefferson Davis Statue," *Washington Post,* July 2, 2018, accessed at https://www.washingtonpost.com/local/virginia-politics/richmond-monument-panel-urges-removing-jefferson-davis-statue/2018/07/02/73636904-7e17-11e8-bb6b-c1cb691f1402_story.html?utm_term=.c470ef07ea15; Michael Levenson, "Protesters Topple Statue of Jefferson Davis on Richmond's Monument Avenue," *New York Times,* June 11, 2020, accessed at https://www.nytimes.com/2020/06/11/us/Jefferson-Davis-Statue-Richmond.html.

24. In response to a suit brought by the Sons of Confederate Veterans, the University of North Carolina agreed to transfer ownership of the statue to the North Carolina Division of the Sons of Confederate Veterans (SCV). The settlement included the University's agreement to fund a $2.5 million charitable trust with private funds, to be used for care and preservation of the statue. In turn, the SCV agreed that the statue would not be displayed in any county in which the University has a campus. In November 2019, a North Carolina Superior Court Judge approved the settlement but on February 12, 2020 voided it on the ground that the SCV "lacked standing" to sue. The SCV was ordered to return the statue to the University and also to return most of trust's funds. See Susan Svrluga, "Silent Sam Will Stay Off the University of North Carolina Campus as the School Turns the Statue Over to a Confederate Group," *Washington Post,* November 27, 2019, accessed at https://www.washingtonpost.com/education/2019/11/27/silent-sam-will-stay-off-university-north-Carolina-campus-school-turns-statue-over-confederate-group/; Michael Levenson, "Toppled But Not Gone: UNC Grapples Anew With the Fate of Silent Sam," *New York Times,* February 14, 2020, accessed at https://www.nytimes.com/2020/02/14/us/unc-silent-sam-statue-settlement.html/.

25. *See* Jordan Green, "N.C. Ban on Removal of Confederate Monuments Is Challenged As Local Councils Continue to Bring Down Statues," *Washington Post,* November 30, 2019, accessed at https://www.washingtonpost.com/national/nc-ban-on-removal-of-confederate-monuments-is-challenged-as-local-councils-continue-to-bring-down-statues/2019/11/29/ab45fe0a-1050-11ea-9cd7-a1becbc82f5e_story.html; Susan Svrluga, "Silent Sam Will Stay Off the University of North Carolina Campus as the School Turns the Statue Over to a Confederate Group," *Washington Post,* November 27, 2019, accessed at https://www.washingtonpost.com/education/2019/11/27/silent-sam-will-stay-off-university-north-Carolina-campus-school-turns-statue-over-confederate-group/.

26. Nor is the removal movement focused on monuments located in Civil War battlefield parks, in museums, or on private property. *See, e.g.,* Sanford Levinson, *Written in Stone: Public Monuments in Changing Societies* (Durham, NC: Duke University Press, 1998), 42, 113 (explaining that Confederate monuments in museums, Civil War battlefields and in cemeteries are not controversial due to their context: cemetery memorials' original purpose was grieving and mourning, they are not normally associated with government imprimatur of the message transmitted by the monument, there is no "captive audience" forced to view them, unlike monuments in a city center, and these monuments are far less likely to breed conflict).

27. Southern Poverty Law Center, *2016 "Whose Heritage?"* 1 (emphasis added).

28. *See* Daniel J. Sherman, "Art, Commerce, and the Production of Memory in France after World War I," in John R. Gillis, ed., *Commemorations: The Politics of National Identity* (Princeton, NJ: Princeton University Press, 1994), 190.

29. Sanford Levinson, "Silencing the Past: Public Monuments and the Tutelary State," 16 *Philosophy and Public Policy Quarterly* 6, 7 (1996).

30. Caroline Janney has argued that some Confederate cemetery monuments did convey a powerful political message. For example, an imposing ninety-foot stone pyramid erected by the Richmond Ladies' Memorial Association in Richmond's Hollywood Cemetery is inscribed "'To the Confederate Dead' and 'Numini et patriae asto' (in eternal memory of those who stood for God and country.") Such calls for ongoing loyalty to the Confederacy was a political call for Confederate nationalism. Yet, location in a cemetery denotes that a monument's primary role is bereavement. *See* Janney, *Remembering the Civil War*, 135 & 135 n. 6.

Chapter 1: History and Memory Distinguished

1. Joseph J. Ellis, *American Sphinx: The Character of Thomas Jefferson* (New York: Alfred A. Knopf, 1996), 21–23, 258–62.

2. See discussion at Eric Foner, *The Fiery Trial: Abraham Lincoln and American Slavery* (New York: W.W. Norton & Co., 2011), 25–26.

3. *See* James McPherson, *The War That Forged a Nation: Why the Civil War Still Matters* (New York: Oxford University Press, 2015), 110–11 (reporting that with respect to what to do about slavery, Lincoln said in 1854 in his famous Peoria speech that, "My first impulse would be to free all the slaves, and send them to Liberia" and in fact Lincoln initiated a program of sending freed slaves to Liberia but few wanted to go).

4. *See* Gary W. Gallagher, "Round Table on Confederate Statues and Memorialization," in Catherine Clinton, ed., *Confederate Statues and Memorialization* (Athens: University of Georgia Press, 2019), 56.

5. Cynthia Mills, "Introduction," in Cynthia Mills & Pamela H. Simpson, eds., *Monuments to the Lost Cause: Women, Art, and the Landscapes of Southern Memory* (Knoxville: The University of Tennessee Press, 2003), xv.

6. *See* Brian Black and Bryn Varley, "Contesting the Sacred: Preservation and Meaning on Richmond's Monument Avenue," in Mills and Simpson, eds., *Monuments to the Lost Cause*, 235.

7. John R. Gillis, "Introduction, Memory and Identity: The History of a Relationship," in John R. Gillis, ed., *Commemorations: The Politics of National Identity* (Princeton, NJ: Princeton University Press, 1994), 3.

8. Eric Hobsbawm, "Introduction: Inventing Traditions," in Eric Hobsbawm and Terence Ranger, eds., *The Invention of Tradition* (New York: Cambridge University Press, 1983), 13. Maurice Halbwachs created the "foundational framework for the study of societal remembrance" what he called "collective memory." Halbwachs showed that "all individual memory was constructed within social structures and institutions . . . Individuals organize and understand events and concepts within a social context, thus they then remember them in a way that "rationally" orders and organizes them through that same social construction." See discussion at Dee Britton, "What is Collective Memory," *Memory Worlds*, accessed at https://memorialworlds.com/what-is-collective-memory/.

9. *See* Dee Britton, "What is Collective Memory;" John Bodnar, *Remaking America: Public Memory, Commemoration, and Patriotism in the Twentieth Century* (Princeton, NJ: Princeton University Press, 1992), 13 (explaining that in an effort to maintain social unity and loyalty to the status quo, cultural leaders or authorities advance interpretations of

the past that "reduce the power of competing interests that threaten the attainment of their goals").

10. See discussion of subjective layers of meaning in Black and Varley, "Contesting the Sacred," 236.

11. *See* Hobsbawm and Ranger, *The Invention of Tradition*, 1–2.

Chapter 2: Distortion-of-History Approach

1. Sanford Levinson, *Written in Stone: Public Monuments in Changing Societies* (Durham, NC: Duke University Press, 1998), 59 (source of the 1:50 estimate); Civil War Trust, *History: Civil War Casualties,* accessed at https://www.civilwar.org/learn/articles/civil-war-casualties (same). Binghamton University historian J. David Hacker's research reveals that the Civil War's dead numbered about 750,000, an estimate that is 20 percent higher than conventional calculations. Rachel Coker, "Historian Revises Estimate of Civil War Dead," *Discover-e Binghamton Research,* September 21, 2011, accessed at https://discovere.binghamton.edu/news/civilwar-3826.html; J. David Hacker, "A Census-based Count of the Civil War Dead," 57 *Civil War History* 307–48 (2011). Richard White, states that "somewhere between 650,000 and 850,000 men died in the Civil War, with a reasonable figure being about 752,000. Richard White, *The Republic for Which It Stands: The United States During Reconstruction and the Gilded Age, 1865–1896* (New York: Oxford University Press, 2017), 28 & n 13. Caroline Janney has adopted 750,000 as the number of dead. Caroline E. Janney, *Remembering the Civil War: Reunion and the Limits of Reconciliation* (Chapel Hill: The University of North Carolina Press, 2013), 30.

2. David W. Blight, "Decoration Days: The Origins of Memorial Day in North and South," in Alice Fahs and Joan Waugh, eds., *The Memory of the Civil War in American Culture* (Chapel Hill: The University of North Carolina Press, 2004), 94; (source of number of Black soldiers in the Union army). The estimates of the percentage of military age dead is from White, *The Republic for Which It Stands,* 28 & 28 n. 13.

3. Civil War Trust, *History: Civil War Casualties.* It is estimated that 50,000 limbs were amputated during the Civil War. See Emily Baumgaertner, "Newly Discovered 'Limb Pit' Reveals Civil War Surgeons' Bitter Choices," *New York Times,* June 20, 2018, accessed at https://www.nytimes.com/2018/06/20/science/civil-war-archaeology-bones-limbs.html.

4. McPherson, *The War That Forged a Nation,* 62.

5. *See* Alan T. Nolan, "The Anatomy of the Myth," in Gary W. Gallagher and Alan T. Nolan, eds., *The Myth of the Lost Cause and Civil War Memory* (Bloomington: Indiana University Press, 2000), 13 (citing James McPherson's summary of the cost of the War to the South found in James M. McPherson, *Ordeal by Fire,* (New York: Alfred A. Knopf, 1982), 476); J. Michael Martinez & Robert M. Harris, "Graves, Worms, and Epitaphs," in J. Michael Martinez, William D. Richardson & Ron McNinch-Su, eds., *Confederate Symbols in the Contemporary South* (Gainesville: University Press of Florida, 2000), 137–38 (stating that the South's share of the national wealth fell from 30 percent in 1860 to 12 percent in 1870 and per capita income in the South after the War fell to less than 40 percent of the Northern average where it remained throughout the nineteenth century).

6. Bruce Levine, *The Fall of the House of Dixie* (New York: Random House, 2013), 3–4.

7. White, *The Republic for Which It Stands,* 13, 23, 30.

8. As Confederate General Patrick R. Cleburne explained soon after the end of the Civil War, losing the war meant that unless the South intervened to massage the

historical record, Southern children will learn the version of the war as written in Northern school books and will learn "to regard our gallant dead as traitors, our maimed veterans as fit objects for derision," Quoted in Lochlainn Seabrook, *Confederate Monuments* (Nashville: Sea Raven Press, 2018), 25.

9. Gaines M. Foster, *Ghosts of the Confederacy: Defeat, the Lost Cause, and the Emergence of the New South* (New York: Oxford University Press, 1987), 3, 22–23, 86. Anxiety over claims that Confederates had acted dishonorably by prosecuting the Civil War had some foundation in accusations coming from other Southerners. For example, J. T. James, an ex-Confederate officer, found God after the war, became a Methodist minister, and circulated a pamphlet castigating the South and calling upon it to repent for waging a war to destroy the American Union, for bringing so much pain to the souls and bodies of those millions it had enslaved, and for undermining the Christian faith in the South. Another Southerner, Rebecca Latimer Felton, in her 1911 book *My Memoirs of Georgia Politics*, argued that secession was wrong, the war had been fought entirely over slavery, and Confederate leaders had misled their citizens in this regard for their own political aggrandizement but also praising the courage of the Confederate soldier. See discussion at Foster, *Ghosts of the Confederacy*, 115 & 115 nn. 1 & 2.

10. In June 1865, a Norfolk grand jury indicted Robert E. Lee for treason, one of thirty-seven ex-Confederate officials whom this grand jury indicted for treason that day. Jefferson Davis had already been indicted for treason, as had John Breckinridge, Confederate secretary of war and former U.S. vice-president under James Buchanan. Article II, section 3 of the United States Constitution provides for punishment for treason, defined as "levying war against [the United States] or in adhering to their enemies, giving them aid and comfort." Lee was indicted for levying war against the state of Virginia, the clearest charge since his Army of Northern Virginia had focused its efforts in the state of Virginia. Lee's invaded Maryland in September 1862, culminating in the Battle of Antietam (Sharpsburg). Thus, treason against the state of Maryland also would have constituted a credible treason charge against Lee. In the *Prize Cases*, 67 U.S. 635 (1863), the Supreme Court had ruled in another context that secession was not a constitutional right, that the Civil War was a "domestic insurrection," and the Confederacy was, thus, not a sovereign power. Given the ruling in the *Prize Cases*, it is likely that the court would have ruled that Confederate leaders were not officials of a sovereign nation and thus could be charged with treason. The question was never adjudicated, however, because none of those indicted were brought to trial for treason, and just prior to leaving office President Johnson pardoned all of them, including Lee who finally was pardoned in the general pardon and amnesty issued on Christmas Day 1868. The 1868 Christmas pardon provided pardon "for the offense of treason against the United States." Even with this pardon, Lee was prevented from holding public office due to the provision in section 3 of the Constitution's Fourteenth Amendment that provides that "No person shall . . . hold any [public] office . . . who, having previously taken an oath as . . . an officer of the United States . . . shall have engaged in insurrection or rebellion against the same, or given aid or comfort to the enemies thereof." *See* John Reeves, *The Lost Indictment of Robert E. Lee: The Forgotten Case against an American Icon* (Lanham, MD: Rowman & Littlefield, 2018), 49, 59–60, 63, 184–85.

11. William A. Blair, *Cities of the Dead: Contesting the Memory of the Civil War in the South, 1865–1914* (Chapel Hill: University of North Carolina Press, 2004), 155–61. *See also* Reeves, *The Lost Indictment of Robert E. Lee*, 16 (pointing out that Lee lacked money for

college and chose West Point at least in part because it provided him a free education).

12. Foster, *Ghosts of the Confederacy*, 26–29, 33, 46.

13. *See* Nolan, "The Anatomy of the Myth," 13; Foster, *Ghosts of the Confederacy* 14, 22, 25–26 & 25, n 8.

14. Foster, *Ghosts of the Confederacy*, 33–34, 66, 194 (concluding that Southerners would not feel fully recognized as equal partners by the North and reconcile unless the North acknowledged the heroism of the Confederate soldier and nobility of the Confederate war effort, and made sincere overtures of respect for the honor of the South). Disquiet and defensiveness reflecting a fear of opprobrium from Northerners was well-grounded for many in the North condemned the ex-Confederates as murderers and traitors, a view of them that challenged Southerners' confidence in their righteousness, honor, and manliness." Foster, *Ghosts of the Confederacy*, 35. Alan Nolan is quite explicit in arguing that ex-Confederates, in particular Jubal Early, "intentionally created the principles and misinformation of the Lost Cause" in order to "hide the Southerners' tragic and self-destructive mistake." Nolan, "The Anatomy of the Myth," 14.

15. Dell Upton, *What Can and Can't Be Said: Race Uplift and Monument Building in the Confederate South* (New Haven, CT: Yale University Press, 2015), 27 (showing that Decoration Day festivities "at first quietly and later more openly [became] occasions for the declaration of continued loyalty to the Southern cause."); Cynthia Mills, "Introduction," in Mills and Simpson, *Monuments to the Lost Cause*, xvi (same).

16. On August 14, 1873, Early had delivered the keynote address at a meeting at White Sulphur Springs attended by fifty-four delegates from twelve states. There, he wove together an heroic narrative of Confederate patriots whose secession was just and honorable, an effort to create a nation and demand their rights and vindicate the constitutional freedoms for which their forefathers had fought. In Early's rendition, the South had fought heroically and nobly until finally worn down by the North's overwhelming numbers and resources. With some refinements, this romantic narrative became the Lost Cause tradition, a "usable past" that vindicated the failed choices made during the Civil War and assisted in ex-Confederates' struggle to overcome Reconstruction. Blight, "Decoration Days," 107.

17. Foster, *Ghosts of the Confederacy*, 47–49, 54–57.

18. Foster, *Ghosts of the Confederacy*, 60.

19. Edward Bonekemper asserts that "the myth of the Lost Cause may have been the most successful propaganda campaign in American history. For almost 150 years it has shaped our view of causation and fighting of the Civil War." But, he argues, it was just a myth—"a false concoction intended to justify the Civil War and the South's expending so much energy and blood in defense of slavery." Edward H. Bonekemper III, *The Myth of the Lost Cause* (Washington, DC: Regnery History, 2015), 255.

20. Foster, *Ghosts of the Confederacy*, 23, 49, 117–18.

21. Quoted in James McPherson, *The War That Forged a Nation*, 10.

22. President James Buchanan, a Southerner and Lincoln's immediate predecessor, made plain in his final message to Congress in December 1860 that the Southern states possessed no constitutional right to secede. No state at its pleasure could dissolve the Union. Even the Articles of Confederation had stated that "the Union shall be perpetual" and the United States Constitution was adopted to form "a *more* perfect Union" than the Articles of Confederation had created. See discussion at James M. McPherson, *Battle Cry of Freedom: The Civil War Era* (New York: Oxford University Press, 1988), 246.

23. *See, e.g.*, Cooper v. Aaron, 358 U.S. 1 (1958) (holding that state courts are bound to enforce the United States Supreme Court's constitutional interpretations even if it disagrees with them); Bush v. Orleans Parish School Board, 364 U.S. 500 (1960) (state legislature may not ban school desegregation in contravention of an order of a federal district court); Ableman v. Booth, 62 U.S. 506 (1859) (state courts cannot issue rulings on federal law that contradict the decisions of federal courts); United States v. Peters, 9 U.S. (5 Cranch) 115, 115 (1809) (state legislature lacks power to nullify a judgment of a federal court because otherwise "the Constitution itself becomes a solemn mockery, and the nation is deprived of the means of enforcing its laws by the instrumentality of its own tribunals").

24. Prize Cases, 67 U.S. (2 Black) 635 (1863).

25. Texas v. White, 74 U.S. (7 Wall.) 700 (1869).

26. *See* John Reeves, *The Lost Indictment of Robert E. Lee: The Forgotten Case Against an American Icon* (Lanham, MD: Rowman & Littlefield, 2018).

27. Sanford Levinson is acknowledged as one of America's most distinguished constitutional scholars, justifiably esteemed for his many insights into our constitutional system of government. Levinson has stated that he would be willing "to proffer a defense of the legitimacy of secession [both] as a general proposition of normative political theory [and] also willing to defend its plausibility even within our particular political system" assuming that a decision to secede resulted from a democratic deliberation and consent of those seceding. Levinson offers the view that it is "not . . . impossible" to provide the Constitutional interpretation that would permit secession and agrees that perhaps Lincoln possessed "more than a trace of 'union mysticism.'" But Levinson agrees that the Civil War and its prodigious loss of life "profoundly shaped" a national decision to reject the possibility of secession today. And he agrees that his offerings on the subject of secession are "musings" that cannot override the reality that the South's attempt to maintain the system of chattel slavery was a sufficient justification "for the suppression of the Southern effort to gain political independence." *See* Levinson, *Written in Stone*, 59–60.

28. *See* Cynthia Mills, "Introduction," in Mills & Simpson, eds., *Monuments to the Lost Cause*, 15–20 (stating that denial of the causal role of slavery in the South's decision to secede and wage war became "a cardinal element of the Southern apologia" (citing Robert F. Durden, *The Gray and the Black* [Baton Rouge: Louisiana State University Press, 1972]); Kirk Savage, *Standing Soldiers, Kneeling Slaves: Race, War, and Monument in Nineteenth Century America* (Princeton, NJ: Princeton University Press, 1997), 129 (observing that "within a remarkably short period of time, White Southerners were not only repudiating the institution [of slavery] that had been central to their society but writing it out of their history of the war [and] a massive and deliberate process of collective forgetting took place.").

29. The South invested considerable intellectual energy laying out a defense of slavery, relying mostly on pseudoscientific-based arguments "that people of African ancestry were inherently biologically inferior and that the racial inferiority of Blacks relegated them to permanently diminished status." The South also defended slavery based on historical arguments (the Greeks and Romans had slavery) and based on the Bible. See Paul Finkelman, *Defending Slavery: Proslavery Thought in the Old South: A Brief History with Documents* (Boston: Bedford/St. Martin's Press, 2003), 5, 6–7, 10–12, 96–128.

30. W. J. Cash argued that Southerners strongly sensed that slavery was not morally defensible and felt shame and guilt because of their participation in the system of human bondage but were not prepared to abandon the benefits of slavery. Therefore, the South mounted a defense to justify itself by constructing "romantic fictions" about slavery. W. J. Cash, *The Mind of the South* (New York: Alfred A. Knopf, Inc., 1941), 73, accessed at https://archive.org/stream/in.ernet.dli.2015.182957/2015.182957.The-Mind-Of-The-South_djvu.txt.

31. Foster, *Ghosts of the Confederacy*, 119 (quoting Hunter McGuire writing to the Grand Camp of Confederate Veterans of Virginia in 1899). *See also* Nolan, "The Anatomy of the Lost Cause," 15 (quoting James L. Roark, *Masters Without Slaves: Southern Planters in the Civil War and Reconstruction* (New York: W. W. Norton, 1977), 195 and stating that "postwar Southerners manifested 'a nearly universal desire to escape the ignominy to slavery'"); Gary W. Gallagher, "Jubal A. Early, the Lost Cause, and Civil War History," in Gallagher and Nolan, *The Myth of the Lost Cause*, 35, 36 (concluding that Early had a "passionate interest in how the future would judge the Confederacy").

32. Upton, *What Can and Can't Be Said*, 18, 31–32 (showing that the early-twentieth-century Confederate memorial landscape was dedicated to "recast[ing] the war as a violent contest among White men over high political principles having nothing to do with slavery"); Foster, *Ghosts of the Confederacy*, 24, 49 (concluding that most ex-Confederate believed that "secession and slavery had measured up to God's moral standards" but feared that posterity would come to an opposite conclusion).

33. Alan Nolan, who tends to speak more directly than some other historians, states that "the assertion . . . of the insignificance of slavery in the sectional conflict seems outrageous and disingenuous in the light of nineteenth-century American political history." Nolan, "The Anatomy of the Lost Cause," 19, 27 (listing extensive evidence of the centrality of slavery in causing the Civil War).

34. *See* Jon Meacham, *The Soul of America: The Battle for Our Better Angels* (New York: Random House, 2018), 54 (concluding that "restrictions on the expansion of slavery lay at the heart of the Republican claim to power"). Among other things, failure to extend slavery to the territories checked the South's political power. Free states would weaken the slaveholder power in Congress. Plus, with more non-slave states there were more states to which the South's slave could flee. See Levine, *The Fall of the House of Dixie*, 34–37.

35. Bonekemper, *The Myth of the Lost Cause*, 33, 35. Slavery expansion was the overarching political controversy of the pre- Civil War period. Most of the slave states seceded due to the anxiety that Lincoln's election threatened the long-term survival of slavery. Moreover, with an independent slaveholding republic, slave owners could confidently look forward to expanding slavery, through acquisition of new territory, into places such as Cuba, more of Mexico, Central America, and even some of the territories acquired by the United States in its war with Mexico. McPherson, *The War That Forged a Nation*, 8, 20–31. *See also* McPherson, *Battle Cry of Freedom*, 52, 241 (demonstrating that prior to the Civil War, slave owners had expanded slave-grown cotton into river valleys of New Mexico and demanded the "liberty" to transfer their slave property, and thus expand slavery, into California and other Western territories to provide labor in mines).

36. *See* Paul Finkelman, *Defending Slavery, 89–95 (emphasis added)* (reprinting the entire "cornerstone" speech). Robert Jeffrey concludes that to defend slavery, Confederate

political and social theory necessarily had to reject natural law's equality principle that "all men are created equal." Jeffrey thus concludes that "the centrality of the rejection of political equality as a regime principle makes one wonder about the claims always made by such partisans that the constitutional issues surrounding state sovereignty were ultimately decisive in the breakup of the Union." Robert C. Jeffrey, "Southern Political Thought and The Southern Political Tradition," in Martinez, et al., *Confederate Symbols in the Contemporary South*, 33–34.

37. The three conditions Georgia placed on not seceding were: respect and uphold the conditions of the compromise of 1859, especially the fugitive slave law; abandon all attempts to ban slavery in Washington, DC, and the territories; and Northern congressmen must be prepared to admit additional slave states into the Union. Levine, *The Fall of the House of Dixie*, 39–40.

38. See discussion at Reeves, *The Lost Indictment of Robert E. Lee*, 27 (emphasis added). This statement coincided with Davis's view that "one of the incidents that led to our withdrawal from the Union was the apprehension that under President Lincoln it was the intention of the United States government to violate the constitutional right of each State to adopt and maintain, to reject or abolish slavery, as it pleased." Quoted at Seabrook, *Confederate Monuments*, 37.

39. Quoted at Levine, *The Fall of the House of Dixie*, 82.

40. Bonekemper, *The Myth of the Lost Cause*, 38, 40–44.

41. Bonekemper, *The Myth of the Lost Cause*, 47–48, 66–67 (citing Charles B. Dew, *Apostles of Disunion: Southern Secession Commissioners and the Causes of the Civil War* (Charlottesville: University Press of Virginia, 2001), 18–19, 32–89 and stating that the commissioners advanced three arguments: the threat of racial equality (the need to preserve the racial foundations of the country's founding as a White supremacist Republic); the threat of race war (the inevitable result of the North's advocacy for racial equality); and the peril of racial amalgamation (racial equality inevitably would lead to a mixing of the races and a threat to the "purity" of Southern women).

42. Bonekemper, *The Myth of the Lost Cause*, 38, 40.

43. *See, e.g.*, Keith S. Bohannon, "'These Few Gray-Haired, Battle-Scarred Veterans:' Confederate Army Reunions in Georgia, 1885–95," in Gallagher and Nolan, *The Myth of the Lost Cause*, 96 (citing references by Confederate veterans at Confederate reunions linking secession with the preservation of slavery such as a Confederate veteran who stated that Northern abolition ideology threatened "the civilization of the South and the purity of our blood and the integrity of our race" and a reunion speaker, a former Confederate officer, who declared that "we fought . . . for the supremacy of the White race in America.").

44. Foster, *Ghosts of the Confederacy*, 23–24, 73. Immediately after the end of the Civil War, both Confederate generals Jubal A. Early and John S. Mosby, "readily admitted that slavery had been the cornerstone of their short-lived nation." Janney, *Remembering the Civil War*, 8.

45. Meacham, *The Soul of America*, 59.

46. Savage, *Standing Soldiers, Kneeling Slaves*, 129 (citing Drew Gilpin Faust, *The Creation of Confederate Nationalism: Ideology and Identity in the Civil War South* (Baton Rouge: Louisiana State University Press, 1988), 59–60).

47. See discussion at John M. Coski, "The Confederate Battle Flag in Historical Perspective," in Martinez, et al., *Confederate Symbols in the Contemporary South*, 89, 96.

48. Joseph Gerteis, *Class and the Color Line: Interracial, Class Coalition in the Knights of Labor and the Populist Movement* (Durham, NC: Duke University Press, 2007), 38.

49. *See* Bonekemper, *The Myth of the Lost Cause*, 28–29, 256 (discussing the "social value of slavery). South Carolina planter and state senator, John Townsend, captured the core of the social value of slavery when he explained that "the color of the White man is now, in the South, a title of nobility in his relations as to the negro. . . . In the Southern slaveholding states, . . . the color of the Black race becomes the badge of inferiority, and the poorest non-slaveholder may rejoice with the richest of his brethren of the White race, in the distinction of color." Quoted in Gordon Rhea, "Address to the Charleston Library Society," January 25, 2011, accessed at https://www.battlefields.org/learn/articles/why-non-slaveholding-southerners-fought. *See also* Bonekemper, *The Myth of the Lost Cause*, 28 & n. 73 (also quoting portion of the Townsend statement).

50. *See* discussion at Joe R. Feagin, *Racist America: Roots, Current Realities, and Future Reparations* (3rd ed.) (New York: Routledge, 2014), 12 (discussing Whites' incentive to preserve the societal structures that provide them "economic and other social privileges often inherited from their ancestors").

51. Meacham, *The Soul of America*, 69.

52. Compare Coski, "The Confederate Battle Flag in Historical Perspective," 96 & 96 n. 28 (concluding that defense of house and region from Northern armies was a prime motive for Confederate enlisted personnel and citing authority) *with* Faust, *The Creation of Confederate Nationalism* (advancing a forceful argument for the centrality of slavery in the creation of Confederate nationalism). Edward Bonekemper points out that "non-slavery rationales for the Civil War certainly are not dead." As recently as the 1988 foreword to a republished edition of Pollard's, *The Lost Cause*, the writer states that of all the reasons advanced for the cause of the Civil War, the "common denominator" was "the growing disaffection between the North and South as they evolved into separate political entities [and] a difference in interpretation of the United States Constitution." Bonekemper, *The Myth of the Lost Cause*, 32–33. *See also* David Kennedy, "Editor's Introduction" to White, *The Republic for Which It Stands* (concluding that "the status of slavery in the far western territories [secured] from Mexico in 1848 had been the proximate cause of the Civil War"); White, *The Republic for Which It Stands*, 13 & 13 n. 5 (concluding that "without slavery there would have been no war. The South fought in defense of slavery; it said so, vociferously and repeatedly").

53. *See* discussion at Levine, *The Fall of the House of Dixie*, 54–56, 78.

54. Bonekemper, *The Myth of the Lost Cause*, 71–72 (explaining Jefferson Davis's assertion fifteen years after the Civil War that the sectional differences were not over slavery; they would have manifested themselves "just as certainly if slavery had not existed . . . or if there had not been a negro in America. . . . The existence of African servitude was in no way the cause of the conflict"). John Coski has stated that "The clearest argument for the centrality of slavery in the formation of the Confederacy is Drew Gilpin Faust, *The Creation of Confederate Nationalism: Ideology and Identity in the Civil War South* (Baton Rouge: Louisiana State University Press, 1988)." *See* Coski, "The Confederate Battle Flag in Historical Perspective," 96 n. 28. *See* Levine, *The Fall of the House of Dixie*, 247 for an argument that only in the last months of the war did the Davis government change the entire substance of the cause of the war, from insulating slavery from the anti-slavery electorate in the North to arguing, for the first time, that the war only was begun to enable the South to preserve "the vindication of our rights to self-government and independence."

55. Lochlainn Seabrook has collected dozens of examples of Confederate monument inscriptions. None reference the defense of slavery as a cause of the war. Rather, in various phrasings, Confederate monument inscriptions plead, as one inscription puts it, for a "just judgment of the cause" for which Confederate soldiers fought. Or inscriptions simply proclaim that the South fought for the "righteous cause.... to keep their country free" or, as another states, "Never braver bled for brighter lands nor brighter land had a cause so grand," or as another states, "They died for right." Seabrook shows that Southern leaders raised monuments with these political purpose in mind, for as one monument states, it stands to tell "The story of the glory of the men who wore the gray." One Confederate monument inscription states the typical refrain found on many other Confederate monuments, that "They gave their lives for us . . . for the rights of the States . . . as they were handed down to us by the Fathers of our common country." See Seabrook, *Confederate Monuments*, 92, 129, 378, 386.

56. *See, e.g.,* Anne C. Bailey, *The Weeping Time: Memory and the Largest Slave Auction in American History* (New York: Cambridge University Press, 2017), 3 (detailing the 1859 slave auction, the largest in American history, of 436 men, women, and children sold by the Butler Plantation estates, the destruction of slave families that resulted, and the "searching earnestly for their loved ones" following Emancipation).

57. *See* Levine, *The Fall of the House of Dixie*, 29; Bonekemper, *The Myth of the Lost Cause*, 14–15, 255–56.

58. *See* Finkelman, *Defending Slavery*, 10, 35; Bonekemper, *The Myth of the Lost Cause*, 15–16 & 16, n. 32.

59. *See* Cash, *The Mind of the South*, 83.

60. See discussion at White, *The Republic for Which It Stands*, 30.

61. Bonekemper, *The Myth of the Lost Cause*, 9–13; Cynthia Mills, "Introduction," in Mills and Simpson, *Monuments to the Lost Cause*, xviii (explaining that the Lost Cause narrative argued that slavery was a benevolent institution for slaves; slaves were generally happy and, in return, were loyal and faithful to their masters).

62. Grace Elizabeth Hale, *Making Whiteness: The Culture of Segregation in the South, 1890–1940* (New York: Pantheon Books, 1998), 48, 54.

63. See discussion at Finkelman, *Defending Slavery*, 11, 39, 160.

64. Finkelman, *Defending Slavery*, 87 (quoting from South Carolina Senator James Henry Hammond's "Mudsill Speech," delivered in the Senate of the United States, March 4, 1858).

65. The instrumental aspects of the faithful slave myth are discussed at Micki McElya, "Commemorating the Color Line: The National Mammy Controversy of the 1920s," in Mills and Simpson, *Monuments to the Lost Cause*, 203, 205.

66. Blight, "Decoration Days," 106–07.

67. *See* Mills, "Introduction," in Mills and Simpson, *Monuments to the Lost Cause*, xvii–xviii; Foster, *Ghosts of the Confederacy*, 51, 57–58, 119–120. As for Gettysburg, the Lost Cause myth made Confederate Lieutenant General James Longstreet the scapegoat, attributing the loss of that battle to his alleged lateness in initiating his attack on the second day of the battle. Longstreet was *persona non grata* to many ex-Confederates, and no statue was ever raised to him, due to his early reconciliation with the North and belief that the South should cooperate with the Republican Party as a way to control the vote of the freedmen. *See* Jeffrey D. Wert, "James Longstreet and the Lost Cause," in Gallagher and Nolan, *The Myth of the Lost Cause*, 127, 129–31.

68. *See* Foster, *Ghosts of the Confederacy,* 57–59.

69. Catherine W. Bishir, "'A Strong Force of Ladies:' Women, Politics, and Confederate Memorial Associations in the Nineteenth Century," in Mills and Simpson, *Monuments to the Lost Cause,* 22–23; David Currey, "The Virtuous Soldier: Constructing a Usable Confederate Past in Franklin, Tennessee," in Mills and Simpson, *Monuments to the Lost Cause* 133, 135–36.

70. W. Fitzhugh Brundage, *The Southern Past: A Clash of Race and Memory* (Cambridge, MA: The Belknap Press of Harvard University Press, 2005), 25–27, 42. *See also* Caroline E. Janney, *Burying the Dead But Not the Past: Ladies Memorial Associations & the Lost Cause* (Chapel Hill: The University of North Carolina Press, 2008), 102–03, 106 (the death of Lee reinvigorated the Confederate memorial movement as memorialization moved "into a more celebratory stage"); Blight, "Decoration Days," 105 (concluding that "by the 1890s hardly a city square, town green, or even some one-horse cross-roads lacked a Civil War memorial of some kind").

71. City of Charlottesville, "Blue Ribbon Commission on Race, Memorials, and Public Spaces: Report to City Council," December 19, 2016, accessed at https://www.charlottesville.org/departments-and-services/boards-and-commissions/blue-ribbon-commissions/blue-ribbon-commission-on-race-memorials-and-public-spaces.

72. See discussion at Blair, *Cities of the Dead,* 127; Foster, *Ghosts of the Confederacy,* 195.

73. Blight, *"Decoration Days,"* 107–08.

74. Blight, *"Decoration Days,"* 110.

75. Blair, *Cities of the Dead,* 118–120, 127; Blight, *"Decoration Days,"* 109–11; Foster, *Ghosts of the Confederacy,* 60.

76. Foster, *Ghosts of the Confederacy,* 104–12 (reporting that by 1896, the UCV had 850 chapters (camps) and 1565 camps by 1904 and while total UCV membership was unclear, one reliable estimate in 1903 found that membership was between 80,000 and 85,000 (about ¼ to ⅓ of all surviving Confederate veterans as of 1903).

77. Blair, *Cities of the Dead,* 51 (stating that Lee both avoided and discouraged Confederate memorial activities).

78. Janney, *Burying the Dead,* 105–09; W. Fitzhugh Brundage, "'Women's Hand and Heart of Deathless Love:' White Women and the Commemorative Impulse in the New South," in Mills and Simpson, *Monuments to the Lost Cause,* 74–75.

79. Caroline E. Janney, *Remembering the Civil War: Reunion and the Limits of Reconciliation* (Chapel Hill: The University of North Carolina Press, 2013), 181–82 (stating that Lee was the "epitome" of the Cult of the Lost Cause and describing how the unveiling and dedication of the Lee monument was viewed as a celebration of Confederate nationalism).

80. Janney, *Burying the Dead,* 111–119, 140–41 (explaining that the male group was led by Jubal Early who desired the approbation and vindication he would achieve by reuniting veterans to win the postwar debate over the "proper" memory of the war and by males leading a successful effort to create a memorial to Lee, which would vindicate male honor—manhood—of the those who had done the fighting but were humiliated by their loss to the North). While the Richmond groups were quarreling over control of the Lee monument, Confederate veterans in New Orleans completed and dedicated a memorial to Lee in 1884. See discussion at Janney, *Burying the Dead,* 118.

81. *See* Savage, *Standing Soldiers, Kneeling Slaves,* 148–53 (stating that on the day of

the laying of the Lee monument cornerstone a local Richmond newspaper argued that "the example of Lee vindicated the Old South and its slave-holding class: 'Was there ever on this planet a nobler class of men'"). *Accord* Janney, *Remembering the Civil War*, 182 (showing that the dedication and unveiling of the Lee monument was a "Confederate-only" Lost Cause affair for White Southerners to promote the ideology of the Confederacy).

82. Savage, *Standing Soldiers, Kneeling Slaves*, 132.
83. See discussion at Savage, *Standing Soldiers, Kneeling Slaves*, 132.
84. Savage, *Standing Soldiers, Kneeling Slaves*, 132–135.
85. *See* Brian Black and Bryn Varley, "Contesting the Sacred: Preservation and Meaning on Richmond's Monument Avenue," in Mills and Simpson, *Monuments to the Lost Cause*, 237.
86. Blair, *Cities of the Dead*, 144–45; Janney, *Burying the Dead*, 141; Janney, *Remembering the Civil War*, 182.
87. *See, e.g.*, David W. Blight, *Race and Reunion: The Civil War in American Memory* (Cambridge, MA: Belknap Press of Harvard University Press, 2001), 265.
88. Blair, *Cities of the Dead*, 155.
89. Blight, *Race and Reunion*, 269.
90. Savage, *Standing Soldiers, Kneeling Slaves*, 138–39. *Accord* Black and Varley, "Contesting the Sacred," 237 (concluding that "The large-scale commemoration of Confederate heroes that began with the huge Lee memorial . . . signified the White establishment's resistance to the new interracial era proposed for a reunited future"); Blight, *Race and Reunion*, 269 (Archer Anderson, the speaker at the Lee dedication, argued that the Lee monument would represent "a perpetual protest against whatever is low and sordid in our public and private objects" and the mantra of the South's Democratic party leadership was that the most "low and sordid" thing a Southerner could do was fracture White unity by abandoning the Democratic Party).
91. *See* Black and Varley, "Contesting the Sacred," 235–37.
92. Quoted at Blight, *Race and Reunion*, 270. On June 4, 2020, during the protests that followed the May 2020 killing of George Floyd, the statue of Jefferson Davis, located on Monument Avenue, and two other of Richmond's Confederate monuments, were pulled down by protesters. Later that month, the Richmond government removed the statues of General Stonewall Jackson and Confederate naval officer Matthew Maury from Monument Avenue. In addition, Virginia governor Ralph Northam announced that the State of Virginia owns the land on which the Lee monument on Monument Avenue is located and that he intended to order that the Lee monument be removed and placed in storage. A Virginia Circuit Court judge temporarily enjoined the monument's removal, pending resolution of issues raised by descendants of the family that donated the land to the state. Aimee Ortiz, "Richmond Begins Removing Confederate Statues from Monument Avenue," New York Times, July 2, 2020, accessed at https://www.nytimes.com/2020/07/02/us/stonewall-jackson-statue-richmond.html. Gregory S. Schneider, "Richmond Judge Extends Order Barring Removal of Lee Statue Indefinitely, Washington Post, June 18, 2020, accessed at https://www.washingtonpost.com/local/virginia-politics/richmond-lee-statue-removal/2020/06/18/492203ac-b106-11ea-856d-5054296735e5_story.html.
93. Foster, *Ghosts of the Confederacy*, 131.
94. Janney, *Remembering the Civil War*, 189.

95. *See* James McPherson, "A Brief Overview of The American Civil War: A Defining Time in Our Nation's History," *American Battlefield Trust*, accessed at https://www.battlefields.org/learn/articles/brief-overview-american-civil-war (concluding that "The Civil War started because of uncompromising differences between the free and slave states over the power of the national government to prohibit slavery in the territories that had not yet become states").

96. Janney, *Remembering the Civil War*, 202.

97. *See* Janney, *Remembering the Civil War*, 187–89. By the turn of the twentieth century, as Jim Crow took ever greater hold on Southern race relations, some monument dedication speakers overtly added White supremacist racial references to their monument dedication presentations. One example is the November 30, 1899 address by J. H. Henderson at the dedication of the Confederate monument at Franklin, Tennessee. Confederate veterans, Henderson stated, are the men we desire to honor [today]. *It is an honor to belong to the race that could produce them.* Quoted in Seabrook, *Confederate Monuments*, 384 (emphasis added).

98. Bishir, "A Strong Force of Ladies," 12. This section on the Raleigh Confederate Monument is informed by the research of Catherine Bishir.

99. Bishir, "A Strong Force of Ladies," 15–16.

100. Bishir, "A Strong Force of Ladies," 16–18.

101. Bishir, "A Strong Force of Ladies," 18.

102. Bishir, "A Strong Force of Ladies," 19–21. One year after the 1895 erection of North Carolina's Confederate Monument, there was a second fusionist victory in North Carolina, which the Democrats reversed in 1898 through a violent White supremacist backlash that "recaptured White voters by pulling out all the stops of the old themes of 'Negro domination,' interracial sex, and Reconstruction horrors." Bishir, "A Strong Force of Ladies," 21.

103. Gary W. Gallagher, "Jubal A. Early, the Lost Cause, and Civil War History," in Gallagher and Nolan, *The Myth of the Lost Cause*, 35–36.

104. See discussion at Foster, *Ghosts of the Confederacy*, 47–49, 54–57. 60.

Chapter 3: The Warping-of-History Approach

1. *See* Stanford University, The Martin Luther King, Jr. Research and Education Institute, *Our God is Marching On!*, accessed at https://kinginstitute.stanford.edu/our-god-marching.

2. William S. McFeely, afterward to C. Vann Woodward, *The Strange Career of Jim Crow*, commemorative ed. (New York: Oxford University Press, (1955) 2002), 223.

3. *See, e.g.*, Dell Upton, *What Can and Can't Be Said: Race Uplift and Monument Building in the Confederate South* (New Haven, CT: Yale University Press, 2015), 29 (stating that "The erasure of African Americans from history [accomplished in part by the raising of Confederate monuments] went hand in hand with their elimination from the political arena").

4. See discussion at C. Vann Woodward, *Tom Watson: Agrarian Rebel* (New York: The Macmillan Co., 1938); C. Vann Woodward, *Origins of the New South* (Baton Rouge: Louisiana State University Press, 1951); Gerald H. Gaither, *Blacks and the Populist Movement: Ballots and Bigotry in the New South* (Tuscaloosa: The University of Alabama Press, 2005); Joseph Gerteis, *Class and the Color Line: Interracial, Class Coalition in the Knights of Labor and the Populist Movement* (Durham, NC: Duke University Press, 2007); Richard

White, *The Republic for Which It Stands: The United States During Reconstruction and the Gilded Age, 1865–1896* (New York: Oxford University Press, 2017).

5. Woodward, *Origins of the New South*, 323.

6. It also was in the interest of White Populists, most of whom strongly opposed Black equality anyway, to support Black disfranchisement as a way to undercut Bourbon race-baiting. It would be more difficult for Bourbons to claim that Populists were attempting to impose Negro domination on the South when Southern African Americans effectively had no right to vote in the first place. The Republican Party, which had ruled during Reconstruction through biracial coalitions, also was vulnerable to Democratic race-baiting. By the 1890s the so-called "Lily-White" faction of the party worked to drive Blacks from the Republican Party, make the Party more "respectable" to Southern Whites, and deny Democrats the ability to successfully race-bait White Republicans. The Lily-White faction thus also supported Black disfranchisement as a way to undercut the Democrat's race-baiting strategy. Woodward, *Origins of the New South*, 276, 323–24.

7. See discussion at White, *The Republic for Which It Stands*, 622, 627.

8. *See* Woodward, *Origins of the New South*, 57–58, 326–27, 347 (quoting a delegate at Mississippi's 1890 constitutional convention who, in an extraordinary admission of illegality, argued for disfranchising Blacks because Black voting power had "forced" Whites to engage in voting manipulation in order to "guarantee the ascendency of White people by revolutionary methods [such as] stuffing the ballot boxes, committing perjury, and . . . carrying the elections by fraud and violence until the whole machinery for elections was about rot down").

9. *See* Woodward, *Origins of the New South*, 327. Woodward has advanced the argument that factionalism in the South in the 1890s centered primarily on a contest for power between hill-country Whites, living in portions of Southern states where slavery never was entrenched and thus where few Blacks lived and the Black belt areas of the state having very large Black populations. Whites in the Black belt sections of the state thus profited primarily from the ability to steal Black votes. Woodward accordingly argues, "It was not Negro domination but White domination from the Black Belt that [disfranchisement] sought to overthrow." Woodward, *Origins of the New South*, 329.

10. In 1875, the Mississippi Plan went into effect. To prevent Black political participation, the state's Democratic Party devised a plan to overthrow the Republican Party by organized violence and thus "redeem" the state of Mississippi. Democrats in South Carolina and Louisiana devised a similar strategy. See Woodward, *Origins of the New South*, 57–58, 321.

11. *See* Henry Louis Gates Jr., *Stony the Road: Reconstruction, White Supremacy, and the Rise of Jim Crow* (New York: Penguin Press, 2019), 28 (quoting Mississippi Senator and future governor, James Kimble Vardaman, that "There is no use to equivocate or lie about the matter. Mississippi's constitutional convention was held for no other purpose than to eliminate the nigger from politics; not the ignorant—but the nigger).

12. Williams v. Mississippi, 170 U.S. 313 (1898) (concluding that no discrimination exists in Mississippi's requirements that voters pass a literacy test and pay poll taxes, as these voting prerequisites were applied to all voters).

13. Woodward, *Origins of the New South*, 321. Before states followed Mississippi's lead in disfranchising Blacks, many already had erected various obstacles to voting by poor Blacks and Whites. The requirement of registering to vote prior to the election and possessing evidence of prior registration at the time of voting posed an obstacle for

those not accustomed to maintaining records and those who were landless and needed to move regularly and were required to re-register upon each move. Some states added petty larceny to the list of crimes that disqualified one from voting and this bar disproportionately impacted on Blacks. Polling places might be moved without notice. But perhaps the most creative obstacle to suppressing poor Black and poor White voting power was the notorious "eight ballot box law" adopted by Georgia and South Carolina. This voting system required voters to execute individual ballots for each of eight offices being contested in the election and then correctly place each ballot in one of eight ballot boxes, each box reserved for ballots for one particular office. Any ballot placed in an incorrect ballot box would not be counted. Election officials constantly rearranged the placement of the ballot boxes so that their order could not be memorized by a literate voter and the information passed on to illiterate voters waiting to vote. Only a literate voter was able to read the office on a ballot box and place the ballot in the correct box. This system disfranchised both illiterate Blacks and Whites but disproportionately affected Blacks since, for example, in South Carolina as late as 1900, 55 percent of Blacks compared to 12 percent of Whites were illiterate. Moreover, the law was more vigorously enforced against Blacks than Whites. See Gaither, *Blacks and the Populist Movement*, 134–35, 199.

14. *See* Terry McAuliffe, *Beyond Charlottesville: Taking a Stand Against White Nationalism* (New York: St. Martin's Press, 2019), 26–27 (quoting Carter Glass, a convention leader, proclaiming that "Discrimination!? . . . That is precisely what we propose. That, exactly, is what this convention was elected for").

15. See Alan P. Grimes, *Democracy and the Amendments to the Constitution* (Lanham, MD: University Press of America, 1978), 134; David E. Kyvig, *Explicit & Authentic Acts: Amending the U.S. Constitution, 1776–1995* (Lawrence: University Press of Kansas, 1996), 351–57; Woodward, *Origin of the New South*, 335–36.

16. Woodward, *Origin of the New South*, 336–40.

17. Harper v. Virginia State Board of Elections, 383 U.S. 663, 666 (1966) (concluding that "[A] state violates the Equal Protection Clause . . . whenever it makes the affluence of the voter or payment of any fee an electoral standard. Voter qualifications have no relation to wealth nor to paying or not paying this or any other tax").

18. Gates, *Stony the Road*, 5, 10 (quoting Rayford W. Logan, *The Betrayal of the Negro: From Rutherford B. Hayes to Woodrow Wilson* (New York: Collier Books, 1954; 1965), 62 (emphasis added).

19. Frederick Douglass, "What the Black Man Wants" (1865) (emphasis added), accessed at Teaching American History, https://teachingamericanhistory.org/library/document/what-the-Black-man-wants/.

20. Gates, *Stony the Road*, 129 (emphasis added).

21. *See* Grace Elizabeth Hale, *Making Whiteness: The Culture of Segregation in the South, 1890–1940* (New York: Pantheon Books, 1998), 54.

22. *See* discussion at Janney, *Remembering the Civil War: Reunion and the Limits of Reconciliation* (Chapel Hill: The University of North Carolina Press, 2013), 199 (arguing that the rising of a Black middle class was a factor in bringing the White South to a "frenzy" of racial animus in the 1890s); Hale, *Making Whiteness*, 200–01.

23. *See* Steven Hahn, *A Nation Under Our Feet: Black Political Struggles in the Rural South From Slavery to the Great Migration* (Cambridge, MA: Belknap Press of Harvard University Press, 2003), 425–26; Dora Apel, *Imagery of Lynching: Black Men, White*

Women, and the Mob (New Brunswick, NJ: Rutgers University Press, 2004), 14 (defining lynching as "murder endorsed by [the] community, regardless of how many or how few people actually committed the crime."); White, *The Republic for Which It Stands*, 742 (defining lynching as "the execution of accused criminals by mobs or posses without official legal sanction").

24. Erika Doss, *Memorial Mania: Public Feeling in America* (Chicago: The University of Chicago Press, 2010), 265. The last publicly acknowledged racially motivated lynching by traditional means was in Mobile, Alabama, in 1981 when the Ku Klux Klan beat and lynched a teenager. Apel, *Imagery of Lynching*, 14–15. Erika Doss argues that the 1998 murder of James Byrd Jr., a Southern African American from Jasper, Texas, was a lynching. Byrd was dragged in chains behind a pickup truck, decapitated, and his limbs were torn from his body. Doss, *Memorial Mania*, 266 (also noting an epidemic of lynching nooses appearing in public places).

25. White, *The Republic for Which It Stands*, 744.

26. Woodward, *Origins of the New South*, 350–52 (also stating that the increased Southern racialization of lynching coincided with a broader, serious deterioration of race relations marked by violent race riots in major U.S. cities); Doss, *Memorial Mania*, 265–67 (describing lynching as a "festering sore throughout the course of American modernity" and stating that the incidence of lynching rose during certain periods of the twentieth century, such as during the Progressive era, after World War I, at the beginning of the Great Depression, immediately after World War II, and during the civil rights era and also reporting that in terms of numbers of lynchings, the cotton belt states of Alabama, Georgia, Louisiana, Mississippi, and Texas surpass all other states, although other states had high numbers of lynchings, such as California with 352 lynchings between 1850 and 1935).

27. *See* Doss, *Memorial Mania*, 284–85 (an epithet inscribed on the walls of the Clayton Jackson, McGhie Memorial in Duluth, Minnesota, a large-scale memorial dedicated to opposition of lynching); "Crowd Pays Respects to Lynching Victims in Downtown Duluth," *Duluth News Tribune*. June 15, 2009, accessed at http://www.duluthnewstribune.com/content/crowd-pays-respects-lynching-victims-downtown-duluth.

28. *See* Apel, *Imagery of Lynching*, 9. In addition to lynching, the other common form of racial violence was "Whitecapping." This entailed bands of armed White men who retaliated against those who were deemed to have violated community norms. In the 1890s their violence often was directed against Southern African Americans who had gained an independent foothold by renting farms, owning land, working for merchants or large planters, or otherwise engaged in acts that White economic competitors perceived as threatening their livelihoods. Whitecappers would flog Black farmers and laborers, destroy crops, and burn buildings. See discussion at Hahn, *A Nation Under Our Feet*, 427.

29. *See* Hahn, *A Nation Under Our Feet*, 426–27. Between 1882 and 1946, less than 25% of lynchings involved rape, or even the accusation of attempted rape, let alone a conviction for rape. White, *The Republic for Which It Stands*, 744 & 744 n. 40 (reporting the findings of turn-of-the-century civil rights activist Ida Wells whose research demonstrated that no matter the original criminal charge, newspapers transformed the crime into a Black man's rape of a White woman and sometimes the rape charge disguised consensual sex).

30. *Atlanta Constitution*, April 14, 1899, quoted in Hale, *Making Whiteness*, 210. *See*

Apel, *Imagery of Lynching*, 9, 10, 14 (concluding that the participants in spectacle lynching in the South were "ordinary people who committed such extraordinary atrocities in the name of community values, [people who] otherwise believed in basic democratic principles [but whom racism] turned into self-exonerating murderers").

31. *See* Jon Meacham, *The Soul of America: The Battle for Our Better Angels* (New York: Random House, 2018), 162 (stating that of 3,500 lynchings since 1900, there had been only sixty-seven indictments and twelve convictions).

32. Apel, *Imagery of Lynching*, 14 (quoting W. E. B. Du Bois with respect to the importance of observing the acts that constituted the crime of lynching); Hale, *Making Whiteness*, 219 (commenting on the broad cross-section of people from Waco, TX, who, "compelled to assert the unity of the White community," participated in the lynching of Jesse Washington).

33. *See* Hale, *Making Whiteness*, 206–07, 210, 223–224 (arguing that the promotion of lynching in the South through advertising of upcoming lynchings through the newspaper, radio, telegraph, and telephone, as well as railroad companies' advertisements in local newspapers that communicated the scheduling of special trains to transport spectators, was central to converting lynching into a more powerful cultural phenomenon of "racial control" and "amusement"); Apel, *Imagery of Lynching*, 15 (stating that one of the most effective methods of advertising an upcoming lynching was through newspaper and radio reports and the memory of the lynching was best captured by the circulation of photographs and display of "relics").

34. *See* New York *Sun*, February 2, 1893, reprinted in Gilbert Osofsky, *The Burden of Race: A Documentary History of Negro-White Relations in America* (New York: Harper and Row, 1967), 181–84. *See also* "Another Negro Burned; Henry Smith Dies at the Stake. Drawn Through the Streets on a Car—Tortured for Nearly an Hour with Hot Irons and Then Burned—Awful Vengeance of a Paris (Texas) Mob," *New York Times*, February 2, 1893, accessed at https://www.nytimes.com/1893/02/02/archives/another-negro-burned-henry-smith-dies-at-the-stake-drawn-through.html. For the photograph of the 1893 lynching of Henry Smith see http://www.americanlynching.com/pic3.htm.

35. Apel, *Imagery of Lynching*, 31. Another estimate is that between 15,000 and 20,000 viewed the lynching of Jesse Washington. *See* Kurt Terry, "Jesse Washington Lynching," *Waco History*, accessed at http://wacohistory.org/items/show/55. For the lynching of Thomas Brooks in Somerville, Tennessee, in April 1915 "[p]eople in automobiles and carriages came from miles around to view the corpse hanging from the end of a rope. . . . Women and children were there by the score. At a number of schools, the day's routine was delayed until boy and girl pupils could get back from viewing the lynched man." Doss, *Memorial Mania*, 265.

36. Apel, *Imagery of Lynching*, 3, 7, 31; Hale, *Making Whiteness*, 223 (reporting the prolonged, ten-hour torture of Claude Neal); Doss, *Memorial Mania*, 265 (describing "barbaric public performances which involved stabbing, shooting, dragging, hanging, burning, and cutting human bodies). Dora Apel has researched the lynching death of Jesse Washington. Washington confessed to the killing of a women for whom he worked. A rape charge was added after his arrest but never substantiated. Once caught, Washington was first beaten with shovels and bricks and then castrated in front of at least one child, with persons carrying proof in a handkerchief showing the contents to onlookers. Then Jesse Washington's ears were severed and he was hanged from a tree by a chain over a roaring fire. Still alive he tried to climb the hot chain to escape the

flames and his tormentors cut off his fingers to preclude this escape. He was repeatedly lowered into the flames and then pulled out again, apparently with the intent to avoid his immediate death from burning in an effort to prolong his pain. He eventually died and a famous picture of his charred corpse, hanging by the chain, shows both feet completely burned away, one leg burned away almost to the knee and one arm burned away to the elbow. Following his death, Washington's charred remains were attached to a rope and he was dragged through town by a horse and rider "followed by a group of young boys." Apel, *Imagery of Lynching*, 31. Photographs were taken of the massive crowd of spectators at the lynching of Jesse Washington and of the charred body of Jesse Washington hanging from a tree by a chain. Visual documentation is available at http://murderpedia.org/male.W/w/washington-jesse-photos.htm.

37. *See* discussion at Gode Davis and James M. Fortier, *American Lynching: A Documentary Feature* (Revised September 2005), accessed at http://www.americanlynching.com/treatment.htm (also describing how two brothers, one thirteen and one eleven collected fingers and toes from the "burnt hulk" of Zack Walker following his lynching and being burned alive by a mob of 5000 of the boys' neighbors on August 13, 1911 many of whom then posed with other spectators for a photograph). *See also* Hale, *Making Whiteness*, 210 (reporting that prior to the 1899 lynching of Sam Hose, one member of the lynch mob stated to a reporter, "whatever death is most torturous, most horrifying to a brute, shall be meted out; let him burn slowly for hours").

38. Doss, *Memorial Mania*, 265.

39. Hale, *Making Whiteness*, 208; Doss, *Memorial Mania*, 253.

40. *See* James Allen, ed., *Without Sanctuary: Lynching Photography in America* (Santa Fe: Twin Palms Publishers, 2000); Apel, *Imagery of Lynching*, 1, 3, 7–10 (describing an exhibition of James Allen's lynching photographs produced between 1880–1960 and first shown in a small Manhattan gallery in 2000 and subsequently shown in several other U.S. cities).

41. Apel, *Imagery of Lynching*, 7.

42. See discussion at Hale, *Making Whiteness*, 213–14, 218 (also recounting the experience of W. E. B. Du Bois who, following the lynching of Sam Hose, was walking to the offices of the local newspaper to deliver a reasoned statement concerning the lynching, but turned back to his office in disgust when he learned that the knuckles of Sam Hose were on display at the local grocery store). *Accord Imagery of Lynching*, 22 (stating that among the most prized souvenirs were pieces of clothing and the hanging rope).

43. *See* White, *The Republic for Which It Stands*, 745 (describing spectacle lynching as "group entertainment").

44. *See* Hahn, *A Nation Under Our Feet*, 427 (arguing also that White perception of African Americans' boundary violations is the best explanation for why rape charges and allegations of miscegenation so often arose "in the discourse of lynching" since these charges touched on "the most intimate and fundamental [color] boundaries [set by Whites] . . . despite the record showing that other forms of assault were more commonly the issue"); Doss, *Memorial Mania*, 265. Dora Apel has argued that White Southern males found interracial sex loathsome because of the fear that it invited social equality that would undermine the racial hierarchy that maintained White men's political, social and economic power). Apel, *Imagery of Lynching*, 26.

45. Doss, *Memorial Mania*, 266–68 (also stating that spectacle lynching was related to

patriarchy. "In protecting White women from Black men, elite White men maintained their own power and authority").

46. W. J. Cash, *The Mind of the South* (New York: Alfred A. Knopf, Inc., 1941), 119, accessed at https://archive.org/stream/in.ernet.dli.2015.182957/2015.182957.The-Mind-Of-The-South_djvu.txt

47. Hahn, *A Nation Under Our Feet*, 430.

48. Gates, *Stony the Road*, xviii.

49. Quoted in Hale, *Making Whiteness*, 221, 228–29 (also observing that spectacle lynching "worked by ritualistically uniting White Southerners, by embodying the community into action" but in addition, "[lynchings] conjured Whiteness . . . through their spectacle of a violent African American otherness [and Black "otherness"] became the foundation for White racial identity"). *Accord* Doss, *Memorial Mania*, 266, 271–72, 275–78 (showing that racial terrorism, encouraged and legitimated by late-nineteenth century and twentieth century lynching, was "a regulating instrument of racialized difference," and was a "means of maintaining White elite patriarchy . . . in the early twentieth century"—derogatory of Blackness and demonstrative of White supremacy by showing that Black men were clowns (*e.g.* Black face mistral shows), childlike, primitive and pre-modern).

50. *See* Apel, *Imagery of Lynching*, 10 (correlating lynching with the power hierarchy rooted in slavery "when Blacks were reduced to objects [and] compelled to assume the mantle of invisibility, to erase all traces of their subjectivity . . . so that they could be better, less threatening servants").

51. *See* Hale, *Making Whiteness*, 202–03; Hahn, *A Nation Under Our Feet*, 430 (emphasis added). *Accord* Doss, *Memorial Mania*, 265 (concluding that "Following the Civil War and throughout the twentieth century, American racists made full use of acts and images of racial terrorism to extend the dehumanizing inequities of slavery and to sustain assumptions of White racial superiority").

52. Hale, *Making Whiteness*, 203. The scavenged items from lynchings that participants removed as mementoes, as well as the thousands of gruesome picture postcards of lynchings, were circulated within the local communities and beyond, serving an ongoing function of expanding the geographic reach of spectacle lynching's message of White superiority and the "otherness" of Southern African Americans. Hale, *Making Whiteness*, 226–27.

53. Woodward, *The Strange Career of Jim Crow*, 25–65 (gives as examples that in some jurisdictions during Reconstruction, Blacks served on juries, as judges, and in legislative councils; Blacks voted and enjoyed economic equality in the marketplace; traveled freely with Whites on public conveyances; the races ate together at a common table; worked together; sat together in the same room and makes the point that Blacks did not press their rights, not seeking entry, for example, in hotels and restaurants where they were not welcome, and Whites reduced or ended their patronage at desegregated facilities). *See also* Hale, *Making Whiteness*, 45, 124 (stating that following Reconstruction, "the form that postbellum Southern race relations would take remained uncertain" and even after the advent of Jim Crow, "the forms if not the fact of modern White supremacy remained unsettled."). Following Reconstruction, the Redeemer governments enforced segregation that developed during Reconstruction but did not significantly alter the segregation already present. This degree of segregation coexisted, uneasily, with new experiments in interracial contact, association, and equality until the arrival of Jim

Crow laws and disfranchisement. The point is not that these examples of interracial cooperation were typical or even particularly common, nor that this endured very long, but that some interracial cooperation existed for a time even as White supremacists were working against it. Woodward, *The Strange Career of Jim Crow*, 28, 31–33.

54. Woodward, *The Strange Career of Jim Crow*, 33–34 (showing that, e.g., prior to the turn of the twentieth century there was no universal demand by Whites that Blacks be disenfranchised or barred from White sections of public conveyances). *Accord* White, *The Republic for Which It Stands*, 363-4 (concluding that in those sections of the South where Black suffrage still survived, it was possible to assemble alliances among Black voters, Republicans, and the agrarian wing of the Democratic Party).

55. Woodward, *The Strange Career of Jim Crow*, 34–41. North Carolina is an excellent example. In 1890 North Carolina, there remained potential for reform—gender, race and class reform. The North Carolina Republican Party was effective in 1890: Whites were Republicans in the state's western hill country and African Americans were Republicans in the Eastern sections of the state. North Carolina had an upwardly mobile biracial middle class and small farmers who were chronically restive. Richard White argues that in the early 1890s, "North Carolina represented one possibility of interracial cooperation for the South." White, *The Republic for Which It Stands*, 739–40. Indeed, in the election of 1890, reform candidates for political office were extraordinarily successful: more than forty were elected to the House of Representatives "where they dominated the delegations of Georgia and the Carolinas." Reform candidates also were elected to the United States Senate in the 1890 election and "controlled legislatures in seven Southern states." H. W. Brands, *American Colossus: The Triumph of Capitalism 1865–1900* (New York: Doubleday, 2010), 437.

56. *See* Hahn, *A Nation Under Our Feet*, 450–51 (arguing that accelerating state-sanctioned segregation at the turn of the twentieth century became possible once the South had disfranchised Southern African Americans and that this development "marked the true end of Reconstruction"). For an analysis of the factors that explain the rise of extreme racism at the dawn of the twentieth century, see Woodward, *The Strange Career of Jim Crow*, 67–75 (citing three factors: the declining effectiveness of Northern liberalism, the decline in the influence of traditional Southern conservatives, and the emergence and subsequent decline of Southern radicalism).

57. Gates, *Stoney the Road*, xix.

58. For example, mobs of roving Whites freely looted and murdered Blacks in the late 1890s in Atlanta; Wilmington, NC; South Carolina; and New Orleans. Woodward, *The Strange Career of Jim Crow*, 87–89.

59. Plessy v. Ferguson, 163 U.S. 537, 550–51 (1896). Critics have understood the Court's upholding of enforced separation of the races in *Plessy* as judicial vindication of a view of African Americans' biological differences "with skin colors designating dissimilar temperaments, [a result] established by nature, not law." See White, *The Republic for Which It Stands*, 741. For a discussion of the Court's denial that its endorsement of African American otherness suggested African American inferiority, see Walter F. Pratt Jr., "Plessy v. Ferguson," in Kermit L. Hall & James W. Ely Jr., eds., *The Oxford Guide to United States Supreme Court Decisions*, 2d ed. (New York: Oxford University Press, 2009), 277–78.

60. Gates, *Stoney the Road*, xix.

61. See discussion of group libel at Woodward, *The Strange Career of Jim Crow*, 93–96;

Gates, *Stoney the Road*, 1–184 (detailing group libel of African Americans over a "painfully long period following Reconstruction . . . across a baffling array of media and through an extraordinary variety of forms, from print to art").

62. Woodward, *The Strange Career of Jim Crow*, 6–7.

63. Woodward, *The Strange Career of Jim Crow*, 8, 11, 98–99. For a detailed discussion of state-sponsored segregation and discrimination in employment, education, recreation, travel, and housing, see Woodward, *The Strange Career of Jim Crow*, 98–102.

64. Quoted in Bruce Levine, *The Fall of the House of Dixie* (New York: Random House, 2013), 297 & 297, n 62 (citing W. E. B. Du Bois, *Black Reconstruction in America: An Essay Toward African Americans History of the Part Which Black Folk Played in the Attempt to Reconstruct Democracy in America, 1860–1889* (Cleveland: Harcourt Brace, (1935) (reprint, 1968), 30.

65. Woodward, *The Strange Career of Jim Crow*, 108 (quoting Edgar Gardner Murphy who expressed this view in 1911).

66. White, *The Republic for Which It Stands*, 76.

67. Hahn, *A Nation Under Our Feet*, 367.

68. Hale, *Making Whiteness*, 8–9, 200.

69. After the Civil War, the Bourbons, the planter/ruling class in the South, had much to answer for to the South's yeoman and laboring classes. For example, the conscription laws that until 1863 permitted one to purchase a substitute and thereby avoid Confederate military service altogether, an option primarily available only to the wealthy. In addition, the Confederate Congress exempted from conscription one White male on any plantation with twenty or more slaves, creating a special privilege made available only to those in the Confederate population from families that were wealthy enough to own such a large number of slaves. Many Confederate soldiers in the yeoman and laboring class interpreted this "twenty-Negro law" and the substitute provision in the conscription law as powerful evidence that the war to preserve slavery was to be fought for rich men by poor men. Or as one Confederate soldier from the ranks put it, "in this war 'poor soldiers' were 'fighting for the rich man's negro.'" See James M. McPherson, *Battle Cry of Freedom: The Civil War Era* (New York: Oxford University Press, 1988), 612–13; Levine, *The Fall of the House of Dixie*, 84–85, 209–10.

70. One example of the malleability of post-Reconstruction politics in the South is the Readjuster Movement of late 1870s. Throughout the South, state bonds worth millions of dollars remained unpaid. In every Southern state other than Mississippi and Kentucky, powerful movements arose to have these bonds repaid at full value. Bondholders, mostly Northern capitalists and elites of the class that controlled the Southern Democratic Party, the so-called Funders, argued that a state's obligation to bondholders should be honored, even if funding repayment of the bonds meant diverting funds otherwise allocated to funding public education. Those who opposed full repayment of the bonds, so-called Readjusters, formed a biracial political coalition in some states, such as Virginia, and "bridged the racial divide" to pluck political power from the Conservative Democrats for several years until consumed politically by a violent backlash orchestrated by the conservative elite who had first redeemed Virginia and who continued to control the Democratic Party. See discussion at William A. Blair, *Cities of the Dead: Contesting the Memory of the Civil War in the South, 1865–1914* (Chapel Hill: University of North Carolina Press, 2004), 128–30; White, *The Republic for Which It Stands*, 363–64; Woodward, *Origins of the New South*, 48, 61, 86–102, 105.

71. *See, e.g.,* discussion at Gerteis, *Class and the Color Line. See generally* Gaither, *Blacks and the Populist Movement.*

72. Gaither, *Blacks and the Populist Movement,* 17.

73. See discussion at Hahn, *A Nation Under Our Feet,* 367.

74. For a discussion and analysis of the "new leadership class" within the Black community—the "young, educated, post-slavery, modern culturally sophisticated, and thoroughly middle class [who] would be more effectively equipped . . . to combat the mounting injustices that the mass of Black people were facing as [anti-Black racism] became more deeply entrenched throughout the South," see Gates, *Stoney the Road,* 185–246.

75. See discussion at Hale, *Making Whiteness,* 200, 284.

76. This view and the following argument that the cultural power of Jim Crow was in the message of Black inferiority *communicated to Whites,* is adapted from the thesis persuasively developed by Elizabeth Hale. *See* Hale, *Making Whiteness.*

77. *See* Brian Black and Bryn Varley, "Contesting the Sacred: Preservation and Meaning on Richmond's Monument Avenue," in Cynthia Mills and Pamela H. Simpson, eds., *Monuments to the Lost Cause: Women, Art, and the Landscapes of Southern Memory* (Knoxville: The University of Tennessee Press 2003), 236–37.

78. Hale uses the metaphor of Jim Crow "turn[ing] the entire South into a theater of racial difference." As a play on the theater metaphor, Hale argues that "Southern Whites created a modern social order in which [racial] difference would . . . be continually performed [to make] reality conform to script." Hale, *Making Whiteness,* 284.

79. *See* J. Michael Martinez & Robert M. Harris, "Graves, Worms, and Epitaphs," in J. Michael Martinez, William D. Richardson & Ron McNinch-Su, eds., *Confederate Symbols in the Contemporary South* (Gainesville: University Press of Florida, 2000), 147–49 (concluding that "[a]lmost all twentieth-century Confederate monuments in the South have been erected by the UDC").

80. Karen L. Cox, "The Confederacy's 'Living Monuments,'" *The New York Times,* October 6. 2017, assessed at https://www.nytimes.com/2017/10/06/opinion/the-confederacys-living-monuments.html; Micki McElya, "Commemorating the Color Line: The National Mammy Controversy of the 1920s," in Mills and Simpson, *Monuments to the Lost Cause,"* 204; Martinez & Harris, "Graves, Worms, and Epitaphs," 49; Gaines M. Foster, *Ghosts of the Confederacy: Defeat, the Lost Cause, and the Emergence of the New South* (New York: Oxford University Press, 1987), 172.

81. McElya, "Mammy Controversy," 204; David Currey, "The Virtuous Soldier: Constructing a Usable Confederate Past in Franklin, Tennessee," in Mills and Simpson, *Monuments to the Lost Cause.* 140.

82. Janney, *Burying the Dead,* 173–75; Janney, *Remembering the Civil War,* 8, 269; W. Fitzhugh Brundage, *The Southern Past: A Clash of Race and Memory* (Cambridge, MA: The Belknap Press of Harvard University Press, 2005), 28–31, 36–41, 117–20 (also pointing out that Confederate monuments, sometimes explicitly and always implicitly transmitted the view that the overthrow of Reconstruction was one of the great achievements of Southern White manhood and emblematic of Anglo-Saxon superiority and the South owed a great debt to the redeemers many of whom became the subjects of commemoration in Confederate monuments).

83. Quoted in Lochlainn Seabrook, *Confederate Monuments,* 384 (Nashville, TN: Sea Raven Press, 2018).

84. Karen L. Cox, *Dixie's Daughters: The United Daughters of the Confederacy and the Preservation of Confederate Culture* (Gainesville: University Press of Florida, 2003), 6.

85. *See* Hale, *Making Whiteness*, 61–62; Janney, *Burying the Dead*, 171–73; Janney, *Remembering the Civil War*, 39–40; Brundage, *The Southern Past*, 32 (concluding that appeals to the supremacy of the Anglo-Saxon "race" by women organized in UDC chapters "provided crucial ideological ballast for White supremacy by rooting the contemporary racial hierarchy in a seemingly ordained historical narrative").

86. David W. Blight, *Race and Reunion: The Civil War in American Memory* (Cambridge, MA: Belknap Press of Harvard University Press, 2001), 273.

87. *See* Foster, *Ghosts of the Confederacy*, 197.

88. Karen L. Cox, "The Confederate Monument at Arlington," in Mills and Simpson, *Monuments to the Lost Cause*, 150; Janney, *Remembering the Civil War*, 261; Foster, *Ghosts of the Confederacy*, 153–54. In 1887, Democratic President Grover Cleveland's suggestion to return captured regimental flags created a firestorm of protest. The regimental colors were returned in 1905 after Southerners rallied around the nation in the War with Spain and "Union veterans reciprocated by calling for the return of the captured flags [to the Confederate regiments that had lost them during the Civil War]." John M. Coski, "The Confederate Battle Flag in Historical Perspective," in Martinez, et al., *Confederate Symbols in the Contemporary South*, 104–05.

89. Cox, *The Confederate Monument at Arlington*, 151; Janney, *Remembering the Civil War*, 261–62.

90. Cox, *The Confederate Monument at Arlington*, 154–60 (source of reference to "textbook in bronze"); Janney, *Remembering the Civil War*, 263–64; Doss, *Monument Mania*, 11.

91. W. Fitzhugh Brundage, "'Women's Hand and Heart of Deathless Love:' White Women and the Commemorative Impulse in the New South," in Mills and Simpson, *Monuments to the Lost Cause*, 64–65, 69–70 (concluding that "armed with the privilege of Whiteness and affluence, commemorative activists employed the full array of cultural resources at their disposal . . . to insinuate their memory into the public realm"); Brundage, *The Southern Past*, 37–44, 106.

92. William M. S. Rasmussen, "Planning a Temple to the Lost Cause: The Confederate 'Battle Abbey,'" in Mills and Simpson, *Monuments to the Lost Cause*, 168–69. For a discussion of the backlash among Lost Cause advocates, especially members of the UDC, arising from the 1922 dedication of the Lincoln Memorial, see Janney, *Remembering the Civil War*, 290.

93. Brundage, *The Southern Past*, 33; McElya, "Mammy Controversy," 203, 216; Janney, *Remembering the Civil War*, 292–93; Tony Horwitz, "The Mammy Washington Almost Had," *The Atlantic*, May 31, 2013, accessed at https://www.theatlantic.com/national/archive/2013/05/the-mammy-washington-almost-had/276431/; *Histories of the National Mall: Faithful Slave Mammies of the South Memorial*, accessed at http://mallhistory.org/items/show/512.

94. *See* Kirk Savage, *Standing Soldiers, Kneeling Slaves: Race, War, and Monument in Nineteenth-Century America* (Princeton, NJ: Princeton University Press, 1997), 155–59 (explaining the loyal slave myth as a "self-delusion" that solidified the South's retreat from the brutality of slavery by spinning slavery as "a kind of golden age of race relations, built on intimate bonds between Blacks and Whites, the bond of mammy and child, of young master and his Black playmates, of soldier and body servant").

95. McElya, "Mammy Controversy," 205–06. *Accord* Brundage, *The Southern Past*, 33 (observing that underlying Whites' projection of domestic harmony and Black subservience were "lurking anxieties about the brittle state of Southern race relations").

96. *See* Horwitz, "The Mammy Washington Almost Had" (also recounting a cartoon in the *Baltimore Afro-American* mocking the mammy monument proposal: "a frowning Mammy perched atop a wash tub instead of a pedestal, her empty hand extended above the inscription: 'In Grateful Memory to One We Never Paid a Cent of Wages During a Lifetime of Service'"). Horwitz also reports that "Blacks also bristled at the stereotype of benignly affectionate relations between masters and hefty, aging mammies, who seemed never to have families of their own. A truer monument, one paper suggested, would be a statue to a 'White Daddy,' sexually assaulting a young Black woman as a mammy looks helplessly on." Horwitz, "The Mammy Washington Almost Had."

97. *See* Meacham, *The Soul of America*, 104–116.

98. *See* G. Kurt Piehler, "The War Dead and the Gold Star: American Commemoration of the First World War," in John R. Gillis, ed., *Commemorations: The Politics of National Identity* (Princeton, NJ: Princeton University Press, 1994), 169 (explaining the breadth of historical examination of "how the First World War exacerbated the divisions of class, ethnicity, religion, and region in the United States.); McElya, "Mammy Controversy," 204–05, 208, & 208 nn. 14 & 18.

99. In the early twentieth century, many Southern writers and speakers stressed the core tenets of the Lost Cause: the right of secession, the righteousness of the Confederate cause, the valor and devotion of the Confederate soldier, and in particular the loyalty of the "childlike slaves." LaSalle Corbell Pickett, the widow of famed Confederate General George E. Pickett, invested much of the fifty years following her husband's death advancing these themes to the Lost Cause faithful, often at Confederate monument dedications. Faithful slaves were "prominently featured" in her writings, lectures, and dedication presentations at the turn of the century and into the early decades of the twentieth century. Her "literary identity was deeply rooted in the plantation South. It was a mystical place of deference, paternalism, stability, and peace." She portrayed plantation life as "idyllic" with contented slaves cared for by kind masters and understanding mistresses. "Until a handful of mischief-making Northerners interfered . . . [the] family's slaves were obedient and respectfully submissive to Whites. . . . Her racist characterization of slaves depicted Blacks as uniformly superstitious and crude, childish and comical, and happily ignorant and simple-minded." Lesley F. Gordon, "'Let the People See the Old Life As It Was:' LaSalle Corbell Pickett and the Myth of the Lost Cause," in Gary W. Gallagher and Alan T. Nolan, eds. *The Myth of the Lost Cause and Civil War Memory* (Bloomington: Indiana University Press, 2000), 173–74.

100. *See* Joe R. Feagin, *Racist America: Roots, Current Realities, and Future Reparations* (3rd ed.) (New York: Routledge, 2014), 43 & 43 n. 28 (discussing the prevalence of White-on-Black rape as a form of "social and sexual control of men and women," and reporting that "it is estimated today that at least three-quarters of "Black" Americans have at least one "White" ancestor"). In the 1930s, the WPA interviewed ex-slaves. These interviews established that slaves nursed White babies while still girls, and the older Black women looked after the children of those who labored in the fields. One former slave described to the WPA interviewers a rape by sons of a slave owner. Another, an ex-slave from Georgia, stated that she "'went into the house as a waiting or nurse girl' between the ages of nine and twelve." "I can tell you," she said, "that a White man laid

a nigger gal whenever he wanted." Horwitz, "The Mammy Washington Almost Had."

101. See discussion at McElya, "Mammy Controversy," 208, 212–13 (showing that the Black press thus linked the mammy commemoration effort to White-on-Black violence, in particular the epidemic of lynching African Americans in the South and arguing that both constituted examples of Whites protest of African Americans' quest for freedom and racial justice and represented "profoundly vicious [and] brutal act[s] of domination").

102. McElya, "Mammy Controversy," 211.

103. See Janney, *Remembering the Civil War*, 293 (discussing the communicative power of a mammy monument and its potential to "reduce the history of slavery to the mammy figure").

104. *See* Caroline E. Janney, *Remembering the Civil War: Reunion and the Limits of Reconciliation* (Chapel Hill: The University of North Carolina Press, 2013), 268–69; Foster, *Ghosts of the Confederacy*, 120 (stating that by 1920 Confederate heritage groups shifted focus from celebrating the White supremacy of Confederate culture to portraying the Confederate veteran as a "role models for society, especially the young").

105. For example, World War I entailed an orgy of death, with Western Europe "destroying its youth in blood-soaked fields," prompting both Blacks and Whites, "to reconsider the presumptive supremacy of Anglo-European civilization." African Americans understandably questioned the belief many previously held that "they should measure their progress against the standard of Western civilization." The war also made Whites question the validity of the previously-held view that "the Black masses were an uncouth child-like race, striving to overcome the legacy of their barbarous ancestors and the peculiar institution while ascending the ladder of civilization." Brundage, *The Southern Past*, 102–03.

106. Elizabeth Gillespie McRae, *Mothers of Massive Resistance: White Women and the Politics of White Supremacy* (New York: Oxford University Press, 2018), 2–8, 7 n. 15 (collecting authorities on schools as sites of reproduction of race hierarchies and the role played by American history in school textbooks and curriculum in reflecting Southern racial values).

107. *See, e.g.,* Upton, *What Can and Can't Be Said*, 53 (reporting that New Orleans' 1891 "Liberty Monument" (a monument commemorating the city's White League and bedecked with racist passages) was used as "both a place of reverence for New Orleans elite . . . and a rallying point for White supremacists").

108. Confederate monuments were self-consciously built in prime public locations such as town squares and adjacent to the courthouse, in places "where children from all the public schools had to pass" so that they "'might know by daily observation of this monument' the cause for which their ancestors fought.'" Cox, *Dixie's Daughters*, 68. The same was true of Civil War memorials erected in the North. For example, Cleveland placed the Soldiers' and Sailors' Monument, dedicated in 1894, in the center of the city so that "people would pass it every day and be reminded of 'love of country' and "the duty that each citizen had to his native land." John Bodnar, *Remaking America: Public Memory, Commemoration, and Patriotism in the Twentieth Century* (Princeton, NJ: Princeton University Press, 1992), 3.

109. *See* McRae, *Mothers of Massive Resistance*, 41. *See also* Cox, *Dixie's Daughters*, 5, 14, 163 (showing the reciprocal relationship between the "cult of Anglo-Saxonism" and promoting the Cult of the Lost Cause—each reinforced the other); Jordan Green, "N.C.,

Ban on Removal of Confederate Monuments Is Challenged As Local Councils Continue to Bring Down Statues," *Washington Post,* November 30, 2019 (reporting the view that Confederate monuments operate as "a constant reminder of the brutality, second-class status, and political power the White population has and can exercise over our citizen neighbors with dark skin"), accessed at https://www.washingtonpost.com/national/nc-ban-on-removal-of-confederate-monuments-is-challenged-as-local-councils-continue-to-bring-down-statues/2019/11/29/ab45fe0a-1050-11ea-9cd7-a1becbc82f5e_story.html.

110. Blight, *Race and Reunion,* 282.

111. *See* McElya, "The National Mammy Controversy," 205.

112. November 30, 1899, address by J. H. Henderson at the dedication of the Confederate monument at Franklin, Tennessee, quoted in Seabrook, *Confederate Monuments,* 383.

113. *See* James M. McPherson, "Long-Legged Yankee Lies: The Southern Textbook Crusade." in Alice Fahs and Joan Waugh, eds., *The Memory of the Civil War in American Culture* (Chapel Hill: The University of North Carolina Press, 2004), 65–66; Janney, *Burying the Dead,* 139–42, 159.

114. McPherson, "Long-Legged Yankee Lies," 66–67.

115. Other "measuring rods" for identifying an acceptable textbook were that textbooks must teach that 1) Reconstruction was a tragic mistake; 2) American imperialism was a gift to nonWhite people as it brought them the uplift of civilization; 3) the nation had progressed due to the wisdom and hard work of Anglo-Saxon Protestants; and 4) the road to greater prosperity lay in the commitment of all classes working together without conflict. Foster, *Ghosts of the Confederacy,* 108–16; Brundage, *The Southern Past* 19–21, 121; McRae, *Mothers of Massive Resistance,* 41–44. Rutherford Committees also placed Confederate battle flags in nearly every public school and hung thousands of pictures of Confederate heroes, such as Robert E. Lee and Jefferson Davis. Committee members made regular school visits to monitor what children were taught about Southern culture, organized pro-Confederate programs honoring Southern heroes such as Lee, Jackson and Davis, worked with teachers to develop history lesson plans, and generally ensured that the schools were "toeing the Lost Cause line." Cox, *Dixie's Daughters,* 121, 127.

116. McPherson, "Long-Legged Yankee Lies," 67–70; Karen L. Cox, "The Confederate Monument at Arlington," in Mills and Simpson, *Monuments to the Lost Cause,* 158 & n. 36.

117. McRae, *Mothers of Massive Resistance,* 44. One effect of the UDC textbook campaign was that some national textbook publishers removed "disagreeable" matter from all of their U.S. history textbooks so that they could sell the books in both the North and the South. Unsatisfied with these modifications to Northern-published textbooks, the UDC arranged for the writing and publication of "correct" textbooks by Southern writers. These home-grown Southern textbooks conformed more perfectly to the various aspects of the Lost Cause narrative, in particular that the conduct of the Confederate soldier and his leaders was thoroughly honorable, not stained by any base motives. These textbooks painted slavery as a mutually beneficial arrangement embodying the kindest relations between the races: the South received the labor and the slave received civilization—a reprieve from his or her savage environment and an introduction to Christianity McRae, *Mothers of Massive Resistance,* 46–47; McPherson, "Long-Legged Yankee Lies," 68–70; Brundage, "Women's Hand and Heart of Deathless

Love," 74 (stating that the UDC textbook campaign included "intimidating [Northern] textbook publishers").

118. James McPherson, *The War That Forged a Nation: Why the Civil War Still Matters* (New York: Oxford University Press 2015), 37–38, 47, 49 (reporting that Confederate soldiers killed more than one-hundred Black soldiers after they had surrendered at the Battle of Fort Pillow and engaged in a similar murder of Black Union prisoners at the Battle of the Crater, within 500 yards of Robert E. Lee). In addition, partisans under the command of notorious guerrilla leader Champ Ferguson scoured the battle field following the October 1864 Battle of Saltville, Virginia, killing both Black and White wounded Union soldiers but especially targeting Black soldiers. After the Civil War, Ferguson was apprehended, tried, and hanged. See Janney, *Remembering the Civil War*, 26, 80. *See also* McPherson, *Battle Cry of Freedom*, 793 (stating that "hundreds [of Black Union soldiers] were massacred at Fort Pillow, Poison Spring, the Crater, and elsewhere").

119. Cox, *Dixie's Daughters*, 122.

120. McRae, *Mothers of Massive Resistance*, 48.

121. Janney, *Burying the Dead*, 172–73; Cox, *Dixie's Daughters*, 124–27 (concluding that Susan Pendleton Lee's history textbook portrayed the South as having had a greater impact on the nation's development than the North and described the Civil War in ways fully consistent with the Lost Cause myth).

122. McRae, *Mothers of Massive Resistance*, 49–50.

123. Brundage, *The Southern Past*, 46.

124. Quoted in McPherson, "Long-Legged Yankee Lies," 75–76.

125. McRae, *Mothers of Massive Resistance*, 56.

126. McRae, *Mothers of Massive Resistance*. 56–57.

127. Cox, *Dixie's Daughters*, 125, 161 (also concluding that one "sad reality" of the UDC textbook campaign was that the racist textbooks assigned to White Southern school children were cast off and used in Black schools exposing Black students to their teachings of Black inferiority).

128. McRae, *Mothers of Massive Resistance*, 58.

129. See discussion at Cox, *Dixie's Daughters*, 160–61.

130. *See, e.g.,* Paul Duggan, "Sins of the Father: The Confederacy Was Built on Slavery—How Can So Many Southern Whites Still Believe Otherwise?," *Washington Post,* November 28, 2018, accessed at https://www.washingtonpost.com/news/magazine/wp/2018/11/28/feature/the-confederacy-was-built-on-slavery-how-can-so-many-southern-Whites-still-believe-otherwise/?utm_term=.f296ffa49bf6 (quoting a Southern heritage advocate from the state of Virginia, over the age of 70, whose "core belief" is that slavery was not the main reason for the Civil War. "Instead, secession was a constitutionally permissible response to years of unfair tariffs and taxes imposed on the South by a tyrannical federal government").

131. McRae, *Mothers of Massive Resistance*, 60.

132. Quoted in Brundage, *The Southern Past*, 138–40.

Chapter 4: The Racial-Reckoning Approach

1. See Kirk Savage, *Standing Soldiers, Kneeling Slaves: Race, War, and Monument in Nineteenth-Century America* (Princeton, NJ: Princeton University Press, 1997), 129–30 (concluding that "the business of Confederate commemoration after the War was to

smash [the] equation [of the inseparable connection between slavery and the cause of Southern independence]. Personal and institutional memories had to be thoroughly revised [with slavery made to disappear.] A nation formed expressly to protect slaveholding . . . sought to redefine itself as an abstract moral cause [with] Confederate monuments erected [that] commemorated an old order that never existed . . .—a slave society without the moral impediment of slavery").

2. See Hilary N. Green, "Julian Carr's Speech at the Dedication of Silent Sam," accessed at http://hgreen.people.ua.edu/transcription-carr-speech.html (transcript of the dedication speech of Julian S. Carr, "Unveiling of Confederate Monument at University. June 2, 1913").

3. Savage, *Standing Soldiers, Kneeling Slaves.*

4. Savage, *Standing Soldiers, Kneeling Slaves,* 4.

5. See W. Fitzhugh Brundage, *The Southern Past: A Clash of Race and Memory* (Cambridge, MA: The Belknap Press of Harvard University Press, 2005), 106 (explaining that prior to 1900, White Democratic state governments faced strong challenges from White Republicans, Black Republicans, and Populists. They did not wish to provide funding that any of these opposing political groups might use "to promote historical narratives that were anathema to the Democratic Party and its supporters").

6. Savage, *Standing Soldiers, Kneeling Slaves,* 5.

7. See Caroline E. Janney, *Burying the Dead But Not the Past: Ladies Memorial Associations & the Lost Cause* (Chapel Hill: The University of North Carolina Press, 2008), 142; John Bodnar, *Remaking America: Public Memory, Commemoration, and Patriotism in the Twentieth Century* (Princeton, NJ: Princeton University Press, 1992), 209 (Stating that standing soldier monument transformed "ordinary foot soldiers . . . into model human beings who followed their leaders and fought for the larger political structures in which they lived").

8. Savage, *Standing Soldiers, Kneeling Slaves,* 6; Brundage, *The Southern Past,* 106 (stating that White voluntary associations "secured the imprimatur of state prestige by mobilizing the 'public' behind campaigns for monuments").

9. UDC leaders were intent to preserve the image of the UDC's reputation as an organization whose membership "exemplified upper-class or patrician values." Achieving a leadership position in the UDC represented an envied social achievement. See Karen L. Cox, *Dixie's Daughters: The United Daughters of the Confederacy and the Preservation of Confederate Culture* (Gainesville: University Press of Florida, 2003), 2, 5, 23, 29–37 (also explaining that the first generation of UDC members was mostly born after 1850, were daughters of mothers who had been active in LMAs, now wanted to establish their place in the "new order" in the South, and their opinions about the war were shaped in large measure by those who were bitter over the loss suffered by the South in the Civil War and Reconstruction); Brundage, *The Southern Past,* 37; Micki McElya, "Commemorating the Color Line: The National Mammy Controversy of the 1920s," in Cynthia Mills and Pamela H. Simpson, eds., *Monuments to the Lost Cause: Women, Art, and the Landscapes of Southern Memory* (Knoxville: The University of Tennessee Press 2003), 204–05 (concluding that by 1900 the UDC was a very successful women's organization among upper-class women who shared a "'loyalty to White supremacy [and] also sharply delineated class distinctions among Whites.' . . . The UDC carefully policed the boundary of its membership by defining who could *not* be part of its honorable South—African Americans and the poor of any race'").

10. *See* Brundage, *The Southern Past*, 44 & n. 40; Savage, *Standing Soldiers, Kneeling Slaves*, 6; William Blair, *Cities of the Dead: Contesting the Memory of the Civil War in the South 1865–1914* (Chapel Hill, University of North Carolina Press, 2004), 127–31 (showing that this shift in memorialization focus to the common soldier is best explained as a response to "an urgent need for leaders to maintain the political loyalty of followers").

11. Savage, *Standing Soldiers, Kneeling Slaves*, 6–7.

12. Karen Cox has described the Confederate monument at Arlington National Cemetery as "no less than a pro-Southern text illustrated in bronze." Cox states that the Arlington Confederate Monument reads like a pro-Southern textbook. No soldier appears worn and defeated. A faithful Negro body servant happily accompanies his master to war. A young Confederate officer consigns his children to the protective care of a loyal Black mammy, demonstrating the mutual trust and respect of the Southern master and slave. Karen L. Cox, "The Confederate Monument at Arlington," in Mills and Simpson, *Monuments to the Lost Cause*, 158.

13. *See* Janney, *Burying the Dead*, 142.

14. Savage, *Standing Soldiers, Kneeling Slaves*, 210 (concluding that the silent, aging image of the common soldier on the village green was a daily reminder year after year of the heroism of the ordinary White male who stood up for his community at a time of peril).

15. Savage, *Standing Soldiers, Kneeling Slaves*, 162–65, 181–84, 210.

16. Brundage, *The Southern Past*, 2.

17. Brundage, *The Southern Past*, 5.

18. Brundage, *The Southern Past*, 6–7.

19. Brundage, *The Southern Past*, 7

20. Brundage, *The Southern Past*, 7–9.

21. *See* Brundage, *The Southern Past*, 58–59 (showing that "illiteracy remained pervasive" and Black communities lacked the financial resources, or the political influence, to erect marble monuments in choice public spaces in Southern towns and cities).

22. Brundage, *The Southern Past*, 9–10 (observing that Southern Whites did not acknowledge African Americans' counternarrative to the White version of Southern history in part because to do so would have risked exposing to public scrutiny "the social fact of Black resistance" thus undermining White Southerners' goal of projecting a "smooth surface" of Southern race relations).

23. Brundage, *The Southern Past*, 57, 107, 115–16, 121–22.

24. *See* Kathleen Clark, "Making History: African American Commemorative Celebrations in Augusta, Georgia, 1865–1913," in Mills and Simpson, *Monuments to the Lost Cause*, 47–48 (reporting that instead of erecting permanent monuments, African Americans shaped their own historical memory through annual ceremonies and transferred this as oral tradition to their descendants).

25. Grace Elizabeth Hale, *Making Whiteness: The Culture of Segregation in the South, 1890–1940* (New York: Pantheon Books, 1998), 15–16 (concluding that "slaves had managed to carve love and even joy from . . . their oppression" and refused to permit physical slavery to become "spiritual slavery").

26. *See* Janney, *Burying the Dead*, 46–47; Blair, *Cities of the Dead*, 35–41.

27. James M. McPherson, *Battle Cry of Freedom: The Civil War Era* (New York: Oxford University Press, 1988), 38.

28. Caroline E. Janney, *Remembering the Civil War: Reunion and the Limits of Reconciliation* (Chapel Hill: The University of North Carolina Press, 2013), 33.

29. See discussion of Southern African American freedom celebrations and political rallies at Blair, *Cities of the Dead*, 23–48.

30. See discussion at Brundage, *The Southern Past*, 55. *See also* Juneteenth.com, "History of Juneteenth," accessed at http://www.juneteenth.com/history.htm (describing the history of Juneteenth, its pre-1900 celebration in Texas, the decline of Juneteenth activities after 1900, the resurgence of Juneteenth celebrations during the 1960s Civil Rights movement of the 1950s and 1960s, and the Texas legislature's 1980 declaration of Juneteenth as a state holiday).

31. Brundage, *The Southern Past*, 92–93. John Hope, a highly regarded African American educator who was born in 1868, recalled that in Augusta, Georgia, of his youth, throngs of freemen participated in massive parades that clogged the streets and filled the parks and squares with celebrations as orators spoke of emancipation, freedom, and liberty. These African Americans commemorative celebrations occurred in the decades immediately following the Civil War in many Southern cities on the anniversary of emancipation. Clark, "Making History," 46.

32. Brundage, *The Southern Past*, 93–97.

33. Brundage, *The Southern Past*, 59–62.

34. See discussion of the execution of surrendering Black Union troops at Bruce Levine, *The Fall of the House of Dixie* (New York: Random House, 2013), 168–70, 225–26.

35. See John Hope Franklin, *Reconstruction After the Civil War* (Chicago: The University of Chicago Press, 1961), 24; James McPherson, *The War That Forged a Nation: Why the Civil War Still Matters* (New York: Oxford University Press, 2015), 102.

36. Brundage, *The Southern Past*, 72. The North did not remedy this failure to recognize Black participation in the Civil War through statuary. In the nineteenth century, "only three monuments . . . depicted Blacks in military service, all appearing in the last decade of the century and none of them generic war memorials." In nineteenth-century Civil War memorials, only the Shaw memorial in Boston depicted a Black soldier in full military dress. *See* Savage, *Standing Soldiers, Kneeling Slaves*, 192–208.

37. *See* David W. Blight, *A Slave No More: Two Men Who Escaped to Freedom, Including Their Own Narratives of Emancipation* (New York: Houghton, Mifflin, Harcourt Publishing Co., 2007), 2, 14, 67, 172; McPherson, *The War That Forged a Nation*, 103–06. See Levine, *The Fall of the House of Dixie*, 298 for an argument that White racism notwithstanding, Black families prevailed in forming strong family ties, that Black institutions grew to help create strong Black communities, and that political action by Blacks built organizations that would fight for Black civil and political rights throughout the South and the nation.

38. When Blacks laid claim to a share of the public space, some Whites responded with threats and violence, including physically assaulting African Americans and banning Blacks from laying flowers on the graves of Union soldiers. See Clark, "Making History" 53.

39. Brundage, *The Southern Past*, 63–69, 73 (also explaining that Whites deployed an out-of-sight-out-of-mind strategy: Whites would shutter themselves in their homes or travel to visit out-of-town friends and relatives for the day when a Black outdoor celebration was planned or, less often but sometimes, join Blacks in these celebrations).

40. Clark, "Making History," 50–55.

41. *See* Eric Foner, *Who Owns History: Rethinking the Past in a Changing World* (New York: Hill & Wang, 2003), 16–19 (demonstrating the active role of Blacks in obtaining emancipation and asserting their post-Civil War freedom, stating the conviction "that the freed people were [not] simply victims of manipulation or passive recipients of the actions of others, [but rather] they were agents of change, whose demand for individual and community autonomy helped to establish the agenda of Reconstruction politics" and concluding that the treatment of Black political leaders in the South during Reconstruction and after its demise by past historians "strikingly illustrated how racism and a commitment to maintaining White supremacy in the South had warped scholarly writing").

42. Levine, *The Fall of the House of Dixie*, 88–89, 92–102; 105–06, 178.

43. McPherson, *The War That Forged a Nation*, 101–03 (citing Vincent Harding, *There Is a River: The Black Struggle for Freedom in America* (New York: Harcourt Brace & Co., 1981); Richard White, *The Republic for Which It Stands: The United States During Reconstruction and the Gilded Age, 1865–1896* (New York: Oxford University Press, 2017), 29–30); Blight, *A Slave No More*, 1, 81, 84, 184 (from post-emancipation "slave narratives" recounting that slaves attempting to escape and reach union lines and freedom confronted swamps and poisonous snakes along their journey).

Chapter 5: Confederate Monuments and Contemporary Institutional Racism

1. For a discussion of the South's physical environment to support Black inferiority see Jennifer L. Eberhardt, *Biased: Uncovering the Hidden Prejudice That Shapes What We See, Think, and Do* (New York: Viking, 2019), 166, 171.

2. *See, e.g.*, Dell Upton, *What Can and Can't Be Said: Race Uplift and Monument Building in the Confederate South* (New Haven, CT: Yale University Press, 2015), 18.

3. Joe R. Feagin, *Racist America: Roots, Current Realities, and Future Reparations* (3rd Ed.) (New York: Routledge, 2014), 144–46.

4. Eberhardt, *Biased: Uncovering the Hidden Prejudice*, 6.

5. Feagin, *Racist America*, 146.

6. *See* Davis Wessel, "Racial Discrimination: Still at Work in the U.S.," *Wall Street Journal*, September 4, 2003, accessed at https://www.wsj.com/articles/SB106262466678910800; Feagin, *Racist America*, x, 91 & 91 n. 82, 105, 126–29. For a discussion of "just-get-over-it claims, see Feagin, *Racist America*, 127 (detailing a recent PEW survey showing that a majority of Blacks report discrimination in jobs, housing, and other "major social areas" but finding that a majority of Whites deny any significant Black discrimination and also discussing a CNN/ORC poll showing that 61 percent of African Americans polled reported that racial discrimination remains a serious problem, compared to 25 percent of Whites).

7. One overt manifestation of outright bigotry is the alarming persistence of lynching nooses that have appeared in public spaces in recent years. *See, e.g.*, Erika Doss, *Memorial Mania: Public Feeling in America* (Chicago: University of Chicago Press, 2010), 266 (concluding that "in recent years lynching nooses have resurfaced [on a monument to an African-American hero, at schools, at post offices and in fire houses and even] hanging on the office door of an African Americans professor at Columbia University Teachers College"). In addition, "White supremacy has become increasingly public in its expressions." Kenneth J. Saltman, "'Privilege-Checking,' 'Virtue-Signaling,' and 'Safe Spaces,'" 26 Symploke 403, 403–07 (2017), accessed at https://www.jstor.org/stable/10.5250/symploke.26.1-2.0403.

8. Feagin, *Racist America*, 9–10 & 10 n. 28.

9. Upton, *What Can and Can't Be Said*, 23.

10. See discussion at Eugene Robinson, "The GOP Is Complicit in Demagoguery," *Washington Post*, November 6, 2018, accessed at https://www.sltrib.com/opinion/commentary/2018/11/06/eugene-robinson/ (assembling evidence supporting a claim of an "openly bigoted" Republican Campaign during the 2018 mid-term national elections, and citing references by President Trump "demonizing . . . Latinos as predatory criminals" and stating that "[President] Trump encourages his base to hold and express racist views about African Americans"). *See also* Michael M. Grynbaum and Niraj Chokshi, "Even Fox News Stops Running Trump Caravan Ad Characterized as Racist," *The New York Times*, November 5, 2018, accessed at https://www.nytimes.com/2018/11/05/us/politics/nbc-caravan-advertisement.html (discussing a political TV ad "by President Trump's political team . . . portraying immigrants as a violent threat . . . widely denounced as racist and misleading" and rejected by television networks as racially inflammatory).

11. *See, e.g.*, Jan Miles, *The Post-Racial Negro Green Book* (New Orleans: Brown Bird Books, 2017) (state-by-state compilation of reported racial bias against African Americans for the years 2013 to 2016).

12. I am indebted to the years of work represented in the facts and insights assembled in Professor Joe R. Feagin's book, *Racist America*. Unless otherwise indicated in footnotes, all of the examples of White racial framing, and the associated commentary, in the following section are drawn from pages 143–89 of *Racist America*.

13. See discussion of this study at Wessel, "Racial Discrimination: Still at Work in the U.S."

14. Wessel, "Racial Discrimination: Still at Work in the U.S."

15. Racial discrimination in employment exploits Black workers who are forced to work for less than they would if they had equal access to employment. White employers therefore are able to keep for themselves "more of the value of the labor of workers of color than comparable White workers." Feagin, *Racist America*, 188.

16. See discussion at Carlos Lozada, "Let's See Some I.D.," *Washington Post*, October 21, 2018, at B2, accessed at https://dougchayka.com/filter/washington-post/Let-s-See-Some-I-D (reviewing Austin Channing Brown, *I'm Still Here: Black Dignify in a World Made for Whiteness* (New York: Convergent Books, 2019)).

17. Feagin, *Racist America*, 104–05, 169 (the 1940 and the 2010 data show that on average African Americans live in urban census areas that are only 35 percent White).

18. Eberhardt, *Biased: Uncovering the Hidden Prejudice*, 159 (also reporting studies showing a direct correlation between the increasing Black density in a community and White perception of crime in that community, "regardless of whether statistics bear that out").

19. Feagin, *Racist America*, 172–73.

20. Feagin, *Racist America*, 173.

21. Feagin, *Racist America*, 175.

22. Feagin, *Racist America*, 175.

23. Feagin, *Racist America*, 156.

24. See American Civil Liberties Union, Carl F. Horowitz, and Marc Mauer, *The Persistence of Racial and Ethnic Profiling in the United States: A Follow-up Report to the U.N. Committee on the Elimination of Racial Discrimination,* (New York: National Legal

and Policy Center, 2009), accessed at https://www.aclu.org/report/persistence-racial-and-ethnic-profiling-united-states.

25. *See* Ian Ayers, "Racial Profiling and the LAPD: A Study of Racially Disparate Outcomes in the Los Angeles Police Department," (2008), accessed at http://www.aclu-sc.org/lapdracialprofiling.

26. Michelle Alexander, *The New Jim Crow: Mass Incarceration in the Age of Colorblindness* (revised ed.) (New York: The New Press, 2012), 133.

27. American Civil Liberties Union, Carl F. Horowitz, and Marc Mauer, "The Persistence of Racial and Ethnic Profiling in the United States," 13–15.

28. American Civil Liberties Union, Carl F. Horowitz, and Marc Mauer, "The Persistence of Racial and Ethnic Profiling in the United States," 35.

29. Alexander, *The New Jim Crow*, 133 & 133 n. 101.

30. American Civil Liberties Union, Carl F. Horowitz, and Marc Mauer, "The Persistence of Racial and Ethnic Profiling in the United States," 44.

31. *See* Alexander, *The New Jim Crow*, 133 & 133 n. 102.

32. Eberhardt, *Biased: Uncovering the Hidden Prejudice*, 102.

33. Alexander, *The New Jim Crow*, 134.

34. *See also* Michael R. Cogan, "The Drug Enforcement Agency's Use of Drug Courier Profiles: One Size Fits All," 41 *Cath. U. L. Rev.*, 943 (1992).

35. *See* Alexander, *The New Jim Crow*, 134 & 134 nn. 103–105. Racial profiling litigation in drug enforcement had been brought primarily pursuant to Title VI of the Civil Rights Act of 1964, which bans racial discrimination by federally funded programs such as police organizations, including actions that have a disparate racial impact (thus obviating the need to prove intent). Title VI disparate impact litigation effectively came to an end following the Supreme Court's decision in *Alexander v. Sandoval*, 532 U.S. 275 (2001). In that case, the Supreme Court held that there is no implied private right of action for individuals to sue under Title VI to challenge racial bias on a theory of disparate impact.

36. Unless otherwise indicated, the data and commentary in this section is drawn from the work of Michelle Alexander. Her careful analysis of the reality of drug-related incarceration of African Americans cited below is found in Michelle Alexander, *The New Jim Crow: Mass Incarceration in the Age of Colorblindness* (revised ed.) (New York: The New Press, 2012), 8–9, 60, 98–100.

37. Alexander, *The New Jim Crow*, 9 & 9 n. 20.

38. Alexander, *The New Jim Crow*, 102.

39. Alexander, *The New Jim Crow*, 60 & 60 nn. 1–3 (emphasis in the original).

40. Alexander, The New Jim Crow, 98.

41. Shaila Dewan, "Maryland Will Stop Prosecuting Marijuana Possession Cases," *The New York Times*, January 20, 2019, accessed at https://www.nytimes.com/2019/01/29/us/baltimore-marijuana-possession.html.

42. Ezekial Edwards, Will Bunting, and Lynda Garcia, *The War on Marijuana in Black and* White (New York: The American Civil Liberties Union, 2013), 3, 8 (cited at Feagin, *Racist America*, 159).

43. Alexander, *The New Jim Crow*, 5–7, 98–99.

44. Feagin, *Racist America*, 118, 158 (finding that overall, "Whites make up 70 percent of illegal drug-users. In addition, the majority of drug couriers are likely to be White, as are the majority of drug pushers.).

45. *See* Feagin, *Racist America*, 118, 157–58; Alexander, *The New Jim Crow*, 104–06.

46. Alexander, *The New Jim Crow*, 99–101 (also showing that racial disparity in incarceration is not explained by differences in the violence associated with drug offenses because mass incarceration of African Americans has soared irrespective of the increase or decrease of violent crime in America and, in any event, homicides account for a fraction of the increase in the rates of incarcerations).

47. *See* Gates, *Stoney the Road*, 94, 129–130, 141 (demonstrating how nineteenth and early-twentieth-century imagery created the stereotype of the "nature of Black people," their "natural propensity" as dangerous and criminally-inclined and the "nagging staying power and inertia of racist stereotypes" and how they "continue to 'do work' within our psychological and subterranean racial landscape"); Eberhardt, *Biased: Uncovering the Hidden Prejudice*, 60–66, 81 (explaining the role of ongoing racial bias in creating the contemporary "Black-crime association"—the cultural stereotype of Black males capacity to do harm).

48. Feagin, *Racist America*, 158.

49. The following summary of cognitive bias research drawn from Alexander, *The New Jim Crow*, 106–07.

50. Eberhardt, *Biased: Uncovering the Hidden Prejudice*, 81.

51. See discussion at Feagin, *Racist America*, 105, 108–09, 131–34.

52. See discussion at Alexander, *The New Jim Crow*, 106 & 106 n. 43.

53. See discussion of this experiment at Eberhardt, *Biased: Uncovering the Hidden Prejudice*, 66–68 (also showing that when the experiment was conducted with police officers, it was found that "police officers are faster to shoot Blacks with guns than Whites with guns, which demonstrates that [as with the larger population] police officers associate Blacks with crime and danger").

54. *See* Alexander, *The New Jim Crow*, 107.

55. *See* Feagin, *Racist America*, 106–07.

56. *See* Feagin, *Racist America*, 107–08.

57. The Constitution of the United States, art. 3, s. 3, defines treason against the United States "to consist only in levying war against them, or in adhering to their enemies, giving them aid or comfort."

58. Upton, *What Can and Can't Be Said*, 32.

59. John D. Foster, *White Race Discourse: Preserving Racial Privilege in the Post-Racial Society* (Lanham, MD: Lexington Books, 2013), 7 (cited at Feagin, *Racist America*, 134 & 134 n. 97).

60. Terry McAuliffe, *Beyond Charlottesville: Taking a Stand Against White Nationalism* (New York: St. Martin's Press, 2019), 48–49, 58 (also concluding that White extremists, such as the KKK use the protection of Confederate monuments as "a vehicle to ... spew their hatred").

61. Gates, *Stony the Road*, xxii.

Chapter 6: The Case Against Monument Destruction

1. *See, e.g.*, discussion at Cynthia Mills, "Introduction," in Cynthia Mills & Pamela H. Simpson, eds., *Monuments to the Lost Cause: Women, Art, and the Landscapes of Southern Memory* (Knoxville: The University of Tennessee Press 2003). xxiii–xxiv.

2. Charles R. Lawrence III, "If He Hollers Let Him Go: Regulating Racist Speech on Campus," 1990 *Duke L.J.* 431, 439–40 (showing that the underlying principle of the

Court's decision in *Brown v. Board of Education* was that segregated education, like all segregation, constitutes a "demeaning, caste-creating practice").

3. *See* Susan Svrluga, "Silent Sam Will Stay Off the University of North Carolina Campus as the School Turns the Statue Over to a Confederate Group," *Washington Post*," November 27, 2019 (discussing the objection to the decision of the University of North Carolina to transfer ownership of the University's "Silent Sam" Confederate statue to a Confederate heritage group and provide a $2.5 million trust fund for its maintenance off campus on private property, arguing that "preserving [the statue] in another location [will] harm another community"), accessed at https://www.washingtonpost.com/education/2019/11/27/silent-sam-will-stay-off-university-north-Carolina-campus-school-turns-statue-over-to-confederate-group/.

4. *See* "Whites Ferry," accessed at https://www.visitloudoun.org/listing/Whites-ferry/56/.

5. Erika Doss, *Memorial Mania: Public Feeling in America* (Chicago: The University of Chicago Press, 2010), 9.

6. Matthew Dessem, "How Did We Treat Monuments to White Supremacists When They Weren't *Our* White Supremacists?" *Slate*, August 13, 2017, accessed at https://slate.com/culture/2017/08/read-the-allied-order-to-destroy-nazi-monuments-in-germany.html (containing the text of Directive No. 30).

7. *See* The Famous Pictures Collection, "Fall of Saddam Hussein's Statue," accessed at http://www.famouspictures.org/fall-of-saddam-husseins-statue/.

8. See discussion at Arthur S. Marks, "The Statue of King George III in New York and the Iconology of Regicide," 13 *The American Art Journal* (Summer 1981), 62 (discussing the destruction of the King George III statue and the famous 1852–1853 painting by Johannes Adam Simon Oertel, which is located in the collection of the New York Historical Society, immortalizing the event and can be seen at https://www.nyhistory.org/exhibit/pulling-down-statue-king-george-iii-new-york-city); Rick Atkinson, *The British Are Coming: The War for America, Lexington to Princeton, 1775–1777* (New York: Henry Holt & Company, 2019), 349–50.

9. See Jacey Fortin, "Toppling Monuments, A Visual History," *The New York Times*, April 17, 2017, accessed at https://www.nytimes.com/2017/08/17/world/controversial-statues-monuments-destroyed.html (Concluding that "History is littered with the shattered remains of toppled statues").

10. Harold Holzer, "Lincoln, Monuments, and Memory," *Civil War Times*, November 21, 2017, reprinted in Catherine Clinton, ed., *Confederate Statues and Memorialization* (Athens: University of Georgia Press, 2019), 103, 105–06 (also recounting the toppling of statues by the Egyptians of their only female pharaoh, by Roman emperors of their predecessors, by the French of Napoleon, and by the Canadians and the East Indians of Queen Victoria).

11. Fortin, "Toppling Monuments."

12. A recovery strategy built on the notion "out of sight out of mind is a great transitional step to help someone move on." The strategy does not eliminate the source of the pain but it "allows [one] to live [a] life without dealing with the pain." Krissy Brady, "Does out of sight out of mind really work?" May 11, 2014, accessed at https://www.psychologytoday.com/us/blog/the-friendship-doctor/201203/friendship-out-sight-out-mind.

13. Doss, *Memorial Mania*, 362.

14. *See* Holzer, "Lincoln, Monuments, and Memory," 103.

15. W. Fitzhugh Brundage, "Round Table on Confederate Statues and Memorialization," in Clinton, *Confederate Statues and Memorialization*, 23–24, 36.

16. James J. Broomall, *Commentary*, in Clinton, *Confederate Statues and Memorialization*, 118–19.

17. *See* Office of the President, "Report of the Committee to Establish Principles on Renaming." November 21, 2016, at 4, accessed at https://president.yale.edu/advisory-groups/presidents-committees/committee-establish-principles-renaming-o.

18. Holzer, "Lincoln, Monuments, and Memory," 108–09.

19. "If there is a bedrock principle underlying the First Amendment, it is that government may not prohibit the expression of an idea simply because society finds the idea itself offensive or disagreeable." Texas v. Johnson, 491 U.S. 397, 414, (1989) (upholding the constitutional right to burn an American flag).

20. Virginia v. Black, 538 U.S. 343 (1996) (cross-burning is a constitutionally protected activity unless done with the intent to intimidate). *See* Roger C. Hartley, "Cross Burning–Hate Speech as Free Speech: A Comment on Virginia v. Black," 54 Cath. U. L. Rev. 1 (2004).

21. Cohen v. California, 403 U.S. 15, 26 (1971).

22. See discussion at J. Michael Martinez and William D. Richardson, "Introduction, Understanding the Debate over Confederate Symbols," in Martinez, *et al.*, *Confederate Symbols in the Contemporary South*, 6–7; J. Michael Martinez, "Traditionalist Perspectives on Confederate Symbols," in Martinez, *et al.*, *Confederate Symbols in the Contemporary South*, 244; Dell Upton, *What Can and Can't Be Said: Race Uplift and Monument Building in the Confederate South* (New Haven, CT: Yale University Press, 2015), 33.

23. *See* Martinez, "Traditionalist Perspectives on Confederate Symbols," 243 (showing that "White Southerners who cherish Confederate symbols are not necessarily racists or members of extremist 'hate' groups as some reconstructionists might have us believe"); Hannah Natanson, "Virginia Man Sues Over Story Detailing Family's Past," *Washington Post*, September 30, 2019, at B1 (reporting a defamation lawsuit by an individual who was one of thirteen plaintiffs suing to prevent removal of Charlottesville Virginia's Confederate monuments who alleged he was not a racist but claimed in this defamation action that a newspaper story of his family's slave-owning history implicitly accused him of being a racist), accessed at https://www.pressreader.com/.

24. *See* Robin W. Winks, "A Place for Liberty Monument," *New Orleans Times-Picayune*, August. 17, 1992, at B7. *See also* Sanford Levinson, *Written in Stone: Public Monuments in Changing Societies* (Durham, NC: Duke University Press, 1998), 64–66 (describing Winks view a "sophisticated" analysis of the issue of what to do with Confederate monuments); Office of the President, "Report of the Committee to Establish Principles on Renaming," at 3 (citing the Winks approach with approval).

25. Office of the President, "Report of the Committee to Establish Principles on Renaming," at 3.

26. Office of the President, "Report of the Committee to Establish Principles on Renaming," at 3.

Chapter 7: The Trouble with Contextualization

1. *See, e.g.*, Dell Upton, *What Can and Can't Be Said: Race, Uplift, and Monument Building in the Contemporary South* (New Haven, CT: Yale University Press, 2015), 179 (reporting the view of an opponent of removing a Confederate monument and urging instead construction of "additional monuments on public land to aid in telling the story of the war from all sides.").

2. See discussion at Upton, *What Can and Can't Be Said*, 21.

3. Editorial, "Liberty Monument: Then, Now," *New Orleans Times-Picayune*, February 15, 1974, cited at Upton, *What Can and Can't Be Said*, 55 & n. 66.

4. Upton, *What Can and Can't Be Said*, 196.

5. Upton, *What Can and Can't Be Said*, 211–212.

6. Erika Doss, *Memorial Mania: Public Feeling in America* (Chicago: The University of Chicago Press, 2010), 293 (showing the predominance of narratives depicting post-Civil War racial uplift and . . . Black middle class respectability").

7. Upton, *What Can and Can't Be Said*, 22, 196.

8. Upton, *What Can and Can't Be Said*, 177–79, 195–96.

9. Upton, *What Can and Can't Be Said*, 22, 178–204.

10. Upton, *What Can and Can't Be Said*, 15–21 (emphasis in the original). Unless otherwise stated, the description of the political realities that compromise contextualization as an option to removal of Confederate monuments is taken from Upton, *What Can and Can't Be Said*.

11. Upton, *What Can and Can't Be Said*, 18–19 (citing as an example the slogan adopted by the city of Atlanta, Georgia, "The City Too Busy to Hate").

12. Upton, *What Can and Can't Be Said*, 15–17, 24, 29, 34–50 (detailing the controversy over the monument of Confederate General Nathan Forrest and demonstrating how monument supporters deployed the language of multiculturalism, heritage, and history to resist removal of the monument from Selma, Alabama).

13. Upton, *What Can and Can't Be Said*, 33–34, 44–45 (also showing how defenders of the monument to Confederate General Nathan Forrest described the effort to remove the statue from its public space in Selma, Alabama, as "discriminatory and violations of civil rights by attacking the 'integrity of the Confederate heritage'").

14. Upton, *What Can and Can't Be Said*, 22.

15. For a discussion of the controversy over the Faithful Slave Memorial at Harpers Ferry, see Paul A. Shackel, "Heyward Shepherd: The Faithful Slave Memorial," 37 *Historical Archeology*, 138–48 (2003).

16. Doss, *Memorial Mania*, 46–47.

17. Doss, *Memorial Mania*, 47–49, 356–59.

18. Doss, *Monument Mania*, 293–97.

19. Philip Kennicott, "Riding Off to Richmond," *Washington Post*, September 27, 2019, at C1, accessed at https://www.washingtonpost.com/entertainment/museums/with-a-brass-band-blaring-artist-kehinde-wiley-goes-off-to-war-with-confederate-statues/2019/09/27/178bbb04-e16c-11e9-be96-6adb81821e90_story.html.

20. See discussion at Kennicott, "Riding Off to Richmond," 1, 8.

21. In some instances, there are practical, financial considerations that preclude

removing a Confederate monument. Some Confederate monuments are so vast that they cannot, as a practical matter, be moved, and should not be destroyed. For these, the best recourse may well be to add contextualization. The massive bas-reliefs carved into the side of Stone Mountain, Georgia, may be the paradigmatic example, a Confederate monument that one historian has referred to as "a billboard to White nationalism." Other Confederate monuments consume thousands of square feet of space and are too vast to be moved. *See* Rick Hampson, "American's 'Confederate Infrastructure': Too Big to Hide, Move or Raze," *USA Today*, August 17, 2017, accessed at https://www.usatoday.com/story/news/2017/08/17/americas-confederate-infrastructure-too-big-hide-move-raze-trump-tweets/574759001/.

Chapter 8: Relocation and Its Critics

1. *See, e.g.*, W. Fitzhugh Brundage, *The Southern Past: A Clash of Race and Memory* (Cambridge: The Belknap Press of Harvard University Press, 1) (reporting disparagement of Whites as the reaction by a member of The Southern Party of Virginia on the occasion of Richmond, Virginia, changing the names of two bridges from Confederate generals to civil rights leaders).

2. Brian Black and Bryn Varley, "Contesting the Sacred: Preservation and Meaning on Richmond's Monument Avenue," in Cynthia Mills and Pamela H. Simpson, eds., *Monuments to the Lost Cause: Women, Art, and the Landscapes of Southern Memory* (Knoxville: The University of Tennessee Press, 2003), 234–35.

3. While trifecta originally referred to a form of betting in which the better selects the first three finishers in exact order, today the term trifecta has been expanded to include any achievement involving three successful outcomes.

4. Erika Doss, *Memorial Mania: Public Feeling in America* (Chicago: The University of Chicago Press, 2010), 360.

5. See discussion at J. Michael Martinez, "Traditionalist Perspectives on Confederate Symbols," in J. Michael Martinez, William D. Richardson, & Ron McNinch-Su, eds., *Confederate Symbols in the Contemporary South* (Gainesville: University Press of Florida, 2000), 252; Sanford Levinson, *Written in Stone: Public Monuments in Changing Societies* (Durham, NC: Duke University Press, 1998), 63; Doss, *Memorial Mania*, 354.

6. For example, following the fall of the Communist government in 1989, some monuments were destroyed, but the Budapest City Council chose to preserve and relocate in excess of twenty monuments, including those of Marx and Engels, moving them from downtown locations to a statue park to house the monuments. *See* Kenneth E. Foote, Attila Toth, and Anett Arvay, "Hungary After 1989: Inscribing A New Past on Place," 90 *Geographical Review* 301 (2000); Nuala Johnson, "Cast in Stone: Monuments, Geography, and Nationalism," 13 *Environmental and Planning D: Society and Space* 52 (1995).

7. *See* Daniel J. Sherman, "Art, Commerce, and the Production of Memory in France after World War I," in John R. Gillis, ed., *Commemorations: The Politics of National Identity* (Princeton, NJ: Princeton University Press, 1994), 190 (concluding that location matters because "a public position [for a civic monument] serve[s] clearly to identify the community with [the] monument").

8. Sanford Levinson, "Silencing the Past: Public Monuments and the Tutelary State," 16 *Philosophy and Public Policy Quarterly* 6 (1996), 7.

9. *See, e.g.*, Walker v. Texas Division, Sons of Confederate Veterans, Inc., 576 U.S. 200 (2015) (explaining that a Confederate heritage organization prefers that Texas place

its private message, containing a Confederate battle flag symbol, on a Texas specialty license plate rather than having the message placed on a bumper sticker next to the license plate and explaining why Texas has the right to reject the heritage organization's proffered design for a specialty license place on the grounds that the design is "offensive" and Texas chooses not to be associated with this offensive symbol). *See also* Walker v. Texas Division, Sons of Confederate Veterans, Inc., 576 U.S. 200, 221 (2015) (Alito J., dissenting) (stating that "governments have long used monuments as a means of expressing a government message [and] long experience has led the public to associate public monuments with government speech").

10. Walker v. Texas Division, Sons of Confederate Veterans, Inc., 576 U.S. 200, 221 (2015) (Alito J., dissenting).

11. Pleasant Grove City v. Summum, 555 U.S. 460, 471–72 (2009).

12. Southern Poverty Law Center, "Whose Heritage?: Public Symbols of the Confederacy," 10 (2016), 1 (emphasis added), accessed at https://www.splcenter.org/20160421/whose-heritage-public-symbols-confederacy (2016, "Whose Heritage").

13. Levinson, *Written in Stone*, 21–22, 137.

14. New Orleans, for example, decided to remove several Confederate monuments from its public spaces, concluding that the monuments "had stolen the identity of New Orleans" and misrepresented contemporary New Orleans and its current citizens. See discussion at Mitch Landrieu, *In the Shadow of Statues: A White Southerner Confronts History* (New York: Viking, 2018), 171, 178–79. Virginia's political leadership has concluded that the state had worked hard to send a message "that the state was open to everyone. The last thing we wanted was for people to think that Virginia was for haters. . . . That puts up a 'not wanted' sign for businesses." Terry McAuliffe, *Beyond Charlottesville: Taking a Stand Against White Nationalism* (New York: St. Martin's Press, 2019), 52 (stating that Confederate monuments are "culturally offensive and a symbol of White supremacy" and they therefore undermine the substantial financial investment by the state to "show that [Virginians] are open and welcoming"). Universities also have concluded that continued association with and conferring an honor on certain individuals is no longer warranted because such a linkage compromises the institution's central educational mission. *See, e.g.*, Susan Svrluga, "Memo on 2017 Calhoun Naming Decision," (February 11, 2017) (announcing that the name of Yale University's Calhoun College will be changed because "John C. Calhoun's legacy as a White supremacist and a national leader who passionately promoted slavery as a 'positive good' fundamentally conflicts with Yale's mission and values"), accessed at https://www.scribd.com/document/339066721/Memo-on-2017-Calhoun-naming-decision#from_embed.

15. There is a certain irony in the fact that Confederate monument supporters advance the accusation that a proposal to remove/relocate a Confederate monument is tantamount to an attempt to rewrite/erase history since the monuments they seek to preserve pervert history by transmitting the tenets of the Lost Cause myth. This irony brings the psychological principle of projection to mind. Projection in psychology is defined as the tendency to ascribe to another person feelings, thoughts, or attitudes present in oneself, or to regard external reality as embodying such feelings, thoughts, etc., in some way. For a discussion of Freud's early development of the theory of projection, see Jean-Michel Quinodoz, *Reading Freud: A Chronological Exploration of Freud's Writings* (New Library of Psychoanalysis Teaching Series) (New York: Routledge, 2005), 24.

16. Kirk Savage, "The Politics of Memory: Black Emancipation and the Civil War

Monument," in Gillis, *Commemorations: The Politics of National Identity*, 135–36; Levinson, *Written in Stone*, 90.

17. See discussion of the desire to preserve White privilege as an explanation of why Whites resist changes in the racial *status quo* at Joe R. Feagin, *Racist America: Roots, Current Realities, and Future Reparations* (3rd. Ed.) (New York: Routledge 2014), 129.

18. *See* Doss, *Memorial Mania*, 316, 354.

19. Brundage, *The Southern Past*, 336.

20. *See* Alan T. Nolan, "The Anatomy of the Lost Cause," in Gary W. Gallagher and Alan T. Nolan, eds. *The Myth of the Lost Cause and Civil War Memory* (Bloomington, Indiana University Press, 2000), 12–13 [citing and agreeing with D. W. Brogan, "Fresh Appraisal of the Civil War," in Alfred Kazin, ed., *The Open Form* (New York: Harcourt, Brace, and World, 1965), 174.]

21. *See* Martinez, "Traditionalist Perspectives on Confederate Symbols," 243 (concluding that "traditionalists who refuse to acknowledge the racial connotations of Confederate symbols displayed in a modern context are either remarkably naive or disingenuous in ignoring historical developments since Appomattox").

22. See discussion at Beth Reingold and Richard S. Wike, "Confederate Symbols, Southern Identity, and Racial Attitudes: The Case of the State Flag, Part Two," in Martinez, *et al.*, *Confederate Symbols in the Contemporary South*, 323.

23. Martinez, "Traditionalist Perspectives on Confederate Symbols," 243.

24. See discussion at J. Michael Martinez & William D. Richardson, "Introduction: Understanding the Debate over Confederate Symbols," in Martinez, *et al.*, *Confederate Symbols in the Contemporary South*, 6–7; Martinez, "Traditionalist Perspectives on Confederate Symbols," 244.

25. *See, e.g.,* Martinez & Richardson, "Introduction: Understanding the Debate over Confederate Symbols," 11 (concluding that "southern history holds many meanings for different audiences because each audience approaches it from a different vantage point; accordingly, not all expressions of Southern culture necessarily hold racist, offensive messages. . . . [Thus] there will be no single perception of Confederate imagery [and] political disputes naturally arise").

26. *See* Martinez & Richardson, "Introduction: Understanding the Debate over Confederate Symbols," 7.

27. *See* Kirk Savage, *Standing Soldiers, Kneeling Slaves: Race, War, and Monument in Nineteenth Century America* (Princeton, NJ: Princeton University Press, 1997), 151 (stating that on the day of the laying of the Lee monument cornerstone a local Richmond newspaper argued that "the example of Lee vindicated the Old South and its slaveholding class). *Accord* Caroline E. Janney, *Remembering the Civil War: Reunion and the Limits of Reconciliation* (Chapel Hill: The University of North Carolina Press, 2013), 182 (showing that the dedication and unveiling of the Lee monument was intended as an event for Whites to promote the ideology of the Confederacy).

28. The Confederate memorial at Shiloh battlefield is entitled *Victory Defeated by Death and Night* and is located at the high-water mark of the Confederate advance against the Union troops. Erected by the United Daughters of the Confederacy, it was unveiled in 1917. Various objects were placed in the cornerstone of that monument when it was constructed, including a photograph of two local dignitaries "in Ku-Klux regalia." See Tony Horwitz, *Confederates in the Attic: Dispatches from the Unfinished Civil War* (New York, Vintage Books, 1998), 172.

29. Horwitz, *Confederates in the Attic*, 250.
30. Landrieu, *In the Shadow of Statues*, 39–40 (emphasis in the original).
31. Quoted in Horwitz, *Confederates in the Attic*, 43–44.
32. James Forman Jr., "Driving Dixie Down, Removing the Confederate Flag from Southern State Capitols," in Martinez, et al., *Confederate Symbols in the Contemporary South*, 210 (relating how, as a teenager, Forman attempted to rid his mind of the pain of state-sponsored bigotry by "clos[ing] my eyes tightly, clench[ing] my fists, and . . . slowly forc[ing] from my mind images of the flag, of the Ku Klux Klan, of Bull Connor and George Wallace—of Black people in chains, hanging from trees, kept illiterate, denied the opportunity to vote [and the concluding that] overcoming the [bigotry represented by the Georgia state] flag has taken a piece of me—a piece that I will not easily recover").
33. *Brown v. Board of Education*, 347 U.S. 483, 494 (1954).
34. Lawrence, *If He Hollers Let Him Go: Regulating Racist Speech on Campus*, 1990 Duke L. J. 431, 439 & n. 37 (citing *Plessy v. Ferguson*, 163 U.S. 537, 560 (1896) (Harlan, J., dissenting).
35. Horwitz, *Confederates in the Attic*.
36. Quoted in Horwitz, *Confederates in the Attic*, 23–24, 35, 78–98.
37. Karen L. Cox, *Dixie's Daughters: The United Daughters of the Confederacy and the Preservation of Confederate Culture* (Gainesville: University Press of Florida, 2003), 4, 67.
38. See discussion at Horwitz, *Confederates in the Attic*, 36–39.

Chapter 9: The Legal Framework Protecting Confederate Monuments

1. See discussion at Jess R. Phelps & Jessica Owley, "Etched in Stone: Historic Preservation Law and Confederate Monuments," 71 *Fla. L. Rev.* 627, 640 (2019).
2. *Pleasant Grove City v. Summum*, 555 U.S. 460, 464, 471–72 (2009) (stating that "the placement of a permanent monument in a public park is best viewed as a form of government speech and is therefore not subject to scrutiny under the Free Speech Clause."). *See* Columbia Broadcasting System, Inc. v. Democratic National Committee, 412 U.S. 94, 139, n. 7 (1973) (Stewart, J., concurring) ("Government is not restrained by the First Amendment from controlling its own expression").
3. *See* Keller v. State Bar of Cal., 496 U.S. 1, 12–13 (1990); *Johanns v. Livestock Marketing Assn.*, 544 U.S. 550, 574 (2005) (Souter, J., dissenting) ("To govern, government has to say something, and a First Amendment heckler's veto of any forced contribution to raising the government's voice in the 'marketplace of ideas' would be out of the question."). This right of government to subsidize its own speech through taxation is not to be confused with efforts by government to compel private persons themselves to convey the government's speech, something the Free Speech Clause prohibits. *See, e.g.*, Walker v. Texas Div., Sons of Confederate Veterans, 576 U.S. 200, 219 (2015); Wooley v. Maynard, 430 U.S.705, 715 (1977).
4. *Pleasant Grove City v. Summum*, 55 U.S. at 467–68, 470.
5. *Monumental Task Committee, Inc. v. Foxx*, 157 F.Supp.3d 573, 594 (E.D. La. 2016).
6. *Board of Regents of Univ. of Wis. System v. Southworth*, 529 U.S. 217, 235 (2000).
7. *Personnel Administrator v. Feeney*, 442 U.S. 256 (1979).
8. The academic literature contains arguments that government's maintaining a Confederate monument in a public space can be viewed as a violation of the Equal Protection Clause. *See, e.g.*, Zachary Bray, "Monuments of Folly: How Local Governments

Can Challenge Confederate "Statue Statutes," 91 *Temp. L. Rev.* 1, 18 (2018). These arguments depend on a judicial finding that every Confederate monument denigrates racial minorities by implicitly transmitting the message that is "something akin" to a sign stating, "This town is for Whites only." That may be the *effect* of Confederate monuments, as this book argues. But that is not the message Confederate monuments convey *on their face*. A court is likely to follow Supreme Court precedent and distinguish between *de jure* and *de facto* discrimination. Accordingly, for any Confederate monument that on its face does not discriminate racially, no equal protection violation will be found absent the unlikely finding of extrinsic evidence that not removing the monument was motivated by a desire to create the negative racial stereotyping that in fact the monument creates.

9. 54 U.S.C. § 302101; *National Register of Historic Places*, U.S. Gen. Servs. Admin., https://www.gsa.gov/real-estate/historic-preservation/historic-building-stewardship/national-register-of-historic-places.

10. See discussion at Phelps & Owley, "Etched in Stone," 643.

11. See 54 U.S.C. § 306108; 36 C.F.R. § 800.1 (2018); *Protecting Historic Properties: A Citizen's Guide to Section 106 Review*, ACHP, https://www.achp.gov/sites/default/files/documents/2017-01/CitizenGuide.pdf [https://perma.cc/4BWT-VMMS],

12. Phelps & Owley, "Etched in Stone," 645.

13. *See* Coliseum Square Association, Inc. v. Jackson, 465 F.3d 215, 225 (5th Cir. 2006); Business & Residents Alliance of E. Harlem v. Jackson, 430 F.3d 584, 591 (2d Cir. 2005) (holding that the NHPA "does not itself require a particular outcome, but rather ensures that the relevant federal agency will, before approving funds . . . consider the potential impact of that undertaking on surrounding historic places").

14. Monumental Task Committee, Inc. v. Foxx, 157 F.Supp.3d 573, 594 (E.D. La. 2016) (holding that "Plaintiffs have not demonstrated any nexus between a federally-funded project . . . and the removal of the monuments at issue. Therefore, Plaintiffs . . . fail to demonstrate a likelihood of success on the merits of their NHPA claim.), *affd. sub nom*, Monumental Task Committee, Inc. v. Chao, 678 Fed.Appx. 250 (Mem.) (5th Cir. 2017). *See also* Phelps & Owley, "Etched in Stone," 649 (concluding that the NHPA only applies "1) where federal funding is used for removal or modification [of a monument] and (2) where the monument is located on federal land").

15. Pub. L. No. 101-650, 104 Stat. 5128 (1990) [codified as amended at 17 U.S.C. § 106A (2012)].

16. See also discussion of state visual arts protection legislation at Phelps & Owley, "Etched in Stone," 657–58 (explaining that some state VARA legislation expands the number of years that visual art is protected and sometimes prohibits removal and relocation).

17. See discussion at Phelps & Owley, "Etched in Stone," 656 (discussing the California Environmental Quality Act (CEQA) as an example of a state environmental policy act with a substantive component and *League of Protection of Oakland's Architectural & Historic Resources v. City of Oakland*, 60 Cal. Rptr. 2d 821, 829 (Ct. App. 1997), that prohibited demolition of a historic house after rejecting placing historic markers and documentation as alternative adequate mitigation).

18. The seven states that had enacted monument-specific legislation as of mid-2020 are Alabama (2017), Georgia (early 20th century, updated 2001), Kentucky (2015), Mississippi (2004), North Carolina (2015), South Carolina (2000), and Tennessee (2013, updated 2016). Virginia enacted such a ban in 1904, and updated it in 2010, but repealed

its legislation, effective July 1, 2020. *See* Laura Taylor, "Bill to Repeal Discriminatory Language and Replace Confederate Statues Becomes Law in Virginia," *WSET News* April 11, 2020 (Reporting that the governor of Virginia had signed legislation repealing Virginia's law banning the removal of Confederate monuments and permitting removal as of July 1, 2020), accessed at https://wset.com/news/at-the-capitol/bills-to-repeal-discriminatory-language-and-replace-confederate-statues-become-law-in-va.

19. Ala. Code § 41-9-231.

20. See Brief for Appellees at 12, State of Alabama v. City of Birmingham, No.1180342 (Sup. Ct. Ala. May 21, 2019), 2019 WL 2710813 (Ala.) (Appellate Brief).

21. O.C.G.A. § 50-3-1(b)(2) (2018) (emphasis added). *See also* South Carolina's heritage protection legislation at S.C. Code Ann. § 10-1-165 (2018) (banning removal of monuments erected in remembrance of the "War Between the States" and requiring a two-thirds vote of the legislature to repeal the legislation).

22. Va. Code Ann. § 15.2-1812 (2019) (banning removal of "Confederate or Union" monuments). *See* Shannon Van Sant, "Judge Blocks Removal of Confederate Statue That Sparked Charlottesville Protest," *NPR*, September 14, 2019, accessed at https://www.npr.org/2019/09/14/760876494/judge-blocks-removal-of-confederate-statue-that-sparked-charlottesville-protest. Virginia repealed its legislation banning monument removal, effective July 1, 2020.

23. *See, e.g.*, Tennessee Heritage Protection Act of 2016, Tenn. Code Ann. § 4-1-412 (2019) (providing an option for local governments to apply for a waiver of the removal bar by filing with the Tennessee Historical Commission, to be granted only upon two-thirds vote of the Commission members); Ky. Rev. Stat. Ann. §§ 171.780-.788 (West 2019) (providing for removal bar of monuments designated at a military heritage site and option of local governments to lodge applications for rescission of that such designation of a monument but only upon the unanimous vote of the "Kentucky Military Heritage Commission). For a discussion of North Carolina's "Cultural History Artifact Management and Patriotism Act of 2015," see Kasi I. Wahlers, "North Carolina's Heritage Protection Act : Cementing Confederate Monuments in North Carolina's Landscape," 94 *N.C. L. Rev.* 2176 (2016) (explaining that in North Carolina, Confederate monuments owned by the state and located on public property may not be relocated except under limited circumstances and then only with the concurrence of the North Carolina Historical Commission).

24. See discussion at W. Davis Riddle, "How Devolved Is Too Devolved?: A Comparative Analysis Examining the Allocation of Power Between State and Local Government Through the Lens of the Confederate Monument Controversy," 53 *Ga. L. Rev.* 367, 377–78 (2018) (explaining that Lexington, Kentucky retained jurisdiction to remove its Confederate monuments because they had not been designated as Kentucky Military Heritage sites).

25. *See* Mississippi Military Protection Act, Ch. 4463, 2004 Miss. Laws 496 (codified as amended at Miss. Code Ann. §55-15-8).

26. Bray, "Monuments of Folly," 248–49.

27. Riddle, "How Devolved Is Too Devolved," 383.

28. See discussion at Bray, "Monuments of Folly," 10, 13–14.

29. *See* Jordan Green, "N.C., Ban on Removal of Confederate Monuments Is Challenged As Local Councils Continue to Bring Down Statues," *Washington Post*, November 30, 2019 (also discussing the removal of a Confederate monument in Winston-Salem,

North Carolina on land previously owned by the county but sold in 2014 to a private developer and converted to residential apartments), accessed at https://www.washingtonpost.com/national/nc-ban-on-removal-of-confederate-monuments-is-challenged-as-local-councils-continue-to-bring-down-statues/2019/11/29/ab45fe0a-1050-11ea-9cd7-a1becbc82f5e_story.html.

30. *See* Rust v. Sullivan, 500 U.S. 173, 194 (1991) (supporting government's right to decide its own message through decision to exclude abortion-related services from federally funded pre-conception family planning program).

31. Pleasant Grove City v. Summum, 555 U.S. 460, 464, 471–72 (2009).

32. Walker v. Texas Div., Sons of Confederate Veterans. 576 U.S. 200, 220 (2015).

33. *See* Wooley v. Maynard, 430 U.S. 705 (1977) (unlawful for New Hampshire to criminalize an objection to the view expressed in the motto "Live Free or Die" located on the state automobile license plate by affixing a piece of red tape over the motto); Board of Education v. Barnette, 319 U.S. 624 (1943) (striking down statute requiring public school students to salute the American flag).

34. Pleasant Grove City v. Summum, 555 U.S. at 464 (confirming a local government's right to refuse a demand from a private party that it erect a monument in a public park the town controls).

35. *See* Brief for Appellees at 15, State of Alabama v. City of Birmingham, No.1180342 (Sup. Ct. Ala. May 21, 2019), 2019 WL 2710813 (Ala.) (Appellate Brief) [responding to the State of Alabama's appeal to the Alabama Supreme Court of the decision by the Jefferson County Circuit Court (C. 350–359)].

36. *See* State of Alabama v. City of Birmingham (Ala. S.Ct.), –So. 3d–. 2019 WL 6337424 (2019).

37. *See, e.g.,* Yishai Blank, *City Speech*, 54 *Harv. C.R.-C.L. L. Rev.* 365 (2019).

38. *See, e.g.,* Pleasant Grove City v. Summum, 555 U.S. at 464 (unsuccessful effort by private group to force a town to place a statue in the town's public park); Walker v. Texas Division, Sons of Confederate Veterans, 576 U.S. 200, 220 (2015) (unsuccessful effort by private party to force Texas to place certain pro-Confederate messaging on Texas automobile license plates).

39. A lower state court held that Alabama's heritage protection statute, applied to bar Birmingham, Alabama, from removing its Confederate monument, violated the city's constitutionally recognized free speech rights. *See* Brief for Appellees at 9, State of Alabama v. City of Birmingham, No.1180342 (Sup. Ct. Ala. May 21, 2019), 2019 WL 2710813 (Ala.) (Appellate Brief). This ruling appears to be inconsistent with court of appeals precedent. See *e.g.,* United States v. State of Alabama, 791 F.2d 1450, 1455 (11th Cir. 1986) (holding that while there is no *per se* rule barring suits against a state by governmental entities that are state political subdivisions, and thus creatures of the state, "a city or county cannot challenge a state statute *on federal constitutional grounds*) (emphasis added). The Alabama Supreme Court reversed the lower court on that ground. State of Alabama v. City of Birmingham, –So. 3d–. 2019 WL 6337424 (2019).

40. The Fourteenth Amendment defines "citizen of the United States" as "[a]ll persons born or naturalized in the United States."

41. *See, e.g.,* Citizens United v. Federal Election Commission, 558 U.S. 310 (2010); First National Bank of Boston v. Bellotti, 435 U.S. 765 (1978).

42. *See* Ysursa v. Pocatello Educ. Association, 555 U.S. 353, 363–64 (2009) (emphasis added).

43. *See, e.g.*, United States v. State of Alabama, 791 F.2d 1450, 1455 (11th Cir. 1986) (holding that while there is no *per se* rule barring suits against a state by governmental entities that are state political subdivisions, and thus creatures of the state, "a city or county cannot challenge a state statute *on federal constitutional grounds*") (emphasis added).

44. Pleasant Grove City v. Summum, 555 U.S. at 467 (emphasis added).

45. Ysursa v. Pocatello Educ. Assn., 555 U.S. 353, 363–64 (2009) (emphasis added).

46. *See, e.g.*, Hunter v. City of Pittsburgh, 207 U.S. 161 (1907); City of Trenton v. New Jersey, 262 U.S. 182 (1923); Williams v. Mayor & City Council of Baltimore, 289 U.S. 36 (1933). The Supreme Court has withdrawn somewhat from such a broad statement precluding states' political subdivision from suing the state, holding, for example, that state subdivisions may sue states to enforce rights grounded in sources other than the Constitution's guarantee of individual constitutional rights found in the Fourteenth Amendment. *See, e.g.,* Rogers v. Brockette, 588 F.2d 1057,1068 (5th Cir. 1979) (holding that there is no bar to a suit against a state by one of its political subdivisions based on *federally-granted statutory rights*, but local entity has no constitutional-based rights of its own that it may assert to challenge state law).

47. Singleton v. Wulff, 428 U.S. 106, 114–16 (1976). *Accord* Craig v. Boren, 429 U.S. 190, 196 (1976); Eisenstadt v. Baird, 405 U.S. 438, 443–46 (1972).

48. *See, e.g.*, Caplin & Drysdale, Chartered v. United States, 491 U.S. 617, 623 n. 3 (1989) (attorney granted third-party standing to assert client's Sixth Amendment right in the absence of any obstacle to the client raising the issue).

49. *See, e.g.*, Singleton v. Wulff, 428 U.S. 106, 114–16 (1976) (obstacle found when third-party was a pregnant woman; even though woman could have litigated her own right to obtain an abortion the pregnant woman's absence from court may have been explained by a desire to "protect the . . . privacy of her decision from the publicity of a court suit); Craig v. Boren, 429 U.S. 190, 196 (1976) (requisite obstacle found in case litigating the Equal Protection rights of males below the age of twenty-one who claimed being denied the same right to purchase alcohol as women who were between the ages of eighteen and twenty-one even though males could have themselves sued where on balance the prudential objectives on third-party standing, are not well served by delay and where the litigant before the court has presented the applicable constitutional questions "vigorously and "cogently"); Eisenstadt v. Baird, 405 U.S. 438, 443–446, (1972) (holding that the impact of the governmental action is the critical factor in third-party standing cases and here a distributor of vaginal foam has standing to assert the rights of unmarried persons denied access to contraceptives because their ability to obtain them will be materially impaired by enforcement of the statute). *See also* Caplin & Drysdale, Chartered v. United States, 491 U.S. 617, 623 n. 3 (1989) (holding that the absence of obstacle excused when on balance the litigant before the court has a close relationship with the third party and the challenged government action is likely to have a serious adverse impact on third-party interests).

50. Singleton v. Wulff, 428 U.S. at 114–16.

51. *See, e.g.*, Neil MacFarquhar, "Scrutiny for Extremist Symbols After Attacks in U.S.," *New York Times*, September 26, 2019 (discussing findings that "a more fluid use of [White extremist] symbols ha[s] accelerated since the 1980s"), available at https://www.nytimes.com/2019/09/26/us/White-supremacy-symbols.html.

52. See NAACP v. Alabama, 357 U.S. 449 (1958) (NAACP members' asserted privacy right to withhold their connection to the NAACP could not be effectively vindicated

except through an appropriate representative before the Court because to require that the right be claimed by the members themselves would result in nullification of members' strong desire for anonymity during a very contentious period of civil rights conflict in Alabama).

53. See Ysursa v. Pocatello Educ. Assn., 555 U.S. 353, 363–64 (2009).
54. Gomillion v. Lightfoot, 364 U.S. 339, 344–45 (1960).
55. Gomillion v. Lightfoot, 364 U.S. at 347.
56. Washington v. Seattle School Dist. No. 1, 458 U.S. 457 (1982).
57. Romer v. Evans, 517 U.S. 620 (1996). See also Papasan v. Allain, 478 U.S. 265 (1986) (local school officials could assert a constitutional claim on behalf of itself and school children when the local officials and school children joined to challenge a state law).
58. Wooley v. Maynard, 430 U.S. 705 (1977).
59. Pleasant Grove v. Summum, 555 U.S. 460, 464, 471–72 (2009).
60. Pleasant Grove City v. Summum, 555 U.S. at 470–71.
61. Pleasant Grove City v. Summum, 555 U.S. at 474.
62. Pleasant Grove v. Summum, 555 U.S. at 470–471.
63. Board of Regents of Univ. of Wis. System v. Southworth, 529 U.S. 217, 235 (2000).

Conclusion

1. *See, e.g.*, Theodore Roosevelt IV, *The Man in the Arena: Selected Writings of Theodore Roosevelt-A Reader* (New York: Forge Books (Macmillan), 2016) (Roosevelt quote asserting that "the credit [for social progress] goes to the man who is actually in the arena . . . who spends himself in a worthy cause [who] at the best knows at the end the triumph of high achievement and who, at the worst, if he fails, at least fails while daring greatly").

2. See Richard Fausset and Campbell Robertson, "Beyond College Campuses and Public Scandals, A Racist Tradition Lingers," *New York Times*, February 8, 2019, accessed at https://www.nytimes.com/2019/02/08/us/northam-Blackface-virginia.html (quoting a Republican from Illinois who served as House minority leader, who expressed the view that Blackface was "just a part of life" that "was fun" and a Kansas local politician whose response to criticism of White men in Blackface was "You've got to stop this P.C. nonsense"). Michelle Alexander, *The New Jim Crow: Mass Incarceration in the Age of Colorblindness* (New York: The New Press, 2010).

3. It might also be accurate (perhaps more accurate) to understand the Confederate removal/relocation movement as a continuation of the Civil Rights movement of the 1960s, an ongoing effort to dismantle Jim Crow. See Jonathan I. Leib, Gerald R. Webster, & Roberta H. Webster, "Rebel with a Cause? Iconography and Public Memory in the Southern United States" 52 *GeoJournal*, 303–10 (2000): (explaining the effort to remove Confederate symbols as a "battle" that is part of "the Civil Rights era . . . effort to celebrate the destruction of the segregated 'Jim Crow' South").

Bibliography

Alexander, Michelle. *The New Jim Crow: Mass Incarceration in the Age of Colorblindness* (revised ed.). New York: The New Press, 2012.

Allen, James, ed. *Without Sanctuary: Lynching Photography in America.* Santa Fe: Twin Palms Publishers, 2000.

American Civil Liberties Union, Carl F. Horowitz, and Marc Mauer. *The Persistence of Racial and Ethnic Profiling in the United States: A Follow-up Report to the U.N. Committee on the Elimination of Racial Discrimination.* New York: National Legal and Policy Center, 2009.

Apel, Dora. *Imagery of Lynching: Black Men, White Women, and the Mob.* New Brunswick, NJ: Rutgers University Press, 2004.

Associated Press. "Man in Charlottesville Car Attack Gets Life Sentence Plus 419 Years." *Huffington Post,* July 15, 2019.

Atkinson, Rick. *The British Are Coming: The War for America, Lexington to Princeton, 1775–1777.* New York: Henry Holt & Company, 2019.

Ayers, Ian. "Racial Profiling and the LAPD: A Study of Racially Disparate Outcomes in the Los Angeles Police Department." (2008), http://www.aclu-sc.org/lapdracialprofiling.

Bailey, Anne C. *The Weeping Time: Memory and the Largest Slave Auction in American History.* New York: Cambridge University Press, 2017.

Baumgaertner, Emily. "Newly Discovered 'Limb Pit' Reveals Civil War Surgeons' Bitter Choices." *The New York Times,* June 20, 2018.

Bishir, Catherine W. "'A Strong Force of Ladies': Women, Politics, and Confederate Memorial Associations in the Nineteenth Century," in Cynthia Mills & Pamela H. Simpson, eds., *Monuments to the Lost Cause: Women, Art, and the Landscapes of Southern Memory.* Knoxville: The University of Tennessee Press, 2003.

Black, Brian, and Bryn Varley. "Contesting the Sacred: Preservation and Meaning on Richmond's Monument Avenue," in Cynthia Mills & Pamela H. Simpson, eds., *Monuments to the Lost Cause: Women, Art, and the Landscapes of Southern Memory.* Knoxville: The University of Tennessee Press, 2003.

Blair, William A. *Cities of the Dead: Contesting the Memory of the Civil War in the South, 1865–1914.* Chapel Hill: University of North Carolina Press, 2004.

Blank, Yishai. *City Speech.* 54 Harv. C.R.-C.L. L. Rev. 365 (2019).

Blight, David W. "Decoration Days: The Origins of Memorial Day in North and South," in Alice Fahs and Joan Waugh, eds., *The Memory of the Civil War in American Culture.* Chapel Hill: The University of North Carolina Press, 2004.

Blight, David W. *A Slave No More: Two Men Who Escaped to Freedom, Including Their Own Narratives of Emancipation.* New York: Houghton, Mifflin, Harcourt Publishing Co., 2007.

Blight, David W. *Race and Reunion: The Civil War in American Memory.* Cambridge, MA: Belknap Press of Harvard University Press, 2001.

Bodnar, John. *Remaking America: Public Memory, Commemoration, and Patriotism in the Twentieth Century.* Princeton, NJ: Princeton University Press, 1992.

Bohannon, Keith S. "'These Few Gray-Haired, Battle-Scarred Veterans:' Confederate Army Reunions in Georgia, 1885–95," in Gary W. Gallagher and Alan T. Nolan, eds., *The Myth of the Lost Cause and Civil War Memory.* Bloomington: Indiana University Press, 2000.

Bomboy, Scott. "Confederate Monuments Debate Heads to the Courts," *Constitution Daily,* January 30, 2018.

Bonekemper Edward H., III. *The Myth of the Lost Cause.* Washington, DC: Regnery History, 2015.

Brands, H. W. *American Colossus: The Triumph of Capitalism 1865–1900.* New York: Doubleday, 2010.

Bray, Zachary. "Monuments of Folly: How Local Governments Can Challenge Confederate "Statue Statutes." 91 *Temp. L. Rev.* 1(2018).

Brief for Appellees, State of Alabama v. City of Birmingham, No.1180342 (Sup. Ct. Ala. May 21, 2019), 2019 WL 2710813 (Ala.) (Appellate Brief).

Britton, Dee. "What is Collective Memory," *Memory Worlds,* https://memorialworlds.com/what-is-collective-memory/.

Brogan, D.W. "Fresh Appraisal of the Civil War," in Alfred Kazin, ed., *The Open Form.* New York: Harcourt, Brace, and World, 1965.

Brown, Austin Channing. *I'm Still Here: Black Dignify in a World Made for Whiteness.* New York: Convergent Books, 2019.

Browne, Allan. "The Confederate Monument in Rockville." *Landmarks,* March 26, 2017.

Brundage, W. Fitzhugh. "'Women's Hand and Heart of Deathless Love:' White Women and the Commemorative Impulse in the New South," in Cynthia Mills & Pamela H. Simpson, eds., *Monuments to the Lost Cause: Women, Art, and the Landscapes of Southern Memory.* Knoxville: The University of Tennessee Press, 2003.

Brundage, W. Fitzhugh. *The Southern Past: A Clash of Race and Memory.* Cambridge, MA: The Belknap Press of Harvard University Press, 2005.

Carbone, Christopher. "Which Confederate Statues Were Removed? A Running List." http://www.foxnews.com/us/2018/03/11/which-confederate-statues-were-removed-running-list.html.

Cash, W. J. *The Mind of the South.* New York: Alfred A. Knopf, Inc., 1941.

Civil War Trust. *History: Civil War Casualties.* //www.civilwar.org/learn/articles/civil-war-casualties.

Clark, Kathleen. "Making History: African American Commemorative Celebrations in Augusta, Georgia, 1865–1913," in Cynthia Mills & Pamela H. Simpson, eds., *Monuments to the Lost Cause: Women, Art, and the Landscapes of Southern Memory.* Knoxville: The University of Tennessee Press, 2003.

Clinton, Catherine, ed. *Confederate Statues and Memorialization.* Athens: University of Georgia Press, 2019.

Cogan, Michael R. "The Drug Enforcement Agency's Use of Drug Courier Profiles: One Size Fits All." 41 *Catholic University Law Review* 943 (1992).

Coker, Rachel. "Historian Revises Estimate of Civil War Dead." *Discover-e Binghamton Research,* September 21, 2011.

Coski, John M. "The Confederate Battle Flag in Historical Perspective," in J. Michael Martinez, William D. Richardson, and Ron McNinch-Su, eds., *Confederate Symbols in the Contemporary South*. Gainesville: University Press of Florida, 2000.

Cox, Karen L. "The Confederacy's 'Living Monuments.'" *The New York Times*, October 6. 2017.

Cox, Karen L. "The Confederate Monument at Arlington," in Cynthia Mills and Pamela H. Simpson, eds., *Monuments to the Lost Cause: Women, Art, and the Landscapes of Southern Memory*. Knoxville: The University of Tennessee Press, 2003.

Cox, Karen L. *Dixie's Daughters: The United Daughters of the Confederacy and the Preservation of Confederate Culture*. Gainesville: University Press of Florida, 2003.

Currey, David. "The Virtuous Soldier: Constructing a Usable Confederate Past in Franklin, Tennessee," in Cynthia Mills & Pamela H. Simpson, eds., *Monuments to the Lost Cause: Women, Art, and the Landscapes of Southern Memory*. Knoxville: The University of Tennessee Press, 2003.

Davis, Gode and James M. Fortier. *American Lynching: A Documentary Feature*. (Revised September 2005), http://www.americanlynching.com/treatment.htm.

Dessem, Matthew. "How Did We Treat Monuments to White Supremacists When They Weren't Our White Supremacists?" *Slate*, August 13, 2017.

Dew, Charles B. *Apostles of Disunion: Southern Secession Commissioners and the Causes of the Civil War*. Charlottesville: University Press of Virginia, 2001.

Dewan, Shaila. "Maryland Will Stop Prosecuting Marijuana Possession Cases." *The New York Times*, January 20, 2019.

Domby, Adam. *The False Cause: Fraud, Fabrication, and White Supremacy in Confederate Memory*. Charlottesville: University of Virginia Press, 2020.

Doss, Erika. *Memorial Mania: Public Feeling in America*. Chicago: The University of Chicago Press, 2010.

Douglass, Frederick. "What the Black Man Wants." (1865) *Teaching American History*, https://teachingamericanhistory.org/library/document/what-the-Black-man-wants/.

Du Bois, W. E. B. *Black Reconstruction in America: An Essay Toward African Americans History of the Part Which Black Folk Played in the Attempt to Reconstruct Democracy in America, 1860–1889*. Cleveland, OH: Harcourt Brace, 1935 (reprint, 1968).

Duggan, Paul. "Four Alleged Members of Hate Group Charged in 2017 'Unite the Right' Rally in Charlottesville." *Washington Post*, October 3, 2018.

Duggan, Paul. "Sins of the Father: The Confederacy Was Built on Slavery. How Can So Many Southern Whites Still Believe Otherwise?" *Washington Post*, November 28, 2018.

Durden, Robert F. *The Gray and the Black*. Baton Rough: Louisiana State University Press, 1972.

Eberhardt Jennifer L. *Biased: Uncovering the Hidden Prejudice That Shapes What We See, Think, and Do*. New York: Viking, 2019.

Editorial. "Liberty Monument: Then, Now." *New Orleans Times-Picayune*, February 15, 1974.

Edwards, Ezekial. Will Bunting, and Lynda Garcia, *The War on Marijuana in Black and White*. New York: The American Civil Liberties Union, 2013.

Ellis, Joseph J. *American Sphinx: The Character of Thomas Jefferson*. New York: Alfred A. Knopf, 1996.

Fausset, Richard and Campbell Robertson. "Beyond College Campuses and Public

Scandals, A Racist Tradition Lingers," *The New York Times*, February 8, 2019, accessed at https://www.nytimes.com/2019/02/08/us/northam-Blackface-virginia.html.

Faust, Drew Gilpin. *The Creation of Confederate Nationalism: Ideology and Identity in the Civil War South*. Baton Rouge: Louisiana State University Press, 1988.

Feagin, Joe R. *Racist America: Roots, Current Realities, and Future Reparations (3rd ed.)*. New York: Routledge, 2014.

Finkelman, Paul. *Defending Slavery: Proslavery Thought in the Old South: A Brief History with Documents*. Boston: Bedford/St. Martin's Press, 2003.

Foner, Eric. *The Fiery Trial: Abraham Lincoln and American Slavery*. New York: W.W. Norton & Co., 2011.

Foner, Eric. *Who Owns History: Rethinking the Past in a Changing World*. New York: Hill & Wang, 2003.

Foote, Kenneth E., Attila Toth, and Anett Arvay. "Hungary After 1989: Inscribing A New Past on Place." 90 *Geographical Review* 301 (2000).

Forman, James Jr. "Driving Dixie Down, Removing the Confederate Flag from Southern State Capitols," in J. Michael Martinez, William D. Richardson, and Ron McNinch-Su, eds., *Confederate Symbols in the Contemporary South*. Gainesville: University Press of Florida, 2000.

Fortin, Jacey. "Toppling Monuments, A Visual History." *The New York Times*, April 17, 2017.

Foster, Gaines M. *Ghosts of the Confederacy: Defeat, the Lost Cause, and the Emergence of the New South*. New York: Oxford University Press, 1987.

Foster, John D. *White Race Discourse: Preserving Racial Privilege in the Post-Racial Society*. Lanham, MD: Lexington Books, 2013.

Franklin, John Hope. *Reconstruction After the Civil War*. Chicago: The University of Chicago Press, 1961.

Gaither, Gerald H. *Blacks and the Populist Movement: Ballots and Bigotry in the New South*. Tuscaloosa: The University of Alabama Press, 2005.

Gallagher, Gary W. "Jubal A. Early, the Lost Cause, and Civil War History," in Gary W. Gallagher and Alan T. Nolan, eds., *The Myth of the Lost Cause and Civil War Memory*. Bloomington: Indiana University Press, 2000.

Gallagher, Gary W. "Round Table on Confederate Statues and Memorialization," in Catherine Clinton, ed., *Confederate Statues and Memorialization*. Athens: University of Georgia Press, 2019.

Gates, Henry Louis Jr. *Stony the Road: Reconstruction, White Supremacy, and the Rise of Jim Crow*. New York: Penguin Press, 2019.

Gerteis, Joseph. *Class and the Color Line: Interracial, Class Coalition in the Knights of Labor and the Populist Movement*. Durham, NC: Duke University Press, 2007.

Gillis, John R. "Introduction, "Memory and Identity: The History of a Relationship," in John R. Gillis, ed., *Commemorations: The Politics of National Identity*. Princeton, NJ: Princeton University Press, 1994.

Gordon, Lesley F. "'Let the People See the Old Life as It Was:' LaSalle Corbell Pickett and the Myth of the Lost Cause," in Gary W. Gallagher and Alan T. Nolan, eds., *The Myth of the Lost Cause and Civil War Memory*. Bloomington: Indiana University Press, 2000.

Green, Hilary N. "Julian Carr's Speech at the Dedication of Silent Sam," http://hgreen.people.ua.edu/transcription-carr-speech.html.

Green, Jordan. "N.C. Ban on Removal of Confederate Monuments Is Challenged As Local Councils Continue to Bring Down Statues." *Washington Post,* November 30, 2019.

Grimes Alan P. *Democracy and the Amendments to the Constitution.* Lanham, MD: University Press of America, 1978.

Grynbaum, Michael M. and Niraj Chokshi. "Even Fox News Stops Running Trump Caravan Ad Characterized as Racist." *The New York Times,* November 5, 2018.

Guelzo, Allen C. *Gettysburg: The Last Invasion.* New York: Alfred A. Knopf, 2013.

Hacker, J. David. "A Census-based Count of the Civil War Dead." 57 *Civil War History* 307 (2011).

Hahn Steven. *A Nation Under Our Feet: Black Political Struggles in the Rural South From Slavery to the Great Migration.* Cambridge, MA: Belknap Press of Harvard University Press, 2003.

Hale, Grace Elizabeth. "Granite Stopped Time: Stone Mountain Memorial and the Representation of White Southern Identity," in Cynthia Mills & Pamela H. Simpson, eds., *Monuments to the Lost Cause: Women, Art, and the Landscapes of Southern Memory.* Knoxville: The University of Tennessee Press, 2003.

Hale, Grace Elizabeth. *Making Whiteness: The Culture of Segregation in the South, 1890–1940.* New York: Pantheon Books, 1998.

Hampson, Rick. "American's 'Confederate Infrastructure:' Too Big to Hide, Move or Raze." *USA Today,* August 17, 2017.

Harding, Vincent. *There Is a River: The Black Struggle for Freedom in America.* New York: Harcourt Brace & Co., 1981.

Hartley, Roger C. "Cross Burning—Hate Speech as Free Speech: A Comment on Virginia v. Black." 54 *Catholic University Law Review* 1 (2004).

Hayes, Stephen F. "Where are Trump's 'Very Fine People'?" *The Weekly Standard,* August 17, 2017.

Hobsbawm, Eric. "Introduction: Inventing Traditions," in Eric Hobsbawm and Terence Ranger, eds., *The Invention of Tradition.* New York: Cambridge University Press, 1983.

Holmes, Robert and M. Christine Cagle. "The Great Debate: White Support for and Black Opposition to the Confederate Battle Flag," in J. Michael Martinez, William D. Richardson, and Ron McNinch-Su, eds., *Confederate Symbols in the Contemporary South.* Gainesville: University Press of Florida, 2000.

Holzer, Harold. "Lincoln, Monuments, and Memory." *Civil War Times,* November 21, 2017.

Horwitz, Tony. "The Mammy Washington Almost Had." *The Atlantic,* May 31, 2013.

Horwitz, Tony. *Confederates in the Attic: Dispatches from the Unfinished Civil War.* New York, Vintage Books, 1998.

Janney, Caroline E. *Burying the Dead But Not the Past: Ladies Memorial Associations & the Lost Cause.* Chapel Hill: The University of North Carolina Press, 2008.

Janney, Caroline E. *Remembering the Civil War: Reunion and the Limits of Reconciliation.* Chapel Hill: The University of North Carolina Press, 2013.

Jeffrey, Robert C. "Southern Political Thought and The Southern Political Tradition," in J. Michael Martinez, William D. Richardson, and Ron McNinch-Su, eds., *Confederate Symbols in the Contemporary South.* Gainesville: University Press of Florida, 2000.

Johnson, Nuala. "Cast in Stone: Monuments, Geography, and Nationalism." 13 *Environmental and Planning D: Society and Space* 52 (1995).

Kennicott, Philip. "Riding Off to Richmond." *Washington Post,* September 27, 2019.

Kytle, Ethan J. and Blain Roberts. "Take Down the Confederate Flags, But Not the Monuments." *The Atlantic*, June 25, 2015.

Kyvig David E. *Explicit & Authentic Acts: Amending the U.S. Constitution, 1776–1995*. Lawrence: University Press of Kansas, 1996.

Landrieu, Mitch. *In the Shadow of Statues: A White Southerner Confronts History*. New York: Viking, 2018.

Lawrence, Charles R., III. "If He Hollers Let Him Go: Regulating Racist Speech on Campus." 1990 *Duke Law Journal* 431.

Leib Jonathan I., Gerald R. Webster & Roberta H. Webster. "Rebel with a Cause? Iconography and Public Memory in the Southern United States." 52 *GeoJournal* 303 (2000).

Levenson, Eric and Steve Almasy. *Montgomery, Alabama Elects its First Black Mayor, CNN*, October 9, 2019.

Levenson, Michael. "Toppled but Not Gone: UNC Grapples Anew With the Fate of Silent Sam," *The New York Times*, February 14, 2020.

Levine, Bruce. *The Fall of the House of Dixie*. New York: Random House, 2013.

Levinson, Sanford. "Silencing the Past: Public Monuments and the Tutelary State," 16 *Philosophy and Public Policy Quarterly* 6 (1996).

Levinson, Sanford. *Written in Stone: Public Monuments in Changing Societies*. Durham, NC: Duke University Press, 1998.

Loewen, Jim. "Rockville's Confederate Monument Belongs at White's Ferry." *History News Network*, May 22, 2017.

Logan, Rayford W. *The Betrayal of the Negro: From Rutherford B. Hayes to Woodrow Wilson*. New York: Collier Books, (1954) 1965.

Lozada, Carlos. "Let's See Some I.D." *Washington Post*, October 21, 2018.

MacFarquhar, Neil. "Scrutiny for Extremist Symbols After Attacks in U.S." *New York Times*, September 26, 2019.

Marks, Arthur S. "The Statue of King George III in New York and the Iconology of Regicide." 13 *The American Art Journal* (Summer 1981).

Martinez J. Michael & Robert M. Harris. "Graves, Worms, and Epitaphs," in J. Michael Martinez, William D. Richardson, and Ron McNinch-Su, eds., *Confederate Symbols in the Contemporary South*. Gainesville: University Press of Florida, 2000.

Martinez, J. Michael and William D. Richardson. "Introduction, Understanding the Debate over Confederate Symbols," in J. Michael Martinez, William D. Richardson, and Ron McNinch-Su, eds., *Confederate Symbols in the Contemporary South*. Gainesville: University Press of Florida, 2000.

Martinez, J. Michael. "Traditionalist Perspectives on Confederate Symbols," in J. Michael Martinez, William D. Richardson, and Ron McNinch-Su, eds., *Confederate Symbols in the Contemporary South*. Gainesville: University Press of Florida, 2000.

McAuliffe, Terry. *Beyond Charlottesville: Taking a Stand Against White Nationalism*. New York: St. Martin's Press, 2019.

McElya, Micki. "Commemorating the Color Line: The National Mammy Controversy of the 1920s," in Cynthia Mills and Pamela H. Simpson, eds., *Monuments to the Lost Cause: Women, Art, and the Landscapes of Southern Memory*. Knoxville: The University of Tennessee Press, 2003.

McFeely, William S. "Afterward to C. Vann Woodward, *The Strange Career of Jim Crow*." New York: Oxford University Press, (1955) 2002 (commemorative ed.).

McPherson, James M. "Long-Legged Yankee Lies: The Southern Textbook Crusade," in Alice Fahs and Joan Waugh, eds., *The Memory of the Civil War in American Culture.* Chapel Hill: The University of North Carolina Press, 2004.

McPherson, James M. *Battle Cry of Freedom: The Civil War Era.* New York: Oxford University Press, 1988.

McPherson, James M. *Ordeal by Fire.* New York: Alfred A. Knopf, 1982.

McPherson, James. "A Brief Overview of The American Civil War: A Defining Time in Our Nation's History," *American Battlefield Trust,* https://www.battlefields.org/learn/articles/brief-overview-american-civil-war.

McPherson, James. *The War That Forged a Nation: Why the Civil War Still Matters.* New York: Oxford University Press, 2015.

McRae, Elizabeth Gillespie. *Mothers of Massive Resistance: White Women and the Politics of White Supremacy.* New York: Oxford University Press, 2018.

Meacham, Jon. *The Soul of America: The Battle for Our Better Angels.* New York: Random House, 2018.

Metcalf, Andrew. "Rockville Historic District Commission Grants County's Request to Move Confederate Statue." *Bethesda Magazine,* September 18, 2015.

Miles, Jan. *The Post-Racial Negro Green Book.* New Orleans: Brown Bird Books, 2017.

Mills, Cynthia. "Introduction," in Cynthia Mills & Pamela H. Simpson, eds., *Monuments to the Lost Cause: Women, Art, and the Landscapes of Southern Memory.* Knoxville: The University of Tennessee Press, 2003.

Murray, F. Morris. *Emancipation and the Freed in American Sculpture: A Study in Interpretation.* Freeport, NY: Books for Libraries Press, (1916) 1972).

Natanson, Hannah. "Virginia Man Sues Over Story Detailing Family's Past." *Washington Post,* September 30, 2019.

New York Times. "Another Negro Burned; Henry Smith Dies at the Stake. Drawn Through the Streets on a Car—Tortured for Nearly an Hour with Hot Irons and Then Burned—Awful Vengeance of a Paris (Texas) Mob." *New York Times,* February 2, 1893.

Nolan, Alan T. "The Anatomy of the Myth," in Gary W. Gallagher and Alan T. Nolan, eds., *The Myth of the Lost Cause and Civil War Memory.* Bloomington: Indiana University Press, 2000.

Office of the President. "Report of the Committee to Establish Principles on Renaming." November 21, 2016, https://president.yale.edu/advisory-groups/presidents-committees/committee-establish-principles-renaming-0.

Osofsky, Gilbert. *The Burden of Race: A Documentary History of Negro-White Relations in America.* New York: Harper and Row, 1967.

Phelps, Jess R. & Jessica Owley. "Etched in Stone: Historic Preservation Law and Confederate Monuments." 71 *Florida Law Review* 627 (2019).

Piehler, G. Kurt. "The War Dead and the Gold Star: American Commemoration of the First World War," in John R. Gillis, ed., *Commemorations: The Politics of National Identity.* Princeton, NJ: Princeton University Press, 1994.

Pratt, Walter F., Jr., "Plessy v. Ferguson," in Kermit L. Hall & James W. Ely Jr., eds., *The Oxford Guide to United States Supreme Court Decisions,* 2d ed. New York: Oxford University Press, 2009.

Puhak, Shelley. "Confederate Monumental and Tributes in the United States, Explained," in Catherine Clinton, ed., *Confederate Statues and Memorialization.* Athens: The University of Georgia Press, 2019.

Quinodoz, Jean-Michel. *Reading Freud: A Chronological Exploration of Freud's Writings (New Library of Psychoanalysis Teaching Series)*. New York: Routledge, 2005.

Rasmussen, William M. S. "Planning a Temple to the Lost Cause: The Confederate 'Battle Abbey,'" in Cynthia Mills & Pamela H. Simpson, eds., *Monuments to the Lost Cause: Women, Art, and the Landscapes of Southern Memory*. Knoxville: The University of Tennessee Press, 2003.

Reeves, John. *The Lost Indictment of Robert E. Lee: The Forgotten Case against an American Icon*. Lanham, MD: Rowman & Littlefield, 2018.

Reingold, Beth, and Richard S. Wike. "Confederate Symbols, Southern Identity, and Racial Attitudes: The Case of the State Flag, Part Two," in J. Michael Martinez, William D. Richardson, and Ron McNinch-Su, eds., *Confederate Symbols in the Contemporary South*. Gainesville: University Press of Florida, 2000.

Riddle, W. Davis. "How Devolved Is Too Devolved? A Comparative Analysis Examining the Allocation of Power Between State and Local Government Through the Lens of the Confederate Monument Controversy." 53 *Georgia Law Review* 367 (2018).

Roark, James L. *Masters Without Slaves: Southern Planters in the Civil War and Reconstruction*. New York: W. W. Norton, 1977.

Robinson, Eugene. "The GOP Is Complicit in Demagoguery," *Washington Post*, November 6, 2018.

Saltman, Kenneth J. "'Privilege-Checking,' 'Virtue-Signaling,' and 'Safe Spaces.'" 26 *Symploke* 403 (2017).

Savage, Kirk. *Standing Soldiers, Kneeling Slaves: Race, War, and Monument in Nineteenth Century America*. Princeton, NJ: Princeton University Press, 1997.

Savage, Kirk. "The Politics of Memory: Black Emancipation and the Civil War Monument," in John R. Gillis, ed., *Commemorations: The Politics of National Identity*. Princeton, NJ: Princeton University Press, 1994.

Schneider, Gregory S. "Richmond Monument Panel Urges Removing Jefferson Davis Statue." *Washington Post*, July 2, 2018.

Seabrook, Lochlainn. *Confederate Monuments*. Nashville: Sea Raven Press, 2018.

Shackel, Paul A. "Heyward Shepherd: The Faithful Slave Memorial." 37 *Historical Archeology*, 138–48 (2003).

Sherman, Daniel J. "Art, Commerce, and the Production of Memory in France after World War I," in John R. Gillis, ed., *Commemorations: The Politics of National Identity*. Princeton, NJ: Princeton University Press, 1994.

Southern Poverty Law Center. "Whose Heritage? Public Symbols of the Confederacy." *Southern Poverty Law Center*, 2016.

Southern Poverty Law Center. "Whose Heritage? Public Symbols of the Confederacy." *Southern Poverty Law Center*, 2018.

Stanford University, The Martin Luther King, Jr. Research and Education Institute. "Our God is Marching On!" https://kinginstitute.stanford.edu/our-god-marching.

Svrluga, Susan. "Memo on 2017 Calhoun Naming Decision." (February 11, 2017) https://www.scribd.com/document/339066721/Memo-on-2017-Calhoun-naming-decision#from_embed.

Svrluga, Susan. "UNC Hints That Confederate Memorial Could Be Restored." *Washington Post*, September 1, 2018.

Svrluga, Susan. "Silent Sam Will Stay Off the University of North Carolina Campus as the School Turns the Statue Over to a Confederate Group." *Washington Post*," November 27, 2019.

Taylor, Laura. "Bill to Repeal Discriminatory Language and Replace Confederate Statues Becomes Law in Virginia." *WSET News* April 11, 2020.

Thompson, Matt. "The Hoods Are Off." *The Atlantic,* August 12, 2017.

Turque, Bill. "Confederate Statue Moved from Rockville Courthouse Over the Weekend." *Washington Post,* July 24, 2017.

Upton, Dell. *What Can and Can't Be Said: Race Uplift and Monument Building in the Confederate South.* New Haven, CT: Yale University Press, 2015.

Van Sant, Shannon. "Judge Blocks Removal of Confederate Statue That Sparked Charlottesville Protest." *NPR,* September 14, 2019.

Wahlers, Kasi I. "North Carolina's Heritage Protection Act: Cementing Confederate Monuments in North Carolina's Landscape." 94 *North Carolina Law Review* 2176 (2016).

Wert, Jeffrey D. "James Longstreet and the Lost Cause," in Gary W. Gallagher and Alan T. Nolan, eds., *The Myth of the Lost Cause and Civil War Memory.* Bloomington: Indiana University Press, 2000.

Wessel, Davis. "Racial Discrimination: Still at Work in the U.S." *Wall Street Journal,* September 4, 2003.

White, Richard. *The Republic for Which It Stands: The United States During Reconstruction and the Gilded Age, 1865–1896.* New York: Oxford University Press, 2017.

Winberry, John J. "'Lest We Forget:' The Confederate Monument and the Southern Townscape." 23 *Southeastern Geographer* 107 (1983).

Winks, Robin W. "A Place for Liberty Monument." *New Orleans Times-Picayune,* August 17, 1992.

Woodward, C. Vann. *Origins of the New South.* Baton Rouge: Louisiana State University Press 1951.

Woodward, C. Vann. *Tom Watson: Agrarian Rebel.* New York: The Macmillan Co., 1938.

Woodward, C. Vann. *The Strange Career of Jim Crow.* New York: Oxford University Press, (1955) 2002 (commemorative edition).

Index

Page numbers in italics refer to figures and tables.

Ableman v. Booth (1859), 196n23
African Americans: Black memory in Southern heritage and, 102–8; Black Union troops and, 104–5, 106–8; dehumanization of, 65–66, 67–68; disfranchisement of, 55, 56–59; impact of Confederate monuments on, xiv. See also warping-of-history approach; lynching and, 12–13, 59–67, *62*, 115; mass incarceration of, 117–19, 120–21; mobilization against segregation by, 70–71, 80; monument dedication ceremonies and, 41, 42–46, 48–49, 51–52; opposition to "Mammy Monument" by, 79, 82; "otherness" of, 55, 65–66, 68–72, 83, 119–20, 125. See also racial framing; racist public education and, 88–90; Republican Party and, 40–41, 49–51, 56, 105; rising middle class of, 59, 71; voting and, 56–59. See also Jim Crow racial discrimination; slavery
Alabama: African American political influence in, 187n2; *Gomillion v. Lightfoot* and, 176–77; lynching in, 206n24; *NAACP v. Alabama* (1958) and, 235–36n52; state legislation for protection of Confederate monuments in, 169, 172–73, 232–33n18; *United States v. State of Alabama* (11th Cir. 1986) and, 234n39, 235n43
Alexander, Michelle, 117, 118, 224n46
Alexander v. Sandoval (2001), 223n35
Allen, James, 63, 208n40
Allied Control Authority, 129, 131

American Civil Liberties Union (ACLU), 115, 116, 117
American Revolutionary War, 104
Anderson, Archer, 202n90
Andersonville, GA, 106
Anglo-Saxonism, 52, 53, 73–78, 79. *See also* White supremacist racism
Apel, Dora: on interracial sexual relationships, 208n44; on lynching, 61, 63, 206–7n30, 207n32–3, 207n36, 209n50
Arizona Department of Public Safety (DPS), 116
Arlington Confederate Monument, 93
Arlington National Cemetery, 74–78, *76*
Ashe, Arthur, 154
Atlanta Constitution (newspaper), 61
Atlanta, GA: Georgia state flag in, 155; racial violence in, 210n58; slogan of, 227n11
Augusta, GA, 106, *107*, 220n31
Ayres, Ian, 115
Aztecs, 131

Baghdad (Iraq), 131
Bailey, Anne C., 200n56
Baltimore Afro-American (newspaper), 214n96
Bates, Berk, 187n1
Birmingham, AL, 172–73
Birth of a Nation (film), 13, 68
Bishir, Catherine, 50, 203n102
Black, Brian, 22, 202n90
"Black Lives Matter" movement, 184
Blair, William A., 201n77, 219n10

Blanchard, Terence, 154, 156
Blight, David, 40, 45, 74, 201n70, 202n90, 221n43
Blue Ribbon Commission on Race, Memorials, and Public Spaces, 39
Board of Education v. Barnette (1943), 234n33
Bodnar, John, 192–93n9, 218n7
Bohannon, Keith S., 198n43
Bonekemper, Edward, 33, 195n19, 198n41, 199n49, 199n52, 199n54
Boston, 112
Bourbon Democrats, 56–59
Bourbons, 211n69
Brady, Krissy, 225n12
Breckinridge, John, 194n10
Brogan, D. W., 230n20
Brooks, Thomas, 63, 207n35
Broomall, James, 132
Brown, Austin Channing, 113
Brown, John, 141
Brown v. Board of Education (1954), 13, 23, 54, 155–56, 158
Brundage, W. Fitzhugh: on African Americans commemorative celebrations, 220n36, 220n39; on Confederate monuments, 212n82; on Democratic Party, 218n5; on erasure of African Americans and slavery from collective memory, 100–102, 108; on Juneteenth, 220n30; on relocation of Confederate monuments, 151, 228n1; on UDC textbook initiatives, 90; on United Daughters of the Confederacy, 78, 213n85, 213n91
Buchanan, James, 195n22
Budapest (Hungary), 131, 228n6
Burke, Edmund, 60
Bush v. Orleans Parish School Board (1960), 196n23
Business & Residents Alliance of E. Harlem v. Jackson (2d Cir. 2005), 232n13
Byrd, James, Jr., 206n24

Cagle, M. Christine, 187n6
Calhoun, John C., 229n14
California Environmental Quality Act (CEQA, 1970), 232n17
Cape Town (South Africa), 131
Caplin & Drysdale, Chartered v. United States (1989), 235n48, 235n49
Carr, Julian S., 94
Cash, W. J., 35, 64–65, 197n30
Cave, Robert C., 46–48
cemetery memorials, 10–11, 14–15, 38. *See also* Arlington National Cemetery
censorship, 133
Charleston, SC, 14
Charlottesville, VA: Blue Ribbon Commission on Race, Memorials, and Public Spaces in, 39; R. E. Lee monument in, xi, 160, 169, 190n20; "Unite the Right" rally (2017) in, xi, 14, 169, 190n20
Chatham County, NC, 171
Chicago, IL, 112
Chicago Defender (newspaper), 79
Children of the Confederacy (C of C), 157–58
Chokshi, Niraj, 222n10
Christianity, 35–36, 86–87, 154–55
cinema, 13, 68
Civil Rights Act (1964), 223n35
civil rights movement, 19, 23, 138, 140, 184
Civil War: African Americans as soldiers in, 104–5, 106–8; death toll of, 25; impact on South of, 25–26. *See also* Cult of the Lost Cause
Clark, Kathleen, 219n24
Cleburne, Patrick R., 193–94n8
Cleveland, Grover, 213n88
Cleveland, OH, 215n108
collective amnesia, 22
collective memory: argument against destruction of Confederate monuments and, 134; Black memory in Southern heritage and, 102–8; Cult of the Lost Cause and, 19, 22–23, 37–38, 45–46, 84–85; erasure of African Americans and slavery from, 96–97, 100–102; vs. history, 19–23; as *White* collective memory, 95–100
Colorado, 118

Columbia Broadcasting System, Inc. v. Democratic National Committee (1973), 231n2
complete-history approach, 3–4
Confederate battle flag, 75, 155, 156, 216n115
Confederate Memorial Day, 2, 39–40, 84
Confederate monument debate: phases of removal controversy, 1–10; activists and potential activists and, 181–84; arguments and counterarguments on contextualization of monuments, 7–8, 129, 135–44; arguments and counterarguments on destruction of monuments, 6–7, 129–34; arguments and counterarguments on relocation of monuments. *See* relocation of Confederate monuments; "just get over it" response to, 110–11; Rockville, MD, and, 2–4, 6–10, 37, 130; social movement to remove, 14–15; Southern heritage claims and. *See* Southern heritage; White supremacist racism and, xi–xii, 4–5
Confederate monument debate—legal framework: overview of, 163–64; Constitutional rights and, 164–67; free speech claim and, 171–80; historic preservation laws and, 167–69; state legislation and, 169–80
Confederate monuments: artistic value of, 132; contemporary racial framing and, 109–10, 119–26; dedication ceremonies and, 38–52, 73–74, 76, 84, 94–95, 94, 97, 154, 203n97; disfranchisement of African Americans and, 58; erasure of African Americans and slavery from, 96–97, 100–102, 200n55; funding and fundraising for, 49–50, 73; Jim Crow racial discrimination and, 12–13, 67–72; "monument mania" (1895–1915) and, 11–12, 53, 67–75, 78, 96–100; public spaces and, 38–39, 147–50; scope and seriousness of the deleterious impact of, xiv, 8–9. *See also* racial-reckoning approach; spectacle lynching and, 59–67; symbolic message of White superiority in, 95–100; types and number of, 10–13, 12. *See also* collective memory; Cult of the Lost Cause; United Daughters of the Confederacy (UDC)
Confederates in the Attic (Horwitz), 156–59
contextualization of Confederate monuments, 7–8, 129, 135–44
Cooper v. Aaron (1958), 196n23
Coski, John M., 187–88n8, 199n52, 199n54
Council of Conservative Citizens (CCC), 156–57
Coweta County, GA, 61
Cox, Karen L.: on Confederate monument at Arlington National Cemetery, 77, 219n12; on public location of monuments, 215–16n109, 215n108; on Southern heritage claims, 188n8; on UDC textbook initiatives, 87, 89, 217n121, 217n127; on United Daughters of the Confederacy, 218n9
Craig v. Boren (1976), 235n49
Cullen, Jay, 187n1
Cult of the Lost Cause: collective memory and, 19, 22–23, 37–38, 45–46, 84–85; Confederate monument at Arlington National Cemetery and, 76–78; Confederate monument in Raleigh, NC, and, 48–52, 51; monument dedication ceremonies and, 38–52; origins of, 24–27; racial framing and, 124–26; racist public education and, 83–91; tenets of, 27–38, 59, 66–67, 68–69, 79; White supremacist racism and, 38–39, 52, 68–69

Daughters of the American Revolution (DAR), 73
Davis, Gode, 63, 208n37
Davis, Jefferson, 26, 31, 42–43, 198n38
Davis, Jefferson: monuments: as "hero monuments," 189n9; in Richmond, VA, 14, 202n92; Stone Mountain Confederate Memorial, 13, 13, 190n17, 227–28n21

Declaration of Independence, 131
dehumanization, 65–66, 67–68
Democratic Party: Confederate monument mania and, 12; Cult of the Lost Cause and, 38–39, 48–52; disfranchisement of African Americans and, 56–59; Jim Crow racial discrimination and, 54; racial segregation and, 70. *See also* Bourbon Democrats
denazification, 129, 131
destruction of Confederate monuments, 6–7, 129–34
distortion of history approach, 20–21. *See also* Cult of the Lost Cause
Dittmer, John, 89–90
Doss, Erika: on contextualization of Confederate monuments, 141–42, 227n6; on lynching, 64, 206n24, 206nn26–7, 207n36, 208–9n45, 209n49, 221n7; on Southern heritage claims, 188nn8–9; on White supremacist racism, 209n51
Douglass, Frederick, 49–50, 58
drug offense convictions, 117–19, 120–21
dual heritage ideology, 135–36, 140–44, 146
Du Bois, W. E. B., 66, 69, 207n31, 208n42
Duggan, Paul, 217n130
Duke, David, 14
DWB (driving while Black), 115–16

Early, Jubal A., 27–28, 41, 195n14, 198n44, 201n80
Eberhardt, Jennifer, 122, 222n18, 224n47, 224n53
"eight ballot box law," 205n13
Eisenstadt v. Baird (1972), 235n49
Elkton, KY, 157
Emancipation Day, 103, 106
Emancipation Proclamation (1862), 31, 106–8
employment, 112–13
Equal Protection Clause, 165–67
Establishment Clause, 165

"Faithful Slave Memorial" (Heyward Shepherd Monument), 141
faithful slave myth. *See* loyal slave myth

Fausset, Richard, 236n2
Faust, Drew Gilpin, 199n52
Feagin, Joe R., 110, 199n50, 214n100, 221n6, 222n14, 223n44
Felton, Rebecca Latimer, 194n9
Ferguson, Champ, 217n118
Ferguson, MO, 117
Fields, James, xi
Fifteenth Amendment, 57, 104, 176–77
Finkelman, Paul, 200n64
First Amendment, 173
Floyd, George, 14, 202n90
Foner, Eric, 221n41
Forman, James, Jr., 155, 156, 231n32
Fort Pillow massacre (1864), 87
Fortier, James M., 208n37
Foster, Gaines M., 11, 189n12, 195n14, 197nn31–2, 201n76, 215n104
Fourteenth Amendment, 173
Franklin, TN, 73–74, 203n97
Free Speech Clause, 164
Funders, 211n70
Fusion Party (North Carolina), 49–51, 70, 203n102

Gallagher, Gary, 21
Gallagher, Gary W., 197n31
Gates, Henry Louis, Jr., 58, 65, 126, 204n11, 212n74, 224n47
George III, King of Great Britain and Ireland, 129, 131
Georgia: "eight ballot box law" in, 205n13; lynching in, 61; racial violence in, 210n58; secession and, 31; "standing soldier" monument in, 106, *107*; state flag of, 155; state legislation for protection of Confederate monuments in, 169, 232–33n118; Stone Mountain Confederate Memorial in, 13, *13*, 190n17, 227–28n21
Germany, 129, 131
Glass, Carter, 205n14
Gomillion v. Lightfoot, 176–77
Gone with the Wind (film), 68, 93
Green, Jordan, 215–16n109, 233–34n29
Grynbaum, Michael M., 222n10
Guelzo, Allen C., 188n1

Guthrie, KY, 157

Hacker, J. David, 193n1
Hahn, Steven, 65, 70, 205–6n23, 208n44, 210n56
Halbwachs, Maurice, 192n8
Hale, Grace Elizabeth: on Cult of the Lost Cause, 35; on cultural power of Jim Crow, 59, 70, 212n76, 212n78; on lynching, 65–67, 190n16, 207n32–3, 207n36, 208n37, 208n42, 209n49; on slavery, 219n25; on White supremacist racism, 209n53
Hammerstein, Oscar, II, 131–32
Hampton, VA, 90
Hampton, Wade, III, 189n9
Harding, Vincent, 107–8
Harper v. Virginia State Board of Elections (1966), 205n17
Harpers Ferry, WV, 141
Harris, Robert M., 193n5, 212n79
Hemings, Sally, 20
Henderson, J. H., 73–74, 203n97
Heritage Preservation Act (Alabama, 2017), 169
"hero monuments," 189n9
Heyer, Heather, xi, 14
historic preservation laws, 167–69
history: argument against destruction of Confederate monuments and, 134; vs. collective memory, 19–23; UDC textbook initiatives and, 55, 83–91
Hitler, Adolph, 131
Hobsbawm, Eric, 22
Holmes, Robert, 187n6
Holzer, Harold, 131, 225n10
Hope, John, 220n31
Horwitz, Tony, 156–59, 214n96
Hose, Sam, 61, 208n37, 208n42
housing, 113–14
Hungary, 131, 228n6
Hussain, Saddam, 131

iconoclasm, 129, 130–32, 228n6. *See also* destruction of Confederate monuments
Illinois, 112, 117
implicit association tests (IATs), 123

implicit bias, 110, 121–26
Incas, 131
insurance companies, 114–15
interracial marriage and sexual relationships, 49–50
invented tradition, 22
Iraq, 131

Jackson, Thomas (Stonewall): monuments: as "hero monuments," 189n9; in Richmond, VA, 39–41, *40*, 202n92; Stone Mountain Confederate Memorial, 13, *13*, 190n17, 227–28n21
James, J. T., 194n9
Janney, Caroline E.: on Black middle class, 205n22; on cemetery memorials, 192n30; on Civil War deaths, 193n1; on Lee monuments, 201–2nn79–81, 230n27; on Lee's death, 201n70; on proposal for "Mammy Monument," 215n103
Jasper, TX, 206n24
Jefferson, Thomas, 20, 160
Jefferson Memorial (Washington, DC), 160
Jeffrey, Robert, 197–98n36
Jim Crow racial discrimination (1895–1915), 53–56, 67–72; as antecedent to today's systemic anti-Black racism, xiv; collective memory and, 19; Confederate monuments and, 12–13; *Plessy v Ferguson* and, 12
Johanns v. Livestock Marketing Assn. (2005), 231n3
Johnson, Andrew, 194n10
Juneteenth, 103

Katrina, hurricane (2005), 114
Kemper, James L., 39–41
Kennedy, David, 199n52
Kentucky: state legislation for protection of Confederate monuments in, 170, 232–33n18; White supremacist racism in, 157
Kentucky Military Heritage Commission, 170
Key, V. O., 152

King, Martin Luther, Jr., 53–54, 157, 159
The KKK (Rose), 88
Kodak, 63
Ku Klux Klan (KKK), 13, 14, 88, 94, 157

Ladies' Memorial Associations (LMAs), 27, 41, 49, 73, 84, 192n30
Landrieu, Mitch, 188–89n4
Lawrence, Charles R., III, 224–25n2
Lee, Fitzhugh, 42
Lee, Robert E.: death of, 27, 38, 42; on secession as justified, 30; treason indictment and pardon of, 26
Lee, Robert E.: monuments: in Charlottesville, VA, xi, 160, 169, 190n20; as "hero monuments," 189n9; in Lexington, VA, 42; in Richmond, VA, 42–45, *43*, 154, 202n92; Stone Mountain Confederate Memorial, 13, *13*, 190n17, 227–28n21
Lee, Susan Pendleton, 217n121
legislation. *See* Confederate monument debate—legal framework
Leib, Jonathan I., 236n3
lending institutions, 114
Lenin, Vladimir, 131
Levine, Bruce, 199n54, 220n37
Levinson, Sanford, 149, 191n25, 196n27, 226n24
Lexington, VA, 42
Liberty Monument (New Orleans), 137
Libya, 131
Lincoln, Abraham, 20, 29, 31
Lincoln Memorial (Washington, DC), 20, 79
literacy tests, 57
Longstreet, James, 200n67
Los Angeles, CA, 114
Los Angeles Police Department (LAPD), 115
Lost Cause. *See* Cult of the Lost Cause
Louisiana. *See* New Orleans, LA
loyal slave myth: Cult of the Lost Cause and, 34–36, 59, 214n99; H. Shepherd Monument ("Faithful Slave Memorial") and, 141. *See also* mammies
lynching, 12–13, 55, 59–67, *62*, 115

MacFarquhar, Neil, 187n3, 235n51
mammies: as depicted in Confederate monuments, 93; in *Gone with the Wind* (film), 93; proposal for "Mammy Monument" and, 78–83, *81*
Marks, Arthur S., 225n8
Martinez, J. Michael: on Confederate symbols and White supremacist racism, 187–88n8, 187n6, 226n23, 230n21, 230n25; on cost of Civil War to the South, 193n5; on United Daughters of the Confederacy, 212n79
Maryland, 118
Maryland State Police (MSP), 116–17
Maury, Matthew, 202n92
McAuliffe, Terry, 190n19, 205n14, 224n60, 229n14
McElya, Micki, 79, 83, 214n95, 215n101, 218n9
McKinley, William, 75
McPherson, James: on cost of Civil War to the South, 193n5; on Lincoln, 192n3; on murder of Black Union soldiers, 217n118; on self-liberated slaves, 107–8; on slavery and Civil War, 197n35, 203n95; on UDC textbook initiatives, 87
McRae, Elizabeth Gillespie, 84, 89, 215n106
Meacham, Jon, 197n34, 207n31
Memorial Day, 106
Memorial Preservation Act (Alabama, 2017), 172–73
memory. *See* collective memory
Memphis, TN, 171
Miles, Jan, 222n11
Mills, Cynthia, 130, 196n28, 200n61
Mind of the South (Cash), 35
Mississippi: disfranchisement of African Americans in, 57; state legislation for protection of Confederate monuments in, 232–33n18; UDC textbook initiatives in, 88, 89; *Williams v. Mississippi* (1898) and, 204n12
Mississippi Education Association, 89
Mitchell, John, 46
Mobile, AL, 206n24

Montgomery, AL, 187n2
Montgomery County, MD, 2–4, 6–10
"monument mania" (1895–1915), 11–13, 53, 67–75, 78, 96–100
Monumental Task Committee, Inc. v. Foxx (E.D. La. 2016), 168, 232n14
Mosby, John S., 198n44
My Memoirs of Georgia Politics (Felton), 194n9

NAACP v. Alabama (1958), 235–36n52
Natanson, Hannah, 226n23
National Association for the Advancement of Colored People (NAACP), 80, 137, 235–36n52
National Historic Preservation Act (NHPA, 1966), 167–68
National Register of Historic Places, 9–10, 167–68
Nazi Party, 129, 131
Neal, Claude, 207n36
New Hampshire, 234n33
New Jersey, 115–17
New Orleans, LA: Blanchard's reaction to Confederate monuments in, 154; Liberty Monument in, 137; racial violence in, 210n58; removal of Confederate monuments in, 4, 6, 168, 229n14; Southern Historical Society in, 27
News and Observer (newspaper), 49–50
Nolan, Alan T., 193n5, 195n14, 197n31, 197n33, 230n20
Nordicism, cult of, 68
Northam, Ralph, 202n92
North Carolina: Confederate monuments in, 14, 48–52, *51*, 94–95, *94*, 154–55, 225n3; Fusion Party in, 49–51, 70, 203n102; possibility of interracial cooperation in, 210n54, 210n55; public education in, 88; racial violence in, 210n58; removal of Confederate monuments in, 14; state legislation for protection of Confederate monuments in, 170, 171, 232–33n18
North Carolina Monumental Association (NCMA), 49–50

Oakland, CA, 117
obelisks, 11
"Our God is Marching On" (King), 53–54
Owley, Jessica, 232n14, 232nn16–7

packaging, 122
Papasan v. Allain (1986), 236n56
Paris, TX, 61, *62*
Personnel Administrator v. Feeney, 165–67
Phelps, Jess R., 232n14, 232nn16–7
Phillips, Ulruch B., 152
photography, 63, 208n36
Pickett, George E., 214n99
Pickett, LaSalle Corbell, 214n99
Piehler, G. Kurt, 214n98
Pleasant Grove City v. Summum (2009), 164–65, 172, 174, 178–80, 234n33, 234n38
Pledge of Allegiance, 30
Plessy v. Ferguson (1896), 12, 68
policing, 115–19, 120–21
poll tax, 57–58
Pollard, Edward Alfred, 32
Populist Party, 49, 56, 70
Pratt, Jeremiah, 63
Prize Cases (1863), 29–30, 194n10
product packaging, 122
projection (psychological principle), 229n14
public education, 83–91

el-Qaddafi, Muammar, 131

race relations. *See* loyal slave myth
racial discrimination: employment and, 112–13; housing and, 113–14; insurance companies and, 114–15; lending institutions and, 114; policing and, 115–19, 120–21; voting and, 115. *See also* Jim Crow racial discrimination (1895–1915); racial framing
racial framing: concept of, 109, 110; Confederate monuments and, 109–10, 119–26; "just get over it" response and, 110–11; mass incarceration of African American males and, 117–19, 120–21; structural racism and, 111–17

racial profiling, 115–19, 120–21
racial-reckoning approach: overview of, 5–6, 92–95, 108; Black memory in Southern heritage and, 102–8; erasure of African Americans and slavery in Confederate monuments and, 96–97, 100–102; symbolic message of White superiority in Confederate monuments and, 95–100. *See also* racial framing
racial segregation. *See* Jim Crow racial discrimination
racial violence, 206n28, 210n58. *See also* lynching
Raleigh, NC, 48–52, *51*
Ranger, Terence, 22
rape: charges against African American men and, 60–62, 68; enslaved women and, 82
Readjuster Movement, 70, 211n70
Red summer (1919), 80
Reed, Steven, 187n2
Reeves, John, 194–95n11
relocation of Confederate monuments: overview of, 6–7, 8, 145–46; avoid needless provocations of racial strife claim and, 146, 150–52; dual heritage ideology and, 146; respect for southern heritage claim and, 146, 152–59; rewriting/erasing history claim and, 146–50; Rockville, MD, and, 2–4, 6–10, 37, 130; "What About George Washington and Thomas Jefferson" claim and, 159–60
Republican Party: African Americans and, 40–41, 49–51, 56, 105; racial segregation and, 70; slavery and, 31
Rhodes, Cecil John, 131
Richardson, William D., 230n25
Richmond Evacuation Day, 103
Richmond Examiner (newspaper), 31
Richmond Planet (newspaper), 46
Richmond, VA: J. Davis monument in, 14, 202n92; S. Jackson monument in, 39–41, *40*; R. E. Lee monument in, 42–45, *43*, 154, 202n92; M. Maury monument in, 202n92; Monument Avenue's residential district in, 45, 72; proposal for Ashe monument in, 154; protests after Floyd's death in, 202n92; "Rumors of War" statue in, 143–44; Soldiers' and Sailors' Monument in, 46–48, *47*; Southern Historical Society in, 27–28; J. E. B. Stuart monument in, 143–44
Riddle, W. Davis, 233n24
Robertson, Campbell, 236n2
Robinson, Eugene, 222n10
Rockville, MD, 2–4, 6–10, 37, 130
Rodgers, Richard, 131–32
Rogers v. Brockette (5th Cir. 1979), 235n46
Roof, Dylann, 14
Roosevelt, Theodore, 181–82
Rose, Laura, 88
"Rumors of War" (Richmond, VA), 143–44
Rust v. Sullivan (1991), 234n30
Rutherford, Mildred Lewis, 74, 84, 86–87

Salisbury, NC, 154–55
Savage, Kirk: on erasure of African Americans and slavery from collective memory, 196n28; on Lee monuments, 43–44, 201–2n81, 230n27; on loyal slave myth, 213n94; on public location of monuments, 218n8; on public monuments, 150; on racial harm caused by Confederate monuments, 95–96, 97–99, 108, 217–18n1; on slavery and Civil War, 32; on "standing soldier" monuments, 219n14
Seabrook, Lochlainn, 200n55
secession, as justified, 28–30
Second Mississippi Plan, 57
Selma to Montgomery march (1965), 53–54
Shepherd, Heyward, 141
Sherman, Daniel J., 228n7
Shiloh, TN, 230n28
"Silent Sam" Confederate Monument (University of North Carolina), 14, 94–95, *94*, 225n3
Singleton v. Wulff (1976), 235n49
slave narratives, 105
slavery: Cult of the Lost Cause and, 30–36, 46–48, 79; as depicted in Confederate monuments, 92, 93; UDC

textbook initiatives and, 86–87. *See also* loyal slave myth; mammies
Smith, Henry, 61, *62*
Soldiers' and Sailors' Monument (Cleveland, OH), 215n108
Soldiers' and Sailors' Monument (Richmond, VA), 46–48, *47*
Somerville, TN, 207n35
Sons of Confederate Veterans (SCV), 141, 156, 158, 191n24
South Africa, 131
South Carolina: Council of Conservative Citizens in, 156–57; "eight ballot box law" in, 205n13; Mother Emanuel A.M.E. Church massacre (Charleston) in, 14; racial violence in, 210n58; state legislation for protection of Confederate monuments in, 169, 232–33n18, 233n21
Southern agrarian revolt, 70
Southern heritage: argument against destruction of Confederate monuments and, 133–34; Black memory in, 102–8; as claim against relocation of Confederate monuments and, xiii, 9, 10, 146, 152–59; collective memory and, 19; Cult of the Lost Cause and, 34; dual heritage ideology and, 135–36, 140–44, 146
Southern Historical Society (SHS), 27–28
Southern Historical Society Papers (SHSP), 28
The Southern Past (Brundage), 100–102, 108
Southern Poverty Law Center (SPLC), 10–11, **12**, 14–15, 148
Soviet Union, 131
Spanish conquerors, 131
spectacle lynching, 12–13, 59–67, *62*
Stalin, Joseph, 131
"standing soldier" monuments: in Augusta, GA, 106, *107*; characteristics of, 11; erasure of African Americans and slavery from collective memory and, 96–97; in Rockville, MD, 2–4, 6–10, 37. *See also* "Silent Sam" Confederate Monument (University of North Carolina)

Standing Soldiers, Kneeling Slaves (Savage), 95–96, 97–99, 108
state bonds, 211n70
Stephens, Alexander, 31
Stevens, Daisy McLaurin, 77
Stone Mountain, GA, 13, *13*, 190n17, 227–28n21
The Strange Career of Jim Crow (Woodward), 67
structural racism, 111–17. *See also* racial discrimination
Stuart, J. E. B., 143–44, 188n1
Supreme Court: *Alexander v. Sandoval* and, 223n35; coerced-government-speech theory and, 173; *Gomillion v. Lightfoot* and, 176–77; on "more perfect Union," 124; *Personnel Administrator v. Feeney* and, 165–67; *Pleasant Grove City v. Summum* and, 164–65, 172, 174, 178–80, 231n2, 234n33, 234n38; *Plessy v. Ferguson* and, 12, 68; *Prize Cases* and, 29–30, 194n10; on public monuments, 148; *Walker v. Texas Division, Sons of Confederate Veterans, Inc.* (2015) and, 172, 228–29n9, 234n38; *Ysursa v. Pocatello Education Association* and, 174–76
Svrluga, Susan, 225n3, 229n14

Taylor, Laura, 232–33n18
Tennessee: lynchings in, 207n35; state legislation for protection of Confederate monuments in, 170, 171, 232–33n18, 233n23
Tennessee Heritage Protection Act (2016), 233n23
Texas: Juneteenth celebrations in, 103; lynchings in, 61–63, *62*, 206n24, 207n32
Texas v. Johnson (1989), 226n19
Texas v. White (1869), 30
textbooks, 55, 83–91
Times-Picayune (New Orleans), 137
Tripoli, Libya, 131
Tuskegee, AL, 176–77
Twenty-fourth Amendment, 58

"Unite the Right" rally (Charlottesville, VA, 2017), xi, 14, 169, 190n20

United Confederate Veterans (UCV), 41–42
United Daughters of the Confederacy (UDC): Anglo-Saxonism and, 73–78, 79; Children of the Confederacy (C of C) and, 157–58; collective memory and, 19, 97; Confederate monument at Arlington National Cemetery and, 74–78, 76; Confederate monument in Rockville, MD, and, 2; Confederate "monument mania" and, 53, 75, 78; Confederate monuments in Richmond, VA, and, 14; control of Confederate memorialization by, 3–4, 23, 52; Jim Crow racial discrimination and, 55; origins of, 41–42, 73; proposal for "Mammy Monument" and, 78–83, 81; racial framing and, 109; H. Shepherd Monument ("Faithful Slave Memorial") and, 141; Shiloh battlefield memorial and, 230n28; state legislation for protection of Confederate monuments and, 171; textbook initiatives by, 55, 83–91
United States Department of Housing and Urban Development, 114
United States v. Peters (1809), 196n23
United States v. State of Alabama (11th Cir. 1986), 234n39, 235n43
University of North Carolina. *See* "Silent Sam" Confederate Monument (University of North Carolina)
University of Virginia, 54
Upton, Dell: on Confederate memorial landscape, 109–10, 195n15, 197n32, 215n107; on contextualization of Confederate monuments, 137–39, 140; on erasure of African Americans and slavery from collective memory, 203n3; on removal of Confederate monuments, 227n1

Vardaman, James Kimble, 204n11
Varley, Bryn, 22, 202n90
Victory Defeated by Death and Night (Shiloh, TN), 230n28
Vietnam Veterans Memorial (Washington, DC), xii–xiii

Virginia: disfranchisement of African Americans in, 57; on Lee monument removal (Richmond), 202n92; monument removal ban in, 169; post-Civil War politics in, 39–41; Readjuster Movement in, 70, 211n70; removal Confederate monuments in, 229n14; state legislation for protection of Confederate monuments in, 232–33n18. *See also* Charlottesville, VA; Richmond, VA
Virginia coalition, 28
Virginia Museum of Fine Arts (Richmond, VA), 143–44
Virginia v. Black (1996), 226n20
Visual Artists Rights Act (VARA, 1990), 168
Volusia County, Florida, 117
voting, 56–59, 115, 204–5n13

Waco, TX, 61–63, 207n32
Wahlers, Kasi I., 233n23
Walker, Zack, 208n37
Walker v. Texas Division, Sons of Confederate Veterans, Inc. (2015), 172, 228–29n9, 234n38
war on drugs, 117–19, 120–21
warping-of-history approach: overview of, 4–5, 52, 91, 93; Confederate "monument mania" and, 53; disfranchisement of African Americans and, 55, 56–59; Jim Crow racial discrimination and, 53–56, 55, 67–72; lynching and, 55, 59–67, 62; UDC textbook initiatives and, 55, 83–91. *See also* United Daughters of the Confederacy (UDC)
Washington, DC: Jefferson Memorial in, 160; Lincoln Memorial in, 20, 79; proposal for "Mammy Monument" in, 78–83, 81; Vietnam Veterans Memorial in, xii–xiii; Washington Monument in, 160
Washington, George, 131, 160
Washington, Jesse, 61–63, 207–8n36, 207n32
Washington Monument (Washington, DC), 160
Webster, Gerald R., 236n3

Webster, Roberta H., 236n3
Wells, Ida, 206n29
White Farmers' Alliance, 70
White, Richard: on Civil War deaths, 193n1; on cost of Civil War to the South, 25–26; on lynching, 208n43; on possibility of interracial cooperation in North Carolina, 210n54, 210n55; on slavery and Civil War, 199n52
White supremacist racism: collective memory and, 19; Confederate monument at Arlington National Cemetery and, 75–78; Confederate monument debate and, xi–xii, 4–5; Confederate "monument mania" and, 53; Cult of the Lost Cause and, 38–39, 52, 68–69; Mother Emanuel A.M.E. Church (Charleston) massacre and, 14; UDC textbook initiatives and, 83–91. *See also* Jim Crow racial discrimination (1895–1915); United Daughters of the Confederacy (UDC)

Whitecapping, 206n28
Wiley, Kehinde, 143
Williams v. Mississippi (1898), 57, 204n12
Wilmington, NC, 210n58
Wilson, Woodrow, 13
Winberry, John, 11–12
Winks, Robin, 134
Woodward, C. Vann: on disfranchisement of African Americans, 204nn8–9; on group libel of African Americans, 210–11n61; on Jim Crow racial discrimination, 54, 67, 210n56; on lynching, 206n26, 209–10nn53–4
Wooley v. Maynard (1977), 234n33
Works Progress Administration (WPA), 214–15n100
World War I, 80, 215n105

Yale University, 229n14
"Yellow Peril" school of literature, 68
Ysursa v. Pocatello Education Association (2009), 174–76